NEW YORK
HISTORICAL MANUSCRIPTS:
DUTCH

COMMITTEE ON PUBLICATION

NEW YORK
HISTORICAL MANUSCRIPTS:
DUTCH

Translated and Annotated
By
ARNOLD J. F. VAN LAER

Edited with Added Indexes by
KENNETH SCOTT
and
KENN STRYKER-RODDA

Published under the Direction of
The Holland Society of New York

Volume IV

Council Minutes, 1638-1649

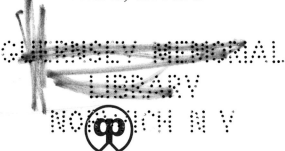

GENEALOGICAL PUBLISHING CO., INC.
BALTIMORE 1974

Genealogical Publishing Co., Inc.
Baltimore, 1974

Library of Congress Catalogue Card Number 73-14890
International Standard Book Number 0-8063-0587-8

Made in the United States of America

VOLUME IV

COUNCIL MINUTES, 1638-1649

COUNCIL MINUTES

Being the executive, legislative and judicial proceedings
of the Director General and Council of New Netherland

---

[1]   On [Thur]sday, [April 8, 1638]

The Honorable Director Kieft and Council [having considered
the small number] of councilors, have deemed it necessary to
[choose an] experienced parson to strengthen their number [and]
in consideration of the ability of Doctor Johannes [la Montagnie],
the said Montagnie has therefore been appointed by us a political
councilor of New Netherland at fl. 35 a [month], commencing on
the date hereof.

In accordance with a certain document presented by the late
Dire[ctor] van Twiller, it is resolved and concluded [that the]
cattle on Farm No. 1 shall remain for the [behoof] of the said
van Twiller, on condition that the cattle be not removed from
the Man[hates], the present director to make an inventory of
said cattle and the matter at issue to be referred to the honorable masters, the directors of the West India Company, chamber
of Amsterdam.

Symen Dircksen from Durickerdam, engaged as skipper of the
ship Harinck, shall receive wages according to the ship's articles.

Adriaen Dircksen, engaged as first mate, instead of
Symen Jansen, shall receive wages as above.

Jan Symensen from Amsterdam, engaged as second mate, ut supra.

The farmers on farms Nos. 4, 5 and 6 are granted permission to remove their cattle from said farms on condition that the same remain within the jurisdiction of the Manhates, the council having been unable to refuse them, in as much as others have heretofore been allowed to remove their cattle and the more so as no other cattle are to be had here.

Upon the request of Jacob Planck, officer of the colony of Mr. Renselaer, called Renselaerswyck, to be allowed to remove certain horses to the aforesaid colony. Whereas many cattle have heretofore been transported from the island of the Manhates and there are no other cattle at the Manhates except those on the farm of the late Director van Twiller, the other five farms being entirely vacant and stripped of animals and not fit for cultivation on account of lack of animals; therefore, the honorable director and council, after mature deliberation, have denied Planck his request and only granted him permission to remove a few goats.

[2] [Upper part of manuscript destroyed]

Several free persons having arrived by the yacht [Dolphyn] and made complaint about the food [   ], it is resolved that the kettles, bowls and cupboards shall be inspected by both the cooks of the ship Har[inck and] the yacht Dolphyn and that we shall govern outselves according

The cooks, aforesaid, after inspection of the yacht Dolphyn, declare the bowls to be of proper size and the cook of the said Dolphyn has also declared under oath that he served them full as

required, so that the said passengers are bound to pay unless
they bring further proof.

Ordinance prohibiting trade in furs, regulating intercourse
with ships in port, establishing court days and prohibiting immorality [1]

Whereas the honorable director and council of New Netherland
find that many persons, as well servants of the Company as freemen, undertake to trade privately in furs and to commit other
irregularities; Therefore, in order to prevent any one at any
time from engaging therein and from suffering damage, the aforesaid honorable director and council, wishing to provide against
this in time, have prohibited and forbidden, as they do hereby
prohibit and forbid, all persons who have taken the oath of the
Company, be their station, capacity or condition what it may,
henceforth to carry on any trade in furs in any manner whatsoever, on pain of forfeiting all their wages and the claims which
the offenders have against the Company, together with the confiscation of the merchandise which shall be found in their
possession.

Likewise, all free persons not in the Company's service
shall govern themselves according to the granted charter and are
hereby warned not to violate the same on pain of forfeiting the
goods and further of being arbitrarily punished.

Moreover, no person belonging to any ship, yacht or sloop
shall be at liberty to remain on shore at night without the
consent of the honorable director, but on the contrary shall

---

[1] Translation revised from Laws and Ordinances of New
Netherland, pp. 10-12.

return on board by sundown; likewise, no ship's boats or other craft shall go at night from any ship to the shore, or from the shore to shipboard, wherefore all skippers and other officers are expressly charged to see to this, and if any person act contrary hereto, he shall be punished as the honorable director and council shall think proper.

No person shall be at liberty to go on board of any ship which may arrive from sea without express order from the honorable director.

All master carpenters, overseers of workmen and all others are expressly commanded to go to and [3] [from their work] at the appointed hours without any [loss of time], and [duly to attend to those] under their charge, on pain of forfeiture of their monthly wages.

Likewise, no sailors shall refuse to perform any necessary work for the service of the Company; in case of failure to do so they shall be punished as rebellious and obstinate persons.

All persons are hereby also notified, in case any cause of action arise, be it civil or criminal, that they may make their complaints and solicit justice every Thursday, being the appointed court day.

Furthermore, each and every one must refrain from fighting; from adulterous intercourse with heathens, blacks, or other persons; from mutiny, theft, false testimony, slanderous language and other irregularities, as in all such matters, according to the circumstances of the case, the offenders shall be corrected and punished as an example to others.

Thus done and published and posted in Fort Amsterdam, the day and year above written.

On Thursday, being the 22d of April

Claes van Elslandt, plaintiff, vs. Symen Jansen, skipper, that is to say, Symen Dircksen, defendant. The parties are ordered to appear on the next court day, unless they come to an agreement in the meanwhile.

Tomas Bescher, Englishman, vs. Cornelis Lamberteen Cool, defendant, about the purchase of a certain plantation. Defendant is ordered to pay the purchase money to the plaintiff.

The late director Twiller requesting the Roode Hoeck, situated south of Noten Island, to use the same for such purpose as it may be fit, his request is granted on condition that he must surrender the same when the Company shall have need of the land.

Mr. Lasle, tobacco planter, plaintiff, vs. Abraham Nieuman, defendant. Default. Is ordered to appear this day week.

[4] On Thursday, being the 29th of April

Mr. Laslee, tobacco planter, plaintiff, vs. Abraham Nieuman. Default. Is ordered to appear to-morrow and if he remains in default he shall be compelled by the court to serve the plaintiff.

Hendrick Jansen, tailor, offers himself as surety and principal for the judgement in the suit between the fiscal and Jan Cornelis from Rotterdam on account of the crime committed.

Anthony Jansen from Salee, plaintiff, vs. Hendrick Jansen, tailor, defendant, in a case of slander. Case put over to the next court day.

Uldrick Lupoldt, plaintiff, vs. Jan Cornelisen from Rotterdam, defendant, as above.

On Friday, being the 30th ditto

Mr. Laslee, tobacco planter, plaintiff, vs. Abraham Nieuman, defendant.

The defendant having three times in succession remained in default, he is ordered to agree with the plaintiff as best he can.

On Saturday, the first of May

The court resolves that Abraham Nieuman, defendant, vs. Mr. Lasle, plaintiff, is bound to serve the plaintiff if he was not under contract to Jacob van Corlaer when he, the defendant, hired himself out to the plaintiff and, if he was not free, he must pay twenty-five pounds of tobacco or furnish another man in his stead to fulfill his term of service and that at once, without any delay.

On Thursday, being the 6th of May

Anthony Jansen from Salee, plaintiff, vs. Hendrick Jansen, tailor, defendant, in a case of slander. Parties ordered henceforth to live with each other in peace as becomes neighbors and, if either party act contrary hereto, he shall be fined 25 gl.

Ulrich Lupoldt, fiscal plaintiff, vs. Jan Cornelisen from Rotterdam, defendant. The defendant is condemned to pay 25 gl. for the dog which he stabbed and moreover a fine of 25 gl. and the costs of the suit.

[5], [Claes], gunner on the ship [Harinck, plaintiff, vs. Bare]nt Dircksen, baker, defendant, about the purchase of [a house] and some cattle. The plaintiff demands [restitution?] inasmuch as the defendant refuses to give the present which he promised him. Therefore, the defendant is condemned to pay the

plaintiff 3 Jacobuses [1] in cash and consequently the purchase
is void.

[2] I, Willem Kieft, director general of New Netherland, residing on the island of the Manhates and in Fort Amsterdam, within
the jurisdiction of their High Mightinesses the lords States
General of the United Netherlands and the chartered West India
Company, chamber at Amsterdam, make known to your honor, Pitter
Minuit, who style yourself commander in the services of her Royal
Majesty of Sweden, that the entire South river of New Netherland
has been for many years in our possession and secured above and
below by forts and sealed with our blood, which took place during
your honor's administration of New Netherland and is well known
to your honor. Now, whereas your honor intrudes between our
forts and begins to build a fort there to our disadvantage and
prejudice, which shall never be suffered by us and we are also
well assured that her Royal Majesty of Sweden has not given you
any orders to build fortifications on our rivers or along our
coasts; Therefore, in case your honor proceeds with the building
of fortifications, the cultivation of the soil and the trade in
furs, or attempts to do anything to our injury, we hereby protest
against all costs, damages and loss, as well as all accidents,
shedding of blood and trouble which may arise therefrom in the
future, intending to maintain our rights in such way as we deem
best. Done ....

---

[1] English gold coin worth 25 shillings.
[2] Revised from Doc. Rel. Col. Hist. N. Y., 12:19.

Ordinance against immoderate drinking and harboring seamen on shore at night [1]

[6] On Monday, being the 17th of May

Whereas the Honorable Director Willem Kieft and the council of New Netherland have observed that much evil and mischief is daily occasioned by immoderate drinking; Therefore, the said honorable director and council, wishing to provide against the same, have prohibited and forbidden, as they do hereby prohibit and forbid, all persons from selling henceforth any wines, on pain of forfeiting twenty-five guilders and the wines which shall be found in their houses; excepting only the store, where wine can be procured at a fair price and where it will be issued in moderate quantities.

Also, no person shall be allowed to lodge at night or after sundown any of the Company's servants who are detailed on the ships and sloops, unless with the consent of the honorable director, upon forfeiture of a like sum of 25 gl. Furthermore, all seafaring persons are commanded to repair before sunset to the ship or sloop to which they are assigned and no one may remain on shore without permission. And whosoever shall act contrary hereto shall the first time forfeit two months' wages and for the second offense forfeit all his wages and be dismissed from the Company's service. Thus done in Fort Amsterdam and published the day and year above written.

---

[1] Translation revised from Laws and Ordinances of New Netherland, pp. 12-13.

On the 27th of May Anno 1638

Symen Pos, plaintiff, vs. Barent Dircksen, baker, defendant, about a certain agreement concerning fishery. Parties ordered to appear on the next court day and to bring proper proof.

Jan Damen, plaintiff, vs. Lenaert Arentsen, defendant, about the hire of his son Aelbert Lenarts. The defendant's son ordered to fulfil his [contract of] service and the plaintiff ordered to treat the boy as his own son; and if the boy should again run home the defendant shall be bound to return the boy each time on pain of making good the loss and damage which Jan Damen shall suffer thereby.

[7] The fiscal, plaintiff, vs. Jan S[chepmoes], Jan [   ] and Jurgen [   ], defendants, for having contrary to the ordinance lodged persons over night. Defendants fined according to the ordinance and to settle with the fiscal.

The fiscal, plaintiff, vs. Hendrick Jansen, tailor, defendant, in a case of slander against Anthony Jansen from Vaes. The fiscal ordered to inquire who uttered the slander and the defendant to furnish proper affidavits that he was asleep at the time the slandering occurred.

The fiscal, plaintiff, vs. Jan Dircksen from Hamb[urg], defendant, for having traded in furs contrary to his oath. The fiscal ordered to obtain further information in regard to the furs as well as the cloth and the defendant prohibited from leaving the Manhates

Ordinance against clandestine trade [1]

The deputies to the Assembly of the XIX of the Chartered
West India Company, by virtue of the charter and the amplifications
thereof granted to the Company by the High and Mighty Lords the
States General, make known:

Whereas it has heretofore not only been sufficiently well
known, but has now recently become manifest to all the world,
that that many self-seeking persons in New Netherland, flagrantly
violating our good ordinances and commands by their private and
clandestine trade and traffic, have acquired and diverted from
the Company to their own private profit many, nay, more peltries
and skins, of better condition and quality, than those that are
purchased there and sent over on the Company's own account and
have bartered them for wares and merchandise taken with them from
here or ordered by them to be sent in the Company's own ships,
clandestinely and secretly, without the knowledge of the Company;
whereby on the one hand the ships are filled and rendered incapable
of carrying the Company's goods and those entered by the patroons
and colonists and on the other hand the Company is defrauded of
the freight thereof; so that they have not only spoiled the trade
of the Company in that country by paying more for the skins and
peltries than the Company, which they are able to do by reason
of their being free from all charges and expenses, both as to
freight and equipment, and not having to bear the [8] daily cost
of maintaining so many people and fortifications and other heavy
burdens which the Company is carrying there; which Company in

---

[1] Translation revised from Laws and Ordinances of New
Netherland, pp. 13-15.

consequence has been able to obtain but few furs or been forced to submit to a like advance in price, while they in this country have also brought the furs and peltries into disrepute and caused them to be sold at a low price, the Muscovy and other traders being furnished by them with better goods and at a lower price; and whereas the Company is besides reliably informed that many have exchanged their poor furs for the best furs of the Company, or at least have bought up the best furs for themselves and not for the Company, all to the great and immense damage and loss of the Company and without once considering the great expense incurred by the Company as well for the equipment and cargoes as for the support and payment of the very people who have deprived the Company of the returns therefrom and thus caused the prosperity of New Netherland to decline considerably; We, therefore, in order to provide against this, renewing our former ordinances, placards and commands issued here by us and there by our director and council against said private trade, have thought fit to order and decree, as we hereby do order and decree, that henceforth no persons, of whatever condition or capacity they may be, residing here or within the limits of New Netherland, shall be at liberty to convey thither any wares or merchandise, be the quantity large or small, either in their own or in the Company's ships, whether openly or secretly, under any cover or pretext whatsoever, without the cognizance or knowledge of the Company, on pain of confiscation of said wares, cargoes and merchandise for the benefit of the Company; also, that none of the above mentioned persons shall be at liberty to carry on at any place any private trade in furs, either by themselves or by others, directly or indirectly, in any manner whatsoever, on pain of confiscation of the traded furs and arbitrary correction at the discretion of the Company, or of the director and council there, and in addition of all their salary and monthly wages.

We therefore order and command our director and council of New Netherland and all other [9] officers to govern themselves accordingly and strictly to enforce the contents hereof, without any connivance, dissimulation or compromise and, in order that no one may plead ignorance, to publish this at the accustomed places and to cause it to be posted everywhere there and also in the respective colonies.

Thus done and published in Fort Amsterdam, this 7th of June anno 1638. [1]

On the 3d of June 1638

Cornelis Jacobsen from Martensdyck, plaintiff, vs. Andries Hudden, defendant, for the payment of the sum of [   ]. As the defendant acknowledges the debt, he is condemned to pay within three weeks.

Jan Damen, plaintiff, vs. Lenaert Arentsen, defendant, in a case of protest. Parties having been heard, in virtue of the oath taken by the plaintiff, the defendant is condemned to restore his son to the plaintiff to complete his bounden service and in case of default he shall be punished as a disobedient person.

---

[1] Judging from its place in the record, it would seem that the ordinance was spread on the minutes immediately after its receipt from Amsterdam and before its actual publication in New Netherland.

Everardus Bogardus, plaintiff, vs. Anthony Jansen from Vees, defendant, for payment of the sum of fl. 319. The defendant is condemned to pay within the time of three months, as he admits the claim.

Symen Dircksen Pos, plaintiff, vs. Barent Dircksen, baker, defendant. Parties being heard and the agreement which they made with each other being open to dispute, Claes van Elslant and Jan Damen are ordered to settle the matter as referees, the parties to be satisfied with the decision of the referees.

Hillebrant Pietersen, plaintiff, vs. Symen Pos, defendant. The defendant is ordered to satisfy the plaintiff's claim.

Hendrick Jansen, tailor, plaintiff, vs. Anthony Jansen, from Veesen, defendant, for slander. Parties being heard and plaintiff having produced but one witness, the case is dismissed and parties are ordered to live in peace as heretofore.

[10] On [the 3d? of June] [1]

The honorable director and council observing the ability of [Cornelis] van Tienhoven, up to the first of April bookkeeper of the Book of Monthly Wages, have engaged him as secretary and bookkeeper of monthly wages at fl. 36 per month and fl. 200 annually for board money, commencing the 1st of April anno 1638.

Hendrick Pietersen, mason, has since the 10th of May anno 1638, as his bounden time had expired, earned as master mason fl. 20 a month and fl. 100 for board.

Hendrick Gerritsen, a boy, has man's wages since the 20th of May anno 1638.

---

[1] The following memoranda were apparently made at different times and afterwards copied at this point in the engrossed minutes. O'Callaghan's translation is in Doc. Rel. Col. Hist. N. Y., 14:8-9.

Pieter Pietersen from Amsterdam was engaged as a man on the 20th of May anno 1638, at fl. 8 a month.

Lourens Lourensen from Amsterdam engaged as a man on the 10th of May anno 1638, at fl. 8 a month.

Claes van Elslant, commissary of provisions, was engaged on the 1st of April anno 1638 by the honorable director and council at fl. 36 a month, as his term of service had expired, particularly on account of the certainty we have of the person's ability and fitness for his charge and the good satisfaction he has given us. Jan Jansen, gunner, engaged on the 15th of May anno 1638, at fl. 16 a month, as gunner (constapel) in Fort Amsterdam.

Jan Dircksen van Bremen engaged as assistant gunner (bosschieter) on the 7th of May 1638, at fl. 10 a month.

Tomas Walraven engaged as carpenter from the 1st of August 1638, at fl. 18 a month and fl. 100 a year for board.

Jacob Stoffelsen's pay was increased by the honorable director and council on the 15th of May anno 1638 to fl. 30 a month, as his bounden time had expired and there is no fitter person to be had here to be overseer of laborers, he being diligent and faithful in all work entrusted to him in the service of the Company.

Jan Pietersen van Essendelft earns as surgeon (barbier) at the South river fl. 10 a month since the 10th of July 1638.

Adriaen Dircksen from Maersen is engaged as assistant at Fort Orange, as he speaks the Mohawk language very well and thoroughly understands the trade there, at fl. 12 a month and fl. 100 for board, from the 15th of July anno 1638.

Dirck Stipel engaged as quartermaster (<u>wachtmeester</u>) at said fort at fl. 10 a month, from July 15, 1638.

[11] [On the 24th of June] [1]

[Whereas the master] house-carpenter [is about to leave for the fatherland and] there are but few carpenters here fit to succeed in his place; therefore, having observed the ability [of] Gillis Pietersen van [der] Gouw, we have appointed him master carpenter, at fl. 38 a month, from the 1st of June anno 1638.

Nicolaes Coorn is engaged as sergeant at fl. 18 a month and fl. 100 a year for board, from the 15th of September anno 1638, as it is necessary to have some one to drill the soldiers in the proper use of arms.

Jeuriaen Rodolff is engaged as sergeant in the place of Coorn, at fl. 18 a month and fl. 100 for board, on the 7th of December anno 1638. [2]

On the 10th of June

Cors Pietersen, plaintiff, vs. Adam Roelantsen, defendant, regarding the inheritance of the late Adam Roelantsen's wife, who is the plaintiff's wife's mother. The court having examined the inventory signed by the notary and witnesses and all debts, claims, and furniture, etc. being deducted, it is decided that 12 gl. 10 st. are still due to Cors Pietersen and no more.

_____

[1] Date supplied from <u>Doc</u>. <u>Rel</u>. <u>Col</u>. <u>Hist</u>. <u>N</u>. <u>Y</u>., 14:9.
[2] Nicolaes Coorn was reduced to the ranks on December 2, 1638. See the entry in the minutes under that date.

Jan Schepmoes ordered henceforth not to lodge any sailors or to tap wine, on pain, in case he acts contrary thereto, of being obliged to leave the Manhattes, it being recommended that he support himself by farming.

On the 24th ditto

Wolphert Gerritsen, plaintiff, vs. Jan Evertsen, defendant. Default.

Cornelis Lambertsen Cool, plaintiff, vs. Cornelis van Vorst, defendant, for payment of fl. 4. Default.

Cornelis Lambertsen Cool, plaintiff, vs. Jan van Vorst, defendant, for payment of fl. 25. Default.

Various free men having petitioned the council for grants of the land which they at present cultivate, the request of the petitioners is granted, provided that at the expiration of ten years after taking possession of their plantations they shall pay yearly to the Company one-tenth of all the produce which God shall grant to the soil; also, for the house and garden from now on yearly one pair of capons. [1]

[12] Thursday, being [the 1st of July]

It is resolved in council, in as much as the caravel De Hoop is not needed here at present for the service of the Company, to send the same to the island of Curaçao to carry from there hither cattle, salt and Negroes, or such goods as may be deemed best for the use of the Company.

Hendrick Jansen, tailor, plaintiff, vs. Jan Jansen Damen, defendant, for delivery of cattle. Parties referred to referees, namely: Claes van Elsl[an]t and Wybrant Pietersen.

---

[1] Revised from Laws and Ordinances of New Netherland. p. 16.

On Thursday, being the 8th of July

Pieter Jansen, plaintiff, vs. Willem, the cooper, defendant. The defendant is condemned to pay the plaintiff fl. 21.

A certain petition being presented to the council by Everardus Bogardus, requesting leave to depart for the fatherland to answer charges brought against him by Lubbert van Dincklagen, we have deemed it necessary to keep the minister here in order that the Church of God may daily grow in strength.

Hendrick Jansen, plaintiff, vs. Jan Damen, defendant. Parties referred to Cornelis Tonisen and Wybrant Pietersen.

Hendrick Jansen, plaintiff, vs. Jan Damen, defendant. After taking the oath, the defendant is condemned to pay the plaintiff fl. 10 for damage to peas.

Jan Willemsen Schut [was] appointed on the 7th of April as assistant to the Commissary of Provisions at fl. 15 a month and fl. 100 a year for board.

[13] [On Thursday], being the 15th of July

Tonis Nyssen, plaintiff, vs. Gerrit Jansen from Oldenborgh, defendant, about delivery of a cow. Defendant condemned to deliver the cow to plaintiff or to satisfy him in cash or otherwise.

Symon Jansen, skipper of the Harinck, plaintiff, vs. Andris Hudden, defendant. As it appears that Hudden has no claim against the skipper, the attachment by the defendant of the plaintiff's property is null and void.

Ulrich Lupolt, fiscal, plaintiff, vs. Gysbert from Beyerlandt, defendant, for drawing his knife. The defendant is condemned to drop three times from the yard of the yacht De Hoop and to receive three lashes from each sailor of the aforesaid yacht.

On Thursday, being the 21st of July

Hans Schipper, soldier, plaintiff, vs. Willem Bredenbent, defendant. Plaintiff and defendant are comdemned each to pay the just half of the surgeon's fee for treating the wound.

Jan Damen, plaintiff, vs. Abraham Isaacksen Planc and Dirck Holgersen, Noorman, defendants. The plaintiff requests to be master of his house and that the defendants be ordered to acknowledge him as such and to stay away from the plaintiff's house. The defendants are ordered to keep away from the plaintiff's house and to leave him master in his own house.

Dirck Holgersen, Noorman, plaintiff, vs. Jan Damen, defendant, for assault. Parties are ordered to submit testimony, the case being put over to the next court day.

[14] On the 5th of August 1[6]38

Cornelis Dircksen, plaintiff, vs. Adriaene [Cuveliers], [1] defendant. The defendant is ordered to satisfy the plaintiff's [claim].

Cornelis Lambertsen Cool, plaintiff, vs. Jan van Vorst. The defendant is condemned by virtue of his declaration to pay the plaintiff fl. 3 and no more.

Ditto Cool, plaintiff, vs. Vroutjen Ides. Default.

---

[1] Manuscript destroyed. In the calender entry the name is given as "Cuvelzeers," but this is probably a mistake. In Dutch records the name is frequently spelled "Cuvilje," which is probably a phonetic rendering of the French name "Cuvelier," of which "Cuveliers" is either a variant or the possessive form. It is also possible, however, that the Dutch form "Cuvilje" should be interpreted as "Cuville," it all depending on whether the final e was accented or not.

Jan Loosrecht, plaintiff, vs. Jan Eversten Bout, defendant, for recovery of earned monthly wages. The defendant is condemned to pay the plaintiff for the period of service rendered, namely, fl. 50.

Abraham Page, plaintiff, vs. Barent Dircksz, baker. Defendant condemned to pay plaintiff what he owes him.

Ulrich Lupolt, plaintiff, vs. Gillis Pietersen, chief boat-swain and butler of the caravel De Hoop, defendant, for having as a rascal and contrary to his oath left the service of the Company and gone over to the English. Ordered that all the defendant's monthly wages be confiscated and furthermore that his name be posted as that of a rascal.

On the 12th of August

It having been resolved in council to appoint two inspectors of the tobacco which shall be grown in the district of New Nether-land in order that the tobacco culture here may not lose its reputation, we have appointed and commissioned, as we do appoint and commission, Claes van Elslandt and Wybrant Pietersen inspectors; and henceforth no tobacco shall be exported out of this province without having been inspected by the inspectors and declared to be good merchandise. For which they shall receive a salary of 10 stivers per 100 pounds.

Master Gerlyn, plaintiff, vs. Hendrick Pietersen from Wesel, defendant, for payment for goods delivered to him. Parties are ordered to bring proper proof tomorrow.

On the 19th of August, being Thursday

Everardus Bogardus, minister, plaintiff, vs. Loosrecht, farm hand, defendant. The plaintiff demands that the defendant shall be at his service, as he bound himself to the plaintiff. The defendant having admitted the same is ordered by the director and council to place himself at the service of the plaintiff or to come to further agreement with him.

Adam Roelantsen, plaintiff, vs. Jan Kant [   ], in an action of slander. Cant having threatened to make complaint against the [plaintiff] before the director and council, he gave for answer that he cared for no one in the country.

Declaration of Hendrick Jansen, locksmith, that he heard Adam Roelantsen say that he had enough of every one in New Netherland.

Declaration of Jan Jansen, from Bremen, that he heard said Adam say that he had enough of the country and all that concerned it.

Declaration of Remner Jansen that he heard Adam Roelants say that he had enough of the country and the council. Whereupon Jan Cant said, "Do you mean the director also?" Thereupon Adam kept still.

[16] Adam Roelantsen from Dockum, plaintiff, vs. [Jan] from Bremen, Tomas Walraven, Jan Jansen, gunner, defendants, for slander. Case put over to the next court day and parties ordered to bring proper proof.

————————————

Ordinance for the inspection of tobacco and drawing up
       legal instruments [1]

Whereas it is deemed necessary by the director and council of New Netherland to frame an order respecting the planting of tobacco, since many tobacco planters seek only to raise a large

————————————

[1] Revised from Laws and Ordinances of New Netherland, pp. 16-17.

crop of tobacco without caring whether it be good, well cured or properly made, whereby our tobacco entirely loses the good reputation which it enjoys in other countries; Therefore, in order to prevent this, all persons are hereby notified, warned and commanded to make well conditioned tobacco, to properly remove all superfluous leaves, see that the tobacco is well cured and to use as little water as possible even for that which is spun. Furthermore, all tobacco which is to be shipped or sent out of New Netherland must first be brought to the appointed warehouse, there to be inspected, marked and weighed and payment to be made there also of the Company's duties on all exported goods, to wit, five of every 100 pounds, according to the tenor of the Freedoms granted by the Company; for which purpose we have appointed two sworn inspectors, who shall make the inspection and receive the duties thereon; and whoever shall act contrary hereto shall forfeit all his tobacco and furthermore be arbitrarily punished.

Likewise, henceforward, no instruments, whether contracts, obligations, leases, or bills of sale, or other writings of whatever nature they may be, and concerning which any dispute may arise, shall be held valid by the director and council unless they shall be written by the secretary of this place. Let every one take warning and guard himself against loss.

Thus done and published in Fort Amsterdam, this 19th of August 1638.

On the 26th August, being Thursday

Claes Cornelissen Swits, plaintiff, vs. Cornelis Lambertsen Cool, defendant. Plaintiff demands delivery of the horses which he bought of the defendant. The plaintiff is ordered to bring sufficient proof that the purchase took place in proper form.

Jan Kant, plaintiff, against Adam Roelantsen from Dockum, defendant for slander. Plaintiff demands proof of the slander which the defendant uttered against him, or, in case he has no proof, to restore his honor. The defendant declares in the presence of the court that he had nothing to say against the plaintiff and that he acknowledged and considered him to be an honorable man.

Jan Jansen, gunner, plaintiff, vs. Adam Roelants from Dockum, defendant, for slander. Plaintiff demands vindication of his honor. Parties are condemned to pay each 25 st. to the poor.

Jan from Bremen, defendant, vs. Adam Roelants, plaintiff, for slander. Jan from Bremen is condemned to pay 25 st. to the poor.

Tomas Bescher, plaintiff, vs. Maryn Adriaensen, defendant, for slander. Parties are ordered to bring proper proof on the next court day.

Master Gerlyn, plaintiff, vs. Nicolaes, Corl[ae]r's servant, defendant, for slander. Defendant declares that he has nothing to say against the plaintiff.

Master Philip Teyler, plaintiff, vs. Nicolaes Martens, for slander. Defendant declares he has nothing to say against the plaintiff.

[18] On the 26th of August 1638

Claes Cornelissen S[wits], plaintiff, vs. Montang[ne, defendant]. The plaintiff complains that the defendant beat [plaintiff's] wife. The defendant, having admitted the same, is condemned to compound with the fiscal.

Johannes La Montangnie, plaintiff, vs. Claes Cornelisen, defendant, for slander. Case put over to the next court day.

Symen Dirckson Pos, plaintiff, vs. Philip de Truy, defendant, demanding payment of fl. 4:10. Case put over to the next court day as the defendant denies the claim.

On the 2d of September

Claes Cornelissen, wheelwright, plaintiff, vs. Cornelis Lamberts Cool, defendant. The plaintiff demands delivery of the horse bought by him from the defendant. The plaintiff having produced satisfactory proof that the purchase took place in proper form, the defendant, by virtue thereof, is condemned to deliver the said horse to the plaintiff, on condition that the plaintiff furnish sufficient security for the payment, unless parties shall agree otherwise.

Symen Dircksen Pos, plaintiff, vs. Philip de Truy, defendant, for payment of fl. 4:10. The defendant answers that he does not owe so much. Parties agree together, one releasing the other, provided that Philip de Truy deliver to the plaintiff as much fish as he has in his house.

Johannes La Montaenje, plaintiff, vs. Claes Cornelissen, defendant, for assault. Is condemned to pay fl. 6 to the poor and to satisfy the fiscal.

[19] On the 16th of September anno 1638,

being Thursday

Everardus Bogardus, defendant, vs. Johannes La Montaengne, plaintiff. Whereas the defendant has a power of attorney from Geertrujt Bornstra, widow of the late Hendrick de Foreest, plaintiff's brother-in-law, to demand the goods and effects of the said Foreest, the plaintiff requests that the defendant take possession of the house together with the cattle and appurtenances of the plantation, provided the defendant pay the plaintiff the balance of the amount due him by de Foreest, according to the account thereof. Parties are ordered to submit their complaint and answer in writing on the next court day.

On the 30th of September, being Thursday

The director and council of New Netherland having seen the criminal action and demand of the fiscal against Jan Gysbertsen from Rotterdam, charged with manslaughter committed in killing Gerrit Jansen, gunner, before the gate of Fort Amsterdam on Saturday, being the 15th of May 1638, about 4 o'clock in the afternoon, and having examined the testimony of witnesses together with the reports of the surgeons who examined the body, the personal summons and defaults taken against him and the conclusion of the fiscal, and the aforesaid writings have been duly weighed and considered by us, after invocation of the name of God; therefore, we, wishing to do justice, have debarred the delinquent from all exceptions, defenses and pleas whatsoever which he might have made use of in the aforesaid matter, and therefore declare Jan Gysbertsen aforesaid in every way liable to arrest if he can be apprehended for the aforesaid ugly crime committed against the highest majesty of God and his supreme rulers as well as against the blood relations of the deceased, whom he, the delinquent, murderously robbed of their friend and relative; all of which in a land of justice can in no wise be tolerated of suffered but ought to be punished with all rigor as an example to others.

[20] Therefore, we have condemned, as we do condemn hereby, the delinquent, in case he be apprehended, to be punished by the sword in such way that death shall ensue, with confiscation of all his movable and immovable property, none excepted, and including all his earned monthly wages which are due him by the West India Company, the just half to be paid to the widow of the deceased Gerrit Jansz or his heirs, one quarter part of the Company and one quarter part to the fiscal, the delinquent also to pay the costs of the suit. Thus done and sentenced in Fort Amsterdam this [   ], anno 1638.

Johannes la Montaengne, plaintiff, vs. Everardus Bogardus, defendant, for the delivery of the property belonging to Hendrick de Foreest, deceased, or his heirs.

Having seen the demand of the plaintiff and the answer of the defendant, it is ordered that the property aforesaid shall publicly be sold to the highest bidder on the 7th of October, being Thursday, at Fort Amsterdam, for the benefit of the widow, and the defendant, in virtue of his power of attorney from the widow of the late de Foreest, is condemned to repay to La Montaengnie such moneys as he has advanced for the benefit of the farm.

Anthony Jansen, plaintiff, vs. Everardus Bogardus, minister, defendant, for the payment of fl. 74 which the defendant owes the plaintiff. The defendant expressly denies the plaintiff's claim. The plaintiff gives the defendant the choice of taking the oath, whereupon the defendant has declared under oath before the court that he owes no more than 7 gl. Upon the oath of the defendant the plaintiff's claim for the remaining fl. 67 is denied and he is condemned to pay the costs of the trial.

[21] On the 7th of October

Everardus Bogardus, minister, plaintiff, vs. Anthony Jansen
from Salee, defendant, for slander.

Declaration of Philip de Truy, made in court at the request
of Bogarde, that on the departure of the ship Soutberch, anno
1633, the said Truy, going to the strand to draw water, heard and
saw the following: Grietjen Reyniers, wife of Anthony Jansen
aforenamed, being likewise on the strand, the crew of the
Soutbergh aforesaid called to her, "Whore, Whore, Two pound
butter's whore!" Whereupon Grietjen, paying little attention to
this, lifted up her petticoat and [turning to] the crew pointed
to her behind.

Declaration of Symon Dircksen Pos that on last Thursday he
heard Griet Reyniers say that Bogarde, the minister, owed her
some money and that he had taken oath that he did not owe her
anything, she saying further, "Although he has taken the oath,
nevertheless he is indebted to me."

Declaration before the court of Hans Schipper and Jochem
Beeckman, both soldiers, that last Thursday they both heard
Grietjen Reyniers, the wife of Anthony Jansen, say that the
minister, Bogardus, had taken a false oath. On the other hand,
Anthony Jansen alleged that the minister had said that his present
wife before he married her had earned a skirt of fl. 40.

Case adjourned to the next court day, in order meanwhile
to examine the evidence and testimony of witnesses.

By virtue of the judgment given on the 3d of June last
against Anthony Jansen, Ulrich Lupoldt, fiscal, is hereby

authorized to levy execution on the property of Anthony Jansen
up to [the amount required for] the payment of Bogarde.

[22] On the 14th of October, being Thursday

Ulrich Lupoldt, fiscal, plaintiff, vs. Anthony Jan[sen]
from Zalee, as husband and guardian of his wife, Grietjen Reyniers,
for slandering the minister, Bogardus.

Parties being heard and the documents having been carefully
examined, Griet Reyniers is condemned to appear next Saturday,
being the 16th instant, in Fort Amsterdam, in order then at the
ringing of the bell to make public acknowledgment that the
minister is an honorable and honest man and that she has lied
falsely; furthermore she is condemned to pay the costs of the
trial and fl. 3 to the poor.

Anthony Jansen from Salee is hereby forbidden to carry any
arms, whatever they may be called, on this side of the Fresh
water, with the exception of a knife and an axe; also, he shall
refrain from giving the least offense to Domine Bogardus either
by word or deed, on pain of corporal punishment, and he is
further condemned to pay a fine of fl. 12 for the benefit of
the fiscal.

Tobias Tonisen and Willem Fredricksen, plaintiffs, vs.
Johan La Montaenje, defendant.

The plaintiffs ask to be released from their contract of
service, maintaining that they are not bound to serve the defendant, as they were hired by his uncle and not by the defendant.

The defendant produces the contracts made between the
plaintiffs and Geraert de Foreest from which it appears clearly
that the plaintiffs are bound to serve the said de Foreest or

his agents for three consecutive years after their arrival here in New Netherland; furthermore, the defendant shows a power of attorney and authorization from the aforesaid de Foreest to employ the plaintiffs in his service at the expiration of their term of service. All of this having been duly considered, the plaintiffs are condemned to serve out their bounden time without any gainsay with La Montaenje, who also promises at the expiration of their bounded time to tender and pay them here in New Netherland the wages which shall then be due to them.

[23] On the [1]4th of October [anno] 1638

Johannes La Montaenje, plaintiff, vs. Tobias Tonissen, defendant, for slander.

The plaintiff demands proof that the ration meat was dried at his house and sent away without the defendant having eaten or had his share thereof as well as the plaintiff.

The defendant declares under oath before the court that what he has spoken in regard to La Montaenje is untrue, namely, that he had dried and carried away the meat without giving his servants any of it to eat, acknowledging that he had his share of the meat as well as the plaintiff.

On the 16th of October, being Saturday

Griet Reyniers appeared in court and declared the following in the presence of the hereinafter mentioned persons:

"I, Griet Reyniers, acknowledge in the presence of the commander and council and all other persons present that I lied what I said regarding Domine Bogardus, namely, that the same was a perjurer, and I pray God, the court and Bogardus for forgiveness, promising that I shall hereafter comport and conduct myself in such a way that the commander and council and everybody else shall be satisfied."

On Thursday, being the 21st of October

Everardus Bogardus, minister, husband and guardian of Anna Jåns, plaintiff, vs. Anthony Jansen from Salee, defendant, for slander.

Anthony Jansen, appearing in court, declares that he has nothing to say against Anna Jans, wife of Bogardus, acknowledging and considering her to be an honorable and virtuous woman and promising henceforth to say nothing to the prejudice of the plaintiff or his wife.

Ulrich Lupoldt, fiscal, plaintiff, vs. Jan Evertsen, Hendrick Cornelissen van Vorst and Gerrit Dircksz, defendants.

Plaintiff demands that the defendants be punished, alleging that they have traded in furs contrary to their oath. The defendants deny that they have traded any furs. Parties to reappear 14 days hence to produce clear proof.

[24] On Thursday, being the 28th of October anno 1[6]38

Ulrich Lupoldt, fiscal, plaintiff, vs. Anthony Jan[sen] from Salee, defendant. He charges the defendant with having stolen the wood which Phi[lip] de Truy had cut in the woods. The defendant says that he is not guilty of the charge. Case put over until the next court day, the parties meanwhile to bring proper proof of everything.

Ulrich Lupoldt, fiscal, plaintiff, vs. Cors Pietersen, defendant. The plaintiff, by virtue of the complaint of the Indians and the deposition of two persons, demands that the defendant be punished for assault and theft. The defendant answers that he has never seen the Indians here, much less taken from them any seawan or cloth. Sivert Cant declares in court

that it was the same Indian whom Cors Pietersen threw overboard.
Fredrick Lubbertsen declares that he well knows the Indian and
received from him a half fathom of seawan to procure from the
defendant the return of the cloth which was taken from him. Case
adjourned to the next court day.

On Thursday, being the 5th of November anno 1638

The fiscal, plaintiff, vs. Cors Pietersen, defendant, for
assault. Plaintiff demands judgment and justice against the
defendant. The case between the plaintiff and the defendant
being carefully considered, the defendant is condemned to restore
what he took from the Indians and to pay 50 stivers for the
benefit of the fiscal and costs.

On Thursday, being the 18th of November anno 1638

Nicolaes Coorn, plaintiff, vs. the soldiers, defendants.
The plaintiff states that not all the soldiers are thieves, but
only Hans Schipper, Jochem Beeckm[an] and Jacob Swart. Case put
over to the next court day.

[25] On Thursday, being the 25th of November anno 1638

Cornelis Lambertsen Cool, plaintiff, vs. Jan Celes, defendant.
The plaintiff demands reparation of the damage which the defendant's
hogs have caused the plaintiff. Parties are ordered to settle
with each other and each to keep his hogs penned in.

Ulrich Lupoldt, plaintiff, vs. Nicolaes Coorn, defendant.
Whereas the defendant is accused by the soldiers of theft, as
appears by their testimony and the deposition of van Curler, the
plaintiff demands that the said Coorn be punished according to
the merits of the case. The defendant is suspended from his
office for the period of eight days.

Ulrich Lupoldt, plaintiff, vs. Hans Schipper, Jochem Beeckman
and Jacob Swardt, defendants. Whereas the defendants are accused
of theft by their sergeant Coorn and partly admit their theft,
the plaintiff demands that they be punished as an example to
other soldiers. Case adjourned to the next court day so that
parties may bring further evidence in the matter.

Ordinance for the recovery of public property, protection of
    private garden and henroosts and prohibiting persons in
    the public service to quit the island of Manhattan
    without permission [1]

Whereas the honorable director and council of New Netherland
observe that there are persons here who seek to enrich themselves
with the Company's goods and effects, taking possession of the
same as if they were their own property, and whereas such tends
to the prejudice of the aforesaid Company; Therefore, all persons
who at present have any property in their hands belonging to the
Company, be it large or small, are warned to return the same
within the space of eight days unless they have purchased it
from the former honorable directors, without proof of which no
excuse shall be accepted; and if hereafter it be found that any
one is in possession of property belonging to the Company, he
shall suffer the punishment usually administered to thieves and
unfaithful servants who steal their masters' property.

[26] And whereas complaints are made by many persons that
their gardens have been robbed and their poultry taken away, if
there be any one who can give information of the thieves, he
shall be paid by the honorable director twenty-five guilders as

---

[1] Revised from Laws and Ordinances of New Netherland.
pp. 17-18.

a reward, and in case he has been guilty himself be pardoned and
his name concealed.

Likewise, every one of the Company's servants, of whatever
rank or capacity he may be, is commanded not to leave the island
of Manhatans without the express consent of the honorable commander. Whoever shall be found to have acted contrary hereto
shall forfeit three months' wages. Thus done in council and on
this date, being the 25th of November, and published and posted
in Fort Amsterdam.

On Thursday, being the 2d of December anno 1638

Gerreken Hessels, plaintiff, vs. Anthony Jansen from Salee,
defendant, for having attached the sum of fl. 24 and 4 stivers.
The plaintiff demands that the attachment of the fl. 24, 4 st.
in the hands of the defendant, sued out by Jan Claesen Alteras,
be vacated, since he, the plaintiff, does not owe Jan Claessen
anything now, except for a hog for which the payment will become
due on the 1st of May anno 1639, which payment Alteras aforesaid
can not claim at present.

Anthony Jansen is ordered to satisfy the plaintiff as the
attachment is null and void and the fl. 24 and 4 st. are deemed
to be not subject to attachment by said Alteras, as the claim
which he has against the plaintiff has not yet become due.

Tomas Bescher, plaintiff, vs. Hendrick Jansen, tailor,
defendant, for slander. Case put over for a week so that parties
may bring further proof.

[27] On Thursday, being the 2d of December anno [16]38
Ulrich Lupoldt, fiscal, plaintiff, vs. Gillis Pietersen, chief
boatswain and butler on the yacht De Hoop, defendant.

Whereas the fiscal makes complaint against the defendant on account of the loss which the Company has suffered by reason of his desertion from the service of the said Company, as more fully appears by the bill of complaint of the plaintiff against the defendant, and whereas notwithstanding three personal citations the defendant has not appeared to make answer and default was taken against him; therefore, all this having been duly considered by us, the defendant's name is posted on the gate of Fort Amsterdam as that of a rascal and oath breaker, with confiscation of all his earned monthly wages which are due him by the chamber of Amsterdam of the honorable West India Company, to wit, one-third part for the benefit of the said Company, one-third part for the poor and one-third part for the fiscal, the defendant being further comdemned to pay the costs of the trial.

Ulrich Lupoldt, fiscal, plaintiff, vs. Nicolaes Coorn, sergeant, defendant, charged with theft and abetting the same; also with adultery.

The plaintiff demands judgment and punishment of the crimes committed by the defendant as hereinafter described, inasmuch as the defendant, who by reason of his office was in duty bound to set a good moral example to his soldiers, has notwithstanding been guilty of bartering with the savages for private gain the axes which were given to him and the soldiers to cut wood and contrary to his oath has hidden the beavers in his bunk.

Likewise, the defendant has at divers times had Indian women and Negresses sleep entire nights with him in his bed, in the presence of all the soldiers.

[28] On Thursday, being the 2d of December anno [16]38

He has rolled a piece of cloth of the Company in a bearskin and stolen it from the Company. The defendant has not been ashamed to command his soldiers to keep out of the way of the commander when they perceived that he intended to give them some order. Moreover, when the soldiers had to his knowledge stolen turnips, chickens and tobacco pipes and other property, he has had his share thereof; all of which are matters which ought not to be tolerated in countries where right and justice is maintained.

All that is hereinbefore written being duly weighed and considered and everything having been clearly proved by the testimony of all the soldiers and the deposition of Mr. Jacobus van Curler and the same being considered matters of serious consequence which can not be tolerated, we therefore, administering justice, depose sergeant from his office, as we do hereby, commanding him to serve the Company as a private soldier until such time as he shall have completed his term of service with the Company.

Ulrich Lupoldt, fiscal, plaintiff, vs. Hans Schipper, Jochem Beeckman and Jacob Swardt, soldiers, defendants, accused of theft. The plaintiff charges the defendants with theft of chickens, turnips and tobacco pipes and asks that the honorable director and council may be pleased to provide therein, in order that the inhabitants of New Netherland shall no longer lose their property through such persons.

Whereas the [crimes] aforementioned are prejudicial to the community and the same are duly proved by the confessions of Hans Schipper and Jochem Beeckman, the same are condemned to ride two hours on the wooden horse.

[29] On Thursday, being the 9th of December anno 1638

Anthony, the Portuguese, plaintiff, vs. Anthony Jansen from Salee, defendant, for injury to a hog. The plaintiff demands reparation of the damage which the defendant's dog caused to the hog. Claes van Elslandt and Barent Dircksen are ordered to appraise the damage, the defendant to pay whatever they shall estimate the damage to be.

Tomas Bescher, plaintiff, vs. Hendrick Jansen, tailor, defendant, for slander. Case put over to the next court day.

On Thursday, being the 16th of December anno 1638

Anthony, the Portuguese, plaintiff, vs. Anthony Jansen from Salee, defendant. Plaintiff demands payment for the damage done to his hog. Defendant is condemned to pay for the damage according to the judgment of the appraisers.

Françoys Lasle, plaintiff, vs. Nidt Wilson, [1] defendant, Parties request that the council be pleased to appoint two persons to appraise their plantation and to examine their accounts. Claes van Elslandt and Tomas Hal are appointed to examine the affairs and accounts of the parties.

Hendrick Jansen, tailor, plaintiff, vs. Tomas Becher, [defendant], for slander. Parties ordered to keep silent on pain of forfeiting fl. 25

[30] Anno 1639

On Thursday, being the 13th of January, in Fort Amsterdam

Cecero Piere, plaintiff, vs. Davidt Pietersen, defendant. Default.

---

[1] Edward Wilson.

Blancke Ael, plaintiff, vs. Adam Rolantsen, defendant, for slander. Parties are ordered not to slander each other any more, on pain of being fined at the discretion of the honorable director and council.

Hans Steen, plaintiff, vs. Tomas Coninck, defendant, for slander. The parties being heard, the defendant does not persist in his slander and acknowledges that he has nothing to say against the plaintiff and admits him to be an honorable and honest man.

On the 20th ditto, being Thursday

Maryn Adriaensen, plaintiff, vs. Everardus Bogardus, minister, as husband and guardian of Anna Jans, defendant. The plaintiff demands payment from the defendant, the defendant's wife having received, as she says, a suit of clothes as a present from Jacob Govertsen. The plaintiff maintains that no one has a right to make a present to or give away his property as long as he has not paid his debts, from which it would follow that inasmuch as Anna Jans, the plaintiff's wife, received the aforesaid [suit] from the late Jacob Govertsen, she must pay his debts. Parties being heard and Anna Jans having taken the oath that the afore-said clothes were presented to her and belong to her, it is ordered that what is due to Maryn Adriaensen and the other creditors of the late Jacob Govertsen shall pro rata be paid by the Company out of the money which is due to the said Jacob Govertsen.

Claes Cornelissen Swits, plaintiff, vs. Jeuriaen Hendricksz, defendant. Default.

Cecero Piere, plaintiff, vs. Davidt Pietersen, defendant. Plaintiff demands payment of his earned monthly wages. Case put over to next week.

[31] On Thursday, being the 27th of January

Davidt Pietersen, plaintiff, vs. Cecero Piere, defendant. The plaintiff maintains that he does not owe anything to the defendant as he ran away as a rascal from the plaintiff's ship. Parties being heard, it is ordered by us that Davit Pietersen shall give Piere Cecero fl. 10 as a present, wherewith he must be satisfied.

Ulrich Lupoldt, fiscal, plaintiff, vs. Marten Cael, skipper of the ship De Liefde, defendant. The plaintiff demands justice against the defendant who bound himself as security for himself and his ship's crew not to sell any merchandise in any way within the limits of the Company. Notwithstanding this, much merchandise is daily sold in the ship, as in a public store. The defendant fails to appear. Default.

On Thursday, being the 3d of February

Ulrich Lupoldt, fiscal, plaintiff, vs. Gysbert Cornelissen Beyerlandt. The plaintiff demands that the defendant be sent to the fatherland and condemned to the usual punishment of trouble makers who wound the soldiers in the Fort, as the defendant has lately done in Fort Amsterdam. [The court] having seen the complaint of the fiscal against Gysbert Cornelissen Beyerlandt and everything being taken duly into consideration, the same is condemned to work with the Negroes for the Company until such time as the first sloop shall sail for the South river and to serve the Company there and furthermore to pay the wounded soldier fl. 15, the surgeon a fee of fl. 10 for his services and the fiscal a fine of fl. 10.

[32] On the 10th of February 1639

The fiscal, plaintiff, vs. Marten Cael, skipper, defendant.
The plaintiff maintains his former complaint. The defendant
answers that it is not known to him that his men have sold any
goods. Case adjourned to the next court day.

The fiscal, plaintiff, vs. Pietter Wyncoop, defendant.
Having taken into consideration the action of the plaintiff, as
it appears thereby that the defendant has fraudulently deprived
the Company of its dues, the seized distilled liquor is confiscated and the defendant is condemned to pay a fine of fl. 12
for the benefit of the fiscal.

Ulrich Lupoldt, plaintiff, vs. Maryn Adriaensen, Hendrick
Jansen, tailor, Dirck, the Noorman, and Jan Lemmet. Whereas the
defendants, contrary to the ordinance, have without consent
been aboard the ship De Liefde, this being their first offense,
they are condemned to pay a fine of 20 stivers each for the
benefit of the fiscal.

Barendt Dircksen, baker, plaintiff, vs. Marten Cael, defendant,
for slander. The plaintiff demands proof of the slanderous
remarks made by the defendant to the plaintiff. Case adjourned
to the next court day.

On Thursday, being the 17th of February

Ulrich Lupoldt, fiscal, plaintiff, vs. Jan Eversen Bout,
Abraham Isaacksen Planck and Gerrit Dircksen, defendants. The
plaintiff demands that the defendants be fined according to the
ordinance as they went on board the ship De Liefde without permission. On the demand of the fiscal and the defendants are condemned to pay a fine of 20 stivers to the benefit of the fiscal.

[33] Mr. Isaack Allerton, plaintiff, vs. Eduwardt Celes, defendant, for payment of fl. 19. The plaintiff demands the payment of fl. 19 which have long been due to him. The defendant admits the aforesaid debt. The defendant is condemned to pay the plaintiff tomorrow, as he is about to leave for New England.

Barent Dircksen, baker, plaintiff, vs. Marten Cael, skipper of the ship De Liefde, for slander. The defendant declares that he has made no remarks about Barent Dircksen.

Ulrich Lupoldt, fiscal, plaintiff, vs. Marten Cael, skipper of the ship De Liefde, defendant. The plaintiff in reply to the answer of the defendant says that it is well known to the defendant that his ship's crew, for whom he is responsible according to the charterparty, have sold divers merchandise in the ship, maintaining furthermore that even if it were true that he, the defendant, had no knowledge whatever of what is aforewritten, he is nevertheless punishable, as he must answer for his crew who thus rob the Company of their freight charges and duties.

Jan Eversen declares that he bought two cheeses from the chief boatswain or his assistant and also from the common sailors of the ship De Liefde one English and one red cap, two pairs of stockings and two pairs of slippers.

Gerrit Dircksen declares that he bought a cheese from the crew.

Abraham Planc declares that he bought a cheese and one pair of slippers from the sailors of the ship De Liefde.

[34] On the 17th of February anno 1639

Having considered the action and the complaint of Ulrich Lupoldt, fiscal, against Marten Cael, Skipper of the ship De Liefde, chartered by the honorable directors of the chartered

West India Company, chamber of Amsterdam, to sail to New Netherland, on condition that neither he, the skipper, nor any of his
crew were to be at liberty to sell any merchandise or do any trading either in New Netherland or elsewhere within the limits of
the charter, [1] for all of which he, Marten Cael, offered as
security the ship and stipulated freight, as will more fully
appear from the charter party made thereof;

And whereas it clearly appears from the seized brandy and
stockings, as well as by the testimony of various persons who
bought goods from some of the sailors of said ship that the
skipper failed to have his crew observe the terms of the charter-
party; and also in consideration of the acknowledgment by the
skipper that he only became aware in New Netherland that his crew
had shipped any merchandise in the said ship;

We, therefore, doing justice, have debarred the aforesaid
skipper Marten Cael from all exceptions, defenses and pleas of
which he might in any way avail himself in this case and condemn
him, as we do hereby, to forfeit one month's stipulated freight
amounting to the sum of 1290 gl., whereof the Company shall
receive 645 gl., 322 gl. and 10 st. to be used for the building
of a new church in New Netherland and 322 gl. 10 st. for the
benefit of the fiscal. Thus done in Fort Amsterdam, the day and
year above written.

---

[1] The charter of the Dutch West India Company, granted
June 3, 1621.

[35] On the 10th of March anno 1639, being Thursday

Hendrick Pietersen, mason, plaintiff, **vs.** Davit Pietersen,
defendant.

The plaintiff demands that the defendant pay his wages
earned on board the ship called <u>De Coninck Davit</u>, amounting to
the sum of six gl.

Defendant shows the account of the aforesaid ship, whereby
it clearly appears that the plaintiff's partner received the
money from the defendant and as the defendant swears to the
correctness of his book, the plaintiff's demand is denied.

Marten Cael, plaintiff, vs. Davit Pietersen, defendant.
Plaintiff demands that the defendant pay him, the plaintiff, for
board received by himself and his servants on the ship <u>de Liefde</u>.
The defendant answers that he is not bound to pay as much as the
board amounts to, **inasmuch** as the skipper has not served
meals as required. Case adjourned to the next court day.

Anthony Jansen from Sale, plaintiff, vs. Wybrant Pietersen,
defendant, for slander. Case put over to the next court day.

On the 24th of March

Jan Cornelissen from Rotterdam, plaintiff, vs. Anthony Jansen
from Salee, defendant, for slander. Default.

Philip de Truy, plaintiff, vs. Anthony Jansen from Salee,
defendant, for slander. Default.

Wybrant Pietersen, plaintiff, [1] vs. Anthony Jansen, defendant,
for slander. Default.

Gerreken Hessels, plaintiff, vs. the same, defendant. Default.

The fiscal, plaintiff, vs. the same, defendant. Default.

---

[1] The original has: <u>ged</u>[<u>acchde</u>], defendant.

[36] On the 31st of March anno 1639

Abraham Pagie, plaintiff, vs. Claes, the tailor, defendant,
for payment of 14 gl. Defendant admits that he owes the plaintiff
14 gl. and is therefore condemned to tender and pay the aforesaid
sum within the space of one month.

Jan Cornelissen, plaintiff, vs. Anthony Jansen from Salee,
defendant, for slander. Default.

The fiscal, plaintiff, vs. Anthony Jansen from Salee,
defendant, for slander. Default.

Wybrant Pietersen, plaintiff, vs. Anthony Jansen from
Salee, defendant, for slander. Default.

Philip de Truy, plaintiff, vs. Anthony Jansen from Salee,
defendant, for slander. Default.

Gerreken Hessels, plaintiff, vs. Anthony Jansen from Salee,
defendant, for delivery of a kid. Default.

[Ordinance prohibiting the sale of firearms to the Indians and
requiring vessels to take out clearances] [1]

Whereas the director and general council of New Netherland
have observed that many persons, both servants of the Company
and inhabitants, contrary to the orders and commands of their
High Mightinesses the Lords States General and the Chartered
West India Company, presume to sell to the Indians in these parts
guns, powder and lead, which has already caused much mischief and,
if no means be adopted by us here to prevent the same, will hereafter cause only greater evil; Therefore every inhabitant of New
Netherland, be his station, quality or rank what it may, is

---

[1] Revised from Laws and Ordinances of New Netherland,
pp. 18-19.

most expressly forbidden to sell any guns, powder or lead to the
Indians on pain of being put to death; and if any one shall inform
against any person who shall act contrary thereto, he shall
receive a reward of 50 guilders.

[37] Furthermore, all persons are hereby notified that no
one shall undertake to sail with boats or other vessels to Fort
Orange, the South river or Fort De Hoop without a permit from
the honorable director and, coming thence, bringing with him
clearances from the commissaries residing at the aforesaid places
on the part of the Company; and in case it be found that any
one has been at the places above named without order as aforesaid,
such vessel and the goods laden therein shall be confiscated for
the benefit of the Company and the person shall in addition be
fined such sum as according to the merits of the case shall be
deemed proper.

And all our dear and faithful commissaries who are in
authority at the places where these presents are sent are ordered
and commanded to post the same in the usual place, in order that
every one may know the contents thereof and guard himself
against loss.

Thus done and published in Fort Amsterdam, this 31st of
March Aᵒ. 1639.

On Thursday, being the 7th of April anno 1639

Ulrich Lupoldt, fiscal, plaintiff, vs. Hans Steen, corporal,
defendant. Plaintiff demands that the defendant be punished as
a whoremonger ought to be punished, as at the guardhouse he has
committed fornication according to the testimony of the following

persons who, being on duty at the guardhouse, saw and heard as
follows:

Balthasar Lourens from Hadderslee, [1] aged 23 years, soldier,
declares that Hans Steen about three weeks ago lay with an
Indian woman at the guardhouse.

Hans Fredrickx from Swynsont, [2] aged 20 years, soldier,
declares in court that about three weeks ago Hans Steen, being
with him on duty at the guardhouse, lay on the bunk with an
Indian woman, the two being almost far enough apart for a man
to have lain between them. Secondly, that on the voyage hither
he hid a small brandy keg for Hans Steen in his chest, without
knowing what was in it.

Hans Noorman from Dronten, [3] aged 20 years, soldier, declares
that about two months ago he lay with Hans Steen in the guardhouse when an Indian woman came and laid her down on the other
side of the said Steen, covering the said Hans Steen with her
blanket. He has also seen here on shore a small keg, which
according to his estimate contained two or three pounds of powder.

[38] On Thursday, being the 7th of April anno 1639

Remmer Jansen from Jeverden, [4] aged 20 years, says that an
Indian woman came to the guardhouse and that Hans Steen desired
her to lie down on the bunk beside him, which took place; also
that Hans Steen ordered the soldiers to put out the fire, which
soldiers put out the fire, and that the aforesaid Indian woman
left the guardhouse in the morning.

---

[1] Hadersleben, a seaport in Schleswig.
[2] Swinesund, an inlet of the Skager Rack, between
Norway and Sweden.
[3] Trondhjem, seaport town of Norway.
[4] Jever, Oldenburg, Germany.

Declaration of Jochem Beeckman from Statyn, [5] aged about
24 years. Hans Steen, seeing an Indian woman, called to her to
come to the guardhouse. When there, said Hans Steen asked her
to lie down beside him on the bunk, which the woman did. He
also forbade the soldiers to make a fire.

Declaration of Jan Andriesen from Basenborch, [6] aged 23 years,
soldier. Declares that another did guard duty for him and that
he was not present.

Declaration of Gregoris [blank], aged 22 years, that he saw
on the ship De Liefde that there was some powder left, but that
Hans Steen stowed it away and that on shore he never saw the
aforesaid powder again, which belonged to the Company.

All that is hereinbefore written having been duly considered
and seeing that this is a matter of consequence which tends to
demoralize the soldiers and might occasion disorder in the guardhouse, we have therefore condemned Hans Steen aforesaid to ride
the wooden horse for three hours and to do guard duty as a
private soldier for 14 days.

The fiscal, plaintiff, vs. Anthony Jansen from Salee, defendant.
Plaintiff demands that the defendant prove that he, the plaintiff,
drew his sword in his house; also that the honorable director and
council be pleased to banish the defendant from the jurisdiction
of New Netherland in as much as the good inhabitants daily
experience much trouble from him and his wife, as appears by the
depositions and also by the former resolution book kept during

---

[5] Stettin, Germany.
[6] Probably intended for Batenborch, or Batenburg, province
of Gelderland.

the administration of the late Mr. van Twiller, which testifies
to their conduct here; all of which the plaintiff requests may
be duly considered.

[39] On Thursday, being the 7th of April anno 1639

Jan Cornelissen from Rotterdam, plaintiff, vs. Anthony Jansen
from Salee, defendant, for slander. Plaintiff demands vindication
of his honor as the defendant can not prove what he has said to
the prejudice of the plaintiff.

Wybrant Pietersen, plaintiff, vs. Anthony Jansen from Salee,
defendant, for slander. Plaintiff demands that the defendant
prove that his books are false as he produced them before the
director and council. Defendant answers that he can not prove it.

Gerreken Hessels, plaintiff, vs. Anthony Jansen from Salee,
defendant. Plaintiff demands payment of a kid which the defendant
owes him for wages. Defendant answers that he delivered the kid
to the plaintiff, but that it died. Plaintiff, replying, says
that the defendant wanted to deliver to him a kid which was lying
sick on a pillow near the fire and which he never received, being
ready to confirm the same by oath. The plaintiff has taken the
oath before the director and council and the defendant is condemned
to deliver the kid to the plaintiff.

Having seen the complaint of Ulrich Lupolt against Anthony
Jansen from Salee and Grietjen Reyniers, his wife, in regard to
their comportment and conduct, as appears from the affidavits,
to wit: Nos. 1, 2, 3, 4, 5, 6, 7, 8, 9. 10, 11, 12, 13, 14, 15
and 16, namely, that on the ship she pulled the shirts of some
sailors out of their breeches and in her house measured the male
member of three sailors on a broomstick; also, that during her

confinement she asked the midwife, Whom does the child resemble,
Anthony or Hudden? Furthermore, that she even went so far as
to call out in the fort, I have long enough been the whore of
the nobility, now I want to be the rabble's whore; and whereas
Anthony Jansen heretofore has pointed a loaded pistol at the
foreman, Jacob Stoffelsen, and he as well as she have committed
various other offenses, according to the affidavits examined here,
and daily make new and unheard of trouble, speaking evil of every
one, on account of all of which he requests that they may be
punished and banished, in order that the few people here in New
Netherland may live together in peace;

Therefore, [the court] having duly considered the said case,
having heard the parties [40] and examined all the evidence and
also taken into consideration that six months ago they were obliged
to pray God, the court and the Reverend Bogardus for forgiveness,
acknowledging that they had lied in what they had said about him,
and promised expressly to conduct themselves quietly and piously
as behooves Christians, and that notwithstanding this the said
Anthony and Grietje have since that time been the cause of various
troubles, especially on the 10th of March last past, when they
came out of the consistory, being drunk, all of which are matters
of serious consequence which to disturb and shock the few
inhabitants here; therefore, we have condemned, as we do condemn
hereby, the said Anthony Jansen from Salee and Grietjen Reyniers
to depart from the jurisdiction of New Netherland within the
space of six months and to remain banished forever, and in addition
to pay the costs of the trial. Thus done and sentenced, the day
and year above written, in council in Fort Amsterdam.

On the 28th of April, being Thursday

Davit Provoost, plaintiff, vs. Harman Dircksen, defendant.
Plaintiff demands that the defendant declare for what reasons
he left his service. The defendant answers that he was not treated
well as to board. Provoost is condemned to pay the defendant
for the service which he has rendered him here in this country.
Defendant is condemned to pay the plaintiff the expenses incurred
for him on the ship De Liefde and in Holland.

Abraham Page, plaintiff, vs. Tomas Bescher, defendant.
Plaintiff demands payment of the 97 pounds of tobacco earned by
working. Defendant acknowledges the debt and is condemned to
pay the plaintiff 97 pounds of good tobacco from the next crop.

Philip de Truy, plaintiff, vs. Anthony Jansen from Salee,
defendant. Plaintiff demands that the piece of land given him
by the defendant be transferred to him. Plaintiff's request
is denied.

Ulrich Lupoldt, fiscal, plaintiff, vs. Symen Huypot, defendant.
The fiscal demands that the peltries which were seized [41] be
confiscated for the benefit of the Company And that the yacht and
Lading be also forfeited as the means wherewith the defendant
intended to defraud the Company. The peltries are provisionally
confiscated for the benefit of the Company and in regard to the
further demand of the fiscal the defendant is granted a delay to
submit his answer.

On the 5th of April, that is to say May, being Thursday 1639

D[e] Coninck, soldier, plaintiff, vs. Hans Steen, defendant,
for slander. Parties ordered to appear next week to present
their case in writing.

On the 19th of May 1639

Tomas Bescher, plaintiff, vs. Willem Willemsen, defendant
for slander.

The defendant declares that in the beginning of last month
of April, on a Sunday night, he saw the plaintiff sitting in a
chair by the fire, being asleep, and Ritsert, the Irishman, lying
with the wife of the plaintiff on the bed in which Bescher and
his wife are in the habit of taking their night rest. Also,
that he could see perfectly that the said Ritsert had carnal conversation with the plaintiff's wife, seeing also that the aforesaid
wife dishonorably manipulated the male member of the aforesaid
Irishman. Which aforesaid declaration the defendant confirmed
by oath before the court of the honorable director and council.

Pieter Breyley, aged 22 years, from Mienjeert, [1] in
Somersetscheer, declares as follows: That about a month or five
weeks ago, on a Sunday night, at about 10 or 11 o'clock, while
Bescher say in the chair and was asleep, one Ritsert Pitser, [2]
an Irishman, lay on the bed of the said Tomes Bescher with the
latter's wife and that they had carnal conversation with each
other. Which aforesaid declaration Piter Breyley has confirmed
by oath before the honorable director and council aforesaid.

Parties to appear on the next court day to make everything
clear and to produce proper and further proof.

---

[1] Minehead?, in Somersetshire.
[2] Richard Gitcher.

[42] On Thursday, being the 19th of May anno 1639

Jan Brouwer, plaintiff, vs. G[e]orge Homs, defendant, for payment of fl. 60. Plaintiff demands payment of what is due him. G[e]orge Homs admits the debt and promises to pay within five or six weeks when Mr. Allerton shall have returned to the Manhates from the North.

Isaac Allerton, plaintiff, vs. Vroutjen Ides, defendant. Plaintiff demands payment of four sheep and fl. 25 in cash, as appears by the bond of Mr. Cock. Defendant admits the claim and is ordered to pay within four or five months.

On the 26th of May

Jan Pietersen, plaintiff, vs. Cornelis Jacobsen Stillen, defendant, for payment of maize. Default.

Ulrich Lupoldt, fiscal, plaintiff, vs. Caspaer van Buren, Dirck Dircksz, the robber. Plaintiff demands that the defendants be punished for violation of the ordinance of the honorable director and council **inasmuch** as contrary to the ordinance they have remained on shore without consent. Defendants admit that they have spent the night on shore without consent. They are therefore condemned to pay a fine of one month's wages each.

On the 16th of June

Ulrich Lupoldt, fiscal, plaintiff, vs. Tobias Pietersen, defendant. Defendant is condemned to pay a fine of fl. 6 to the fiscal and fl. 6 to the poor, **inasmuch** as he has threatened to beat the fiscal, which the defendant has admitted in court.

Casper van Beuren, plaintiff, vs. Cornelis Pietersen, skipper of the <u>Westindise Haven</u>, defendant. Parties have settled their differences in court.

Ulrich Lupoldt, fiscal, plaintiff, vs. Jochem Beeckman, soldier, defendant, accused of manslaughter. The plaintiff demands that the defendant be punished with the sword until death ensue, as an example to others who commit homicide.

[43] Having seen the complaint and conclusion of Ulrich Lupolt, fiscal, against Jochem Beeckman, soldier, charged with the manslaughter of Jacob Jeuriaensz from Dansick, soldier, who was wounded in Fort Amsterdam on [   ], and who died on the 27th of May, [the court find] that the defendant did wound Jacob Jeuriaensen, deceased, but that it appears from the testimony of Hans Kirstede, surgeon, that Jacob Jeuriaensen, deceased, did not die of his wounds, but through his own negligence and excesses, the more so as he did not heed the instructions of the said surgeon, as it appears further by the affidavits of Gillis Pietersen, master house carpenter, aged 27 years, Claes Jansen, tailor, aged 26 years, Arent from Landen, aged 22 years, and Jan Andriessen from Basenborch, aged 24 years, that two or three days after he had been wounded by Beeckman aforesaid he stood before the door in Fort Amsterdam making his water, having his cloak on, kindled a fire, made an omelet and then drank an entire pint of wine at one draft;

All of which aforesaid documents having been duly considered and [the court] having personally examined the witnesses and taken into consideration the law of God, Exodus 21, verse 19, the fiscal's demand is denied and the aforesaid Jochem Beeckman is acquitted, being adjudged not guilty of the death of the said Jacob Jeuriaensen. Thus done and sentenced in council, in Fort Amsterdam in New Netherland, this [   ], anno 1639.

On the 23rd of June anno 1639

Jan Pietersen, plaintiff, vs. Cornelis Jacobsz Stillen, defendant, for payment for some maize. Defendant admits the debt and is condemned to pay within 3 or 4 days.

Claes Cornelissen Swits, plaintiff, vs. Jacob Stoffelsen, defendant. Case adjourned until news is received from the fatherland.

On [   ]

The fiscal, plaintiff, vs. Jan Dondey and Claes, the cabin boy, of the yacht __Westindise Raven__, defendants. Plaintiff demands punishment of the defendants as they cut loose with a knife and took away the seawan which a squaw carried around her waist. The defendants admit the charge and are condemned as follows: Claes, the cabin boy, to be whipped in the Fort at break of day and Jan Dondey, soldier, receiver of the stolen goods, to ride the wooden horse and moreover to forfeit two months' wages.

[44] On the 27th of June 1639

There arrived here from Virginia an Englishman, named Gerrit Sanders, in an open sloop, flying aloft a large forked pennant of the Prince's colors and aft a large red flag bearing the arms of Amsterdam; and whereas this is a matter of grave consequence we have upon due consideration, ordered the pennant and the flag to be taken from his sloop.

On the 14th of July anno 1639

Cornelis vander Hoykens, fiscal, plaintiff, vs. Cors Pietersen, defendant. Case put over to the next court day.

On the 21st of July anno 1639

Cornelis vander Hoykens, having been sent here by the directors to be fiscal in the place of Lupoldt, the aforesaid

Lupoldt is released from his former office and continues in the capacity of councilor and commissary of store goods.

Pedro Negretto, plaintiff, vs. Jan Celes, defendant. Plaintiff demands payment for the trouble he has taken in tending the defendant's hogs. The defendant is condemned to pay the plaintiff 2 schepels of maize.

The fiscal, plaintiff, vs. Gerrit Jansen from Oldenborch, defendant, for eloping with a certain widow. Whereas the defendant admits the elopement, but declares that he was betrothed to the widow, he is condemned to pay fl. 20 to the fiscal as punishment.

Mr. Jonas Bronck, plaintiff, vs. Clara Matthys, defendant. Plaintiff Plaintiff demands that the defendant fulfill the contract made with her, or that she forfeit [her wages] and be made to pay according to the contract.

Having examined the contract made between Clara Matthys and Mr. Bronck, signed by the notary and witnesses, the aforesaid Clara, or in her place Gerrit Jansen from Oldenborch, inasmuch as they intend to marry each other, is condemned to pay to Mr. Bronc whatever he may claim according to the contract.

The fiscal, plaintiff, vs. Tomas Walraven, defendant. Case put over to the next court day.

The fiscal, plaintiff, vs. Jan Steen. Defendant ordered to satisfy the fiscal.

[45] On the 28th of July anno 1639

Tomas Pietersen, plaintiff, vs. Barent Dircksen, baker, defendant. Default.

Jan Jacobsen, plaintiff, vs. Gysbert Rycken, defendant. Parties referred to Jan Jansen Damen and Elslent, appointed referees to settle their differences.

Cornelis van[der] Hoykens, fiscal, plaintiff, vs. Jan Andriessen
from Basenborgh, Jacob Swart, Hans Noorman, Marten Nagel, Balthasar
Lourens, Davit Davitsen, Jan Warnarsen, Jems the Englishman, Hans
the baker, all soldiers, defendants. Plaintiff demands that the
defendants be punished as disobedient soldiers who have broken
their oath, **inasmuch** as they have refused to obey the 111th
article of the regulations and do not observe their oath set
forth in the regulations which they have sworn to.

Having seen the complaint of Cornelis vander Hoykens, fiscal,
vs. Jacob Swart, Jan Andriessen from Basenb[orgh], Hans Noorman,
Marten Nagel, Balthasar Lourens, Davit Davitsen, Jan Warnarsen,
Jems the Englishman and Hans the baker, soldiers, for having
refused to comply with the regulations sworn to by them in repairing Fort Amsterdam, according to article 111 of the regulations,
having on the contrary expressly opposed the same and refused
to lend a helping hand, although they were offered as much as
10 stivers a day, with express promise of receiving a stiver or
two more if they worked well and faithfully; and whereas, after
due notice and protest was served on said soldiers by the fiscal
and the secretary, they nevertheless remained obstinate;

Therefore, having duly considered the matter, which is of
grave consequence and tends to lead to serious mutiny, we have
dishonorably discharged from the service Jacob Swart and Jan
Andriessen, as being the chief instigators and ringleaders of
the said opposition, declaring the same unfit to bear arms or to
serve any potentates, and we condemn, as we do hereby, the said
Jacob Swart and Jan Andriessen from Basenborch to the forfeiture
of all their wages which are due them by the West India Company,

one-third part to be for the benefit of the fiscal and two-thirds
for the benefit of the Company; and we furthermore order them to
embark immediately on the ship Den Harinc, to remain confined
there and to depart with it to the fatherland, on pain of arbitrary
punishment. Thus done and sentenced and also publicly read to
all the soldiers in Fort Amsterdam, this 28th of July 1639.

[46] On the 4th of August anno 1639

Symon Dircksen Pos, plaintiff, vs. Jacob van Curler,
defendant, about delivery of a drag-net. Plaintiff's demand
is denied because the drag-net was found not to be in such shape
as it was represented to be when sold, as appears from the
evidence submitted.

Cornelis vander Hoykens, fiscal, vs. Gregoris Pietersen,
defendant, at present a prisoner. Plaintiff demands that the
defendant receive corporal punishment because he has shown himself not only rebellious to the commands of the honorable director,
but has sought to instigate mutiny among all the soldiers and
in addition, speaking for all the others, said, "What the others
say, I say also."

Having seen the complaint and conclusion of the fiscal
and considering that the crime committed by the defendant tends
to lead to revolt and the total ruin of a well ordered republic,
we have condemned, as we hereby do condemn, the said prisoner to
be brought tomorrow, being the 5th of August, to the usual place
of execution and there to be shot by harquebusiers according to
military law.

Andries Hudden, plaintiff, vs. Anthony Janse from Salee,
defendant. Default.

Gillis de Voocht, plaintiff, vs. Davit Provoost, defendant.
Suit dismissed and the plaintiff ordered to be satisfied with
the defendant's discretion, as he, the plaintiff, claims nothing
but that the defendant be pleased to pay him according to his
discretion.

[Ordinance for the regulation of the workmen in the public
service] [1]

Whereas the honorable director and council daily observe
that many of the machanics and laborers in the Company's service
do not perform their bounded duty by working, but spend much
time unprofitably, yes, frequently waste whole days, all of which
tends to the great injury and damage of the Company;

Every one whom it may concern is hereby notified to repair
to his work when the bell rings and there to perform his duty
until the bell rings again to break off, on pain of paying double
the loss for the benefit of the fiscal and whoever else shall
be entitled to it.

Therefore, we have appointed and do hereby appoint Gillis
de Voocht to be commissary of the workmen and daily to superintend
them and to continually go around and note those who are in
default and report their names.

Done in Amsterdam, this 11th day of August anno 1639.

[47]   On the 11th of August anno 1639

Cornelis vander Hoykens, fiscal, plaintiff, vs. Eduwart
Wilson, defendant. Plaintiff demands that the defendant be
punished as it is customary to punish those who rob gardens, as
well as those who break out of jail. The defendant is

---

1 Revised from **Laws** and Ordinances of New Netherland, p. 20.

provisionally released from irons on condition that he promise
to appear when summoned, the case being put over for further consideration.

Pieter Pia, soldier, plaintiff, vs. Arent van Landen and
Hendric Cornelissen de Boer, defendants.

Arent van Landen says that on Sunday evening, being the 21st
of August, between 4 and 5 o'clock, he went to the house of
Hendric de Boer, where he remained for about a quarter of an hour.
Going from there he went with with Hendrick de Boer aforesaid,
in company with Burgert Jorissen, ti Evert Bisschop's house and
from there to the guardhouse which he, Hendric, entered. Van
Landen called: "Pieter, are you there?" Whereupon they went
straight home, the moon having been up about half an hour.

Hendrick Cornelissen says that on the 21st of August, between
7 and 8 o'clock in the evening, Arent van Landen came to Hendric
Harmansen's house and that together, in company of Burgert Jorissen,
they went to Evert Bisschop's house, where they remained about
an hour or an hour and a half, going from there to the guardhouse
which he, Hendrick, entered while he, Arent, waited below, and
that from the guardhouse they went straight home, it being between
10 and 11 o'clock when he lit his pipe. When they arrived together
at farm No. 5, it was about midnight.

Case adjourned until the next court day.

Arent van Landen says also that he did not run away when
Piter Pia came to the house and Jan van Vorst, but served brandy
to him; also, that he was called back to the house by
Jan van Vorst.

On [blank   ]

Form of the oath taken by all the Englishmen

dwelling on or about the island of Manhatans

You swear that you will be loyal and faithful to their High
Mightinesses the Lords States General, his Highness of Orange and
the honorable director and council of New Netherland; that you
will follow wherever the director or anyone of the council shall
lead; that you will immediately faithfully report all treason
and injury to the country of which you receive any knowledge; and
that you will to the best of your ability help to protect with
your life and property the inhabitants thereof against all
enemies of the country. So help me God.

On the next page follow the signatures [48] of all the
Englishmen who have taken the oath in the form above written.

This is X the mark	Ffrancis Lastley
of G[e]orge Homs	This is T the mark
Richard Brudnill	of Eduwart Wilson
Abraham Newman	This is W the mark
This is X the mark	of Willem Willemsz
of Jan Habbesen	
John Hathaway	

Abraham Pagie, plaintiff, vs. Jan Habbesen, defendant.
Plaintiff demands payment of fl. 27: 14 st. Defendant is ordered
to pay as soon as he receives payment from Davit Pietersen.

Adriaen Pietersen, plaintiff, vs. Claes Cornelissen Swits,
defendant. Plaintiff demands delivery of a certain parcel of
land situated on the East river. Defendant in return demands
that the plaintiff prove that he, the defendant, sold the land
to the plaintiff.

Hendrick Cornelissen, plaintiff, vs. Pieter Pia, defendant. Case put over.

Cornelis van[der] Hoykens, fiscal, plaintiff, vs. Fredrick Lubbersen, defendant. Case put over.

Cornelis van[der] Hoykens, fiscal, plaintiff, vs. Schepmoes and de Veringh, defendants. Case put over.

Cornelis van[der] Hoykens, fiscal, plaintiff, vs. Blancke Ael. Default.

Harman Meyndersen at the request of the fiscal declares in court that while sailing as supercargo on the yacht _Canarivogel_ he saw that in general all the ship's crew received linen and that he was not resolved to take an oath that no linen was divided on the said yacht after the capture of the prize; also that Jan Sytjes and skipper Adriaen bought goods from the ships in the West Indies.

Adriaen Cornelissen, skipper, has declared under oath in court that he did not sell any of the linen that came from the prize.

[49] On the 8th of September

Whereas Governor Onderhil, residing in the North, has requested permission to settle here with some families under our protection, on condition that they shall enjoy the same privileges as other inhabitants here; therefore, the petition of the said Onderhil is granted, provided that he and his associates take the oath of allegiance to their High Mightinesses the Lords States General and his Highness of Orange.

Adriaen Pietersen, plaintiff, vs. Claes Cornelissen Swits, defendant. Default.

Jan Jansen Damen, plaintiff, vs. little Manuel. Case put over to the next court day.

Cornelis vander Hoykens, fiscal, plaintiff, vs. Andries Noorman, defendant. The seized wine is confiscated as it was not entered for the benefit of the Company and [the defendant is] condemned in addition to pay a fine of fl. 8 for the benefit of the fiscal.

Willem Bredenbent, plaintiff, vs. Pieter Smit, defendant, for slander. Case put over.

Hendrick Cornelissen, plaintiff, vs. Pieter Pia, defendant.

On the 15th of September

Whereas the Company is put to great expense both in building fortifications and in supporting soldiers and sailors, we have therefore resolved to demand from the Indians who dwell around here and whom heretofore we have protected against their enemies, some contributions in the form of skins, maize and seawan, and if there be any nation which is not in a friendly way disposed to make such contribution it shall be urged to do so in the most suitable manner.

Adriaen Pietersen, plaintiff, vs. Claes Cornelissen Swits, defendant. Plaintiff demands delivery of the land which the defendant sold to him, the plaintiff. Defendant answering, demands proof of the contract which he made with the plaintiff. Parties to reappear in three weeks unless they can meanwhile come to an agreement.

Tomas, the smith, plaintiff, vs. Aert Tonissen, defendant. Plaintiff demands reparation of the damage done by the defendant's cattle. The court appoints two arbitrators, to wit, Jan Damen and Hendric Harmansen, to estimate the damage.

[50] On the 22d of September

[1] The honorable director and council hereby warn all residents within our limits that they are forbidden to take less than 12 schepels of maize from the Indians for one coat of duffel, until such time as a fixed price shall be set with the heathen by the director. All persons are to govern themselves accordingly, on pain, if they are found to have acted contrary hereto, of paying a fine of fl. 100 and of forfeiting for life the privilege of trading. Let every one guard himself against loss.

Cornelis vander Hoykens, fiscal, plaintiff, vs. Tomas Walraven, defendant, for violence committed in the houses of the blacks. Defendant is condemned to pay fl. 12 for the benefit of the fiscal.

Davit Pietersen, plaintiff, vs. Govert Danielsen, defendant. Plaintiff demands that the defendant complete his term of service. Defendant answers that Davit Pietersen has voluntarily released him from his service and demands payment for the service rendered. Parties have settled with each other in court, so that neither one nor the other has any further claim.

Tomas Bescher, plaintiff, vs. Willem Willemsen, defendant. Default.

Tomas de Coninc and Marritjen Frans from Beets came and appeared before the court and requested to be legally married. Therefore, the aforesaid persons have on this date at their request been joined in the holy state of matrimony in court at Fort Amsterdam.

---

[1] Revised from *Laws and Ordinances of New Netherland*, p. 21.

On the 29th of September

Cornelis vander Hoykens, fiscal, plaintiff, vs. Tomas Sandersen, defendant, for drawing his knife and wounding his helper. Defendant is condemned to pay a fine of fl. 12 and Abraham Isaacsen is fined fl. 6. It is also ordered that Elslandt and Curler, as referees, are to settle the further differences between the parties.

Manuel de Gerrit de Reus, plaintiff, vs. Jan Damen, defendant. Default.

[51] On the 5th of October

Cornelis vander Hoykens, fiscal, vs. Hendrick Jansen from Bremen, gunner's mate on the ship Den Harinck, defendant, for violence committed against an officer of the law. The fiscal demands punishment of the defendant for having wounded his deputy in the head while inspecting the said ship Den Heringh.

[the court] have seen the complaint of the fiscal on account of violence against an officer of the law commited on the 3d of October on board the ship Den Heringh, lying off Staten Island, during the inspection of the said ship, after the skipper, Symon Jansen, had received his clearance papers from the director, to wit:

Willem, the deputy sheriff, walking on deck, was asked by Hendrick Jansen from Bremen, gunner's mate, to go below and have a drink of brandy. Having gone below, a blanket was thrown over his head and he was beaten with a crowbar so that blood flowed, without his knowing who did it, and afterward, as he was going from board with the fiscal and he was climbing down the side of the vessel, an iron [cannon] ball was dropped on his body.

We, therefore, wishing to do justice in the matter, ordered
the ship to return here and caused the said Hendric, gunner's
mate, to be arrested and put to the torture, but he persisted
in his denial, although we felt convinced that he was guilty.
Thereupon the entire crew, except the skipper and the pilot,
came together on shore and wanted to compel us to surrender to
them the said Hendrick, whereupon the soldiers were called to
arms and finally succeeded in sending the sailors back on board.
Upon our promise to pardon the prisoner and his accomplices if
he would confess the truth, but [assurance] that otherwise we
would proceed against him with all rigor, the said prisoner,
being released from torture and irons, has voluntarily confessed
that he coaxed Willem, the deputy sheriff, to go below decks,
where a blanket was thrown over his head and he was beaten with
an iron bar by one Pieter Smit, and that their hatred arose from
the seizure by the deputy sheriff of an anker of brandy, which
they intended to smuggle.

Having considered the mutiny of the crew and the fact that
the ship would have to lose much time, we have in the interest
of the Company and for the sake of the peace of the country
thought fit not to investigate or prosecute the case further,
for weighty reasons us thereunto moving.

[52] On the 13th of October

The director and council of New Netherland order you, Claes
van Elslandt, commissary of provisions, Wybrant Pietersen, late
commissary of store goods, and Jacob van Curler, commissary of
merchandise, to close your books and accounts, to strike a
balance and to have the same ready within the space of one month

from the date hereof, on pain of forfeiture of one hundred guilders
and recovery from you of all loss and damage which the Company
may suffer thereby. Thus done and otdered in council in Fort
Amsterdam, the day above written.

Andries Hudden, plaintiff, vs. Davit Provoost, defendant.
Plaintiff demands that the defendant fulfil the contract made
for the sale of a yawl. It is ordered that the owner, who is
at present in possession of the yawl, convey the defendant this
coming winter back and forth across the East river with the
said yawl.

On the 20th of October

Andries Hudden, plaintiff, vs. Anthony Jansen from Salee,
defendant. The plaintiff having failed to appear, default is
taken against him.

Tomas Sandersen, smith, plaintiff, vs. Willem Hendricksz
from Wesep, [1] defendant. Having heard the complaint and the
defendant's acknowledgment, the defendant is condemned to fulfil
the contract between him and the plaintiff, or to pay the loss
which the plaintiff shall suffer through the defendant's neglect.

The 27th of October

Isaac Abrahamsen, plaintiff, vs. Volckert Eversen, defendant.
Plaintiff demands payment of the maize promised him for the cloth
delivered to the defendant. Defendant is condemned to pay 16
schepels of maize to the plaintiff.

Hendrick Pietersen from Wesel, plaintiff, vs. Jan Harmansen
from De Lemmet, defendant, for slander. Parties ordered to
appear on the next court day to furnish clear proof on both sides.

---

[1] Wesep, an old form of Weesp, a city 8.5 miles S. E. of
Amsterdam.

[53] On the [3d] of November anno 1639

Tonis Cray from Venlo, plaintiff, **vs.** Gysbert Opdyck, defendant. Plaintiff demands payment of maize. Defendant, admitting the debt, is ordered provisionally to pay 20 schepels of maize to the plaintiff, the plaintiff being upon his request promised by the director and council that he shall not lose the cow delivered to Opdyck for the use of the Company.

Hans Nelissen, plaintiff, **vs.** Jan Salomonsz, defendant. Default.

Cornelis Lambersen Cool, plaintiff, **vs.** George Luco, defendant. Parties ordered to appear next court day and to furnish proper proof.

The fiscal, plaintiff, **vs.** Jeuriaen Rodolff, defendant. Plaintiff demands that the defendant restore the seawan taken by him and the soldiers from the savages. The defendant is ordered to produce and restore the seawan.

Willem Bredenbent, plaintiff, **vs.** Aert Tonissen, defendant. The defendant shall pay to the plaintiff 4 glds., wherewith the plaintiff and defendant are agreed as to the fencing in of the cattle.

On the 9th of November

Hendrick Pietersen, mason, plaintiff, **vs.** Barent Dircksz, defendant. Default.

As the defendant has not appeared, the plaintiff asks permission to take an inventory of the goods which he bought from the defendant, in order that the same may not be alienated. Plaintiff's request is granted.

Cornelis van[der] Hoykens, fiscal, plaintiff, vs. Jan Eversen Bout, defendant. Default.

At the request of the fiscal, Gysbert Opdyck, commissary at Fort De Hoop, [1] declares that he handed his Negro boy, called Lourviso Barbosse, a pan to bake cakes and as the fire was too hot for the boy, Opdyck took the pan, giving the knife to the Negro. Thereupon [54] he, Opdyck, ordered the boy to get a platter, who brought one that was dirty, wherefore Opdyck beat the Negro who, to avoid the blows, attacked Opdyck, who thrust him away, so that the boy fell on his left side, pushing him with his foot. The boy ran toward the door where he fell and Opdyck, finding the aforesaid knife bent like a hoop, went to look at the boy who had a wound in his body near the left arm from which he shortly after died.

On the 17th of November anno 1639

Hendrick Pietersen, mason, plaintiff, vs. Barent Dircksen, baker, defendant. Parties are agreed in court that the defendant shall pay the plaintiff fl. 40, on condition that he shall make no further claim.

Pieter vande Linde, plaintiff, vs. Aert Tonissen, defendant. Parties are to furnish proper proof or, in default thereof, the demand of the plaintiff is denied.

Jan Schepmoes, plaintiff, vs. Hendrick Westercamp, defendant. Jan Schepmoes declares that he has nothing to say against the defendant.

---

[1] Fort Hope, the Dutch stronghold on the Connecticut river, where Hartford is now located.

Cornelis van[der] Hoykens, fiscal, plaintiff, vs. Jan Schepmoes, defendant. As the defendant is charged by Fredric Lubbertsen with theft, the plaintiff demands punishment according to his deserts. The defendant admits that he took bread, oil, cheese, and lard and ate the same for sustenance; also that he drank two gills of brandy, without the consent of the said Fredric Lubbersen. Case adjourned to the next court day.

On the 24th of November anno 1639

Jan Schepmoes, plaintiff, vs. Hendrick Westercamp, defendant. Plaintiff demands that the defendant bake for him according to the contract made between them. The defendant is ordered to fulfil his contract, provided the plaintiff furnish him with the wood needed for baking.

[55] On the 24th of November

Cornelis vander Hoykens, fiscal, plaintiff, vs. Jan Schepmoes, defendant, for theft of goods belonging to Fredrick Lubberssen. Plaintiff demands that the defendant be punished for stealing the goods of Fredrick Lubberssen which were entrusted to him and which he was in duty bound zealously to protect in case others should have wished to steal them.

Having seen the complaint of the fiscal and the confession of the defendant that he and Claes de Veringh had stolen bread, lard, oil, cheese and brandy, Schepmoes and de Veringh are condemned to pay for all that Fredrick can prove to have been taken by the defendants, and after due compensation to satisfy the fiscal.

Lourens Haen, plaintiff, vs. Nicolaes, the tobacco planter, defendant. Plaintiff demands payment for or restitution of the canoe loaned by him. Defendant having admitted that he borrowed

the canoe, he is condemned to pay the value of the canoe within
eight days or else to restore the canoe.

Nicolaes, the tobacco planter, plaintiff, vs. Tomas Hal,
defendant, who appears for G[e]orge Homs. The defendant, that
is to say, the plaintiff, says that he delivered to G[e]orge Homs
a small cask of wine for which he demands payment. The defendant
says that G[e]orge Homs received no wine from the plaintiff.
Case adjourned until the next court day.

On the 1st of December, being Thursday

The commissaries Elslandt, Wybrandt Pietersen and Corl[ae]r
are ordered to prepare their accounts within eight days and in
default thereof they shall be proceeded against with all rigor
according to the merits of the case.

Isaac Abrahamsz, plaintiff, vs. Gerrit the Moff, [1] defendant.
default.

The same, plaintiff, vs. Aert Tonissen, defendant. Default.

G[e]orge Peper, plaintiff, vs. Gerrit the Moff, defendant.
Default.

[56] In the name of God, anno 1640, in Fort Amsterdam

On Thursday, the 5th of January 1640

In council, Claes van Elslandt is at his request discharged
from the office of commissary of provisions and Davit Provoost
is appointed in his place at 25 gl. a month and 150 gl. a year
for board.

In the place of Claes van Elslandt and Wybrant Pieterssen,
Jacob van Curler and Davit Provoost have been appointed inspectors

---

[1] A disparaging name for a German.

of tobacco, they to receive a fee of [   ] stivers per hundred pounds from the purchaser and of [   ] stivers from the vendor; whereupon they have taken the oath of fidelity to the Company.

On Thursday, being the 19th of April [1] anno 1640

Adriaen Pieterssen, plaintiff, vs. Pieter vander Linde, defendant. Default.

On Thursday, being the 26th of January

Eduwart Wilson, plaintiff, vs. Jan Pietersen, defendant. Parties are ordered each to present his claim in writing in proper form at the next session of the court.

Andries Hudden, plaintiff, vs. Anthony Jansen from Salee, defendant. Plaintiff does not appear and default is entered against him.

On the 9th of February

Andries Hudden, plaintiff, vs. Anthony Jansen from Salee, defendant. Default.

Eduwart Wilson, plaintiff, vs. Jan Pietersen, defendant. Plaintiff presents an itemized account and demands payment. Defendant gives for answer that more is due him than the plaintiff demands of him. Case adjourned until the next court day in order that the defendant may bring proof of his claim.

[57] On Thursday, being the 23d of February

Barent Dirckssen, baker, plaintiff, vs. Gerrit Jansen from Oldenburch, defendant. Plaintiff is ready to deliver his farm which was bought by the defendant, provided the defendant furnish security for the purchase money. Defendant answers that he was drunk and maintains that he is not held by the purchase. Parties

---

[1] Intended for January.

having been heard, they are referred to referees who are to settle
the matter in dispute.

On Thursday, being the 1st of March

Andries Hudden, plaintiff, vs. Anthony Jansen from Salee,
defendant. Plaintiff presents a certain document from which it
appears that Anthony Jansen was to furnish him three goats for
the term of three years. Defendant is therefore condemned to
make delivery according to the contract or writing.

On the 8th of March, being Thursday

Cornelis Cornelissen, chief boatswain, plaintiff, vs. Laurens
Cornelissen, skipper of the Engel Gabriel, defendant. Plaintiff
demands that he be allowed to sail on the ship Engel Gabriel in
the same capacity as heretofore, as he claims to have conducted
himself well. Defendant says that under God he is master of his
ship and that he does not intend to take the plaintiff with him
inasmuch as he has not conducted himself well in his service.
Parties ordered to settle with each other in friendship.

On the 15th of March, being Thursday

Eduwart Wilson, plaintiff, vs. Jan Pieterssen, defendant.
Parties referred to referees, to wit: Eduwart Wilson chooses
Master Fiscock and Jan Pietersz Jacob van Curler.

[58] On the 15th of March

[1] Whereas many complaints are daily made to us of loss and
destruction done to the corn fields by the goats and hogs against
which fences and rails are of no avail, which tends to injure the
cultivation of the corn and the Company's interests: and whereas
throughout the world it is customary for those who own cattle to

---

[1] Revised from Laws and Ordinances of New Netherland, p. 21.

have the same herded or taken care of; Therefore, in case any
goats or hogs are found in the corn fields, there shall be paid
for the first time for each goat or hog 10 stivers, for the second
time one guilder and for the third time 40 stivers. In addition
the farmer's damage shall be made good before the goats are
released. Thus done in our council and published in Fort Amsterdam
in New Netherland, this 15th of March anno 1640.

On Thursday, being the 12th of April

Cornelis vander Hoykens, fiscal, plaintiff, vs. Adriaen
Pietersz from Alckmaer, defendant, for slander and assault in
the house of Pieter van[der] Linde. Case put over until the
next court day.

On the 19th of April, being Thursday

It is resolved and decided in council to maintain in these
regions of New Netherland the charter granted by their High
Mightinesses to the honorable West India Company and [to that
end] to dispatch Cornelis van Tienhoven, secretary, to the
archipelago to purchase there the surrounding land, to set up
the arms of the Lords States General, to take the savages under
our protection and to prevent any other nation from usurping any
authority within our limits and making further use of our territory.

Willem Bredenbent, plaintiff, vs. Piere Pia and Philip
Gerardy, defendants, regarding the fencing in of their hogs.
Parties are ordered to govern themselves according to the
published ordinance.

Abraham Ryken, plaintiff, vs. Gysbert Ryken, defendant, for
payment of fl. 147. As the defendant admits the debt he is
condemned to pay.

[59] On Thursday, being the 26th of April

Jan Schepmoes, plaintiff, vs. Abraham Ryken, defendant.
Plaintiff demands payment for the goods which the defendant's
wife bought from the plaintiff. Defendant answers that he is
not aware that his wife bought any goods from the plaintiff;
requests therefore that a delay be granted in order that he may
speak to his wife about it. Defendant's request is granted, provided he pay the plaintiff after he has spoken to his wife.

Eduwardt Wilson, plaintiff, vs. Jan Pietersen, defendant.
Default.

Claes Cornelissen, plaintiff, vs. Maryn Adriaensen, for
delivery of a row-boat and building of a yacht. Parties ordered
to exhibit their contract on the next court day.

Jacob Stoffelsen, plaintiff, vs. Domine Bogardus and Jan
Damen, as administrators of the estate of the late Hendrick van
Vorst, for the keep of 15 head of cattle during last winter.
Parties referred to referees, to wit: Jacob Walingen, Huych Aertsen
and Gerrit Wolphersen.

On the 3d of May, being Thursday

Appeared in court Tryntjen Scherenburch, wife of Hendric,
the tailor, requesting in his absence that the administrators of
the estate of the late Hendric van Vorst be ordered not to sell
any cattle or other movables left by the aforesaid van Vorst, until
news is received from Holland whether the said van Vorst made
any last will or testament, or codicil.

At the request of the aforesaid Tryntjen Scheerburch the
administrators of the aforesaid estate are hereby ordered not to
sell, alienate, or otherwise dispose of any cattle until reliable

news about the aforesaid Hendrick van Vorst is received from
Holland, unless any movable effects or other goods be perishable;
if not, everything shall be kept intact.

Eduwart Wilson, plaintiff, vs. Jan Pietersz, defendant.
Second default.

[50] On the 3d of May, being Thursday

Claes Cornelissen Swits, plaintiff, vs. Maryn Adriaensz,
defendant. Parties have amicably agreed with each other in court.

Maryn Adriaensen, plaintiff, vs. Hendric Pietersen, mason
defendant. Plaintiff says that he sold to the defendant a certain
house and plantation and is therefore ready to make delivery.
Defendant claims that he was drunk and does not have any knowledge
of the purchase. Defendant is ordered to furnish proper proof
that he was drunk and that he canceled the purchase within 24
hours; if the contrary appears the purchase shall stand.

The fiscal, plaintiff, vs. Govert Loockmans and Barent
Dircksen, baker, defendants. Plaintiff demands that the defendants
be fined according to the ordinance as contrary to the orders
they went on board the Englishman. Defendants are condemned to
pay a fine of 50 stivers each.

On the 9th of May

[1] Whereas serious complaints are daily made by the Indians
that their corn hills are trampled under foot and uprooted by
hogs and other cattle and consequently great damage will be done
when the maize is growing, as a result of which the corn would
be dear in the autumn and our good people suffer want, the Indians
be induced to remove and to conceive a hatred against our nation,

---

[1] Revised from Laws and Ordinances of New Netherland, p. 22.

and thus **out** of mischief inflict some injury or other upon us,
which we are most expressly ordered by the honorable directors
to prevent; Therefore, the matter having been duly considered,
we, the director and council of New Netherland, hereby charge
and command all our inhabitants whose lands adjoin plantations
of the [61] savages to have their horses, cows, hogs, goats and
sheep herded or else to prevent them by fences or otherwise from
damaging the corn of the Indians, on pain of making good the
damage and of incurring a fine payable to the fiscal, according
to the ordinance published on the 15th of March last. Let everyone take warning and beward of damage. Thus done and ordained
on the island of Manhatans in Fort Amsterdam, the 9th of May 1640.

On the 10th of May

Leendert Arentsen, plaintiff, vs. Volckert Eversen, defendant.
Plaintiff demands that the defendant pay for the keep of his
cattle. Upon admitting the debt, the defendant is condemned to
pay fl. 9:12.

Eduwart Wilson, plaintiff, vs. Jan Pietersen, defendant.
Parties are referred to the previously appointed referees, to
wit: Master Fiscock and van Curler.

Ordinance providing for arming and mustering of the militia [1]

The honorable director and council have deemed it advisable
to ordain that the inhabitants residing near and around Fort
Amsterdam, of whatever station, quality or condition they may be,
shall each provide himself with a good gun and take good care
to keep the same at all times in good order and repair. And

---

[1] Revised from Laws and Ordinances of New Netherland, p. 23.

whereas they live at a distance one from the other, every person
is assigned to a post under the command of a corporal in order
that in time of danger he may appear there with his gun. Should
it happen, which God forbid, that at night any mischief occur,
either from enemies or traitors, the people will be notified by
three cannon shots fired in quick succession, and by the day
means will be found to give warning to every one, who is commanded
thereupon to repair as quickly as possible to his corporal at
the appointed place and then to adopt such measures as the
exigency of the case may require, on pain of being fined 50 guilders.

[62] [1] We, the director and council, residing in New
Netherland on the part of the High and Mighty Lords the States
General of the United Netherlands, his Highness of Orange, and
the honorable directors of the Chartered West India Company,
having express order and command from the aforesaid lords to
purchase in their name from the inhabitants of these parts all
such lands as we may consider most adapted for agriculture and
the raising of all sorts of stock —

Have, therefore, pursuant to the orders of our Sovereign
Lords, purchased from the Great Chief or Sachem named Penhawits,
all the lands lying on Long Island, within the limits of New
Netherland, which he has inherited from his forefathers, with
all such right and title as he may in any wise claim, according
to the deed of purchase and conveyance thereof in existence.
Which aforesaid Panhawits, after some foreigners had settled on
the aforesaid land, about Schout's bay, notified us that some
deserters or vagabonds had come on the land that we had purchased
from him and there begun to build houses, cut trees and do other

[1] Revised from Doc. Rel. Col. Hist. N. Y., 2:144-50.

work, and that said vagabonds had there pulled down their High Mightinesses' arms.

In order to obtain a good and correct report and assurance of what is aforewritten, Jacobus van Curler, commissary of cargoes, was sent thither with the yacht _Prins Willem_, who, coming to the place where their High Mightinesses' arms had been set up, found the same torn off and that on the tree to which they had been nailed a fool's head was carved in the stead of said arms.

All of which appeared strange to us, being a crime of Lese-Majesty and tending to the disparagement of the sovereignty of their High Mightinesses.

[63] We therefore, on the 13th May 1640, after mature deliberation, resolved to send Cornelis van Tienhoven thither with 25 soldiers, to whom we have given the following Instructions here inserted:

Whereas we have certain information that some foreigners have come on Long Island into Marten Gerritsen's bay and Schout's bay, [1] which are the Hon. West India Company's lands, under the authority of the High and Mighty Lords the States-General, and there thrown down the arms of the Lords States, and settled and cultivated the soil, We therefore send you, Secretary Cornelis van Tienhoven, thither, with the under-sheriff, the sergeant and three and twenty men, to inquire into the state of the matter, and you shall regulate yourself as follows:

You shall endeavor to arrive there unexpectedly; 'twill be best, in our opinion, at the break of day, and to surround the English there and prevent the use of any force of arms; and you

---

[1] Now Manhasset (North Hempstead), at the head of Cow bay.

shall forthwith inquire who has knocked down the arms, and who gave them commission to do so, and constrain them to come here and defend themselves. If they refuse, then you shall set about, by force, to bind and to bring them hither, taking an inventory of their goods and making out in writing a careful report of all that has occurred and been done by you; you shall also prevent the soldiers committing any excess, and in case the Indians themselves have removed the arms, and the English are innocent of the matter and willing to depart in your presence, it would not be unwise to let them do so quietly; but then, the chiefs of the Indians must be taken prisoners and brought hither, and, in all cases, it will also be necessary that you take the Indians with you. And if it happen that so many additional English have come (which we do not [64] anticipate) as to prevent you being able to cope with them, you shall make a strong protest against such proceedings, have it served and come back, taking care, above all things, to avoid all bloodshed.

Thus done in our council, the 13th May A⁰. 1640.

Anno 1640, the 14th May, the secretary and five and twenty soldiers, departed with the preceding Instructions from Fort Amsterdam, and on the 15th at break of day arrived at the place where the English had taken up their abode, finding there a small house built by them and another not yet finished.

They were first asked: What they were doing there; by what power or by whose authority they presumed to settle on our purchased soil, and told that they must show their commission.

Eight men, one woman and a little child made answer that they intended to plant there and were authorized thereto by a Scotchman who had gone with their commission to the Roode berch.

Secondly, they were asked, for what reason did they throw down their High Mightinesses' arms and set up a **fool's** face in the stead?

To which some answered: The arms were cut down by a person who is not present. Another answered: Such was done in their presence by order of a Scotchman, and the man who did it was at the Bode berch.

Hereupon six men were brought to Fort Amsterdam, leaving two men and one woman and a child on the ground to take care of their goods; they arrived on the 15th of May.

Examination of divers Englishmen taken on Long Island

[65] On the 16th May 1640, at the house of the honorable director of New Netherland, the following six persons were examined, to wit:

What is your name?	<u>Answer</u>. Jop Cears.
Where born?	<u>Answer</u>. In Bretfortsthier.
How old are you?	<u>Answer</u>. Twenty-eight years.
On what conditions did you go to reside on Long Island, under the English or Scotch?	<u>Answer</u>. Under the English, with authority from Mr. Foret.
Who brought them there, and who was their principal?	<u>Answer</u>. Lieutenant Houw.
What did they intend to do there, and if more folks are to come?	<u>Answer</u>. To plant and build dwellings; does not know for certain how many folks are still to come there.
Where did he reside in New England?	<u>Answer</u>. At Lin, in Matetusje's bay, 8 miles from Boston.

| Did he not see the arms of the States? | Answer. Saw them when cut down; was on board when it was done. |
| Does he not know who did it? | Answer. Lieutenant Daniel Houw and Mr. Foret did it together; does not know which in particular did it. |

All of which he has declared upon oath before the honorable director and council, to be true and truthful, and further knows not.

[66]   Declaration of G[e]orge Wilbe

Where born?	Answer. North Hantomschier. [1]
How old?	Answer. Twenty-five years.
Who was the chief person that brought them, and what did they purpose to do?	Answer. Lieutenant Houw brought them thither, and he did not know the land belonged to the States; they came there by authority of Mr. Foret, a Scotchman.
Would they have been under English or Scotch rule, if they had remained there?	Answer. They should have lived free under their own laws, and would have owed obedience to whoever was lord of the land.
Where did he live in New England?	Answer. In Matetusje's bay, eight miles from Boston.
Did he not see the States' arms?	Answer. Did not see them when he came with the sloop.
Wherefore did they pull down the arms, and who did it?	Answer. Does not know for certain whether Mr. Foret or Lieutenant Houw did it.

---

1 Northamptonshire.

Does he not know who   Answer. He does not know.
carved the fool's face in
the stead of the arms?

All of which he declares to be true and truthful, without
knowing any more, and has before the honorable director, confirmed the same on oath.

Interrogatories for Jan Farington

Where was he born?   Answer. In Bockingamschier.

How old is he?   Answer. Twenty-four years.

Who brought them there,   Answer. Lieutenant Houw, with
and who was their leader that   Mr. Foret's permission, brought
conveyed them thither, and   them to where they intended to
what did they intend to do   plant; it was intended that 20
there, and how many persons   families should come, and if the
more are to come there?   land was good they expected a
                                 great many people.

[67] Were they to   Answer. English, and they have
settle under English or   acknowledged Lord Sterlincx for
Scotch rule?   their Lord; and if 'twere found
                                 that the land belonged to the
                                 States they would have been
                                 subject to them.

Where did he live in   Answer. At Lin, in Matetusje's bay,
New England?   eight miles from Boston.

Did they come there   Answer. He understood so.
with the knowledge and
consent of Mr. Wintrop,
the Governor of the Bay?

Did he not see the arms of the States?	Answer. Saw them when brought on board.
Does he not know who tore them down and conveyed them on board?	Answer. Lieutenant Houw and Mr. Foret brought them on board and he understood that they had torn them off.
Does he not know who carved the fool's face on the tree in the stead of the arms?	Answer. Does not know that any of his people did it.

Declares this to be true and truthful and confirmed the same on oath before the honorable director.

Interrogatory of Philip Cartelyn

Where born?	Answer. In Bockingamschier.
How old are you?	Answer. Twnety-six years.
Who was the principal person that brought them there?	Answer. Lieutenant Daniel Houw.
On what conditions did they come there; under the English or Scotch?	Answer. Under the English with Mr. Foret's permission, as far as he knows.
What did they mean to do there?	Answer. To plant and make a plantation.
Were many people to come there?	Answer. Some were to come to look at the land, and if they liked it they were to settle there; if not, they were to depart; the number he did not know.
[68] Where did he live?	Answer. At Lin, eight miles from Boston.

Did Mr. Wintrop, the Governor of the Bay, know that they were going to plant there?

Answer. Did not know it was States' land; thought that the land belonged to Lord Sterlincx.

Did he not see the States' arms?

Answer. Did not see them before they were torn down, but when they were broken off.

Who tore them off?

Answer. Is not sure whether it was Mr. Foret or Lieutenant Houw; says that one of the two did it, as he believes.

Does he not know who carved the fool's face on the tree?

Answer. Does not know; believes none of the English did it.

All of which he declares to be true and truthful, and has confirmed the same on oath before the honorable director.

Interrogatory of Nataniel Cartclandt

Where was he born?

Answer. In Bockingamscier.

How old is he?

Answer. Twenty-two years.

Who was the chief person that brought them there?

Answer. Lieutenant Houw brought them there with Mr. Foret's consent.

What did they propose doing there, and how many people were to come there?

Answer. They intended to plant, and if the place was good, a great many more were to come.

Where did he reside?

Answer. At Lin, 7 or 8 miles from Boston.

Did he not see the States' arms?

Answer. Mr. Foret and Mr. Houw went ashore and brought the arms on board.

Does he not know who tore them down?

Answer. Does not know who tore them down; but understood from the boy that Mr. Foret and Lieutenant Houw had done it.

Does he not know whether any of their party carved a fool's face on the tree where the States' arms were?

Answer. Does not know who did it, and it was not done by his party.

All of which he declares to be true and truthful, and has confirmed the same by oath before the honorable director.

[69] Interrogatory of Willem Harker

Where was he born?

Answer. In Lingconschier.

How old?

Answer. Twenty-four years.

Who was the principal person that brought them thither, and what did they intend to do on States' ground?

Answer. Lieutenant Houw, master of the bark, with Mr. Foret's consent; they intended to plant.

Were there not many more people to come?

Answer. He does not know.

Did Governor Wintrop know that they were to plant there?

Answer. Yes; and he wrote a letter to Mr. Foret.

Did he not see the States' arms?

Answer. Did not see them on the tree, but when brought on board.

Who tore them down?	**Answer**. Heard Lieutenant Houw say that he had torn them down and that Mr. Foret had lent him a hand.
Does he not know who carved a fool's face in the stead of the States' arms?	**Answer**. Does not know and does not believe that any of their company did it.

All of which he declares to be true and truthful and confirms the same on oath before the honorable director.

On the 19th of May, being Saturday

It is resolved in council inasmuch as the six Englishmen who were brought in were found not to be guilty of having torn down the arms of the Lords States, to discharge them from confinement and to set them at liberty, on condition that they promise to depart forthwith from our territory, and never to return to it without the director's express consent; whereto they shall be obliged to pledge themselves in writing.

Whereas we, Jop Sears, G[e]orge Wilbi, Jan Farington, Philip Cartelin, Nataniel Cartelandt, William Harker, some days ago, came to settle on territory belonging to their High Mightinesses, the States-General, without knowing the fact, being deceived by Mr. Foret, a Scotchman, wherefore the honorable director-general of New Netherland has had us removed and requires us immediately to break up and depart beyond the limits of the honorable Chartered West India Company, which we are bound to do, we promise on our word of honor to set about it forthwith without fail, on pain of being punished as deliberate trespassers, subjecting ourselves not only to this, but to other courts in the world.

In testimony of the truth and sincere good faith, we have subscribed
this with our own hands, in Fort Amsterdam, in New Netherland,
the 19th of May anno 1640. Signed, Jop Ceyrs, G[e]orge Welbe,
John Farington, Philip Cartelandt, Nataniel Cartelandt,
Willem Harker.

On the 7th of June 1640

Maryn Adriaensen, plaintiff, vs. Hendric Pietersen, mason,
defendant, regarding the delivery of a tobacco plantation. Having
seen the complaint and the defendant's answer, the defendant is
condemned to lease the plantation for six years, commencing the
first of January 1641, at fl. 60 a year, provided that the
defendant may deduct from the first payment one pistole.

Symon Pos, plaintiff, vs. Jan Celes, defendant. Plaintiff
demands payment for 24 quarts of peas which he delivered to the
defendant on account against the crop, or at the discretion of
the defendant. The defendant having admitted the claim, he is
condemned to pay the plaintiff fl. 5.

Davit Provoost and Jan Damen, as guardians of Jan van Vorst,
plaintiffs, vs. Jacob Stoffelsen, defendant. Plaintiffs, in the
capacity aforesaid, demand Jan van Vorst's share of his deceased
father's estate. Defendant answers that he has found many claims
against the estate of the late Cornelis van Vorst and requests
two months time [71] to make an accounting of the debts due by
and to the estate. The defendant's request is granted.

Gillis de Voocht, plaintiff, vs. the fiscal, defendant. Plaintiff demands payment of 24 gl. The complaint and answer being heard, the case is adjourned until the next court day.

On the 7th of June Master Hans has caused the court messenger to attach 6 gl. in the hands of Maryn Adriaensen, on account of Hans Steen.

On the 20th of June

Cornelis van[der] Hoykens, fiscal, plaintiff, vs. Hans Fredricxsz, soldier, defendant, regarding a complaint made by Gillis de Voocht. Upon consideration of the complaint and the answer of the defendant Gillis de Voocht and Hans Fredricxsz are each fined 6 stivers to be paid to the poor.

The fiscal, plaintiff, vs. Pietertjen Jans, defendant, for slander. Plaintiff demands proof, or, on default thereof, reparation of the injury. Parties granted 14 days to produce proper proof of the slander.

Tomas Hal, plaintiff, vs. Philip Gerritsen, defendant. Plaintiff demands payment for two schepels of wheat which he delivered to the defendant and which were stolen from the mill. Defendant admits the receipt and is condemned to restore the two schepels of wheat or to pay [for them].

On the 4th of July Willem Hont caused the tobacco of Nataniel Martyn in the hands of Jacob van Corl[e]r to be attached for 6 months, on condition that he is to bring proof from Virginia of the debt of the said Nataniel Martyn.

[72] On the 16th of July 1640

[1] Whereas the Indians dwelling in the Raretangh have heretofore shown themselves very hostile, even to the shedding of our blood, we nevertheless in the year 1634 concluded a firm peace with them, whereupon we have continued to trade with them, especially by sending every spring a sloop thither for beavers. This spring, anno 1640, it happened that they attempted to capture our sloop which had but three men on board, to kill the crew and to take the cargo, but through the grace of God this was courageously prevented, the Indians being driven again from board, with the loss only of our canoe, whereupon they came to Staten Island, shot some of the Company's hogs and plundered the house of the Negro. Wishing to obtain satisfaction therefor, we notified them to come here to indemnify us, but they only laughed at us.

And whereas this is a matter of grave consequence, as well as regards the reputation of the Lords States General, the respect and interests of the honorable Company, and the safety of our lives and cattle, it is resolved to send 50 soldiers and 20 sailors, together with the secretary and the sergeant, with orders to attack them, to cut down their corn and to make as many prisoners as they can, unless they willingly come to an agreement and make reparation. Thus done in council at Fort Amsterdam, this day, the 16th of July anno 1640.

On the 2d of August being Thursday

Tymon Jansen, plaintiff, vs. Lourens Haen, defendant, for slander.

---

[1] Revised from Doc. Rel. Col. Hist. N. Y., 13:7.

Lourens Haen, plaintiff, vs. Davit Provoost, defendant for slander. Cases put over until the next court day.

Pieter Andriessen, plaintiff, vs. Blancke Ael, defendant. Default.

[73] On the 9th of August 1640, being Thursday

1 Whereas daily many servants run away from their masters, whereby the latter are put to great inconvenience and expense, the corn and tobacco spoil in the fields and the entire harvest must come to a standstill, which tends to the serious injury of this country, to the masters' ruin and to bring the government into contempt; we, therefore, wishing to provide against this, command all farm and house servants faithfully, to serve out their time with their masters according to their contracts and in no manner to run away, and if they have anything against their masters to come here and make application to be heard in court on pain of being punished, of making good all loss and damage of their masters and of serving double the time that they lose.

We do also forbid all inhabitants of New Netherland to harbor or feed any of these fugitive servants under the penalty of fifty quilders, one-third for the benefit of the informer, one-third for the new church and one-third for the fiscal.

And whereas daily many abuses occur in consequence of the writing of bonds and other instruments by private persons, we do therefore declare that from this date all such writings, whether bonds or other instruments, which are not drawn up by the secretary or by other persons appointed thereto, shall be null and void.

---

1 Revised from Laws and Ordinances of New Netherland, p. 24.

Whereas some time ago the arms of their High Mightinesses the
Lords States General were set up on Long Island in Marten
Gerritsen's bay and the aforesaid arms were torn down by the
natives of the aforesaid bay and in the place of said arms a
fool's head was set up, we have therefore resolved to send a
sloop with soldiers thither to reduce the said savages to our
obedience and make them pay tribute.

Tymen Jansen, plaintiff, vs. Lourens Haen, defendant, for
slander. Plaintiff demands proof of the charges or in default
thereof vindication of honor.

Defendant, answering, says that about six weeks after the
arrival of the _Harinc_ he heard Davit Provoost say at the house
of Lupoldt, in his and his wife's presence, that he had seen
Dirc Cotsen committ adultery with the wife of Tymen Jansen and
that not for money, but for otters and beavers, and that he had
seen this happen several times.

Davit Provoost expressly denies [having made] the aforesaid
[statement]. Plaintiff ordered to produce proof.

[74] On the 9th of August anno 1640

Pieter Andriessen, plaintiff, vs. Aeltjen Douwes, defendant,
for slander. Defendant has in court prayed the plaintiff for
forgiveness, acknowledging and holding him to be an honest and
honorable man.

Jochem Kaller, plaintiff, vs. Adam Roelantsen, defendant,
for slander. Plaintiff demands reparation of honor. Defendant
having acknowledged that he has nothing to say against the wife
of the plaintiff and that he has nevertheless defamed her, he
is condemned to pay fl. 2:10 to the poor.

Cornelis Willemsen, plaintiff, vs. the wife of Tomas Broen, cadet, defendant, for slander. Having seen the unfounded complaint of the plaintiff and heard the answer of the defendant who declares the plaintiff to be as far as he knows an honest and honorable man, the defendant is acquitted and absolved from liability as to costs.

On the 16th of August

Claes Jansen Ruyter, plaintiff, vs. [   ] Ridder, defendant. Plaintiff, as husband and guardian of his wife, Pietertjen Jans, requests and demands that the defendant prove the defamatory words which he alleges to have heard from others. The defendant, answering, says that he does not know precisely word for word what was said. Parties are ordered to leave each other unmolested and henceforth to live together in peace.

Gregoris Pietersen, plaintiff, vs. Cornelis Lambersen Cool, defendant. Default.

[75] On the 23d of August 1640

Whereas Davit Provoost, commissary of provisions, has, against the orders of the honorable director, alienated the Company's property, left the warehouses and cellars of the Company open during the night and without express consent extended too much credit to every one and furthermore in the end has come short in his accounts, the aforesaid Davit Provoost is hereby dismissed from his office of commissary and Maurits Jansen, thus far assistant, is appointed commissary of provision in the place of Provoost, on condition that he furnish security.

Tymon Jansen, plaintiff, vs. Lourens Haen, for slander. Plaintiff desires and demands proof of the slanderous remarks

which Davit Provoost is said by the defendant to have made. The
defendant persists in his testimony. Davit Provoost declares in
court that he knows nothing of the wife of Tymon Jansen but what
is honorable and virtuous and that he has seen nothing in her
house but what is proper, being ready at all times to confirm
the same under oath.

Having seen the evidence and the insufficiency of the testimony
produced by Lourens Haen to prove the case, the said Provoost is
acquitted and the said Haen condemned to pay a fine of fl. 10
for having, as he says, had knowledge of such scandalous words
so long and kept still about them and not reported the same to
the magistrates according to his oath; one half [of the amount
to be] for the church and the other half for the fiscal, on condition that he furnish the offended party a certificate hereof.

Whereas Peter Draper, by virtue of a letter from Governor
Calvert of Maryland, has come here to find some runaway servants,
among whom is alleged to be one Eduwart Griffins, who has appeared
before us and admits that he ran away from Maryland but says
that he had no master in Maryland and that Captain Claber in
Virginia was his master, which he proves by Hendrick Penninghton,
residing at Hackemac, who thereupon has taken the proper oath,
[76] saying that the said Griffins was not a servant, but a
prisoner in Maryland; that he does not know whether Griffins,
being a prisoner there, has voluntarily bound himself to any one
as a servant, but that it is well known to him, Hendric Pennington,
that he, [said Griffins], was Captain Claver's servant in Virginia;

Therefore, we have ordered that the said Peter Draper shall
agree with the aforesaid Griffins about his freedom and that the

said Draper shall furnish satisfactory security that said Griffins
shall not be molested by said Captain Claber or any one else who
might show his indenture and not suffer any damage. This day,
the 27th of August, in Fort Amsterdam in New Netherland.

On the 20th of August anno 1640

Jan Jacobsen from Vrelant, plaintiff, vs. Davit Davitsen
and Hans Noorman, defendants, for the delivery of fence posts.
The defendants having admitted that they bought 800 posts from
the plaintiff and [declared] that they have not received the same,
the plaintiff is obliged to prove that they have had the said
800 posts in the woods.

Baltasar Lourens and Tomas Broen, plaintiffs, vs. Davit
Provoost, defendant. Default.

On the 6th of September

Jan Jacobsen from Vrelant, plaintiff, vs. Barent Dircksen
from Norden, defendant. Default.

[77] On the 20th of September, being Thursday Jan Jansen Damen
and Davit Provoost, as chosen guardians of Jan van Vorst, plaintiffs,
vs. Jacob Stoffelsen, defendant, regarding the accounting of the
estate of the late Cornelis van Vorst. The defendant requests
time to prepare his accounts. At the request of the defendant
he is granted 14 days to draw up his accounts and then to render
an accounting to the plaintiffs.

Samuel Chandelaer, plaintiff, vs. Jacob Stoffelsen, as
husband and guardian of Vroutjen Ides, widow of the late
Cornelis van Vorst, defendant. Plaintiff demands payment of
the money which the late Cornelis van Vorst owes him by balance
of his account. Parties referred to referees.

Adam Roelantsen, plaintiff, vs. Gillis de Voocht, defendant, for laundry money. Plaintiff demands payment for washing defendant's linen. Defendant says that he is not offering to pay less in payment for the washing, only that the year is not yet expired. Plaintiff is ordered to fulfil the term of the contract and then to demand payment.

On Thursday, being the 4th of October

Cornelio vander Hoykens, vs. Gerrit Jansen from Haerlem and Floris Jansen from Hoochwouw, defendants. Plaintiff complains about the negligence of the defendants in disobeying the commands of their skipper, as the shallop might thereby become damaged. The defendant, Gerrit Jansen, being the more guilty of the two, is condemned to satisfy the fiscal.

[78] On the 4th of October anno 1640

Hester Symons, widow of the late Jacob Vernu, plaintiff, vs. Roelandt Hackwart, defendant, for slander. Plaintiff demands that the defendant retract the slander or prove that she is a whore. Defendant declares in court that he acknowledges the said Hester Symons to be a virtuous woman and that he knows nothing about her but what is good.

Jan Damen and Davit Provoost, chosen guardians of Jan van Vorst, plaintiffs, vs. Jacob Stoffelsen, defendant. Plaintiffs demand from the defendant the accounting which on the 20th of September last he was ordered to make today. Defendant answers that he is ready to render the accounting, provided the plaintiffs give security that they will reimburse him for any debts which may afterward come to light in Holland or elsewhere concerning the estate of Cornelis van Vorst. It is ordered that

the plaintiffs, if they earnestly desire an accounting from the
defendant, give security for the [payment of the] debts which
may yet come to light.

On the 11th of October 1640

Baltasar Lourens and Tomas Broen, plaintiffs, vs. Davit
Provoost, defendant. Second default.

Jan Jacobsen from Vrelant, plaintiff, vs. Barent Dircksz,
baker, defendant. Second default.

[79] On Thursday, being the 25th of October 1640

Whereas Gysbert van Dyc, commissary of Fort De Hoop on the
Fresh river, [1] intends to sail for the fatherland on the ship
Waterhont and his place is become vacant, it is deemed necessary
by us to choose another suitable and experienced person in his
place. Therefore, having considered the ability of Hendric Roesen,
we have engaged him as commissary of Fort De Hoop aforesaid on
the same salary which was paid heretofore, namely 36 gl. a month,
and free board for the commissary.

Cornelio vander Hoykens, fiscal, plaintiff, vs. Abraham
Planc, defendant, for having traded maize contrary to the
ordinance. Plaintiff demands that the defendant be punished as
it is customary to punish those who violate the ordinances of
the [Company] and that the defendant be condemned to pay the
fine provided therefor. Case put over until next week.

On the 1st of November anno 1640

Cornelio van[der] Hoykens, fiscal, plaintiff, vs, Abraham
Planc, Cornelis Lambersen Cool and G[e]orge Rappaelje, defendants,

_____

[1] Fort Hope on the Connecticut river.

for violating the ordinance concerning the trading of maize.
Defendants answer that they have traded from 10 to 11 schepels
of maize. Defendants are ordered to comply with the ordinance
or to settle with the fiscal.

The fiscal is ordered to prove that the wife of G[e]orge
Rappaelje did not trade any maize with the Indians before the
28th of October last.

[80] On the 8th of November anno 1640

Cornelio vander Hoykens, fiscal, plaintiff, vs. Ulrich
Lupholt, defendant. Default.

Jan Jacobsen from Vrelandt, plaintiff, vs. Barent Dircksen
from Norden, defendant. Default.

On Thursday, being the 15th of November

Anna Jans, wife of Jan Snediger, cadet, defendant, that is
to say, plaintiff, vs. Maria Tirry, defendant, for slander. The
fiscal, becoming a party to the case, substitutes himself for
the plaintiff because the defendant beat Anna Jans on the public
highway and he therefore demands that she be tried and punished.
Maria Tirry is condemned to pay the fine to the fiscal and to
reimburse the plaintiff for the expenses incurred by her.

Cornelio vander Hoykens, plaintiff, vs. Ulrich Lupholt,
defendant, for fraud committed by him in pricing the store
goods. The plaintiff, submitting his complaint in writing,
sustains that Lupholt has greatly advanced the prices of goods,
contrary to the regulation; also, that he has been very negligent
in the care of them. The defendant requesting time to answer
the complaint is granted a delay until Thursday.

Nicolaes Coorn, appearing before the council, requests,
inasmuch as Gillis Ros, in his lifetime supercargo of the ship
Neptunes, has died, that he may be engaged as supercargo on the
said ship. In consideration of the capacity of the aforesaid
Coorn we have chosen and appointed him supercargo on the said
ship, on condition that he is to receive the same pay as the
deceased Gillis Ros.

[81] On the 23d of November

Whereas Bastiaen from Pariba, Portuguese, taken on the 15th
of November anno 1638 with a prize, entered the service of the
honorable directors of the Chartered West India Company on the
ship Neptunes and until now has together with other sailors done
his work on said ship, for which he was allowed fl. 8 a month by
the ship's council of the said ship, therefore we, the director
and council of New Netherland, accept and approve the resolution
passed by the said skipper and ship's council that he, Bastiaen,
is to earn fl. 8 a month from the time that he came on the ship
Neptunes. Thus resolved on the day above written.

On the 22d of November, being Thursday Cornelio vander Hoykens,
fiscal, plaintiff, vs. Uldrich Lupholt, defendant. Case put
over until next court day when sentence is to be pronounced.

On the 29th of November

Abraham Pietersen, miller, plaintiff, vs. Hendrick Harmansen,
defendant, for the delivery of farm No. 5. Plaintiff demands
that the defendant remove other people's cattle from the farm.
Defendant answers that the cattle are his own, both those which
he has leased and the others. Parties amicably settled with
each other in court.

Cornelio vander Hoykens, fiscal, plaintiff, vs. Uldrich Lupholt, defendant. Plaintiff demands justice and prompt decision. It is resolved in council to fix the prices of store goods at 50 per cent above the net cost and to post the same in the store; also, to inform the people by handbills that if any one considers himself defrauded he is to examine the prices there. It is also decided not to pass upon the demands of the fiscal until after New Year when the defendant shall have rendered his account and the complaints of the people shall have been heard.

[82] Whereas many complaints have been made by the good inhabitants here that they are charged excessively high prices for the goods of the store, which is contrary to the orders and wishes of the honorable directors and ourselves; therefore, wishing to provide against this, we have caused to be placed in the said store on a board a schedule of the cost of all the goods with the prices at which they must be sold, in order that every one may see whether he has been over-charged and demand the difference back from the merchant in the store or make his complaint to us.

[83] Anno 1641. In the Name of God

On Thursday, being the 17th of January

Cornelio vander Hoykens, fiscal, plaintiff, vs. little Antonio Paulo d'Angola, Gracia d'Angols, Jan of Fort Orange, Manuel of Gerrit de Reus, Anthony the Portuguese, Manuel Minuit, Simon Conge and big Manuel, all Negroes, defendants, charged with homicide of Jan Premero, also a Negro. The plaintiff charges the defendants with manslaughter committed in killing Jan Premero and demands that justice be administered in the case, as this is

directly contrary to the laws of God and man, since they have
committed a crime of lese majesty against God, their prince and
their masters by robbing the same of their subject and servant.

The defendants appeared in court and without torture or
shackles voluntarily declared and confessed that they jointly
committed the murder, whereupon we examined the defendants, asking
them who was the leader in perpetrating this deed and who gave
Jan Premero the death blow. The defendants said that they did
not know, except that they committed the deed together.

The aforesaid case having been duly considered, it is after
mature deliberation resolved, inasmuch as the actual murderer
can not be discovered, the defendants acknowledging only that
they jointly committed the murder and that one is as guilty as
another, to have them draw lots as to who shall be punished by
hanging until death do ensue, praying Almighty God, creator of
heaven and earth, to designate the culprit by lot.

The defendants having drawn lots in court, the lot, by the
providence of God, fell upon Manuel of Gerrit de Reus, who shall
be kept in prison until the next court day, when sentence shall
be pronounced and he be executed.

[84] On the 24th of January, being Thursday

The governor and council, residing in New Netherland in the
name of the High and Mighty Lords the States General of the United
Netherlands, his highness of Orange and the honorable directors
of the Chartered West India Company, having seen the criminal
proceedings of Cornelio vander Hoykens, fiscal, against little
Antonio Paulo d'Angola, Gracia d'Angola, Jan of Fort Orange,
Manuel of Gerrit de Reus, Antony the Portuguese, Manuel Minuit,
Simon Conge and big Manuel, all Negroes and slaves of the aforesaid

Company, in which criminal proceedings by the fiscal the said
Negroes are charged with the murder of Jan Premero, also a slave,
committed on the 6th of January 1641, which said defendants on
Monday last, being the 21st of this month, without torture or
irons, jointly acknowledged in court at Fort Amsterdam that they
had committed the ugly deed against the slain Premero in the
woods near their houses; therefore, wishing to provide herein
and to do justice, as we do hereby, in accordance with the Holy
Scriptures and secular ordinances, we have, after due deliberation
and consideration of the matter, condemned the delinquents to
draw lots which of them shall be hanged until death ensue. And
after we had called upon God to designate the culprit by lot,
finally, through the providence of God, the lot fell upon
Manuel of Gerrit de Reus, who therefore is thereby debarred from
any exceptions, pleas and defenses which in the aforesaid matter
he might in any wise set up, inasmuch as the ugly murderous deed
is committed against the highest majesty of God and His supreme
rulers, whom he has deliberately robbed of their servant, whose
blood calls for vengence before God; all of which can in no wise
be tolerated or suffered in countries where it is customary to
maintain justice and should be punished as an example to others;
therefore, we have condemned, as we do hereby condemn, the aforesaid Manuel of Gerrit de Reus (inasmuch as he drew the lot) to
be punished by hanging until death follows, as an example to all
such malefactors.

Thus done and sentenced in our council and put into execution
on the 24th of January of this year of our Lord and Savior Jesus
Christ anno 1641.

[85] On the 24th of January 1641

Manuel of Gerrit de Reus having been condemned to be
executed with the rope so that death would follow, standing on
the ladder, was pushed off by the executioner, being a Negro,
having around his neck two good ropes, both of which broke,
whereupon the inhabitants and bystanders called for mercy and
very earnestly solicited the same.

We, therefore, having taken into consideration the request
of the community, as also that the said Manuel had partly under-
gone his sentence, have graciously granted him his life and
pardoned him and all the other Negroes, on promise of good
behavior and willing service. Thus done the day and year above
written, in Fort Amsterdam in New Netherland.

On the 14th of February, being Thursday

Cornelio vander Hoykens, fiscal, plaintiff, vs. Uldrich
Lupholt, defendant. Plaintiff, answering the written denials
of the defendant, bitterly complains about the negligence, fraud,
etc., according to the written bill of complaint. Case put over.

Cornelio vander Hoykens, fiscal, plaintiff, vs. Laurens
Haen, defendant, for unfaithful conduct in the store. Plaintiff,
in writing, demands justice and punishment of the defendant.
Laurens Haen admits in court that he took the Holland linen,
table linen and velours from the store without charging them to
his account.

Jan Snediger declares that he has nothing in his possession
that belongs to Haen except some boards and a straw mattress.

Albert Cuyn affirms in court by oath that he does not have, nor ever had, anything in his possession belonging to Haen, except what the fiscal seized in his house.

The case against Haen is put over until the next court day.

[86] On Thursday, being the last of February 1641

Cornelis vander Hoykens, fiscal, plaintiff, vs. Uldrich Lupholt, defendant. Plaintiff demands judgment against the defendant in accordance with his written replication.

Lupholt acknowledges that he sold many goods too dear and that the rattinet (noppen) which was to cost 13 stivers was sold for 18 stivers.

Cornelio vander Hoykens, plaintiff, vs. Laurens Haen, defendant, for theft in carrying goods out of the store. Defendant admits having carried some goods out of the store, but says that he did not intend to steal these, but to enter them on his new account, as the old account was somewhat high. Case put over until the next court day.

Nidt Wilsoon, [1] plaintiff, vs. Tomas Sandersen, smith, defendant, for damage alleged to have been done to the plaintiff's garden by the defendant's cattle. Plaintiff demands damages. Defendant answers that the land was not cleared and parties are ordered to bring proof as to the damage that was done.

On Thursday, being the 7th of March

Cornelio vander Hoykens, fiscal, plaintiff, vs. Uldrich Lupholt, defendant, on account of faithlessness and fraud committed

---

[1] Edward Wilson.

against the inhabitants. Plaintiff persists in his former charges made in writing and therefore demands judgment; also, that the defendant declare who the persons are that spoke evil of the honorable directors.

[87]   On Thursday, being the 7th of March 1641

Interrogatories on which Lupholt was examined in council

Q. Who put the water in the brandy?

A. Elslandt, and alleges that the fiscal said, "What can I do? The commander has fixed it up with him."

Q. Who violated his oath?

A. Crol, as he sold French wine at 12 stivers which was to sell for 10 stivers.

Q. Who charged fl. 1800 in **addition to the 50 per** cent advance and let the goods spoil which he, Lupholt, had to accept as merchantable?

A. Wybrant Pietersz, former commissary of store goods.

Q. Who was it who called the honorable directors cuckoos?

A. Cornelio vander Hoykens, the fiscal.

Q. Who was it who said, "I have enough to live on; if they put me out of the service now, I do not care?

A. It was Cornelis van Tienhoven.

Q. Who knew two or three months ago that Haen was crooked?

A. The honorable Director Willem Kieft, Lupholt says.

Cornelio vander Hoykens, fiscal, plaintiff, vs. Laurens Haen, defendant, for faithlessness in the store. The fiscal, persisting in the charges made in his former written bill of complaint, demands judgment.

Pieter Cornelisz, formerly a deacon here, declares that one day last October, toward evening, Haen accosted him near the warehouse to ask that fl. 50 of the poor money be lent to him upon interest. Whereupon he said, "There is no money." Haen answered: "There are persons who would be willing to lend it to me, but they do not wish to have their names mentioned." Haen said: "If Mrs. Lupholt comes to your house, please tell her that I borrowed the money from the poor fund upon interest." Pieter Cornelissen has affirmed this under oath before the honorable director and council.

[88] On the 14th of March 1641

The director and council of New Netherland have seen the criminal proceeding by Cornelio vander Hoykens, fiscal, plaintiff, against Uldrich Lupholt from Staden, in the diocese of Bremen, formerly councillor and commissary of store goods here, defendant, from which it appears that the said Lupholt has spoken very contemptuously of the honorable directors of the General Chartered West India Company, saying, "They are but merchants and cause themselves to be called lords," and that he several times defied the director here, saying, "If you dare, send me back; do your best and I shall do my best;" also snapping his fingers, etc.; all of which was forgiven him on promise of good behavior. Notwithstanding this, he has not hesitated grossly to overcharge the people here for the goods in the store, above the usual

50 per cent and costs of the cases, which he was instructed not
to exceed, as appears by his account book, which is full of
changes in prices and blots, and by the accounts in his own
handwriting given to various people, as well as by the affidavits
furnished by various persons at the request of the fiscal;
standard grey cloth which was to sell at 12 gl. was sold at
15 gl. to Tomas Ouwens for cash; an entire case of sugar at 24
stivers which was to bring but 17 stivers; copper kettles 3½
stivers a pound too high; Haerlem goods 5 stivers per yard too
high; all small children's shoes of 18 stivers at 24 stivers;
head dresses (oorysers) of 2½ stivers at 8 stivers; wooden bowls
of 3 stivers at 8 stivers; linen of 16 stivers at 23 stivers;
kersey which should be sold at 36 stivers at 3 gl. and 2 stivers.
No discount was made on silk goods, the price of the same being
considerably raised instead, and that of all other goods accordingly, as appears from his day-book; in selling cloth, linen and
cambric, no numbers were given in his book and of what was sold
for cash no entries were made, while much gold and heavy money
received from various people was kept by him. A private trade
in the Company's goods was carried on with the savages and
Christians, especially in kettles, according to his little
memorandum book; considerable outstanding debts were not entered
in the account book, among them those of Burger Jorissen,
Mr. Allerton, Jan Eversen and others. Furthermore, he has
generally badly received [89] those who came to purchase goods,
refusing to give them many articles which were still plentiful,
such as shoes, shirts, pewterware, etc., not taking proper care
of the goods, but letting everything lie around, without making

any effort to keep things in order. He has also slandered and
spoken disparagingly of the authorities, the minister of the
gospel and the community here, saying that if the English come
into the country he will cut off his relations with the Hollanders
and associate with them; finally, in closing his accounts he has
come short considerable amounts.

Having hereupon taken the advice of the principal inhabitants
here, as appears from the expression of their opinion in our
custody, therefore, after invocation of God's holy name, we hereby
depose and discharge the said Lupholt from his office, declaring
him unfit henceforth to serve the honorable Company in this
country and order that he is to remain under arrest until the
arrival of the first ship, in order to be sent therein to Holland
to be dealt with by the honorable directors. Furthermore, he
is condemned to pay a fine of fl. 200, fl. 150 for the benefit
of the fiscal and fl. 50 for the poor, and in addition the costs
of the trial, after having first given satisfaction to the
honorable directors. Thus done and sentenced in council, the
day and year aforesaid, in Fort Amsterdam in New Netherland.

On Thursday, being the 11th of April anno 1641

Everardus Bogardus and Tymen Jansen, chosen guardians of
the minor children of the late Cornelis v[an] Vorst, plaintiffs,
vs. Jan Damen and Davit Provoost, chosen guardians of Jan van
Vorst, eldest son of the late Cornelis van Vorst, defendants.
Plaintiffs claim that the small minor children should receive
something from the estate of their deceased father in advance
in order that they may be better educated and learn to read and
write; they request that the honorable director may be pleased

to render such decision as they shall think proper, according to
law. It is decided in council that Ide and Anna van Vorst shall
each receive fl. 50 in advance from the estate of their deceased
father and that the residue shall be divided and distributed
according to law.

[90] On Thursday, being the 11th of April

Cornelio vander Hoykens, fiscal, plaintiff, vs. Laurens Haen,
defendant. Plaintiff asks that the case may be expedited. Case
put over.

Cornelis Lambertsen Cool, plaintiff, vs. Sybet Claessen,
defendant. Plaintiff demands delivery of boards which the
defendant has promised to furnish him in exchange for logs.
Parties referred to Gillis Pietersen and Dirc Cornelissen or, in
the absence of one or the other, Pieter Cornelissen, to settle
their dispute.

[1] Whereas complaints are made to us that some of the
inhabitants here undertake to tap beer during divine service and
also make use of small foreign measures, which tends to the
neglect of religion and the ruin of this state; we, wishing to
provide herein, do therefore ordain that no person shall attempt
to tap beer or any other strong liquor during divine service,
or use any other measures than those which are in common use at
Amsterdam in Holland, or to tap for any person after ten o'clock
at night, nor sell the vaen, or four pints, at a higher price
than 8 stivers, on pain of forfeiture of the beer and payment
of a fine of 25 guilders for the benefit of the fiscal and three
months' suspension of the privilege of tapping.

---

[1] Revised from Laws and Ordinances of New Netherland, p. 25.

On Thursday, being the 18th of April

2 Whereas at present very bad seawan is in circulation
here and payments are made in nothing but dirty, unpolished stuff
that is brought here from other regions where it is worth 50 percent less than here, and the good, polished seawan, ordinarily
called Manhattan seawan, is exported and wholly disappears, which
tends [91] to the decided ruin and destruction of this country;
therefore, in order to provide against this in time, we do hereby
for the public good, interdict and forbid all persons, of whatever
state, quality or condition they may be, during the coming month
of May to receive or give out in payment any unpolished seawan
except at the rate of five for one stiver, that is to say, strung,
and thereafter six beads for one stiver. Whoever shall be found
to have acted contrary thereto shall provisionally forfeit the
seawan paid out by him and ten guilders to the poor, the same
applying to the receiver as well as to the giver. The price of
the well polished seawan shall remain as before, to wit, four
[beads] for one stiver, provided it be strung.

On Thursday, being the 2d of May

Everardus Bogardus, minister, and Jan Damen, Davit Provoost
and Tymen Jansen, chosen guardians of the surviving children of
the late Cornelis van Vorst, plaintiffs, vs. Hendric Jansen,
tailor, defendant. The plaintiffs jointly demand that the defendant
be compelled to declare in court whether it is known to him that
Hendric van Vorst was indebted to his deceased father in the

---

2 Revised from Laws and Ordinances of New Netherland,
p. 26.

amount of 1000 guilders. The defendant declares upon his manly
troth in court that he has no knowledge of the matter, being
ready at all times, if required, to confirm the same under oath.

On Thursday, being the 23d of May 1641

Jan Damen and Davit Provoost, plaintiffs, vs. Everardus
Bogardus and Tymen Jansen, chosen administrators of the estate
of the late Hendric van Vorst, defendants. The plaintiffs claim
and maintain that Jan van Vorst, being the full brother of Hendrick
van Vorst, is lawfully entitled to the just half of the estate
before any division is made and that then the remaining half is
to be lawfully divided among himself and his half-brother and
sister, each to have a one-third share.

[92] The defendants maintain and give for answer that two
half-interests of the half-brother and sister constitute a whole
interest and, therefore, that the property should be equally
divided, half and half, between them and their full brother.
Having seen the plaintiffs demand and the answer of the defendants,
it is decided that according to law Jan van Vorst, being the
full brother of the late Hendric van Vorst, shall first of all
receive one-half of the estate and that the remaining half shall
be equally divided and distributed between the plaintiffs as
guardians of Jan van Vorst and the guardians of Ide and
Anna van Vorst.

Jacob Stoffelsen, plaintiff, vs. Everardus Bogardus, Tymen
Jansen, Davit Provoost and Jan Damen, defendants, as guardians
of the children of the late Cornelis van Vorst. Plaintiff demands
that the defendants before they proceed to divide the estate of

the late Hendric van Vorst shall satisfy the debt which the said
van Vorst owes to his father, according to the account book. The
defendants acknowledge that what is written in the account book
is in Cornelis van Vorst's own handwriting and that the same was
confirmed by him at his death. Defendants are condemned to pay
out of the estate of the late Hendric van Vorst what said van
Vorst owes his father, according to the said account book of
Cornelis van Vorst.

Hendrick Jansen, tailor, father and guardian of his daughter
Elsjen Hendricx, plaintiff, vs. the guardians of the heirs of the
late Hendric van Vorst, defendants. The plaintiff demands three
cows which van Vorst promised his daughter by word of mouth in
case he should die on the voyage to the fatherland. Plaintiffs'
claim is denied as he cannot prove that Hendric van Vorst made
the aforesaid promise to his daughter and he is granted fl. 24
for the keeping of two [female] goats and one buck.

[93] On Thursday, being the 30th of May 1641

Fredrick Jansen, plaintiff, vs. Claes Sybrantsen Veringh,
defendant. Plaintiff demands payment of wages earned by him.
The defendant acknowledges the debt and the receipt of his canoe.
The defendant is condemned to satisfy the plaintiff.

Cornelio vander Hoykens, plaintiff, vs. Uldrich Lupholt,
defendant. Plaintiff demands that satisfaction and compensation
be given to the Company. Defendant is granted 8 days to make
answer, without fail.

Cornelio van[der] Hoykens, plaintiff, vs. Cornelis Bartensz.
defendant. Default.

On Thursday, being the 6th of June [1]

Whereas a considerable number of respectable Englishmen with their clergyman have applied for permission to settle here and to reside among us and request that some terms might be offered to them, we have therefore resolved to send to them the following terms:

1. They shall be bound to take the oath of allegiance to the honorable Lords the States General and the West India Company under whose protection they will reside.

2. They shall enjoy free exercise of religion.

3. In regard to political government, if they desire a magistrate, they shall have the privilege of nominating three or four persons from the fittest among them, from which persons so nominated the governor of New Netherland shall choose one, which magistrate shall be empowered in all civil actions to render final judgment not exceeding 40 guilders; above this amount an appeal may be made to the governor and council of New Netherland; and in criminal cases he shall have jurisdiction except in cases involving corporal punishment.

4. They shall not be at liberty to erect any strongholds without permission.

5. The land shall be granted to them in fee, free of charge, and they shall have the use thereof for ten years without paying any dues and at the expiration of the said ten years be obliged to pay tithes.

6. They shall enjoy free hunting and fishing and freedom of trade according to the charter of New Netherland.

---

[1] Revised from Laws and Ordinances of New Netherland, p. 27-28, and Doc. Rel. Col. Hist. N. Y., 13:8.

7. They shall be bound to make use of the weights and measures of this country.

1 [94] On Thursday, being the 6th of June 1641

Whereas the English on the Fresh river of New Netherland commit great depredation and violence against our people there and are not satisfied with usurping and cultivating the lands which were bought and paid for and taken possession of by our people, but in addition come at night and sow with grain the land which our people plow, haul away to their houses the grass which our people mow, come with clubs and mattocks and barbarously treat our people when they are plowing, dig out our fine looking peas and plant Indian corn instead, forcibly take away our horses, cows and hogs and let some of them die of hunger, cut the traces of our plow to pieces and throw the latter into the river, and surround our house with palisades so that one can scarcely get out of it on the land side;

Therefore, all of this having been considered by us and whereas the same is tending to the injury and contempt of our supreme government and the honorable West India Company, whose jurisdiction and authority we are charged to maintain, we have resolved to send thither Dr. Johannes la Montagne, councilor of New Netherland, with 50 soldiers and some sloops, in order to fortify our house De Hoop 2 and to prevent the repetion of such hostilities as the English have wickedly committed against our people and to maintain our soil and jurisdiction.

---

1 Revised from <u>Doc</u>. <u>Rel</u>. <u>Col</u>. <u>Hist</u>. <u>N</u>. <u>Y</u>., 14:34-35.
2 Fort Hope, at Hartford, Conn.

Cornelio van[der] Hoykens, fiscal, plaintiff, vs. Uldrich
Lupholt, defendant. Plaintiff demands that the Company be paid
and that satisfaction be made as soon as possible. Defendant
presents a certain humble petition instead of an answer. Having
seen the humble petition of Ulrich Lupholt requesting that he
may be reinstated in the service of the Company and acknowledging
the offenses committed by him, with promise of better and satisfactory comportment, he is ordered to satisfy the honorable
Company and to make reparation, provided that provisionally he
shall receive his rations until the arrival of the ships.

Cornelio van[der] Hoykens, fiscal, plaintiff, vs. Maryn
Adriaensz, defendant, for slander. Defendant asks forgiveness
from the honorable director for the offense committed by him
before Fort Amsterdam, whereupon his offense is graciously forgiven him for the sake of his wife and children.

[95] On Thursday, being the 13th of June 1641

The chosen guardians of the surviving children of the late
Cornelis van Vorst, plaintiffs, vs. Jacob Stoffelsen, defendant,
as husband of the widow of the late Cornelis van Vorst. Plaintiffs
demand the grain that stood in the field on the farm of the late
van Vorst. Jacob Stoffelsen is ordered to produce evidence concerning the grain which he says was given by Hendric van Vorst
to the widow as far as his part was concerned and the other half
belonging to Jan van Vorst shall be appraised by the mowers.
Jacob Stoffelsen acknowledges that he was indebted to Hendric
van Vorst in the amount of fl. 430; therefore, he is ordered to
pay the same. Also, Maryn Andriaensen is ordered to declare to
whom the cow belonged which he bought from Vroutjen Ides.

Dirck Cornelissen from Wensveen, plaintiff, vs. Jan Eversen Bout, defendant. Plaintiff demands payment of fl. 500 in Dutch or English coin. Defendant admits the debt and says that he is ready to pay in beavers and cannot pay it at present in Dutch or English money; also, that he is not obliged to pay before the plaintiff sails for Holland. Defendant is ordered to pay plaintiff's claim within two months from this date to his satisfaction.

Tomas Hal, plaintiff, vs. Everardus Bogardus, minister, defendant. Plaintiff demands proof that he acted unjustly in connection with the defendant's tobacco. Defendant answers that the plaintiff let the tobacco spoil and demands compensation for the damage and loss suffered thereby.

Jacob van Curler and Francois Lasle are appointed referees to decide the aforesaid case.

Phillip Garaerdy, plaintiff, vs. Jeuriaen Hendricksz, defendant. Plaintiff demands that the defendant fulfil his promise to build his house. As the defendant acknowledges that he is bound to do so, he is ordered to commence within two months from this date and from then on to carry out his contract.

At Fort Orange 16 beaver skins have been seized by Bastiaen Jansen Crol of which the former owner can not be found. According to the order of the honorable directors he is granted 15 stivers apiece for them, which are to be credited to his account.

[96] On the 20th of June 1641

This day, date underwritten, personally appeared before our governor and council of New Netherland Anna Metfoort, widow of the late Willem Quick, making known the insolvent condition of the estate left to her by Willem Quick, deceased, and whereas

she, Anna Metfoort, is a sorrowful widow in a foreign land, without any effects or means of satisfying the creditors, yes, even
does not know where she may find lodging or obtain a morsel of
bread, she declares before us that she neither intends nor is
willing to assume the obligations of heir of the late Willem
Quick, her deceased husband, or to use any of his property for
her benefit, placing everything, whether bed, furniture or other
property, movable and immovable, at the disposal of the creditors.
She, Anna Metfoort, further declares on her conscience that she
is ready to affirm the same upon oath and that she retains nothing
but the clothes which she has on now to cover her nakedness,
leaving the rest for the benefit of the creditors; whereof she
requests a certificate in order that hereafter she not be molested
by any one on that account. Whereupon she has taken the oath in
council before us, the director and concilors, that all that is
hereinbefore written is true and that she possesses nothing more
than is mentioned in the subjoined inventory. Thus done, the
20th of June, in Fort Amsterdam.

Inventory of the estate of the late Willem Quick

1 bed

1 pillow, 3 blankets

1 small mat, 5 bedsheets

2 tablecloths, 2 pillow cases

8 napkins

1 towel

2 pewter platters

1 wooden bowl, 1 pewter cup

2 small pewter saucers

1 salt cellar, 2 small copper kettles

1 flatiron

1 pewter chamber pot

3 spoons

4 skirts

3 woman's shirts

6 undershirts

3 aprons, 10 caps, 12 handkerchiefs

1 chest, 1 small box

3 books

2 pairs of stockings

1 Indian child

[97]   On Thursday, being the 20th of June 1641

Jeuriaen Hendricksen and Nanninck Hansen appeared in court and at the request of Jacob Stoffelsen declared that now about two years ago the deponents mowed grain for Jacob Stoffelsz at Ahasims and that to the best of their knowledge there were about 60 bushels of it, including waste and all. They offer to confirm this on oath.

Gillis de Voocht, plaintiff, vs. the wife of Teunes Tomassen, mason, defendant, about charges for sewing linen. It is ordered that the wives of Albert Cuyn and Adam Roelants shall estimate how much was earned by sewing.

On Thursday, being the 4th of July

[1] Whereas the Indians of the Raretangh are daily exhibiting more and more hostility, notwithstanding they have solicited of

---

[1] Revised from Laws and Ordinances of New Netherland, p. 28-29.

us peace, which we consented to, permitting him to depart unmolested
on his promise to advise us within twelve days of the resolution
of his chief, which has not been done; and whereas the aforesaid
Indians, who experienced every friendship at our hands, have in
the meantime on the plantation of Mr. de Vries and Davit
Pietersen, [2] partners, situated on Staten Island, murdered four
tobacco planters and set fire to the dwelling and tobacco house,
whereby the planters and farmers and other remote settlers stand
in great in great danger of life and property, which we under
the circumstances, on account of the density of the forest and
the small number of men, can not prevent; we have therefore considered it most expedient and advisable to induce the Indians,
our allies hereabout, to take up arms, in order thus to cut off
stray parties who must pass through their territory, so that
they can not reach our farms and plantations without peril or
at least without being discovered; and in order to encourage
them the more we have promised them ten fathoms of seawan for
each head, and if they succeed in capturing any of the Indians
who have most barbarously murdered our people on Staten Island
we have promised them 20 fathoms of seawan for each head.

[98] On Thursday, being the 8th of August anno 1641

Adam Roelantsen, plaintiff, vs. Jan Jansen Damen, defendant,
for damage done by his cattle in plaintiff's garden. It is
ordered that the damage shall be appraised by two impartial men
and that each person, the defendant as well as others, shall pay
in proportion to the number of his cattle.

---

[2] Frederick de Vries, secretary of the city of Amsterdam,
and David Pietersen de Vries. See Van Rensselaer Bowier MSS.,
p. 64.

The guardians of the surviving children of the late Cornelis van Vorst, plaintiffs, vs. Maryn Adriaensen, Hendric, the tailor, Jacob Stoffelsen and Frederic Lubbersen, defendants, on account of debt according to the note in the handwriting of Hendric van Vorst. Maryn Adriaensen and Frederick Lubbersen are provisionally released from the claims against them as they paid Jacob Stoffelsz, as said Jacob Stoffelsz admits in court.

On Thursday, being the 22d of August

Maryn Adriaensen, plaintiff, vs. Jan Andriesz from Tonderen, defendant. Plaintiff demands restitution of what was stolen from him on his yacht. Defendant says that he has no knowledge of the stolen bacon, but acknowledges that he paddled with a canoe around the yacht of the plaintiff. Harman van Nus acknowledges that he has eaten of the stolen bacon, but says that he does not know who stole it and that Jan Andriesz hung the same over the fire to cook.

On the 23d of August

Jan Andriessen from Tonderen acknowledges in court that he took half a pound of bacon out of a tub at the house of Maryn, with the knowledge of Pieter from Hamburg and Harman Nus. Defendant is provisionally released from his irons and ordered to appear on the next court day.

The honorable director general of New Netherland hereby notifies all heads of families or households dwelling here about to be pleased to repair to the Fort on next Thursday, being the 29th of August, in order to resolve there upon some urgent business.

[99] On Thursday, being the 5th of September

G[e]orge Homs, plaintiff, vs. Jeuriaen from Osenbrugge, [1]
defendant, for payment of 17 gl. and 10 stivers. Default.

On Thursday, being the 12th of September

Cornelio van [der] Hoykens, plaintiff, vs. Laurens Haen,
defendant. Plaintiff maintains that the defendant, if he can be
apprehended, is liable to arrest and deserves to be flogged with
rods and demands that he be condemned to pay a fine for the
behoof of such persons as the director and council shall deem
proper.

The director and council of New Netherland having seen the
criminal proceedings instituted at the request of Cornelio van
[der] Hoykens, fiscal, plaintiff, vs. Laurens Haen from Amsterdam,
aged about 23 or 24 years, formerly assistant in the store,
defendant, whereby it clearly appears that the defendant has
not hesitated to take and steal from the honorable directors'
store here, silk, napkins, tablecloths, linen, cambric, velvet,
sugar, terzanelle, [2] spices, etc., and cash which he buried in
various places, such as a certain goat house on the strand near
the land of Davit Provoost, in his garden and at the end of the
Lange Heere wech, as appears from his voluntary confession, made
in writing while free from torture or irons, sent to the honorable
director and council and consisting of seven separate schedules,
some without date and others bearing the day and year; which
defendant, having been placed under arrest on account of said
crimes in order that he might be dealt with according to law and
the matter might be further investigated, escaped from prison

---

[1] Osnabrück, Hanover, Germany.
[2] A corded silk, also called "gros de Naples" and "gros
de Tours."

during the night between the 2d and 3d of May. Therefore, having
first called upon God and duly weighed and considered the aforesaid case, we, administering justice therein, as we do hereby,
find the charges of the fiscal to be true as the money was dug
up in four different places and goods were taken from the houses
of two different persons. Nevertheless, considering his youth,
we declare the aforesaid Laurens Haen liable to arrest if he can
be apprehended elsewhere and furthermore condemn him, as we do
hereby, if he were present, to be publicly placed on the scaffold
and there to be flogged with rods, and further to pay a fine of
150 Carolus guilders for the benefit of the fiscal and the costs
of the trial as an example to all others.

[100] On Thursday, being 12th of September anno 1641

Isaac Allerton, plaintiff, vs. Antony Jansen from Salee,
defendant. Plaintiff demands payment for the goods which he sold
and delivered to the defendant. Defendant acknowledges the debt
and is condemned to pay before he leaves the island of Manhatans.

A certain petition is presented to the council by Oloff
Stevensen praying that inasmuch as he has acted as commissary
of cargoes in the stead of Curler since the 1st of July 1641 he
be granted the same salary as Curler. Whereupon, in view of the
efficiency of the said Oloff Stevensen, we have granted him 30
gl. a month from the time he has performed the duties of the
aforesaid office of commissary.

Cornelio van[der] Hoykens, fiscal, plaintiff, vs. the pilot,
chief boatswain and cook of the ship Engel Gabriel, for having
sold some sugar without entering the same. Parties having been
heard, defendants are ordered to pay the duties to the Company

together with a fine of 40 pounds of sugar for the benefit of
the fiscal.

Cornelio van[der] Hoykens, plaintiff, vs. Uldrich Lupholt,
defendant. Plaintiff requests that the case be expedited and
that Lupholt pay the honorable Company what is due to them.

Having considered the petition of some respectable Englishmen who are on good terms with us here, praying that the defendant
may remain in this country provided he pay and satisfy the
honorable Company, which they promise to do on their part as far
as they are concerned, we deem it advisable to keep him here for
the present in order that the honorable Company may be more fully
satisfied.

Laurens Cornelisz, defendant, vs. Abraham Cloc, plaintiff.
Parties have settled with each other in court.

Jan Damen, plaintiff, vs. Jacob Stoffelsen, defendant.
It is ordered that Maryn and Fredrick Lubbersz declare under
oath that there is no other debt or account between them and
Hendric van Vorst outstanding, except that which arises from the
purchase of the cows which they bought from van Vroutjen Ides.

Jeuriaen Hendricksz, plaintiff, vs. Antony Jansen, defendant.
Antony is provisionally discharged and plaintiff condemned to
pay the costs.

[101] On Thursday, being the 12th of September anno 1641

Whereas some of our men have lately been murdered by the
savages on Staten Island, therefore, to prevent further accidents
and to protect those who are still dwelling there, we have
thought it very useful and advisable to construct on the said
island a small redoubt at as little expense as possible.

On Thursday, being the 24th of September

Cornelio van[der] Hoykens, fiscal, plaintiff, vs. Jan Symonsen, former skipper of the yacht Reael, and his gunner, defendants, for having while drunk fired a cannon loaded with ball after the watch was set. The fiscal is provisionally ordered to put the defendants in irons.

Cornelio van[der] Hoykens, fiscal, plaintiff, vs. Piere Pia and Davit Clement, defendants, for having fought with each other. Parties are ordered to produce their respective witnesses.

Bontjen, plaintiff, vs. Symon Dircksen Pos, defendant, for debt. The defendant says that he does not owe the plaintiff anything, but has paid. The plaintiff leaving the decision to the choice of [the defendant to take] an oath, the defendant swears before the honorable director and council that he does not owe the plaintiff anything, whereupon the plaintiff's claim is denied.

On Friday, being the 25th of September

Cornelio van[der] Hoykens, fiscal, plaintiff, vs. Jan Symonsz and his gunner, defendants. Defendants are ordered to settle with the fiscal.

The same, plaintiff, vs. Piere Pia and Davit Clement, defendants. The defendants are ordered to satisfy the fiscal.

[1] All persons are hereby notified that the director and council of New Netherland have ordained that henceforth there shall be held annually at Fort Amsterdam a cattle fair on the 15th of October and a hog fair on the 1st of November. Whoever has anything to sell or to buy can regulate himself accordingly. On the 30th of September this notice was posted at said fort.

---

[1] Revised from Laws and Ordinances of New Netherland, p. 29.

[102]   On the 3d of October 1641

Borger Jorissen, plaintiff, vs. Jacob Roy, gunner, defendant.
Plaintiff demands payment of fl. 50.   Defendant admits the debt
and requests eight days time.   Defendant is ordered to pay within eight days.

Borger Jorissen, plaintiff, vs. Cornelio van[der] Hoykens,
fiscal, defendant, for damage done to the plaintiff's house by
the careless shooting of Jan Symonsz and his gunner.   The defendant
gives for answer that the plaintiff did not claim any damages and
released Jan Symonsz.   The fiscal is ordered to prove that Borger
said that he did not desire any indemnity and that he had released
[Jan Symonsz of liability for] the damage.

Jan Damen, plaintiff, vs. Lyntjen Adams, defendant, for
slander of Ragel Viengne.   Defendant answers that she has named
no one, but that she heard from Tomas Coninck, the soldier, that
there is a woman in or about the fort who pays money to boot.
Case adjourned.

Jan Damen, plaintiff, vs. Tomas Coninck, defendant, regarding his having made the above statement.   Defendant answers that
about three weeks ago, at the house of Uldrich, the soldier, he
heard Sander Boyer say that there was a woman at the fort who
gave money to boot.   He having asked who it was, said Boyer said,
"If you don't know, it won't hurt you."

Jan Damen, plaintiff, vs. Jan Platneus, [1] alledging that he
is a perjurer and incompetent to give any testimony, because he
has committed adultery with Indian women, according to the
affidavit.

---

[1] Jan Flat Nose.

Cornelis Willemsz, plaintiff, vs. Dirck Volkersz, defendant. Default.

On the 24th of October

Willem Bredenbent, plaintiff, vs. Hendrick the tailor, Evert Bisschop and Burgert Jorissen, defendants, for impounding their goats. They give for answer that the fence was out of repair and that other animals than their goats have been on the land. Defendants are ordered to pay fl. 10 to the deputy sheriff for pound money and fl. 10 to Davit Davitsz to indemnify him for the damage done by the goats, unless the defendants can prove that other animals than their goats did the damage on the land and that the fence was not tight.

Pieter Cock, plaintiff, vs. Jan Eversen, defendant. Default.

[103] On Thursday, being the 31st of October 1641

Davit Davitsz and Tomas Broen, plaintiffs, vs. Borger Jorisz, Hendrick the tailor and Evert Bisschop, defendants. Default.

The defendants are condemned to satisfy the judgment rendered eight days ago, as they failed to prove that the fence was not tight and that the damage was done before by other animals. In default whereof the fiscal is authorized to attach their goats and to sell as many of them publicly in the fort as will satisfy the judgment and the costs of the trial. [1]

[104] On Thursday, [2] being the 1st of November 1641

Cornelio van [der] Hoykens, plaintiff, vs. Lambert Cool, defendant, upon complaint of Altjen Brackonge, alleging that the defendant beat her in her house. Clara Tysens, wife of Gerrit Jansen, aged 31 years, declares at the request of Altjen Brackoengie

---

[1] The remainder of the page is blank.
[2] This should be Friday.

that Lambert said that he had received no powder, saying Altjen
lied; whereupon she beat him on his back and Cool took up a
branding iron and dealt her a blow on the arm and first pulled
Aeltjen's hair; which she offers to confirm on oath.

Articles submitted by the honorable director and council
of New Netherland to the heads of families or householders
residing here under the jurisdiction of the honorable West
India Company

1. Whether it is not just to punish the barbarous murder
of Claes Swits committed by an Indian and, in case the Indians
refuse to surrender the murderer at our request, whether it is
not justifiable to ruin the entire village to which he belongs?

2. In what manner the same ought to be put into effect
and at what time?

3. By whom it may be undertaken?

Answers of the 12 selectmen chosen by the entire community

to consider the aforesaid questions

In regard to the first, they find that by all means the
murderer according to the proposition of the honorable director
should be punished, but that it is advisable to have regard to
God and the circumstances and meanwhile to provide ourselves
with everything that is necessary, especially, that 200 coats
of mail be procured by the director from the North, both for the
soldiers and freemen, who are willing to pay for part of them
themselves.

[105] As regards the second article, that meanwhile
friendly intercourse, yes, even as far as the maize trade, be
maintained, until the opportunity presents itself and the will
of God be made manifest. Also, that meanwhile no one, of whatever condition he may be, shall commit, either on water or on

land, any hostility against any Indians, with the exception of
the murderer, and that meanwhile everyone be on his guard. Likewise, when the Indians are hunting, that we shall divide ourselves
into two parties, to wit, one on land near the Clepela and the
other party at Qiquaeskeck, in order to surprise them on both
sides, and that the honorable director shall employ thereto as
many Negroes from among the strongest and fleetest as he can conveniently spare, and provide them each with a hatchet and a
half-pike.

As to the third article, whereas we acknowledge no other
commander than the director, who is our as well as the soldiers'
chief, therefore, in order to prevent all disorder, [we find it
advisable that] the honorable director shall personally lead
this expedition, for which we offer ourselves to be of personal
service to him.

We also deem it advisable that two or three times more a
sloop be sent by the honorable director to make a friendly request
without threats, for the surrender of the murderer, in order to
execute him, and thus to mislead the savages.

Whereupon the following persons have sworn to keep this
their advice secret: Jaques Bentyn, Maryn Adriaensz, Jan Damen,
Hendrick Jansen, Davit Pietersz de Vries, Jacob Stoffelsz,
Abraham the miller, Fredric Lubbersz, Jochim Pietersz, Gerrit
Dircksz, G[e]orge Rapalje, Abraham Planc; so verily may God
help them.

[106] Willem Kieft, director general, and the council of
New Netherland have summoned the 12 men delegated by the community
to give advice on the matters to be proposed to them and to put

into execution the advice lately given by them if it be thought advisable, as the time and opportunity now present themselves to surprise the Indians on the hunt.

Mr. Jo[c]hum says that it will be best to have patience and to lull the Indians to sleep.

Jaques **Bentyn** says that it will be best to kill the Indians so as to fill them with fear.

Jan Eversen says that he does not think it advisable to undertake anything against the savages but to lull them to sleep so as to avoid suspicion.

Jacob Stoffelsen says that it will be best to wait for a ship to come from the fatherland.

G[e]orge Rapalje, Gerrit Dircksz, Hendrick the tailor agree with the above opinion.

Abraham Pietersz says that he thinks it advisable to begin war and to exterminate the savages if possible.

Fredrick Lubbersen says that the war cannot be carried out successfully as the undertaking against the Raretangs came to a standstill.

Jacob Waltingen says that he is ready to do whatever the director and council may order and think advisable.

Hereupon it is resolved in council by the honorable director and councilors to watch for the proper time and opportunity, it being understood that the barbarous murder must be revenged for the sake and security of our lives and cattle; and if anything be undertaken by us, everyone will be notified as promptly as possible in order then carefully to consider the matter.

[107] On the 7th of November anno 1641

Pieter Cock, plaintiff, vs. Jan Eversen Bout, defendant, for
slander. Plaintiff demands that the defendant prove the slanderous
words uttered by him about the plaintiff. The defendant gives
for answer that the statements made by the plaintiff are mostly
lies and requests that the plaintiff produce reliable witnesses,
offering to substantiate whatever he may have said. Case
adjourned.

On the [14th] [1] of November

Whereas the director of Curaçao, Jan Clasen van Campen,
in his letter dated the 11th of October 1641, which arrived
here by the ship Witte Valck on the 18th of November, writes
earnestly requesting us to send said ship back to him with provisions as they are very much in need of them and can no longer
send their ships out to sea for lack of provisions, it is resolved
in council to aid them and to purchase from the skipper his lading
of salt in order to keep the salt trade in the hands of the
Company; furthermore to agree with the skipper of the said Valck
in the most profitable way about the freight of as many provisions
as may be brought together to take the same to Curaçao.

Paulus Jansen from Vlissingen, plaintiff, vs. Maryn Adriaensz
and Fynhout, defendants. Jan Damen and Cornelis Tonissen are
requested to settle the matter between the parties and if they
cannot come to an agreement the referees are to submit their
opinion to us in writing.

Cornelis van[der] Hoykens, fiscal, plaintiff, vs. Jan Habbesz,[2]
defendant, for theft. The plaintiff produces depositions by four

---

[1] Date left blank in the record.
[2] John Hobson.

witnesses from which it appears that the defendant stole a bed sheet from a bed stead in the city tavern. [3] Defendant answers that he was drunk and does not know about the sheet; he is therefore granted till this afternoon to refresh his memory and if he remains headstrong he is to be put to the torture.

[108] On the [14th] of November anno 1641 in Fort Amsterdam

Cornelis vander Hoykens, fiscal, plaintiff, vs. Gerrit Jansen, cooper, defendant, for stealing wood. The fiscal is ordered to prove his charge against the defendant.

Andries Hudden, as guardian of Lambert Cool, plaintiff, vs. Altjen Brackoenge, defendant. Parties have amicably settled their differences in court.

On the 22d of November

Cornelis van[der] Hoykens, fiscal, plaintiff, vs. Jan Habbesz, defendant, for theft. Plaintiff produces information in the form of [depositions of] six witnesses who have seen that the defendant stole linen from the bed in the city tavern and requests, if the defendant persists in denying the charge, that he be put to the torture. The defendant, having persisted in his denial, is put to the torture and examined on the evidence and after having been tortured and released from torture and irons he acknowledges and confesses that he did steal the sheet from the city tavern, as well as bacon from old Jan, from which he has had his share. Whereupon the plaintiff, ex officio, demands that the delinquent be flogged with rods and banished from the limits of New Netherland.

The director general and council, residing in New Netherland on the part of their High Mightinesses the Lords States General

---

[3] s'lants harbarge; the public tavern at New Amsterdam.

of the United Netherlands, his Highness of Orange and the honorable
Chartered West India Company, having seen the criminal charge and
the conclusion of the fiscal against Jan Habbesen, English carpenter,
together with the information taken against him, from which it
appears that the delinquent on the 19th of November last stole
a sheet from a bedstead in the city tavern which the delinquent
on the 22d inst. acknowledged in our court without torture or
constraint of irons; also that he ate part of the bacon which
was stolen last year from old Jan's house; [109] likewise, that
heretofore he ran away from here as a rascal, taking with him a
canoe and leaving here various debts; all of which are matters
of evil consequence which cannot be suffered or tolerated in places
where justice is customarily maintained; therefore, having called
upon God and duly considered the matter and wishing to do justice
as we do hereby, and having found the complaint of the fiscal to
be true, we have condemned, as we do hereby condemn, the aforesaid
Jan Habbesen, at present a prisoner, to be brought to the usual
place of execution, there to be flogged with rods; furthermore,
the said delinquent shall from now on forever be banished from
the limits of New Netherland and immediately after the execution
of these presents shall depart from here, on pain if he be found
elsewhere within the province of being put in irons and forced
to labor with the honorable Company's Negroes, as an example to
all others of that kind. Thus done in court on the 22d of November
anno 1641, in Fort Amsterdam in New Netherland.

On the 13th of November

John Haes, plaintiff, vs. Master Fiscock, defendant, for
payment of £4. 8 s. sterling due for wages. Defendant says that
the work of the plaintiff was not worth the money. The matter
is referred to referees.

On the 5th of December

Andries Hudden, plaintiff, vs. Dirck Corsen Stam, defendant, in regard to certain goods belonging to the late Henderick de Foreest. Plaintiff demands payment and account of the aforesaid goods. Defendant answers that the plaintiff must prove that he, the defendant, received any goods from the late de Foreest. Parties are ordered to bring proper proof at the next session of the court.

[110]   On the 5th of December anno 1641

Before us, the director and council, appeared Dirck Corsen Stam, who declared that he did not state in Holland that Mr. La Montangne daily went around with his pockets full of ducatoons and Jacobuses.

Johannes La Montangne, plaintiff, vs. Jan Meris, [1] defendant. Plaintiff says that the defendant built the tobacco house which he had engaged him to build so poorly that it blew over, as it stood with its posts loose on the ground. He therefore demands payment for the tobacco which was spoiled in the said house and, furthermore, that the defendant raise the house again at his expense.

It is ordered that two carpenters, one Dutch and one English carpenter, shall inspect the house and render a decision according to their conscience whether in their opinion the house was well or poorly built. Mr. La Montangne chooses Gillis Pietersz and Jan Meris engages Jan Haes, both carpenters, to inspect the work.

---

[1] John Morris.

On the 13th of December 1641

Willem Dircksen, master of the ship De Witte Valck,
plaintiff, vs. Jacob Dircksz, chief boatswain, and Jan Heyn,
defendants. Plaintiff complains that the defendants have been
very disobedient on board; also, that they have gone on shore
without consent and remained there many days, whereby the
plaintiff and the owners of the ship suffer great loss, inasmuch
as the work does not proceed when the chief boatswain, who ought
to be the foreman in all ship's duties, is absent.

The complaint of the plaintiff having been considered by
us and it being found that the matters set forth therein are
prejudicial to the skipper, the defendants at the request of the
plaintiff are dismissed from the ship and ordered to fetch their
belongings from board; furthermore, they are condemmed to pay a
fine of fl. 20, fl. 10 for the fiscal and fl. 10 for the benefit
of the poor, and to pay jail charges and board to the under-sheriff.

[111] In the name of God, Amen. In the year after the birth
of our Lord and Savior Jesus Christ, 1642, Isaack de Foreest,
plaintiff, vs. Isaack Abrahamsen, defendant, for payment of
fl. 57. Parties have settled with each other.

Borger Jorissen, plaintiff, vs. Tonis Nyssen, defendant.
Plaintiff demands payment of fl. 18, due for wages. Defendant
admits the debt and asks that he be given time to pay. He is
granted six weeks, when payment must be promptly made.

Borger Jorissen, plaintiff, vs. Isaack Abrahamsz,
defendant. Default.

Dirck Corsen Stam, plaintiff, vs. Andries Hudden, defendant,
as husband of the widow of the late Hendrick de Foreest.
Plaintiff demands proof of the claim against him on account of
the affairs of the late de Foreest. Ordered, if Hudden proves
his claim to be true, that Dirck Corsen give security to prove
the contrary with his books here within a year from this date or
furnish such proof to the attorney of the said Hudden in Holland.
Hudden offers to prove his claim within 24 hours.

Cornelio vander Hoykens, fiscal, plaintiff, vs. Gerrit
Gerritsz, defendant, on account of cordage which the defendant
is alleged to have stolen from the Company's yachts and sold
according to the depositions. Plaintiff demands that the defendant
be punished according to his deserts. It is ordered that the
defendant be placed under arrest in the guardhouse; also, that
Dirck Holgersz be not allowed to leave the country before the
case is disposed of.

Cornelis Volckersz, plaintiff, vs. Aert Willemsz, defendant,
on account of the killing of a hog by the dog of Mr. Twiller.
Gysbert Cornelissen, aged 24 years, declares that he saw the dog
of Twiller bite the hog and that he pulled him off it. Case is
referred to the farmers' baker [1] and Leendert Arends.

[112]   On the 9th of January anno 1642

Cornelio vander Hoykens, plaintiff, vs. Gerrit Gerritsen and
Dirck Holgersz, defendants. Case put over in order to have the
depositions sworn to.

Philip Gerritsen, plaintiff, vs. Tonis Cray and Gerreken
Hessels, defendants. Plaintiff demands that the defendants

---

[1] De boere backer, meaning Barent Dircksen.

fulfil the contract made with them for the delivery of fire wood. Defendants acknowledge the justice of the claim and are therefore condemned to fulfil the contract or in default thereof the plaintiff shall be at liberty to purchase wood at their expense.

Jochim Kirsteede, plaintiff, vs. Pieter Pia, defendant, for slander. Plaintiff demands proof of the slander or reparation. Defendant declares in court that he has nothing to say about the plaintiff but what is to his honor and credit. Defendant is condemned to pay the costs of the trial.

Hans Rodewick, plaintiff, vs. Andries, the chief boatswain, defendant. The plaintiff demands the return of a certain canoe which the defendant is alleged to have detached and to have set adrift. Case adjourned until the owner of the canoe shall have arrived here.

Cornelis Willemsz, plaintiff, vs. Maryn Adriaensz, defendant. First default.

Dirck Corsen, plaintiff, vs. Andries Hudden, defendant. First default. The plaintiff demands and requests that the defendant [113] prove what he promised on the 2d of January to prove within 24 hours, to wit, that his claim was just; the more so as the plaintiff intends and expects to leave for Virginia and should not like to suffer loss in this matter through delays and postponements on the part of the defendant who even this day has caused default to be taken against him, thus seeking excuses. The plaintiff also requests that as the defendant has produced no proof according to his promise, that he be permitted to proceed on his intended boyage at the first opportunity without molestation. The request of Dirck Corsz

being taken into consideration, the said Dirck Corsen is granted
permission to depart at the first opportunity if Andries Hudden
does not proceed with his case.

On the 16th of January 1641

Cornelio vander Hoykens, fiscal, plaintiff, vs. Jan Tomasz
and Philip Geraerdy, defendants, for having contrary to the
ordinance sold beer 2 stivers higher per gallon than is required.
Parties ordered to agree with each other.

Gerrit Jansen, plaintiff, vs. Cornelio van[der] Hoykens,
fiscal, defendant. Plaintiff demands proof of the charges ex-
officio brought against him by the defendant. Defendant proves
by two witnesses that Donminge called the plaintiff a wood thief.
Plaintiff has sworn before the honorable director and council of
New Netherland that he is not guilty of the theft of the wood.
The fiscal's demand is therefore denied and the plaintiff acquitted.
What was done by the fiscal was done ex-officio.

Cornelio van[der] Hoykens, fiscal, plaintiff, vs. Gerrit
Gerritsen and Dirck Hollegersz defendants. Dirck Volkersz
declares under oath in court that he bought rope from Gerrit in
good faith and did not know but that it was his own. Gerrit and
other sailors on the yacht Real are ordered to appear next
Thursday to draw lots as to who of them shall be punished or
meanwhile to satisfy the fiscal.

[114] On the 23d of January 1642

Gregoris Pietersz, plaintiff, vs. Tomas Coninck, defendant.
Plaintiff demands payment for an elk skin which cost him 8 gl.
Defendant answers that he warned the plaintiff that the breeches
were made out of the elk skin. He is ordered to prove the same.

Hans Steen, plaintiff, vs. Hans Schipper, defendant, for
slander. Case is referred to the ensign and the sergeant to

dispose thereof and to cause satisfaction to be given to the
offended party as they shall see fit.

Cornelis Willemsz, plaintiff, vs. Maryn Adriaensz, Second
default.

Hendrick Jansen, plaintiff, vs. Jeuriaen Hendricksz, defendant.
First default.

Sybolt Classen, plaintiff, vs. Jeuriaen Hendricxsz,
[defendant]. First default.

The 30th of January

Cornelio vander Hoykens, fiscal, plaintiff, vs. Abraham
Planck, defendant. Deponents have confirmed their depositions
by oath, whereupon it is resolved properly to examine the same.

Cornelis Willemsz, plaintiff, vs. Maryn Adriaensz. Third
default.

[115] On the 13th of March anno 1642

Johannes Winckelman, plaintiff, vs. Abraham Pietersen,
defendant. Plaintiff says that Abraham Pietersz to his great
loss makes his servant, Jacob Bouwensen, whom he brought from
Holland at great expense to his masters, dissatisfied in his
service, inasmuch as he has made a contract with him to take
his place as head farmer on farm No. 5, thereby causing him
great loss and damage. Plaintiff demands that the aforesaid
Jacob Bouwensen be forced to serve out his bounden time according
to the contract made with him at Utrecht.

Having seen the complaint and the answer of the parties
with the depositions submitted on both sides, and the matter
having been duly considered by us, Jacob Bouwensen is ordered
to serve out his time according to the contract made at Utrecht
and signed by him.

Cornelio vander Hoykens, fiscal, plaintiff, vs. Maryn
Adriaensz, defendant, for drawing a knife. Plaintiff demands
that Maryn pay such fine as is imposed by law for knife drawing.
Defendant denies expressly that he drew a knife and says that he
has had no quarrel with anyone.

Sybert Clasen, plaintiff, vs. Jeuriaen Hendricxz. Second
default.

On the 20th of March

Baltasar Lourens, plaintiff, vs. Jan Tomassen, smith,
defendant. Plaintiff says that he sold to the defendant a small
house and demands that the defendant accept delivery thereof.
Defendant admits the purchase of the house. Having seen the
demand of the plaintiff and acknowledgment of the defendant that
final purchase took place and that part payment was made, the
defendant is condemned to receive the house according to the
contract made between him and the plaintiff.

[116] On the 20th of March anno 1642

Cornelio vander Hoykens, fiscal, plaintiff, vs. Jan Seles,
defendant. Plaintiff charges the defendant with having shot
other people's hogs in the woods, maintaining that this causes
great loss to the inhabitants and proving the truth of the
accusation by depositions. The fiscal is ordered to have the
witnesses personally appear before us in order to confirm their
depositions by oath. Meanwhile the defendant shall remain in
custody, unless he furnish bail for his appearence before he
leaves the Fort. Tomas Hal becomes bail for Jan Celes to appear
a week from today.

Andries Hudden, plaintiff, vs. Dirck Corsen Stam, defendant.
Plaintiff does not appear and default is taken against him and
if he does not appear before noon it is decided that the suit
against the defendant shall be dismissed.

Maryn Adriaensen, plaintiff, vs. Tomas Hal, defendant.
Default against the plaintiff, as he does not appear.

On the 27th of March

Andries Hudden, plaintiff, vs. Dirck Corsen, defendant.
Whereas the plaintiff for the second time has failed to appear
and two defaults have been taken against him and whereas time
does not permit further delay, the director and council decide
that the defendant according to our previous resolution may continue his voyage without being prevented from doing so by the
plaintiff. The plaintiff's claim against the defendant is hereby
dismissed, so that the defendant shall hereafter be free from
any further action by the plaintiff on that account.

[117] On the 27th of March anno 1642

Cornelio vander Hoykens, fiscal, plaintiff, vs. Jan Celes,
defendant, for shooting hogs according to the depositions. The
defendant admits having shot a hog which was not his in the mouth,
being white, which hog he says he gave to the planters of Dirck
the Noorman. Hendrick de Boer [1] says that he does not know that
it was another man's hog which was shot. Ordered that the fiscal
shall cause the planters of Dirck the Noorman to appear on the
next court day to be then personally examined.

Cornelio vander Hoykens, fiscal, plaintiff, vs. Hendrick
Hansen Curffanger, formerly gunner on the Witte Valck, defendant,
for insolence committed by him at the house of Hendrick Jansen,

---

1 Hendrick, the farmer.

locksmith. The defendant admits having committed the offense.
The defendant is condemned to serve the honorable Company one
month in such capacity as the honorable director shall see fit
and to pay a fine of fl. 10 to the fiscal, and costs.

Cornelio vander Hoykens, fiscal, plaintiff, vs. Philip
Geraerdy, soldier, defendant. Plaintiff demands that the
defendant be punished according to military rule because he left
his post during the night without consent. The defendant admits
having left his post without consent and prays for forgiveness.
Having seen the demand of the fiscal and the matter having been
duly considered, the defendant is condemned to ride the wooden
horse when the soldiers are on parade, having a tankard in one
hand and a naked sword in the other.

Abraham Ryken, plaintiff, vs. Jaques Bentyn, defendant, for
alleging that stolen hogs were eaten at his house. First default.

[118] On the 27th of March anno 1642

Maryn Adriaensen, plaintiff, vs. Tomas Hal, defendant, about
the delivery of a certain plantation which the plaintiff sold to
the defendant for fl. 1000, to be paid one-third New Year anno
1643, one-third New Year 1644 and one-third New Year anno 1645.
Parties have settled in court.

Cornelio vander Hoykens, fiscal, plaintiff, vs. Hendrick
Jansz, tailor, defendant, Default.

On the 1st of April, being Tuesday

Davit Provoost declares in court that it is known to him
that the widow of the late Hendrick de Foreest and Dirck Corsen
sued each other at Amsterdam, but that he does not know for
what cause.

Interrogatory upon which Dirck Corsen was examined in court

Whether he was not arrested   Dirck Corsen answers, No.

at Amsterdam and left in spite

of the writ of arrest?

Whether he has ever been will-   Answers, that this has never

ing to render an accounting   been proposed to him.

regarding the matters submitted

to him in court by the schepens?

Whether he left the books and   Answers, that the accounts

papers concerning him, Dirck   thereof are in the custody of

Corsen, Jan Tepkens and   Renselaer and Jan T'Jepkens. [1]

Hendric Foreest in company

at the house of Renselaer?

The original record was signed: Dirck Corsen Stam.

[119] On the 3d of April 1642 [1]

Whereas our territory on the Fresh river of New Netherland, which we purchased, paid for and took possession of, and which in the year 1633, long before any Christians were on the said river, was provided with a blockhouse, garrison and cannon, has now for some years past been forcibly usurped by some Englishmen and given the name of Hartford, notwithstanding we duly protested against them, and whereas they moreover treat our people most barbarously, beating them with clubs and mattocks, even to the shedding of blood, hoe up our corn, sow by night the fields which our people plow by day, draw away by force the hay which is mowed

---

[1] Dirck Corsen Stam was supercargo, Jan Tiepkens, skipper, and Hendrick de Forest, mate, of the ship Rensselaerswyck, which sailed from Amsterdam on Sept. 25, 1636. See Van Rensselaer Bowier MSS., pp. 345, 355-89.

[1] Revised from Laws and Ordinances of New Netherland, pp. 29-30.

by our people, cast our plow into the river and forcibly take
possession of our horses, cows and hogs, so that there is no
cruelty, insolence or violence left but it is practised against
us, who nevertheless have treated them with all moderation, yes,
even at great hazard have demanded and sent back home their women
who were carried off by the savages; and although we are commanded
by the States General, his highness of Orange and the honorable
West India Company to maintain our limits and uphold our rights
by every means, which we also have the power to do, yet, we have
rather chosen patiently to suffer violence and to prove by deeds
that we are better Christians than they who go about clothed with
the outward semblance thereof, until in its time the measure
shall at last be full.

Therefore our order and command provisionally is and we do
hereby ordain that our inhabitants of New Netherland are most
expressly forbidden to purchase, either directly or indirectly,
by two or three successive shipments or any manner whatsoever,
any produce that has been raised on our land near Fort Hope on
the Fresh river, on pain of arbitrary correction until they know
their rightful master; and the sellers of the produce which shall
have arrived from our Fresh river of New Netherland and from New
England shall first declare upon oath where the produce has been
grown, whereof a certificate shall be given them and thereupon
everyone shall be at liberty to buy and to sell. And all persons
are hereby warned so that no one may hereafter plead ignorance
and let everyone guard himself against damage.

Thus done in council and published at Fort Amsterdam.

[120] [1] On the 3d of April 1642

Whereas all the subjects of the High and Mighty Lords the
States General who pursue their trade or commerce here in New
Netherland are bound to pay in Holland before they can ship their
goods a duty of 10 percent to the West India Company, which was
granted to said Company by their High Mightinesses in consideration
of the great war which the honorable West India Company is carrying on and the heavy expenses it has to bear; and whereas the
honorable directors have learned that many goods are brought
hither from divers places upon which no duty has been paid any-
where, which tends to the serious injury of the honorable Company
and great damage of the good inhabitants of New Netherland who
have to bear even heavier burdens than foreigners; wherefore we
are expressly commanded to collect said duty here on all imported
goods on which nothing has been paid in Holland, Brazil, Guinea
and the West Indies and on exported goods so much as is authorized
by the Freedoms granted to this country.

Therefore, we have ordained and enacted, as we do hereby
ordain and enact, that from now and henceforth all persons who
import here any wares for purposes of sale shall enter their
goods and pay a just tenth part either in kind or in money and
on the exported goods according to the list thereof included in
the Freedoms, to the receiver of the Company's revenues or whoever shall be appointed thereto, on pain of forfeiture of the
same goods not only by the seller but by the buyer and the
parties in whose hands they may be found. Thus done, published
and posted in Fort Amsterdam, dated as above.

---

1 Revised from Laws and Ordinances of New Netherland, p. 31.

[121] On the 10th of April anno 1642

At the request of the fiscal the following persons have declared in court as follows:

Maurits Jansen, commissary, says that on Sunday evening he heard the landlady in the tavern say that Abraham Pietersz, the miller, called the director a rascal.

Marritjen Liuwens, landlady of the tavern, declares at the request of the fiscal that on Sunday last Abraham Pietersz called the director a rascal and a liar, which he said he was ready to prove, offering to confirm the same on oath.

Claes van Elslandt declares at the request of the fiscal that Abraham Pietersen, going with him from the tavern to the Smith's Valley, called the director a rascal, vilifying the entire council.

Cornelio vander Hoykens, fiscal, plaintiff, vs. Abraham Pietersz, defendant, for slandering the director. Plaintiff demands that the defendant be punished according to Imperial Statutes, folio 296, as the offense committed is clearly proven by the preceding declarations.

Abraham Pietersz is ordered to go to the house of Maurits Jansen and to take up his abode there until such time as he shall have defended his case.

Captain Patrick, plaintiff, vs. Josop Schocht, defendant, for slander and false accusation. Mr. Josop Schot is ordered to prove his statements within a month and meanwhile to give security for such loss or damage as Captain Patrick may suffer in consequence of this case and Captain Patrick is granted permission to go meanwhile wherever he pleases.

[122] On the 10th of April 1642

Cornelio vander Hoykens, fiscal, plaintiff, vs. Jan Celes, defendant, in regard to the shooting of a hog. [The court] having seen the complaint of the fiscal and the depositions connected therewith, the case is adjourned until a week from today, when judgment will be pronounced, according to which the defendant will have to govern himself.

Tobias Teunessen, plaintiff, vs. Hendrick van Dyck, defendant, in regard to a certain dispute. Parties have agreed with each other.

Abraham Ryken, plaintiff, vs. Jaques Bentyn, defendant. The defendant proves that hogs were eaten at the house of the plaintiff.

On the 13th of April [1]

Whereas many persons come here in New Netherland daily both from New England and Virginia who carry their passports under foot and have run away from their masters and who afterward occasion much trouble here, as has been shown recently in several instances; Therefore, to prevent all disorders, we have prohibited and forbidden, as we hereby do prohibit and forbid, all our good inhabitants here from this time forward to lodge any strangers in their houses, or to furnish them more than one meal, or to harbor them more than one night, without first obtaining a permit from the director and having their names recorded, so that it may be known what sort of people are here and whence

---

[1] Revised from Laws and Ordinances of New Netherland, p. 32.

they came, under penalty of 50 guilders and responsibility for
the actions of the person whom they harbor. Let every one be
warned hereby and save himself from damage.

Thus done in our council and published in Fort Amsterdam
on the date above written.

[123] On the 15th of May anno 1642 [1]

Whereas we have reliable information that some Englishmen
have presumed to enter our South river and to settle on the
Schuylkill, obliquely opposite our Fort Nassau, without having
any commission from any potentate, which is a matter of serious
consequence which tends to bring their High Mightinesses into
disrepute and to cause great damage to the West India Company,
as thereby their trade which they have on the south river becomes
unprofitable; Therefore, we have resolved in council and deemed
it to the best interest of the aforesaid Company to expel the
aforesaid Englishmen from the said Schuylkill in the most convenient way possible.

Andries Roulofsz, plaintiff, vs. Govert Lookmans, defendant.
Plaintiff demands payment for digging a cellar. Defendant answers
that he did not let the contract to the plaintiff but to someone
else. Plaintiff's demand is denied and he is ordered to seek
redress from the person who put him to work.

Catrina Bartram, plaintiff, vs. Tomas Jacobsz, defendant,
for slander. Tomas Jacobsz declares in court that he knows
nothing whatever to the discredit of the plaintiff and that he
acknowledges the said Catrina to be an honorable and virtuous

---

[1] Revised from Doc. Rel. Col. Hist. N. Y., 12:23.

woman. The plaintiff likewise declares that she acknowledges Tomas Jacobsz to be an honorable young man.

Cornelio vander Hoykens, fiscal, plaintiff, vs. Abraham Planc, defendant. Jan Damen becomes bail for the appearance of the defendant at the appointed time. Jan Damen is ordered to cause the defendant for whom he becomes responsible to appear at the next session of the court.

[124] On the 15th of May 1642

Cornelio vander Hoykens, fiscal, plaintiff, vs. Jan Celes, defendant, for shooting hogs belonging to other people. Plaintiff asks and demands that the defendant be punished, as by the shooting of hogs many inhabitants might suffer damage, so that it is necessary to make timely provision against this.

Having seen the complaint and conclusion of the fiscal and the depositions whereby it appears clearly that Jan Celes has shot hogs and given them away, which cannot be tolerated, as thereby many people might suffer loss, we therefore condemn, as we do hereby condemn, the aforesaid Jan Celes to pay for the hog which belonged to Everardus Bogardus, minister, so much as referees shall judge it to have been worth at the time it was killed; and as much as he shall have to pay to Everardus Bogardus the fiscal shall receive by way of fine. Furthermore, he is to pay the costs of the trial.

On the 22d of May 1642

Instructions according to which Jan Jansen Ilpendam, commissary on behalf of the Chartered West India Company on the South river of New Netherland, shall have to govern himself

As soon as the yachts Real and St. Merten shall have arrived, there, Jan Jansen shall proceed with one or both yachts if he

considers it necessary, accompanied by as many people as he can
conveniently assemble, up the Schuylkill to the place where the
English have recently taken possession, [125] go immediately on
shore, demand the commission of the said Englishmen and ask by
what authority they have presumed to take away our rights, lands
and trade. If they have no expressed royal commission to settle
in our limits, nor any formal copy thereof, he shall compel them
immediately to depart in a friendly way in order that no blood
be shed and, if they refuse to do so, he shall secure their
persons and put them on board the yachts in order that they may
be brought here. He shall further take care that he remain
master of the situation, maintain the reputation of their High
Mightinesses and the honorable West India Company and, after the
departure or capture of the English, raze the said settlements
to the ground, he, Jan Jansen, taking care that the English
suffer no loss as to their furniture but that a suitable
inventory thereof be made in their presence. Thus done in our
council in Fort Amsterdam in New Netherland on the date above
written.

Cornelio vander Hoykens, fiscal, plaintiff, vs. Abraham
Isaacksen Planck, defendant, for tearing down a placard. The
fiscal asks that the case be expedited and that the defendant be
punished according to the ordinance.

Having seen the complaint and the conclusion of the fiscal,
Cornelio vander Hoykens, against Abraham Planck for disloyalty
in deliberately tearing down the placard posted in Fort Amsterdam, in the presence of the sentinel and other witnesses, and
denouncing the principal officers of the Company, which is a

matter of grave consequence which tends to mutiny and revolt and can in no way be tolerated in a well ordered state, we have therefore condemned, as we do hereby condemn, the defendant to pay a fine of fl. 300, to be applied one-third part to the West India Company; one-third part to the building of the new church and one-third to the fiscal; and he is further forbidden on pain of banishment to express himself in word or deed to the prejudice of this State or of our masters. Thus done in our council in Fort Amsterdam in New Netherland, on the 22d of May 1642.

[126] **On the 19th of June 1642**

Davit Pietersen, plaintiff, vs. Hendrick Jansen, tailor, defendant, for payment of a certain bond signed by the defendant. Defendant answers that he has a counterclaim against the plaintiff. The defendant is ordered on the next court day to produce his counterclaim in due form.

It is resolved in council to engage Uldrich Lupolt in the service of the Company, to be employed where he might be most serviceable to the Company, for which he is to receive a salary of fl. 20 a month and fl. 120 a year for board.

Hendrick Jansen, tailor, plaintiff, vs. Dirck Cornelisz, defendant, for slander.

Hans Rodichwich declares that he heard Dirck Cornelisz call Hendrick's daughter names, saying she is a whore and Hendrick, securing affidavits to that effect, said "You will end by marrying a whore."

Gerrit Jansen, cooper, declares that he heard Dirck Cornelisz say to Hendrick, the tailor, "Your daughter is a whore." Hendrick said: "Such a whore you will not get." This was confirmed by oath.

Harmen Bastiaensen said that he heard that Dirck drank to the health of the bride and bridegroom, saying to Hendric, "Here is to Hoorn and Enckhuysen." Whereupon Hendrick said, "Do you mean to say that my daughter is a whore? You will not marry such a whore." Dirck, replying, said, "If I marry a whore, your daughter is a whore." This was confirmed by oath.

Hendrick van Dyck declares that Dirck Cornelisz called Hendrick the tailor's daughter a whore. Which was confirmed by oath.

The aforesaid case having been duly considered by us and the declarations having been examined it is resolved and decided that the persons who were present when Dirck slandered the daughter of Hendrick Jansen shall be assembled here and that he shall declare before them that he has nothing to say about the daughter nor about her bridegroom that reflects in any way on their honor or virtue. And he shall appear before them and request their forgiveness. Furthermore, the defendant is condemned to pay fl. 50 to the church and fl. 50 to the fiscal.

[127] On the 19th of June 1642

I, Dirck Cornelisz, acknowledge that I have injured Elsjen Hendrickz and her bridegroom in their reputation and have said more than I can prove. I therefore request them to forgive me and I declare before God, the court and all those who are present that I know nothing about them except what is consistent with all honor and virtue. Thus done in the presence of Hendric van Dyck, Hans Rodewich, Harman Bastiaensen, Gerrit Jansen, cooper, and the entire council.

Richert Brudnil, plaintiff, vs. Jan Celes. First default.

Cornelio vander Hoykens, fiscal, plaintiff, vs. Merry Terry, defendant, for violence committed by the defendant against Jan Eversen in taking away his hat. The defendant is ordered to the return the hat to the place from which she took it and is condemned to pay fl. 6 to the fiscal.

Jacob Roy, gunner, plaintiff, vs. Claes de Veringh, defendant. Default.

Cornelio vander Hoykens, fiscal, plaintiff, vs. Cornelis Volkersz, defendant. The defendant is condemned to pay fl. 9 duty on beavers to the Company and furthermore to settle with the fiscal; and it is ordered that henceforth he comply with the law upon such penalty as shall be deemed proper according to the merits of the case.

On the 26th of June

Jacob Roy, gunner, plaintiff, vs. Claes de Veringh, defendant. Plaintiff demands payment of fl. 55. The defendant admits that he is duly indebted in the aforesaid sum and requests time in order meanwhile to make arrangements for the payment. The defendant is granted two months, at the expiration of which he is ordered to pay promptly without delay.

[128] On the 26th of June 1642

Davit Pietersen from Hoorn, plaintiff, vs. Hendrick Jansen, tailor, defendant, for payment of a certain account outstanding between the parties, amounting to fl. 173:19, which sum the defendant admits he owes. He requests time to make payment. The defendant, upon his request, is granted a respite of six weeks to make payment, provided that if there are any items in the defendant's counter claim which heretofore have been paid, he shall be obliged to pay these in addition to the aforesaid sum.

Cornelis Melyn, plaintiff, vs. Johannes Winckelman, defendant. The plaintiff, by virtue of a contract made with the Lord of Nederhorst at Amsterdam, requests that the defendant show him by what authority he came to him last winter on Staten Island with his men and cattle, saying that he came to fulfil the aforesaid contract of which a copy had been given to the defendant, and for what reason he left there and planted another colony behind the Col, without asking for his advice according to the contract.

The defendant answers that he came into this country in the name and on the part of Meyndert Meyndertsz, whose agent he is and for whom he is establishing a colony behind the Col, according to the orders given him, in accordance with the patent granted to his master by the honorable directors and shown here to the director. Case put over until further information arrives by what authority the defendant came here.

Cornelio vander Hoykens, fiscal, plaintiff, vs. Jan from Meppelen, defendant, for slander. Case put over until the next court day and the skipper ordered to refrain from further abusive language and to prove the statements made by the fiscal.

[129] On the 26th of June

Andries Hudden is engaged by the council as surveyor, for which the Company shall pay him fl. 200 a year, and he has taken the oath before the honorable director and council that in all things he will act honestly, without fear or favor.

Laurens Andriesz is ordered to serve the Company for one month in mowing grain and if he conducts himself well he shall be paid for said service.

On the 11th of July [1]

Whereas we hear daily, God help us, of many accidents caused for the most part by reckless quarreling, drawing of knives and fighting, and the multitude of taverns and low groggeries that are badly conducted, together with the favorable opportunities which all turbulent persons, murderers and other lawless people have for running away and consequently of excaping from condign punishment, against which we should like to provide so as to prevent as much as possible all harm;

Therefore, we hereby ordain, decree and enact, agreeably to the ordinance made last year in Holland by the High and Mighty Lords the States General, that no one shall presume to draw a knife, much less to wound any person, under penalty of fl. 50, to be paid immediately, or, in default thereof, of working for three months with the Negroes in a chain gang; [said penalty to be inflicted] without respect of persons. Let everyone guard himself against damage and take heed. Thus done in council and published on the day above written.

The fiscal, plaintiff, vs. Gerrit Schuyt, defendant.

[130] On this day the 10th of July anno 1642 appeared before us, the director and council of New Netherland, Mr. Weytengh and Mr. Heel, delegated by the governor and council of Hartford, situated on the Fresh river of New Netherland, bearing letters credential who, being properly received, declare that they have been sent to treat with us in regard to the differences which have arisen between us and them concerning the possession of a certain piece of land situated on the Fresh river which they

---

[1] Revised from Laws and Ordinances of New Netherland, p. 33.

maintain to be theirs and which they desire to possess in peace
and quietude.

Whereupon we have answered that the said land was bought by
us in the year 1633 from the lawful owners and paid for, as
appears by contract of sale thereof; also, that in the same year
possession thereof was taken and a fortification built on the
same, provided with a garrison and munitions of war, before any
Christians had been on the aforesaid river, as we proved by
several authentic documents, desiring of the aforesaid delegates
that we might possess and retain our purchased and paid for land
in peace and quietude, or else, that they should acknowledge the
High and Mighty Lords the States General and his Highness of
Orange as their sovereign lords and pay the fee for the possession
of the said land; which the said delegates have provisionally
accepted, requesting time to submit the matter to their governor
and council of Hartford aforesaid, which was granted by us according to the conditions given them. Thus done in council the day
and year aforesaid.

[131]   Conditions [1]

Conditiones á D. Directore Gen. Senatuys Novi Belgii, Dominis
Weytingh atque Hill, Delegatis a nobili Senatu Hartfordiensi,
oblatae:

Pro Agro nostro Hartfordiensi, annuo persolvent Praepotentiss.
D. D. Ordinibus Foed. Provinciarum Belgicarum aut eorum Vicariis,
decimam Partem Reventús Agrorum, tum Aratro, tum Ligone, aliove
Cultorum Medio; Pomariis, Hortisq; Oleribus dicatis, Jugerum

---

[1] William Smith, History of New York, (Albany 1814), p. 22.

Hollandium non excedentibus exceptis; aut Decimarum Loco, Pretium nobile postea constituendum, tam diu quàm diu possessores ejusdem Agri futuri erunt. Actum in Arce Amstelodamensi in novo Belgio, Die Julii 9 Anno Christi 1642.

Translation

Conditions offered by the Director General and the Council of New Netherland to Messrs. Weytingh and Hill, delegates of the noble council of Hartford.

For our Hartford land, they will pay annually to the high and Mighty lords of the Federation of the Netherlands Provinces or their substitutes, one tenth of the return of the lands, whether by plowing or by tilling, or by some other means of cultivation; by orchards and by gardens; by vegetable gardens, not exceeding a Holland yoke (28,000 square feet); or in place of the tenth part, a just price to be arranged afterwards, for as long as they will be possessors of the land.

Done in Fort Amsterdam in New Netherland, this 9th day of July, the the year of Christ 1642.

On the 30th of July

Ritchert Brudnil, plaintiff, vs. Jan Celes, defendant, for slander. Case dismissed and Jan Celes condemned to pay the costs.

On Thursday, the 7th of August 1642

Dirck Corsen Stam, plaintiff, vs. Tymen Jansen, defendant. The plaintiff states that he promised at Amsterdam, according to a certain contract dated the 20th of June 1640, to pay the sum of 520 fl. with interest to Tymen Jansen, which sum he claims to have paid to Tomas Jansen Ses in Virginia, as the said Ses had a power of attorney from Tymon Jansen aforesaid to receive the aforesaid sum; also, that afterward, in the year 1641, the same sum was paid to the said Ses in tobacco by order of the commander of Kiketeyn and on his arrival in New Netherland in 1642 turned over by him to Tymen Jansen according to the receipt thereof. The plaintiff therefore demands the restitution of the aforesaid sum inasmuch as the sum has been paid once here and once in Virginia. The defendant requests a copy of the bill of complaint. The case is put over until the next court day and the defendant shall be furnished with a copy.

Philip Gerritsz, plaintiff, vs. Johannes Winckelman, defendant; plaintiff demands payment of the debt which the defendant owes. The defendant says that the summons was not properly served. It is ordered that the plaintiff shall cause the defendant to be summoned again to appear tomorrow.

[132] On the 7th of August 1642

Tomas Willet, plaintiff, vs. Dirck Cornelisz, defendant. Default.

On the 14th of August

Tomas Seyl, plaintiff, vs. Goetman Lengh, defendant. It is
ordered that if Tomas Seyl furnish security to the owner to
release the defendant the plaintiff's claim shall be paid.

Tomas Willet, plaintiff, vs. Dirck Cornelisz from Wensveen,
defendant, for slander. Dirck Cornelisz declares that he has
nothing to say that in any way reflects upon the plaintiff. It
is ordered that the defendant shall at his discretion put something in the box for the poor,

Tymen Jansen, defendant, vs. Dirck Corsen, plaintiff. The
defendant denies that Doctor Ses was paid until he is shown
better and further proof for, in the first place, the plaintiff
according to the power of attorney which he had from the defendant
ought to have exerted himself to procure from the heirs of
Dr. Ses surrender of the latter's power of attorney or in default
of payment to attach his property.

In the second plave the plaintiff ought to have an
authentic and formal certificate signed by the commander and
council there, written by the secretary, in which the commander
and council certify that the men have acknowledged under oath
before them that they paid Dr. Ses for the plaintiff by virtue
of a power of attorney which Dr. Ses had from the defendant.

In the third place, the promise of restitution of the money
is not absolute, but coupled with the condition that the cattle
must be delivered to the defendant, with which condition the
plaintiff was satisfied.

In the fourth place, the defendant entertains great
suspicion as regards all the assertions, as the plaintiff

several times put him off with lies, which the defendant can
prove, for instance, that in the presence of various people he
has said that the plaintiff was not aware that Dr. Ses in Virginia
had been paid and satisfied on his account.

[133] The defendant is condemned to pay, provided the
plaintiff furnish a perfect affidavit or receipt from the late
Dr. Ses that he paid him by virtue of a power of attorney from
the defendant and that the plaintiff produce satisfactory proof
that he made every effort to demand payment from the heirs of the
late Dr. Ses, according to the power of attorney granted him for
that purpose by the defendant. And the defendant is ordered to
furnish security.

On the 21st of August 1642

Steven Harpele, plaintiff, vs. Cosyn Gerritsz, defendant.
Plaintiff demands payment of the wages earned by him. The
defendant acknowledges the debt and promises to pay fl. 20 within eight days, which the defendant is ordered to carry out. He
is also to pay the costs.

Jan Jacobsz Carpenel, plaintiff, vs. Jan Jacobsz, defendant.
Default.

On the 28th of August

Cornelio vander Hoykens, fiscal, plaintiff, vs. Uldrich
Lupolt, defendant, for breaking the Company's seal with which his
chest at his house was sealed and taking away the money that
was in it.

Lupolt declares that the seal was not broken by him nor by
anyone for him, nor that he has advised anyone to do so. It is
ordered that the defendant and his wife shall confirm under oath
that they have not broken said seals and that it happened without

their knowledge. Which they have confirmed by oath.

[134] On the 28th of August 1642

Cornelio vander Hoykens, fiscal, plaintiff, vs. Jan from Meppelen, defendant, for slander. The defendant is ordered to present proof that the plaintiff slandered him first.

Cornelio vander Hoykens, plaintiff, vs. the gunner of the Sevensterre, defendant, for having beaten his skipper. Defendant is ordered to pay a fine of 5 gl. to the fiscal.

Cornelio van[der] Hoykens, plaintiff, vs. Hans Nicola, defendant. It is ordered that the fiscal shall further investigate the matter.

Having seen the complaint of the fiscal with regard to the great loss which the honorable Company sustains on account of the spoiling of the trade with the savages by the English within our limits and usual places of trading, especially by one George Lamberton residing at the Rodeberch, notwithstanding we have expressly protested against him, we have resolved not to allow this unless he, Lamberton, pay the duties to the Company. The fiscal being hereby authorized to constrain him thereto.

Tomas Smith, plaintiff, vs. Jan Pietersz from Amsterdam, defendant. The plaintiff demands a gun which the defendant is ordered to bring to the courtyard within the Fort and thereupon they are to settle their account.

Willem Cornelisz Coster, plaintiff, vs. the skipper of the Houttyn, for leakage of wine and ruination of cloth. Eslant, Opjyk and the skipper Laurens are appointed referees to inspect the damage.

[135] On the 4th of September 1642

Davit Pietersen, plaintiff, vs. Hendrick Jansen, the tailor,
defendant. Default.

Whereas Hendrick Jansen on the 26th of June last was condemned
to pay and was cited on that account by the plaintiff, but has
not appeared and has suffered default to be taken against him,
we therefore condemn the aforesaid Hendric Jansen, as we do
hereby, to pay the costs and damage which Davit Pietersz has
already suffered and in case the defendant continues to refuse
to pay, the fiscal is authorized to obtain a writ of execution
against him to sell so much of the defendant's property as is
needed to satisfy the amount of the debt and costs. Thus done
and ordered in Fort Amsterdam of New Netherland on the day
above written.

On the 6th of September

Robbert Pinoyer, plaintiff, vs. Tomas Sandersz, defendant,
complaining that he was beaten when he came to get his clothes
and tools. The defendant answers that Pinoyer tried to force
his door. The plaintiff admits that it took place. Pinoyer is
provisionally put under arrest and the fiscal is ordered to
seek information.

Abraham Grevenraet, plaintiff, vs. Dirck Corsz Stam, defendant.
The plaintiff presents a petition and a bond, demanding payment.
The defendant says that he is to pay in Virginia and that the
plaintiff is bound to serve him. The plaintiff replies that he
was never bound to serve the defendant and demands proof.
Parties are ordered to furnish mutual security, one for the payment and the other that he was not bound at Amsterdam, where he
is to settle the same with the owners.

[136] Robbert Cock from Middlesex in old England, aged 18 years. He is asked in court whether he does not know where his master Jan Brint is and when he went away. Answers, that his master on the day he went away ordered him to get buttermilk at Hendric Pietersz', between 9 and 10 o'clock. He then left in the house his master and Rebecca his wife and Eduwart Oyens and heard that Jan Brent wanted to go to Goodman Steyl for money. Having been away about an hour he found no one in the house but Ritchert Brudnil and Jan Smit, furthermore nothing but 3 cheeses, a bushel of flour and cooper's tools. Having asked Brudnil and Smit whether they knew what had become of his master and wife they answered, No. He, the deponent, thereupon asked to be permitted to go with them, which was refused so that his master would not be angry with them. They were prevented by the tide so that they were obliged to stay there. Arriving at Brudnil's he found Eduwart Oyens and his wife and Rebecka, his master's wife. Ritchert Brudnil called Rebeca to the door and staid out about one-quarter of an hour. Coming into the house he asked them aloud what they were doing there. They answered that her husband had sent them there as he was in the woods splitting staves. Brudnil asked, "Where are the goods? Your husband has apparently taken them with him." She answered, No. Whereupon they resolved to report the same to the director.

Rebecca Raetse, aged 18 years, wife of Jan Brent, says that her husband sent her to Brudnil's and that he had gone cutting staves; and that she went with Eduwart Oyens from her house to Brudnil's, where they arrived toward evening without having taken any goods with them, only some linen to cover her head.

The same evening Ritchert told her that her house was empty,
whereupon the next day she went with Brudnil and found the house
empty of everything but a Bible.

[137] Rittchert Brudnil, aged 33 years, from Bedford, says
and declares that sometime ago he, the deponent, in company with
Jan Smit, went shooting and found the house of Jan Brint quite
empty. They then saw a boy coming with milk. They asked him
where his master was and he said he did not know and that he
left his wife and Eduwart Oyens in the house. Coming home about
9 o'clock he found the wife and Eduwart Oyens at his house. He
asked her, "Where is your husband?" She answered, "He has gone
out to cut staves", and that he would be away for 10 days and
that he had ordered her to go to the deponent's house. Rebecca
had brought a little linen with her.

Jan Smit from Oxford, aged 25 years, deposes that he went
out shooting with Ritchert Brundil and came to the house of Jan
Brent, who was at home with his wife, the boy and Eduwart Oyens.
Having gone from there into the woods and remaining there about
one-quarter of an hour they returned and found no one but the boy,
who brought back milk. Having asked the boy, "Where is your
master?" he said, he did not know. From there they went to the
house of Brundil where they found the wife of the cooper.

On the 11th of September anno 1642

Cornelis Melyn, plaintiff, vs. Egbert Woutersz, defendant,
on account of his stepdaughter having become engaged to marry
before her time was up.

Elsjen Jans, aged 17 years, declares that her mother and
another woman on a Sunday morning came to Staten island with
Adriaen Pietersz and desired that she should promise to marry him.

Whereupon she said "I do not know the man". But finally, upon the request, persuasion and desire of her mother she accepted Adriaen Pietersz' troth. She declares, however, that she does not want him and has no desire to marry, the more so as she does not know the young man and is well treated by her master.

[138] On the 11th of September

Whereupon Elsjen Jans in court has returned the pledge of troth, being a handkerchief.

Engel Jans acknowledges in court that she contracted with Melyn at Amsterdam to go with him to New Netherland, upon promise that Melyn would give her so much land on Staten island as she would need for a garden or farm on which to support herself and her children, in return for which Engel Jans promised to serve him, Melyn, according to the best of her ability.

Tomas Hal binds himself as bail for Pieter Barnevelt and takes him into his custody, promising if necessary to deliver him again into our hands and meanwhile to prevent him from committing any mischief or rascality.

Eduwart Oyens from Wales, aged 21 years, declares that Jan Brent, the cooper, went out without letting him, the deponent, know where he went, leaving in his house the deponent, Isaac Abrahamsen and Eduwart, the carpenter, his wife and the boy. When the cooper went out he desired Eduwart Oyens to take his wife to Brundil's house, as he intended to go out working for some time without saying where.

Between 11 and 12 o'clock he left the house with the wife and they came about half past one in the evening at Brundil's. They took with them a box, a bushel of flour, as many cooper's tools as a man could reasonably carry under his arm, and butter and cheese. Owing to contrary current they were held up at Varken Eylant, [1] which is the reason they were so long on the way, where they heard from Brundil and Jan Smit that all the goods were gone. Brudnil asked what had become of the husband. They answered that he was working for a farmer.

It is ordered that Ritchert, that is to say, Eduwart Oyens shall be put under arrest until further information is received regarding the cooper.

[139] On the 11th of September

Rebecca Raetse says that because she and her husband were in debt he had gone to South Hampton on Long island to request assistance from her former master, who was a man of influence, taking with him some provisions and some tools.

Between 11 and 12 o'clock she left her house with Eduwart Oyens in a canoe for Brudnil's, but owing to contrary current they could make no progress and remained on Long island. She said that she put the other goods in the woods, fearing to get into trouble, and that since that time she has [not] seen the goods that were in the woods.

Samuel Chandelaer, aged 33 years, declares that Rebecca said that she knew that her husband would return but that she would not live with him any more.

Margariet Fransum declares that Rebecka said before she was married that she would play her husband a trick and that she would not stay with him and that the marriage which took place here in the church was of no value.

---

[1] Hog Island.

Eduwart Fiscock, plaintiff, vs. Jan Haes, defendant. Default.

On the 18th of September

Dirck Corsen, plaintiff, vs. Jochim Kirsteede, defendant, on account of a foresail which was stolen from the plaintiff in Virginia by the crew of Lieutenant Vrientschup and which was bought here by the defendant. It is ordered that if the plaintiff proves that it is his foresail and that it was stolen from him, the defendant shall return the foresail or the value thereof and have the right to recover the amount from the sellers.

At the request of Dirck Corsen, Davit Pietersen is ordered to take the oath that according to his book 45 gl. remain due him by Lady Harwee or, in default thereof, he shall lose his right; this to be communicated to him before his departure.

Eduwart Fiscock, plaintiff, vs. Jan Haes. Second default.

[140] On the 25th of September 1642

Whereas Captain Davit Pietersz has appeared before us and requested the attachment of a sum of 4 pounds 14 shillings sterling due him from the estate of the late Captain Ritchert Stevens for linen sold to Lady Harwee, at that time the wife of Captain Stevens, all of which was sworn to by the aforesaid Davit Pietersz in court at Fort Amsterdam, the 25th of September anno 1642 in New Netherland;

It is resolved that the money in our hands shall be attached until an answer is received from Lady Herwey.

Dirck Corsen Stam, plaintiff, vs. Jochim Kirstede, defendant, regarding a certain foresail stolen by the crew of Lieutenant Frinschup.

Having seen the complaint of the plaintiff and the depositions
signed by three persons from which it clearly appears that the
foresail bought by Jochim Kirsteede was stolen from Dirck Corsen's
bark, the defendant is therefore condemned to return the said
sail in as good a condition as it was, or else to satisfy the
plaintiff therefor and to recover the amount from the persons who
sold it, either out of their goods or the boat with which it was
stolen, the value being estimated at 25 guilders.

Robbert Bello, plaintiff, vs. Barent Dircksen, defendant,
for damage done by hogs. Parties are referred to such referees
as they shall choose to inspect and estimate the damage.
Abraham, the miller, and Tomas Hal are chosen by parties as
referees.

[141] On the 25th of September 1642

Whereas some dispute has arisen on the South river between
our people and Mr. Lammerton, who came there within our limits
without our permission and against our will, we have approved
the action of our people and to that end granted these presents
to Maryn Adriaensen as we understood that our people are threatened
by those of the Rodeberch. Therefore all those to whom these
presents shall be shown are warned to leave the bearer unmolested
and if they have anything to say regarding the matter aforesaid
to be pleased to refer the same to us, we being at all time
ready to answer their complaints.

On the 2d of October 1642

Whereas Mr. Trochmarten and his Company ask permission to
settle with 35 families under the jurisdiction of their High
Mightinesses the Lords States General and to live in peace, provided they enjoy the same benefits as other inhabitants and have

the free exercise of their religion; therefore, having considered
the request of the aforesaid Mr. Trochmarten and taken into consideration the desire of the honorable Company, inasmuch as this
request does not tend to injure this country, the more so as the
English intend to settle about three miles from us [their said
request is granted.]

On the 9th of October 1642

Cornelis Melyn, plaintiff, vs. Egbert Woutersz, as husband
and guardian of Engel Jans, defendant, for certain damage done
him according to the bill of complaint filed by the plaintiff,
requesting redress for the violence committed in carrying off his
servant girl by night from his land and firing guns and muskets,
which is said to have been done by Adriaen Pietersz.

Adriaen Pietersz admits that he took the maid in the yawl
with her consent from Melyn's land. Parties having been heard
it is ordered that the pretended bride Elsjen shall be delivered
into our hands next Thursday forenoon, and that the fiscal shall
make further inquiry. Meanwhile Adriaen shall remain under arrest
on this island until the case is decided and be furnished with
a copy of the bill of complaint.

[142] On the 9th of October anno 1642

Pieter Cornelisz, plaintiff, vs. Johannes Winckelman, defendant,
for payment of 435 gl. The defendant admits the debt, but says
that he has no money for the present. He offers to pay in duffel
according to market value. The defendant is condemned to pay in
money or goods to the value thereof.

Jacob Roy, plaintiff, vs. Jan Pietersz, defendant, for payment of fl. 54. The defendant admits the debt and is condemned
to pay, also 12 stivers for the summons.

Piere Cecero, plaintiff, vs. N. N., Englishman, tailor, defendant. First default.

Piere Cecero, defendant, vs. Jan Haes, plaintiff, First default.

On the 16th of October 1642

Andries Hudden appeared in council and requested a certificate showing how much pay he might demand of those who employ him as surveyor. He is granted 3 gl. a day and furthermore 2 stivers per morgen and free transportation by ferry and expenses.

Elsjen Jans declares in court that she was forced to speak of Cornelis Melyn and his wife as she did on the 11th of September; also that Melyn's wife said that Adriaen had a wife and 3 children in Holland and that he was engaged here in this country and that the clothes which he wore were borrowed; furthermore, that she had given her brother on a Sunday on Staten island a shilling to be given to Adriaen Pietersz with the request that said Adriaen should come the next monday. He came there in the evening about 8 o'clock and she departed immediately with him for the strand, finding there a small yawl in which was the boy of Jan from Rotterdam and no one else. She is ordered to appear on the next court day and to bring Auken with her.

[143] On the 19th of October anno 1642

Piere Pia, plaintiff, vs. Barent Dircksz, defendant, as surety for Willem Willemsz in the sum of fl. 26:6. Plaintiff proves by Aert, the smith, and Tomas Broen that the defendant became surety for Willem Willemsz in the sum of fl. 26:6. No appearance on the part of the defendant; first default.

Mr. Wilcock, plaintiff, vs. Robbert Pinoyer, defendant. First default.

Whereas persons who are summoned show much neglect in failing to appear for minor reasons, thus allowing default to be taken against them, and whereas this tends to bring the council into disrepute, we have therefore ordained, as we do ordain hereby, that henceforth 6 stivers shall be paid for the first default, 12 stivers for the second default and that on the third and last default judgment shall be given against him. Thus done in council on the date above written.

On the 17th of October

Jannitjen Martens, widow of the late Jan Tomasz Mingal, declares that Jan from Meppelen, skipper of the <u>Sevenster</u>, promised to marry her, before God, and on that condition slept with her and had carnal conversation with her, with promise of van Meppelen that he would never leave her and that the banns would be published here and that on arriving safely at Curaçao he would marry her there.

Jan van Meppelen says that the first evening when he asked to sleep with Jannitjen Mertens she asked, "Do you intend to marry me?" To which he replied, "Do you think I have any other intentions?"; having nothing with him to give to her.

Claes Eversen from Amsterdam, aged 22 years, says that Jan van Meppelen five or six weeks ago came to the house of Jannitjen Mertens, who said, "Jan, people say that you will not marry me." The skipper said, "Do you believe other people rather than me?"; promising that he would marry her at Curaçao and would have the banns published here.

The parties are allowed time to think the matter over until
the next court day, in order then to take the oath.

[144] On Thursday the 23rd of October anno 1642

Cornelis Melyn, plaintiff, vs. Adriaen Pietersz, defendant.
The fiscal, against the same for carrying off Melyn's maid. It
is ordered that Adriaen Pietersz shall bring here in our presence
Elsjen, the plaintiff's maid, and deliver her into the hands of
the said Melyn and receive her back from him, on condition that
he give security for all damage and expenses which the plaintiff
has incurred thereby.

Pieter Pia, plaintiff, vs. Barent Dircksen, baker, defendant,
for security of fl. 26: [6]. Parties and witnesses having been
heard, the defendant is condemned to pay the amount and costs.

On the 30th of October 1642

Having consulted with each other in council regarding the
proposition of the fiscal and the consequences thereof, it is
decided that it is necessary to bind the newly arriving people
to the services of the Company as otherwise this country will
come to ruin and the people remain in a miserable state. We
trust that the honorable directors will approve of this our
resolution inasmuch as the welfare of the country depends upon
it and the honorable Company will suffer no damage except for
the short period that the outstanding earnest money must remain
idle.

Jan Jacobsz Carpenel, plaintiff, vs. Jan Jacobsz, soldier,
defendant, for having borrowed a canoe. The defendant admits
having borrowed the canoe in company with two Swedes. The
defendant is condemned to pay for the canoe and to seek redress
from the Swedes.

Maurits Jansen van Broeckhuysen, plaintiff, vs. Everardus
Bogardus, as guardian of the surviving children of the late
Cornelis van Vorst, defendant, for the recovery of fl. 50 which
the plaintiff furnished to Jan van Vorst in Holland according to
the note. The defendant requests that Maurits declare that he
has no private account with Jan van Vorst. Case put over to the
next court day.

[145] On the 30th of October 1642

Eduwart Oyen, plaintiff, vs. Ritchert Brudnil, defendant,
concerning the account outstanding between the parties. Parties
producing each his account, confirm the same by oath.

Cornelio vander [H]oykens, fiscal, plaintiff, vs. Hendrick
Jansen, tailor, defendant, for slander uttered by him to the
detriment of the honorable director. The fiscal demands that
the defendant be punished according to his deserts and be placed
under arrest, so that he may make further inquiry and then proceed
against him as may seem fit.

It is ordered that the defendant be put in irons and that
the fiscal make further inquiry.

Ritchert Brudnil, plaintiff, vs. Eduwart Oyen, defendant.
Default.

6th of November

Laurens Cornelissen, plaintiff, vs. Paulus Jansen, defendant,
for spading his land which the defendant agreed to do and for
which he received 4 gl. hand money. The defendant answers that
the land is not workable. It is ordered that if the land can be
spaded the defendant shall be held to do the work or, in default
thereof, the plaintiff shall cause to have it done at the expense
of the defendant.

Adriaen vander Donck, plaintiff, vs. Jannitjen Teunes, defendant.
Plaintiff says that the defendant made a contract with Mr.
Renselaer and demands that the defendant fulfil the same, as
his patroon desires that the people intended for his colony shall
go there. The case is adjourned until next spring, as the defendant
is married and in the last stages of pregnancy, provided she
give security for the fulfilment of the contract and the repayment
of the money advanced.

The fiscal, plaintiff, vs. Hendrick Jansen, tailor, defendant,
for slander. The defendant asks a copy of the charge against him.
The request is granted and a copy shall be furnished him by the
secretary so that he may make answer thereto next Thursday.

[146] Appeared in court at Fort Amsterdam, Arent van Curler,
secretary in Renselaerswyck, who at the request of Cornelio van-
[der] Hoykens, fiscal, attests, testifies and declares that he,
the deponent, on the 27th of October, being with others at the
house of Burger Jorissen, heard Hendrick Jansen, the tailor,
make the following statements, namely, that he, the tailor, sold
to the honorable director hogs, which were sows and with which
the honorable director was not well pleased; also, that he had
asked the director for duffel, which was refused him unless he
gave money, in which case he Hendrick would receive the duffel.
Hendrick said, "If I could scrape and bow like Frenchmen and
Englishmen I would have credit all right; in short, they seek to
oppress the Netherlanders and foreigners are helped along,"
snapping his finger against his thumb, saying, "I have had enough
of it." He, the deponent, upon further reflection testifies as
before at the request of the fiscal that Hendrick Jansen, speaking of Director Kieft, said, "I wonder what the rascal means?"

All of which the deponent declares to be true and truthful and
that he knows nothing more of the matter; also, that this is done
by him to give testimony to the honest truth, which every
Christian is bound to do, especially when requested so to do, to
no one's benefit or injury, without any regard of persons,
personal hatred or favor.

The above deposition was confirmed by oath by Arent van
Curler in court, on the 13th of November 1642, at Fort
Amsterdam.

Appeared in court Laurens Cornelisz, aged 31 years, who at
the request of Cornelio van[der] Hoykens, fiscal, attests, testifies
and declares, as he does hereby, that he the deponent, on the
27th of October last, at the house of Burger Jorisz, heard
Hendric Jansen, tailor, say that he had sold hogs to the director
which were sows, with which the director was not well pleased.
He, Hendrick, said further, "I wonder if he thinks that sows
are not hogs?"

The deponent being again asked in court what Hendrick Jansen
said about the honorable director or what names he called him,
the deponent, answering, said that Hendrick in addition to the
aforesaid statements said, "I wonder what the rascal means?"
or words to that effect, but he immediately retracted his words
saying "I do not mean that."

All of which the deponent declares to be true and truthful
and that he knows nothing more than is hereinbefore written and
that this is done by him in order to testify to the truth to no
one's benefit or injury. All of which Laurens Cornelisz has
confirmed on oath on the 13th of November anno 1642, before the
honorable director and council of New Netherland in court at Fort
Amsterdam.

[147] The 6th of November

There appeared in court Philip Gerritsz from Haerlem, tavern
keeper, who declares at the request of the honorable fiscal that
on the 27th of October last he heard Hendric, the tailor, say
many words at the house of Burgert Jorisz, but that in truth he
does not know what there is of the matter, as he did not stand
still but went back and forth. Declares that he knows nothing
else.

There appeared in court in Fort Amsterdam, Jan Damen, aged
35 years, who at the request of Cornelio van[der] Hoykens, fiscal,
attests, testifies and declares, as he does hereby, that on the
27th of October last at the house of Burger Jorisz he heard
Hendrick Jansen, the tailor, who was quite intoxicated, say,
"The director is a rascal and the woman who gave birth to the
director is a whore," for which the deponent berated the aforesaid
Hendrick, saying: "Hendrick, do not say that; she is an honorable
woman, I have been at her house." All of which the deponent
declares to be true and truthful and that he has done this to
testify to the truth as everyone is requested to; also, that
this is done without any personal hatred or favor and to no one's
benefit or injury. Which the deponent has confirmed in court
before the honorable director general and council, to be the
truth, in Fort Amsterdam in New Netherland, the 19th of
November, anno 1642.

[148] On the 12th of November 1642

Whereas criminal charges and suit for slander between Adriaen
vander Donck, officer of Renselaerswyck, and Frans Allersz, cooper,
have been brought before us in which the honor of the parties

is attacked; therefore, the parties having entered into an amicable
and a friendly agreement, acknowledge that they know nothing of
each other but what redounds to their honor and virtue. Consequently the case is dismissed.

Hendrick Jansen from Oldenborch, aged 20 years, soldier,
acknowledges that he bought from the gunner 2 pounds of powder
to be used at <u>Achtert Col</u>, where he was commanded to go, which
powder he sold to Schepmoes; also 8 yards of linen out of the
store of which he sold 4 yards to the wife of Jan Pieteräz for
fl. 3:10.

Hendric Jansen is ordered to perform his guard duty as required
and to remain in the Fort until next session of the court.

On the 14th of November 1642

Whereas Tomas Pop and Rogier Jorissen, both soldiers in the
service of the Chartered West India Company, forgetting their
honor and oath, have presumed to leave their respective companies
without furlough or passports, all of which is directly contrary
to the articles sworn to by them, is unservicable to the country
and tends to lessen the military discipline and respect for the
high authorities; therefore, the aforesaid soldiers are summoned
to appear by the beating of the drum and called upon to justify
themselves in respect to these desertions, on pain, if after
having been three times summoned they do not appear, of being
proceeded against by the honorable fiscal as according to
military law shall be found necessary. This proclaimed by the
beating of the drum.

[149] On the 18th of November anno 1642

Messrs. Jaques Bentyn, Jochim Pietersen, Hendrick van Dyck, ensign, and Gysbert van Dyck, commissary, are requested by the honorable director and council of New Netherland to repair next Thursday, being the 20th of November, to the house of the said Mr. Willem Kieft to hear there, in company with the honorable councilor La Montangne, the complaint of the fiscal against Hendrick Jansen, tailor, for certain slanderous statements made by him, and there to pronounce their opinion as according to law they shall find proper to which they are hereby authorized and empowered and we shall hold their sentence as binding, lawful and irrevocable. Thus done in Fort Amsterdam on the date above written.

On the 19th of November anno 1642

Jan Damen, aged 35 years, declares in court that he knows nothing more of the matter of Hendrick, the tailor, than he has heretofore testified, which testimony is recorded above. Dated as above.

In court at Fort Amsterdam appeared Burger Jorissen, farrier, who at the request of the fiscal declares, testifies and attests, as he does hereby, by true Christian words that it is true and truthful that he, the deponent, heard Hendrick, the tailor, say at his house on the 27th of October last, "He is a rascal", saying immediately afterward, "I do not mean it." He declares that he heard nothing more, except something about "giving birth," but there were other words before and after this which the deponent did not hear. All of which the deponent confirmed by oath before the honorable director and councilor of New Netherland on the 19th of November anno 1642.

[150] On the 21st of November, being Thursday

Hendrick van Dyck, plaintiff, vs. Willem Cornelisz Coster, defendant. The plaintiff demands according to his power of attorney three beavers which the defendant bought from Schepmoes, who obtained from one Tourbay, who had stolen and sold them. The defendant admits having bought the beavers from Schepmoes without knowing that they were stolen. The defendant is condemned to deliver the three beavers next Thursday to the court in the fort, retaining the right to recover the loss from Schepmoes.

Jan Eversen Bout, plaintiff, vs. Wolphert Gerritsz, defendant, for payment of fl. 50. The defendant requests time until the next court day to reply in writing.

Cornelis Volckersz, plaintiff, vs. Samuel Chandelaer, defendant, for fl. 85 spent by the defendant for entertainment at his house. The defendant admits the debt and promises to pay one-half within a month and the other half in two months.

Johannes Winckelman, plaintiff, vs. Cornelis Lambersz Cool, defendant. First default.

Borger Jorisz declares in court at the request of the fiscal that he heard Hendrick, the railor, speak of "giving birth" and "he is a rascal," saying immediately after it, "I do not mean that." He also says that he heard nothing more, but that there were other words spoken before and after which he did not hear. All of which the deponent has confirmed by oath.

Hendrick Jansen is asked in court whether he has anything to say against the hereinafter named persons and why the same should not be allowed to testify to the truth, to wit: Arent van Curler, Laurens Cornelisz, Jan Damen, Borger Jorisz. Answer, No.

[151] On the 21st of November 1642

Cornelio vander Hoykens, fiscal, plaintiff, vs. Hendrick
Jansen, tailor, defendant, for slander. The plaintiff requests
in writing that the case may be expedited. The defendant requests
a copy of the charges against him. The copy is granted in order
to present a written answer thereto on the next court day, on
pain of having the plaintiff proceed with the case.

On the 27th of November 1642

Cornelis vander Hoykens, fiscal, plaintiff, vs. Jan Schepmoes,
defendant, who bought three stolen beavers and two pounds of
powder from a soldier. Plaintiff demands that the defendant be
punished as the thief who stole the beavers deserves. Schepmoes
is ordered to restore to Coster the money and the goods which he
received from Coster. The defendant, refusing to do this, is
placed under arrest until such time as he shall have restored
the money.

Michiel Picet, plaintiff, vs. Piere Pia, defendant, for
slander. Parties are ordered to prove the slander.

Nicolaes Stander, plaintiff, vs. Jaques Bentyn, defendant,
in regard to a certain contract. The defendant says he made no
contract with the plaintiff, but with Goodman Lengh and Messingjour.
Goodman Lengh and Messingjour are ordered to appear on the next
court day and prove the injury done to Bentyn.

Mr. Smit, plaintiff, vs. Andries Hudden, defendant. Default.

[152] On the 27th of November 1642

Cornelio vander Hoykens, fiscal, plaintiff, vs. Hendrick
Jansen, tailor, defendant, for slander. The fiscal exhibits his
written bill of complaint and thereby demands lawful punishment
and justice.

Having seen the criminal proceedings of the fiscal, plaintif,
against Hendrick Jansen, tailor, defendant, together with the
depositions of various creditable witnesses confirmed by oath
whereby it clearly appears that he the defendant on the 27th of
October last at the house of Burger Jorissen called his lawful
superior, the honorable Director Willem Kieft a rascal, and also
spoke in a very scandalous manner saying, "The woman who gave
birth to the director is a whore;" which is a matter of grave
and dangerous consequences which cannot be tolerated or suffered
in countries where it is customary to maintain justice, inasmuch
as the same not only tends to create disrespect for the honorable
director aforesaid but also brings into disrepute their High
Mightinesses the Lords States General, his Highness of Orange
and the honorable directors, in whose name he, the director,
holds the aforesaid office, which aforesaid slander is punishable
according to God's law and the imperial statutes;

Therefore, wishing to provide herein, having first called
upon God, we have after mature consideration of the matter found
the aforesaid Hendrick Jansen guilty of the charges brought against
him by the fiscal, ex officio, in reparation of which we have
condemned, as we do hereby condemn, the defendant to declare
before the door of the aforesaid honorable director in the fort,
with uncovered head, after the ringing of the bell, that these
infamous words were falsely and scandalously spoken by him, and
then there to pray God, justice and his opponent for forgiveness.
In case of refusal he, Hendrick Jansen, is ordered at the first
opportunity to leave the jurisdiction of New Netherland, being
forbidden on pain of corporal punishment to return within six

consecutive years within the aforesaid region. He is furthermore condemned to pay a fine of 300 Carolus [153] guilders and the costs of the trial. Thus done in court and published in Fort Amsterdam in New Netherland, the 27th of November anno 1642.

The above sentence is pronounced by La Montangne, councilor, Jaques Bentyn, Jochim Pietersz, Hendrick van Dyck, ensign, Gysbert van Dyck, commissary, all of whom were requested and authorized thereto by the honorable director and council. Dated as above.

Whereas, you, Hendrick Jansen, tailor, yesterday refused to do what you were ordered to do according to the accompanying sentence, which tends greatly to bring the authorities here into contempt, you are hereby notified that you shall make yourself ready to depart for the fatherland by the ship De Pauwe, which lies here in the roadstead; and in case you do not get ready, you will without the slightest warning be compelled to go on board said ship when it is ready to sail. Thus done in Fort Amsterdam in New Netherland, the 28th of November anno 1642.

[154] On the 4th of December anno 1642

Govert Loockmans, plaintiff, vs. Tyman Jansen, defendant. The plaintiff, having power of attorney from Dirck Corsz, demands payment of fl. 550. The defendant, before answering, requests time until next the session of the court; also a written copy of the complaint.

Cornelio vander Hoykens, fiscal, plaintiff, vs. Michiel Picet and Nicola Boet, defendants, for having beaten the wife of Touchyn. It is ordered that Michil and Nicola Boet shall pay the surgeon and fl. 20 to the woman for her pain.

Nicolaes Boet, plaintiff, vs. Michiel Picet, defendant, regarding land which the plaintiff cleared for the defendant. The case is referred to G[e]orge Rapaelje and Jan Montfoort as referees.

G[e]orge Rapaelje, plaintiff, vs. Michiel Picet, defendant, about the biting of a goat. It is ordered that he shall pay the plaintiff fl. 4 for the damage.

Cornelis Volckersz, plaintiff, vs. Gregoris Pietersz, defendant. First default.

Cornelio vander Hoykens, fiscal, is authorized to execute the sentence pronounced at the last session of the court against Hendrick, the tailor, by the honorable councilors and additional members of the court.

On the 11th of December 1642

In view of the multitude of English persons who daily come to reside among us and the fact that many questions arise in connection with litigation and the consequences thereof, which makes it highly necessary for us to have a person who can write English and has some experience in legal matters to assist us therein and now and then to write letters, we have therefore provisionally engaged for this service the person of G[e]orge Bacxter, at a yearly salary of fl. 250.

[155] On the 14th of December 1642

Laurens Cornelisz, plaintiff, vs. Pauwels Jansen from Vlissingen, defendant. The plaintiff demands fulfilment of the contract made with the defendant. He is ordered to obtain a copy of the previous judgment and to govern himself according.

Nicolaes Looper, plaintiff, vs. G[e]orge Rapalje, defendant, and also vs. Hans Hansz. The plaintiff demands the return of a crosscut saw which Hans Hansen has in his house. It is ordered that Hans Hansen bring the saw here on the next court day.

Eduwart Fiscock, plaintiff, vs. Michiel Picet, defendant. First default.

[157]   In the Name of God, Amen
Anno 1643, the 8th of January

Hans Hansen, plaintiff, vs. Nicholaes Sloper, defendant. Plaintiff demands a crosscut saw from the defendant which he claims belongs to him. The defendant denies the claim and offers the plaintiff the choice to take the oath. The plaintiff cannot prove that it is his saw and refuses to take the oath. The defendant takes the oath that the saw belongs to him. The plaintiff's claim is denied and he is condemned to pay the costs.

Jan Dette, plaintiff, vs. Jan Haes, defendant. Plaintiff demands payment of fl. 5:5, which debt the defendant admits. The defendant is condemned to pay.

Cornelio van[der] Hoykens, fiscal, plaintiff, vs. Jan Sneidger, defendant, for violation of the published ordinance regarding weights and measures, which violation is proved by the fiscal. The defendant is condemned to pay the fine according to the ordinance.

Barent Dircksz, baker, plaintiff, vs. Cornelis Willemsz, defendant. Default.

On the 22d of January

Jan Brint, cooper, plaintiff, vs. Mr. Heyl, defendant, concerning some question which has arisen between them. Default.

Barent Dircksen, baker, plaintiff, vs. Robbert Bello, defendant, for payment of fl. 50 for rent of a plantation. The defendant admits the debt, but says that damage was done by hogs through the plaintiff's negligence. The plaintiff and defendant having been heard, the defendant is condemned to pay fl. 25.

Tomas Tailleyr, plaintiff, vs. Jan Forbus, defendant, for payment of fl. 32. The defendant admits the debt and requests that he be released from his surety bond. The defendant is condemned to pay and it is ordered that the defendant be released from the surety bond. The defendant promises to pay this week in tobacco.

Maryn Adriaensz, plaintiff, vs. Paulus Jansen from Vlissingen, defendant. Default.

Mr. Allerton and Tomas Bacxter are authorized by the honorable director and council to satisfy Jan Heyl and Jan Brint, or to give us their opinion as to what would be just.

[158] On the 27th of January 1643

Abel Rendenhasen, [1] aged 26 years, appeared in court and declared at the request of the fiscal that he made the glove of English duffel in the Bay about three years ago and that he never since used such cloth as he used in the Bay, and he says that he does not know for whom he made the same.

Deposition of Geertjen Nannincx, wife of Claes Meutelaer: [2]

---

[1] Abel Reddenhasen.
[2] This is apparently a mistake in the record and should read: Deposition of Geertjen Nannincx, wife of Abel Reddenhasen, made at the request of Claes Meutelaer.

Says that Roelant Hackwaert said at her house in the Bay,
"There are seven pits of maize about a pistol shot from the
wagon path", which she is ready to confirm by oath.

Roelant Hackwaert declares that he saw the savages cover
maize pits at Marechkawieck; whereupon the said Hackwaert was
placed under arrest.

On the 5th of February 1643

Adam Hooft, plaintiff, vs. Hendrick van Dyck, defendant for
slander. Plaintiff demands and requests that Hendrick van Dyck
prove that he did not sit with Markus, at that time a prisoner,
in the tavern. The defendant answers that he will prove it.
The plaintiff says that the defendant is a thief of the Company's
property. The defendant protests against the slander. The case
is adjourned and parties are ordered each to produce his witnesses.

Markus Jansen, plaintiff, vs. Burgert Jorisz, defendant, for
accusing him of theft for which he, the plaintiff, is placed
under arrest, and demands vindication of his honor. The defendant
answers that he never accused or complained against the plaintiff.
The plaintiff is promised in court that if hereafter it be found
that he is not guilty, he shall be granted a certificate to that
effect when he goes to Holland.

Maryn Adriaensz, plaintiff, vs. Claes van Eslant, defendant,
regarding a certain bond for fl. 40 executed by Jan Eversz and
attached in his possession. Eslant is ordered to have the
attachment vacated or else the attachment shall remain in force.

[159] On the 5th of February 1643

Adam Hooft, plaintiff, vs. Hendrick van Dyck, ensign, defendant,
alleging that the defendant called Markus Jansen from Sebu, being

under civil arrest, to him in the tavern, sat and drank with him.
The defendant expressly denies the charge and offers to prove
the contrary. The defendant, that is to say, the plaintiff, says
in court that the ensign robs the Company and offers to prove it.
The ensign protests against the slander. The case is adjourned
and the parties are ordered each to produce his witnesses.

Borger Jorisz, aged about 31 years, declares in court that
about ten days ago, one or two days more or less, he, the
deponent, came into the tavern and there heard some talk about
the ensign. Among other statements the fiscal said, "The ensign
is a murderer." Whereupon the deponent received a shilling from
Adam Hooft to give testimony to the truth. Which the deponent
has confirmed by oath.

Laurens Cornelisz, aged about 32 years, declares in court
that about fourteen days ago the ensign and Markus Jansen sat
together among other company in the large hall of the tavern,
but that he does not know how closely they sat together, which
he offers to confirm on oath.

Philip Gerritsz, aged 27 years, declares in court that last
Saturday evening, between nine and ten o'clock, in the large
hall of the tavern, there was some talk about Markus Jansen.
The fiscal, who was intoxicated, said, "Pay no attention to the
ensign; he is a Company's thief." Which he offers to confirm
on oath.

Gerrit Cornelisz, aged 24 years, declares in court that some
days ago he saw the ensign sit on a bench in the tavern and that
as far as he knows Markus Jansen sat on the same bench, which
he offers to confirm.

Cornelis Cornelisz, aged 22 years, declares in court that last Saturday evening, it being about 8 o'clock, he heard the fiscal, who was intoxicated, say in the tavern, "The ensign is a thief, who takes the Company's property, "which the deponent confirms by oath.

[160] On the 19th of February, being Thursday anno 1643

Jan Celes, plaintiff, vs. Raeff Cardel, defendant. The plaintiff demands payment for 200 pounds of tobacco loaned to the defendant in the year 1641 and to be paid for at 10 stivers a pound. The defendant admits having borrowed 200 pounds of tobacco from the plaintiff and promised to deliver 200 pounds to the plaintiff in return, without any price being stipulated. The plaintiff says that when he loaned the tobacco it was worth 10 stivers a pound and that he should not suffer loss by loaning it longer without profit. The defendant is condemned to pay the plaintiff fl. 102:10, instead of the 200 pounds of tobacco.

Hans Nelissen, plaintiff, vs. Evert Jansen, defendant. Plaintiff demands restitution of certain cloth which the plaintiff gave to the defendant to make a suit of and which in the absence of the defendant was stolen from his house. Hendrick Kip and Gillis de Voocht are invited by the honorable director general and council to settle the matter between Hans Nelissen and Evert Jansen.

Hendrick van Dyck, plaintiff, vs. Adam Hooft, defendant, for slander. The plaintiff exhibits a written bill of complaint. The defendant answers in writing. Having seen the proceedings of both parties it is ordered that the defendant prove the slander, which he offers to do.

Oloff Stevensz, commissary of cargoes and store goods,
appeared in court and requested that inasmuch as until now he
has had charge of the store goods and cargoes, for which a
compensation in addition to his monthly wages was promised him,
the honorable director and council may be pleased to pay him
for his trouble what they shall think proper.

Having taken into consideration the request of Oloff
Stevensen, his fidelity and industry, and also the fact that he
fills the place of a commissary, he is granted 100 guilders a
year as a compensation for his trouble.

[161] Whereas the good inhabitants here have heretofore been
obliged to dwell on their farms in great fear and to cultivate
their fields in constant dread of the Indians who now and then
have treacherously murdered some of our people without having any
reason therefor, and whereas with kindness we have been unable
to obtain any satisfaction for this bloodshed, therefore it is
necessary to take up arms to defend our just cause, in order
that we may live here in peace, fully trusting that God will
bless our resolution, the more so as the community itself, on
the 22d of February 1643, requested the execution thereof;

Therefore, we hereby authorize and empower Maryn Adriaensz
at his request to go with his company on an expedition against
a party of Indians lying behind Curler's hook or plantation and
to treat them as they shall see fit according to time and circumstances. Done the 25th of February 1643.

Sergeant Rodolff is hereby ordered and authorized to command
this troop of soldiers and to lead them across [the river] to
Pavonia to attack there all the Indians who are located behind

Jan Eversen's plantation, but to spare the women and children as
much as possible and to take them prisoners and to bring them
here. He shall himself examine the situation to see in what
manner he might best attack them, for which purpose Hans Steen,
who is acquainted with the place where the savages are located,
shall go with him, and he shall consult with the aforesaid Hans
Steen and all the cadets. This exploit must take place this
night. Furthermore, may prudence be exercised and God grant you
success. This day the 25th of February 1643.

The 27th of February

Whereas the insolence of the heathen dwelling here about
has within the last two or three years greatly increased, notwithstanding the friendship and kindness which has continually
been bestowed upon them, yes, more than could have been shown
to Christians, even taking them under our wing when they were
persecuted by their enemies; and whereas their wickedness has
steadily increased and after having deliberately killed many
goats, hogs, cattle and horses they have now begun to take
Christian blood and innocently killed one after another seven
men, all under the semblance of friendship, so that no one of
the good inhabitants here in the country is safe in his house,
let alone cultivating his fields; and whereas we have made every
endeavor to have the murderers surrendered to us, [162] all of
which has been like knocking on a deaf man's door, their insolence
having on the contrary increased more and more, it was decided
by general consent last year to send a troop of soldiers and
free men to the savages to seek by this means to obtain
satisfaction for the blood which had been spilt. And although

these missed the savages on account of the darkness of the night,
they have nevertheless awakened fear among the savages, who
requested peace on condition that they would surrender the murderer
of Claes, the wheelwright, which was agreed to. However, this
had no result and on the contrary they continued their iniquities
and in the Colony of Achter Col shot down one Gerrit van Vorst,
who was busy putting a roof on his house, and murdered an Englishman who came to their village, without being in any way willing
to surrender the murderer or to punish the same, yes, acting
sufficiently as if they imagined that we had come here to be
their slaves. Finally, they have come in bands of 50 or 100
half a mile from the fort and across the river at Pavonia, not
without giving rise to suspicion that they intended to start a
general massacre, as they have boasted at times and heretofore
has taken place in Virginia and elsewhere.

Our God, not wishing to tolerate these iniquities any longer,
has moved our community to seek justice and to avenge this
Christian blood. To this end some deputies in the name of all
have presented a petition that they might be permitted to take
revenge, since the Lord had placed sufficiently within our power,
and although we, fearing to involve the country in war, pointed
out to them the danger, especially for the houses which are
situated at a great distance and have few inhabitants and which
must necessarily be abandoned as we have not sufficient soldiers
here to guard all the houses, and cited other weighty reasons,
nevertheless, they remained firm in their desire, saying that if
we would not consent to it the blood would be upon our heads, so
that we were forced to grant their request and to assist them
with our soldiers, who on the one side killed a goodly number

while the freemen on the other side did likewise. A party of
savages having made their escape, attacked our houses on all
sides and burned four of them with the cattle and killed as many
as ten Christians, making further attacks on the remaining
settlers, whom we immediately supported with all our soldiers
and sailors, whereby they were partly checked and much trouble
was prevented. However, not having soldiers enough to guard all
places and seeing the great peril in which the country is put,
we have resolved to engage as many planters [163] as are available
here, the more so as they wish to go north, seeing no prospect
of planting here, and also for the sake of saving the country
and putting the heathen a bit in the mouth, in order that we may
plow our fields in peace and this for one or two months, not
doubting that through God's grace in the meanwhile a peace such
as we desire will be concluded. Our settlers are scattered here
over a distance of 10 miles east and west and 7 miles south and
north. So that it is not possible to clear all this land of
woods without having more people than we have had thus far.

On the 4th of March 1643

Whereas we are at present suffering much annoyance from the
heathen and the life and property of many of the inhabitants is
not safe, which without doubt has come upon us through our manifold
sins, the council here has thought fit to ordain that next Wednesday, being the 4th of March, a general fast and day of prayer
shall be held, for which everyone may prepare himself in order
that by due repentence and constant prayer we may move God to
mercy and not suffer that His holy name, by reason of our sins,
may be profaned by these heathen.

Whereas heretofore some quarrels and misunderstandings have arisen between the savages of Long Island and our nation, as a result of which blood has been shed on both sides, houses have been robbed and burned down, cattle have been killed and savages robbed of their maize, therefore, a peace has been concluded between us and them, who now are under the control of the great chief Pennawitz, and all injuries are forgotten and forgiven. Therefore, all our good inhabitants are hereby ordered and enjoined, as we hereby do order and enjoin them in every way to observe the said peace and not to molest in any way any of the savages who live on Long Island, unless they should commit any hostility against our people, in which case everyone shall be at liberty to defend himself, to which end the savages are also forbidden to come with any weapons near our people. All this on pain of arbitrary correction and punishment as disturbers of the public peace. Thus done and published in Fort Amsterdam, the 25th of March anno 1643, new style.

[164] Whereas Maryn Adriaensen, a resident of this place and formerly one of the freebooters and sailors of Compaan, [1] has at different times behaved very insolently here, as in endeavoring to force his way on board ahead of the Company's sloops when ships arrive and in accosting the director three times with an unbearable arrogance and abusing his good will and affection for the community, it has at last come to pass that the said Maryn in the afternoon of the 21st of March 1643,

---

[1] Claes Gerritsen Compaen, a notorious freebooter.

under the pretext that some member of the community had called
him "murderer" and had reproached him for being the cause of the
damages now committed by the Indians in the country, because he
with some others had signed the petition praying that they might
be permitted once to avenge the Christian blood which was so
treacherously shed by the Indians and of which it was said that
the director now disavowed the responsibility and shifted all on
the signers of the petition, which, however, was not true, left
his house in a rage, armed with a sword and a loaded and cocked
pistol, and came to the house of the director and went to his
bedroom. Pointing his pistol at the director to shoot him, he
said: "What devilish lies are you telling of me?" Monsr. La
Montagne, being at the time with the director, caught the pan
with such quickness that the cock snapped on his finger, preventing thus through God's mercy this atrocious design. Meanwhile,
the fiscal and several others having come into the chamber, they
disarmed Maryn, and Jan Harmensen from Lemmet, each armed with
a musket and a pistol, came to the fort, where the director was
walking up and down. He was informed of their coming and retreated
to his house, which he had barely entered when Jacob Slangh fired
at him, so that two bullets passed through the gate into the wall.
The sentry before the door immediately fired at Jacob Slangh and
killed him, God having in his mercy saved the director a second
time within an hour and a half and preserved the community from
a cruel massacre. Shortly after this fearful event about 25
persons, residents of Manhattan, among them some of said Maryn's
accomplices, appeared at the door of the director; advised to
delegate a few of their number to present their petition, they

sent four men to the director to ask [165] pardon for the criminal,
to which the answer was given that the director would be satisfied
to leave the matter in the hands of the community, who should
decide according to their conscience; they might choose some men
for this purpose (as may be seen by their petition, marked No. -).
But instead of communicating with the community, numbering more
than 500 men, they showed it only to the aforesaid 25 or 30 men,
who immediately demanded the freedom of the prisoner. This having
been refused for good reasons, they elected eight men, of whom
one had been convicted of a crime, who without having been presented
to the council for confirmation promptly pronounced sentence that
the criminal should pay fl. 500 and be set free on condition of
remaining away from Manhattan for three months. When they submitted this sentence to us, we represented to them that it was
impossible that they had judged with a clear conscience according
to our answer, as they had acted without having heard the complaint of the assaulted party, the motion of the fiscal, the confession of the criminal, the depositions of the witnesses and
other evidence necessary in such proceedings; that this case
was of too great importance to be figured out on the fingers
(as the saying is). We admonished them to consider the matter
more deliberately and we would furnish them with all the evidence.
Instead, however, of correcting their hasty action, they contented
themselves with arguing some points in the director's complaint
which were explicit enough to be understood, traversing the motion
of the fiscal, written by himself, and making other irrelevant
remarks, as may be seen under No. -, in such a way that we were
compelled for the sake of maintaining the respect due to justice,

as being the foundation of a republic, to take the case in our own hands and to reinforce the council, numbering only two members in criminal cases. But we could find nobody willing to assist us and in order to avoid the charge of being moved by passion, having through God's mercy sufficient papers to Holland, to await there his trial, I mean sentence, as the courts may decide. Done in council at Fort Amsterdam, the 28th of March A°. 1643.

[166]   The 22d of April 1643

Between Willem Kieft, director-general and the council of New-Netherland of the one side and Oratamin, Sachem of the savages living at Achkinkes hacky, [1] who declared himself commissioned by the savages of Tappaen, Rechgawawanc, Kichtawanc [2] and Sintsinck, of the other side a firm peace was concluded today in the following terms:

All injuries done by the aforesaid tribes to the Dutch or by the Dutch to them shall henceforth and forever be forgotten and forgiven.

They promise mutually not to molest each other any more in the future, but if the Indians learn that any tribe not mentioned herein had evil intentions against the Christians, they will faithfully forewarn them and not admit such within their limits.

For the confirmation and ratification of this treaty presents were mutually given.

We pray God, that this peace may be kept unbroken by the savages.

---

[1] Hackensack, N. J.
[2] Sleepy Hollow.

On the 30th of April 1643

Cornelis Lambertsen Cool, plaintiff, vs. Jan Damen, defendant,
demands restitution of the land which the plaintiff alleges
belongs to him and which at present is cultivated by the defendant.
The defendant expressly denies this. It is ordered that the
plaintiff prove his claim.

Michiel Picet, plaintiff, vs. Piere Pia, defendant. Plaintiff
demands payment of fl. 20. The defendant admits the debt and says
that he has a counter-claim against the plaintiff. Andries Hudden
and Elslandt are ordered to examine the account and to settle
the matter.

Nicola Boet, plaintiff, vs. Michiel Picet, defendant, demanding payment according to the decision of referees. First default.

Abraham Rycken, plaintiff, vs. Michiel Pouwelsz, defendant.
First default.

Cornelio van[der] Hoykens, fiscal, plaintiff, vs. Dirck
Cornelisz, defendant, for having taken away the sentinel's hat
and nailed it to a post. The defendant is granted eight days
to make proof to the contrary.

[167] On Thursday, the 6th of May 1643

Abraham Rycken, plaintiff, vs. Michiel Pauwelsz, defendant.
Plaintiff demands the first payment for the land sold to him, the
defendant, by Borsjen and which was due last Easter. The defendant
is ordered to make two payments next Easter, unless he give
sufficient security for the payment of 200 guilders next Easter
1644 and the balance two years from now.

Hendrick Jansen, plaintiff, vs. Willem Adriaensz, cooper,
defendant, for delivery of the said plaintiff's house which the

defendant bought, as appears by the contract of sale. The case
is put in the hands of Andries Hudden and Govert Loockmans as
referees to make the parties come to an agreement.

Cornelio van[der] Hoykens, fiscal, plaintiff, **vs.** Dirck
Cornelisz from Wensveen, defendant, for insolent conduct toward
the sentinels before the house of the director. The defendant
calls upon the gunner, Schram, and Hendrick Pietersz Kint as
witnesses. It is ordered to have the depositions of the witnesses
put in writing by the secretary.

Hendrick Jansen, plaintiff, vs. Burger Jorisz, defendant.
First default.

On the 21st of May

Cornelio van[der] Hoykens, fiscal general of New Netherland,
plaintiff, vs. Adriaen van[der] Donck, officer of Renselaerswyck,
defendant, for violation of the charter of this country. Having
seen the citation of the said van Donck made at the request of
the said fiscal of New Netherland, personally to appear before
us within six weeks after the receipt of the said citation and
that the defendant after having been summoned three times has
not appeared, we have therefore entered default against him and
ordered that the said van Donck shall be cited again to appear
personally before us within four weeks after the date hereof to
defend his cause.

[168] On Thursday, being the 11th of June 1643

Ritchert Elias, plaintiff, vs. Waterduyve, defendant.
Ordered that the defendant shall pay fl. 5 and that the plaintiff shall return the skins.

Hendrick Li, plaintiff, vs. Gregoris Pietersz, defendant. The plaintiff demands payment of fl. 5 which the defendant promised to pay to Jan Smit. The defendant admits the debt and is condemned to pay.

Hendrick Lie, plaintiff, vs. Jan Forbus, defendant, for payment of fl. 38 The defendant says that the money in his hands was attached at the request of Dirck Volkersz and if Dirck is willing to vacate the attachment, he is willing to pay.

Jems Jaspaer declares under oath that the half of the aforesaid money is due him, whereupon Forbus is condemned to pay fl. 19 to him. The rest will be left until eight days from now, unless Dirck proves that the attachment was sued out at the proper time.

Abraham Rycken, plaintiff, vs. Marten, the mason, defendant. First default.

The fiscal, plaintiff, vs. Oule Pouwelsen, defendant, for insolent conduct at the house of his master. The fiscal is ordered provisionally to keep him in confinement at the expense of Dirck Volckersz, his master, and meanwhile to examine the witnesses.

G[e]orge Rapalge requests in court that the land which is used by Tymen Jansen may be restored to him. Rapalge is ordered to show the bounds of his land, whereupon justice will be done.

[169] The director and council of New Netherland having out of extreme consideration granted Hendrick Jansen, tailor, permission to remain until the first opportunity of ships, in order the better to settle his affairs in this country, notwithstanding he was ordered to depart on the yacht De Pauw, therefore we, the

director and council aforesaid, order you, Hendrick Jansen, as
we do hereby, to depart without any delay for the fatherland by
the yacht Prins Maurits which is ready to sail, as otherwise you
will be compelled to go aboard by the officers of the law. And
this sent to you in order that you may not plead ignorance. Thus
done in Fort Amsterdam in New Netherland, the 17th of June 1643.

On the 18th of June

Whereas large quantities of strong liquors are daily sold
to the Indians, from which practice serious difficulties have
already arisen in this country and it is to be feared further
calamities may result; therefore, in order to prevent the same
as much as possible, we, the director general and council of New
Netherland, do hereby forbid all tapsters and other inhabitants
henceforth to sell, either directly or indirectly, whether
personally or through others, any liquors to Indians. If any
one shall be found to have acted contrary hereto, he shall for
the first offense forfeit fl. 25; for the second offense double
the amount; and for the third time be arbitrarily punished.
Thus done and published in Fort Amsterdam, the day and year
above written.

On this day, the 18th of June 1643, was renewed and published
the ordinance against those who run away from their lords and
masters, heretofore published and posted on the gates of Fort
Amsterdam on the 13th of April of the year 1642.

[170] On Thursday, being the 18th of June 1643

Abraham Rycken, plaintiff, vs. Michiel Pauwelsz, defendant.
Plaintiff demands payment according to the contract of sale of
his plantation. As the defendant has failed to appear the
plaintiff is authorized to again take possession of his property

as it now is, unless the defendant or anyone on his part pay the purchase price and costs.

Antony Jansen, plaintiff, vs. Barent Dircksen, baker, defendant. The defendant is ordered to bring proof in regard to an entry of fl. 10 which he claims to have loaned to the plaintiff or otherwise let the matter be decided by oath. Upon refusing to take the oath and failure to produce proof Barent is condemned to pay within eight days for the plow share and the parties to govern themselves according to the contract.

Hendrick Lie, plaintiff, vs. Dirck Volckensen, defendant. The plaintiff's demand is denied as the attachment was sued out at the proper time.

Jeuriaen Hendricksz, plaintiff, vs. Antony Jansen, defendant, for payment of fl. 15 due for wages. Antony Jansen says that the plaintiff has not earned as much, but that Jeuriaen must still make one door and two windows for him. It is ordered that if Jeuriaen Hendricksz can prove that the [extra] work which he has done is worth more than the work of the door and windows would amount to, then the defendant shall be held to satisfy the plaintiff's claim.

[171] On the 25th of June, being Thursday, 1643

Isaack Allerton, plaintiff, vs. Hendrick Jansen, tailor, defendant. Demands payment of about fl. 500, not knowing the exact amount by heart, as they have not adjusted their accounts exactly. The wife of the defendant admits the debt and promises to pay promptly within two months. She is condemned to pay within two months, the length of time allowed her.

Isaac Allerton, plaintiff, vs. Piere Pia, defendant, for payment of some 55 or 56 gl. The defendant says that he does not owe so much and has not gome over his accounts, with the plaintiff. Parties are ordered to settle their accounts.

Markus Jansen, plaintiff, vs. Philip Gerritsz, defendant. Borger Jorisz is condemned to pay 10 days' board for Markus.

Jacob Reynsen, plaintiff, vs. Wessil Eversz, defendant.

Whereas Master Moor of Virginia through our efforts got hold of two Englishmen who seized and made off with a bark on the South river, Nicolaes Sloper and Matheuw Nicola, came on board said Moor's bark where the aforesaid Englishmen were kept prisoners and by using force set said prisoners free under pretext that they wished to deliver a letter in Virginia, whereupon said Sloper and Matheu Nicola have been placed under arrest, as it clearly appears by the depositions that they are guilty, which is confirmed by oath.

G[e]orge Bacxter has become bail for the prisoners, who have promised to deliver again to Mr. Moor the Englishmen whom they released.

Nicola Boet, plaintiff, vs. Michil Picet, defendant. Default. The plaintiff is authorized to have the defendant summoned for tomorrow morning and if he does not appear then, his property shall be attached and sold.

[172] On the 2d of July anno 1643

Burger Jorissen, plaintiff, vs. Jaques Bentyn, defendant, for payment of fl. 48. The defendant admits being indebted, but says that he does not know that the sum is so large. The case is adjourned until Burger's arrival when their account shall be adjusted.

Jaques Bentyn, plaintiff, vs. Willem Adriaensz, cooper, defendant. Parties are ordered first to adjust their accounts, in order to know exactly what is due to the plaintiff.

Eduwart Griffis, plaintiff, vs. Jan Celes, defendant, for fl. 187 and a pair of shoes earned by the plaintiff in working [for the defendant]. The defendant promises to pay within two months. The defendant is condemned to pay within six or eight weeks.

Barent Jansen, plaintiff, vs. Cornelis Melyn, defendant. The defendant says that his contract made with the plaintiff at Amsterdam was not fulfilled and that another contract was made. The plaintiff says that the contract was fulfilled. The defendant offers to confirm by oath that as far as the land was concerned the contract was not fulfilled; which the defendant confirms by oath. The defendant having taken the oath that he did not release the plaintiff from his contract as far as the land was concerned, the plaintiff is condemned to continue to reside on Staten island according to the aforesaid contract.

On the 9th of July

Cornelio van[der] Hoykens, fiscal, ex officio plaintiff, vs. Adriaen van[der] Donc, officer of Rensselaerswyck, defendant. The officer, Verdonc, having been legally summoned at the request of the fiscal and the defendant having twice failed to appear, the second default was entered against him after his name had three times been called by the court messenger, the aforesaid messenger being authorized to summon the said Verdonc for the third and last time to appear four weeks from date in Fort Amsterdam to hear the complaint of the fiscal general of New Netherland.

[173] On Thursday, the 9th of July 1643

Abraham Jacobsz from Steenwyck, plaintiff, vs. Anna Gerrits, defendant. Demands payment of what remains due to his wife from her father's estate, as entered on the books of the orphan chamber.

Andries Hudde and Hendrick Kip are requested to hear the demand and answer of the parties and if possible to get them to agree; if not, to give their opinion in writing.

Isaack de Foreest, plaintiff, vs. Pieter van [der] Linden, defendant. Plaintiff says that one cask of tobacco is found missing.

Andries, the chief boatswain, being examined in court, answers that Adam Hooft told him in the Oude Kerck [1] that he had still eight casks of tobacco standing there and that he, Hooft, took nine casks out of it. The chief boatswain says that he warned said Hooft not to take more than his own tobacco, whereupon Hooft answered, "The numbered casks are mine." All of which he has confirmed by oath before the director and council.

Case dismissed and Isaack de Foreest ordered to bring his action against Adam Hooft.

Briant Killy, plaintiff, vs. Willem Lachem. First default,

On the 6th of August

Fredrick Jansen from Flensborch, plaintiff, vs. Philip Gerritsz, defendant. Plaintiff demands payment for a dog, which was shot dead by mistake. The defendant admits that it happened by mistake. Ordered that the defendant pay the plaintiff fl. 5.

[174] [On the 20th of] August 1643

Jacob Roy, plaintiff, vs. Jan Pietersz from Amsterdam, defendant. Plaintiff demands payment of fl. 5. Defendant admits the debt, whereupon he is condemned to pay.

---

[1] Meaning the Old Church at Amsterdam.

Jan Hadduwe, plaintiff, vs. Tomas Sael, defendant, for payment of fl. 20. Defendant admits the debt, but [states] that he has a counter claim. Defendant is condemned to pay, but allowed to deduct what is due him on condition that he produce proper proof thereof.

On the 27th of August

Tonis Cray, plaintiff, vs. Piter van [der] Linden, defendant, for damage done by hogs on Cray's plantation. Plaintiff demands payment of damages.

Barent Dircksen, baker, and Tomas Hal are requested by the honorable director and council to view the fence of Tonis Cray's plantation and if they can not satisfy the parties to report their opinion to us.

Gillis de Voocht and Jan Eversz, plaintiffs, vs. Teunes Tomasz, mason, on account of the purchase of a house. Ordered that the purchase shall stand, provided that the plaintiffs furnish payment between this day and next Saturday before sundown, wherewith Teunes is satisfied.

Jan Pitersen from Amsterdam, plaintiff, vs. Barent Dircksz, baker, on account of an attachment. It is adjudged that the attachment was wrongfully issued.

Aert Willemsen promises to pay within two months from this date to Wolphert Gerritsz for Frans Allersz of Amsterdam the sum of fifty-eight guilders, for which he gives security in court.

[175] On the 3d of September 1643

Gillis de Voocht, plaintiff, vs. Teunes Tomassen, mason, defendant. Plaintiff demands delivery of the house which he bought from the defendant. The plaintiff offers beavers, being

the most current article, for which one can get money or other
goods.

The honorable director and council having seen the testimony
on both sides and also heard the parties in person, decide that
the [contract of] purchase concluded between the parties shall
have **its** full effect and that Gillis de Voocht shall pay the
defendant within the time of twenty-four hours in money or
beavers at such price as the merchants here receive the same
instead of money.

Tonis Cray, plaintiff, vs. Piter van [der] Linden. Default.

On the 8th of September

Jan Schepmoes, guardian of the surviving child of Marritjen
Piters, plaintiff, vs. Claes Calff, defendant. The defendant
requests time to confer with the co-heirs of Brant Pelen. The
case adjourned until the defendant shall have visited the colony
of Van Renselaer and consulted the co-heirs and he is granted
time until the arrival of the first sloop.

Jacob Roy, plaintiff, vs. Claes Calff, defendant, for payment of fl. 48:2 according to a bond signed by Brant Pelen under
date of July 8, 1643. Ordered that the heirs of the said Brant
Pelen shall be obliged to pay the amount out of the estate.

On the 10th of September, being Thursday

Whereas the ships Sevenstar and Neptunes have arrived from
Curaçoa in New Netherland, which ships were sent purposely to
provide the said island of Curaçoa and its ships with provisions,
and whereas since last spring we had counted on the arrival of
some ships and, owing to the long delay of the same, much of our
supplies were consumed, especially pork and fish, which would

otherwise have spoiled; therefore, we have thought fit immediately to dispatch the yacht _Real_ to New England, there to purchase dried fish, for which we shall use beavers from the warehouse, having no other effects with which we might purchase anything; of pork, beef and peas we shall with God's blessing obtain enough here in New Netherland.

[176] On the 15th of September 1643

Jochim Pitersz, Barent Dircksen, Abraham Planck, that is to say, Abraham Pitersz, Isaack Allerton, Tomis Hal, Gerrit Wolphersz and Cornelis Melyn, being chosen by the commonalty, appeared before the council and requested that Jan Damen, who was also chosen with them by the inhabitants, may be excluded from their meeting because Jan Damen had signed a certain petition in the name of the commonalty. Jan Damen protests against the aforesaid persons.

In council, each of the aforesaid said seven persons having also cast his vote, it is resolved to commence war against the Indians, either by force or by strategy; that is to say, against the Indians who are our enemies, and leave those on Long Island undisturbed so long as they do not show any hostility. And it is further thought advisable, if any of the Long Island Indians can be prevailed upon to secure the heads of the murderers, to take steps to that effect.

Permission is granted by the select men to have the freemen enroll as many soldiers as can conveniently be done. Every Saturday afternoon these men shall appear here to discuss what is to be done and if five of them are present, whatever shall be decided by them shall be held valid.

29th of September 1643

Whereas Jochim Gerritsz Blenck, skipper of the ship Fortuyn, having taken on a cargo of wine at the Canary islands, claims to have sailed from there to the West Indian islands and thence to New England and from there to have come hither and anchored at Fort Amsterdam without passport or permission from the honorable directors of the West India Company, being come, as he said, for want of water and victuals, for which reason he presented a petition to the director and council of New Netherland praying for permission to sell 3 or 4 pipes of wine to pay his pilot and to buy necessaries, on condition that he would pay duty to the Company, [177] he was allowed to do so without prejudice to any claim that the honorable directors might set up against him in the fatherland.

Nevertheless, the said Jochim Gerritsz refused to pay the duty, but set sail and anchored far beyond the ordinary roadstead, between the fort and Staten Island, where he is said to have discharged a quantity of wine into the bark of Mr. Isaack Allerton, an Englishman, for which reason the honorable fiscal, assisted by the secretary of this province, went on board Jochim Gerritsz ship and there formally protested against him and issued an attachment against him and his ship and ordered him to return to the ordinary roadstead, declaring that they would proceed against him according to law in case he refused and failed to appear. But instead of appearing, he set sail by night without obeying the court, which, being a matter of grave consequences which ought not to be tolerated in places where justice is administered, therefore, wishing to provide therein and taking

into consideration the demand and conclusion of the fiscal, after
having examined the papers in the sloop and other documents and
weighed the consequences thereof, we have declared the above
mentioned Jochim Gerritsen Blenck in contempt for refusing to
obey the orders of the court and for usurping the rights of the
Company, wherefor we condemn him, as we hereby do, to pay a fine
of 300 guilders, one-third for the benefit of the Company, one-
third for the fiscal, and one-third for the poor, and moreover
we have confiscated the above mentioned ship and her cargo for
the benefit of the honorable directors and condemn the defendant
to pay the costs of the proceedings.

Oath taken by the English officers and soldiers

We promise and swear allegiance to the High and Mighty Lords
the States General, the Prince of Orange, the Chartered West
India Company and the honorable director general and council of
New Netherland, to risk life and limb for them and in the
country's service and furthermore to obey the honorable director
as faithful officers and soldiers are bound to obey their commander.
So truly help us God Almighty.

[178] Whereas Adriaen vander Donck, officer of Renselaerswyck,
on the 6th of November 1642, seized on the bark of the patroon
of said colony, coming from Fort Amsterdam, some goods belonging
to Jan Laurensz, the duty on which was paid in Holland, which
goods the said Jan Laurensz, had put on board the said yacht to
be discharged at Fort Orange and to be delivered to his partner
trading there, and whereas Officer Verdonck sold said goods on
his own authority, without the consent of the court there, as
appears by the certificate on the 5th of March 1643, for which
reason Verdonck was summoned by the fiscal general of New Netherland

to appear in person before the director and council of New Netherland to answer for this violation and infringement of the law and
liberty of New Netherland, after which summons by reason of his
failure to appear default was entered against him and for greater
precaution he was formally summoned for the second and third times.

Therefore, we, the director and council, having heard the
complaint and demand of the fiscal and considered the consequences
of the case, have declared the aforesaid Verdonck contumacious
and in contempt of court and hence condemn him to restore the
goods seized by him or the value thereof according to the
pliantiff's invoice, with the damage thereto, estimated at fifty,
say sixty guilders, and in addition a fine of 100 guilders and
the costs of the suit; hereby enjoining and prohibiting him from
doing such things again on pain of being discharged from his
office and of being arbitrarily punished. Thus done in council
in Fort Amsterdam in New Netherland, the 8th of October 1643.

[179] On the 14th of October 1643

Albert Cornelisz, plaintiff, vs. Hendrick Jansen, tailor.
Plaintiff says he sold an account to the defendant on which he
claims he lost fl. 22 and demands payment or restitution of the
account. Defendant acknowledges that he bought the account, on
condition that the plaintiff was to remain surety for its payment
by the lord of Horst. [1] The defendant is condemned to turn over
to the plaintiff the money or the account, unless he prove within
eight days that the lord of Horst was not bound to pay said account.

---

[1] Heer vander Horst; meaning Godard van Reede, lord of
Nederhorst.

On the 17th of October

Resolved in council in the presence of Captain Johan Onderhil, Ensign de Leu, [2] Cornelis Melyn, Tomas Hal and Isaack Allerton to make a hostile attack upon the chief of the Wiquaeskecks, and his band.

On the 24th of October

Piter Colet, plaintiff, vs. Tonis Nyssen, defendant. First default.

On the 12th of November, being Thursday

Sybolt Claessen, plaintiff, vs. Hendrick Pitersen, defendant, about an attachment. Plaintiff demands payment of wages earned in working for the defendant. Defendant answers that the plaintiff has not earned as much as he claims. Gillis Pitersz and Dirck Cornelisz, carpenters, are ordered to examine the work and to judge what plaintiff should receive for work done for Hendric Pitersz. Meanwhile, the attachment shall remain in force until the matter is settled.

Tonis Nyssen, plaintiff, vs. Piter Colet, defendant. Plaintiff says that the defendant's boy has injured a young cow. Ordered that when the boy shall have lived two months with the defendant he shall pay to the plaintiff fl. 15 for the damage and if the boy should happen to die in the meantime the sum to be paid shall be in proportion to the time.

---

[2] Ensign Gysbert de Leeuw.

[180] Ordinance framed by the honorable director and council according to which all the Company's servants and freemen shall have to regulate themselves while on duty in the Burger guard [1]

1. If any one on duty in the Burger Guard take the name of God in vain, he shall forfeit for the first offense 10 stivers, for the second offense 20 stivers, and for the third time 30 stivers.

2. Whoever on the Burger guard speaks ill of a comrade shall forfeit 30 stivers.

3. Whoever comes fuddled or intoxicated on guard shall for each offense forfeit 20 stivers. Whoever is absent from his watch, without lawful reason, shall forfeit 50 stivers.

4. After the watch is duly performed and daylight is come and the reveille beaten, whoever discharges his gun or musket without orders of his corporal, shall forfeit one guilder. The 16th of November 1643.

On the 19th of November

Manuel of Gerrit de Reus and big Manuel declare in court at the request of the fiscal that Jan Selis cut the cow of little Manuel with a chopping knife, producing a large wound, and that old Jan drove many cows and horses into the swamp; which they have confirmed by oath in court.

On the 26th of November

The fiscal, plaintiff, vs. old Jan Selis, for having chased and wounded cattle, especially little Manuel's cow. Jan Selis is condemned to pay the owner for the damage which was done to

---

[1] Revised from Laws and Ordinances of New Netherland, p. 35.

the animal and is forbidden on pain of banishment to injure any persons or cattle and is condemned to pay a fine of fl. 25 to the fiscal and costs.

The fiscal, plaintiff, vs. Borger Jorisen, for payment of duty. Ordered that Borger Jorisz within 14 days shall pay the duty to the fiscal on all that he has conveyed from and to the North since he began to trade; and he is forbidden to depart or come ashore without first entering everything correctly with the fiscal, on pain of confiscation of the sloop and goods.

[181] On the 26th of November

Joris Dircksen, plaintiff, vs. Claes Lambertsen Cool, defendant, for service rendered to the defendant by the plaintiff. Plaintiff demands payment. Case adjourned until the defendant shall have come home.

On the 28th of November

Briant Killi and Jan Masten become bail for Robbert Eden's appearance in the fort next Monday when the English troop shall be assembled there, to confess the crime committed against his lieutenant, and there to ask forgiveness of God, the court and his officer.

We, Willem Kieft, director general and council of New Netherland, certify and declare at the request of Hendrick van Dyck, ensign, that on the 5th of October last he went the rounds before midnight with some musketeers in the public service and was then shot through his right arm with a bullet which grazed his right breast. This we declare to be in fact true, to which end this is signed by us on the 5th of December anno 1643, at Fort Amsterdam of New Netherland.

The 15th of December

Jan Percel, plaintiff, vs. Piere Pia, charging him with theft. Ordered to produce proof of the charge at the next session of the court.

The 21st of December 1643

Piere, the Italian, and partner, plaintiffs, vs. Tonis Nyssen, for payment of fl. 180 earned in drawing hay. Case adjourned until the witnesses of both sides shall have returned from the expedition.

Jan Percel, plaintiff, vs. Piere Pia, defendant. Piere Pia and his wife declare that Jan Percel came drunk into their house with another Englishman and there went to sleep and that they had not seen any of his money.

[182] In the year of our Lord and Savior, 1644, on the 14th of January, being Thursday

Dirck Cornelissen, plaintiff, vs. Piter Cornelissen, defendant. Plaintiff demands payment of fl. 32:10. Defendant admits the debt and requests delay of one month. The defendant is ordered to pay in one month.

Piere Pia, plaintiff, vs. Pircel, defendant, on account of accusation of theft to the detriment of the plaintiff. Ordered, if the defendant cannot prove within 8 days that he brought his money to Piere Pia's house, that Piere Pia and his wife shall be heard and take the oath that they are innocent. And then the defendant shall make reparation for the injury to character.

Jochim Kiersteede, plaintiff, vs. Sybolt Claesz, defendant, for payment of fl. 72 for a share in a small yacht. Ordered that the defendant prove that the plaintiff did not deliver the yacht complete with its appurtenances and that he have his man,

Barent Dircksz, to whom he appeals, appear on the next court
day; or, in default thereof, that Sybolt Clasz shall pay.

The 28th of January, Thursday

Andries Tomassen, plaintiff, vs. Jeuriaen Otsen, heir of
Hans Nelisen, defendant, for some goods belonging to him, which
Hans Nelisen is alleged to have lost, to which the plaintiff
makes oath. Ordered that fl. 25 be paid out of Hans Nelisen's
estate.

Piere Cecer, the Italian, plaintiff, vs. the widow of Jan
Manje, regarding his legacy from Manje, deceased. The widow
says that she delivered to the plaintiff the legacy which was
promised to him, to wit: one bed, two pillows, one green blanket,
a folding chair, a purple coat lined with crimson baize, fl. 15
worth of boratto, and a flatiron, the receipt of all of which
Piere Secer acknowledges; wherewith the case is dismissed.

[183] The 28th of January

Cornelis Volckertsen, plaintiff, vs. Barent Dircksen, baker,
defendant, for fl. 3:3, for which the defendant has become surety.
Defendant acknowledges the debt and is condemned to pay.

Luyck Cock, plaintiff, vs. Tymon Jansen, defendant.
Defendant appears and plaintiff is in default.

The 1st of February

The fiscal, plaintiff, vs. Jan Haes, defendant, for theft.
Jan Haes admits in court that he shot a hog and stole a gun
from Davit Pietersen; also, that after Laurens the Noorman had
been wounded by the Indians he took off his shoes and sold them
for 3 guilders.

Jan is pardoned in consideration of the fact that he served the country as a soldier on that occasion, on condition that he give security for the damage done by him and that which he might do in the future and that if he commits similar crimes again he shall be hanged without mercy.

The 4th of February

Jochim Kersteede, plaintiff, vs. Sybolt Clasen, defendant. Plaintiff demands payment for his share in the bark sold to the defendant in company with Lambert Huybersz and Dirck Dircksz for fl. 75. Defendant is ordered to pay fl. 75 and to seek his remedy against the farmers' baker (boere backer).

Piere Pia, plaintiff, vs. Jan Percel, defendant. Plaintiff again requests proof of the accusations made by the defendant. Case is adjourned until the arrival of the secretary to examine the documents in the matter.

The 25th of February

[1] We, Willem Kieft, director general, and the council of New Netherland, having considered the petition of the Negroes named Paulo Angolo, Big Manuel, Little Manuel, Manuel de Gerrit de Reus, Simon Congo, Antony Portuguese, Gracia, Piter Santomee, Jan Francisco, Little Antony and Jan Fort Orange, who have served the Company for 18 or 19 years, that they may be released from their servitude and be made free, especially as they have been many years in the service of the honorable Company here and long since have been promised their freedom; also, that they are burdened with many children, so that it will be impossible for them to support their wives and children as they

---

[1] Revised from Laws and Ordinances of New Netherland, pp. 36-37.

have been accustomed to in the past if they must continue in the
honorable Dompany's service; Therefore, we, the director and
council, do release the aforesaid [184] Negroes and their wives
from their bondage for the term of their natural lives, hereby
setting them free and at liberty on the same footing as other
free people here in New Netherland, where they shall be permitted
to earn their livelihood by agriculture on the land shown and
granted to them, on condition that they, the above mentioned
Negroes, in return for their granted freedom, shall, each man
for himself, be bound to pay annually, as long as he lives, to
the West India Company or their agent here, 30 schepels of maize,
or wheat, pease, or beans, and one fat hog valued at 20 guilders,
which 30 schepels and hog they, the Negroes, each for himself,
promise to pay annually, beginning from the date hereof, on
pain, if any one shall fail to pay the annual recognition, of
forfeiting his freedom and again going back into the servitude
of the said Company. With the express condition that their
children, at present born or yet to be born, shall remain bound
and obligated to serve the honorable West India Company as
slaves. Likewise, that the above mentioned men shall be bound
to serve the honorable West India Company here on land or water,
wherever their services are required, on condition of receiving
fair wages from the Company. Thus done, the 25th of February
1644, in Fort Amsterdam in New Netherland.

On the 3d of March 1644

Marritjen Livens, plaintiff, vs. Jan Snediger, defendant,
for slander. Case put over to the next court day, the parties
on both sides meanwhile to bring in their evidence.

Cornelis Volckersen, plaintiff, vs. Tonis Cray, defendant, for payment of fl. 10:15 st. Whereas the defendant admits that he owes something and says that he has paid something, he is ordered to pay the balance which he owes and to produce proof of the payment already made by him.

[185] This day, the 10th of March 1644.

Adriaen Willemsen, plaintiff, vs. Piter Wyncoop, defendant, alleging that the defendant said that the plaintiff informed the fiscal that there were dutiable goods in Mr. van Renselaer's ship. Defendant says that the chief boatswain said so. The chief boatswain says that he knows who told him. Ordered that the chief boatswain produce the man and discharge Piter Wyncoop.

Nicolaes Coorn, plaintiff, vs. Lubbert Jansen, defendant, alleging that the defendant caught and ate the plaintiff's rooster for which the defendant had promised him, the plaintiff, something. Defendant declares in court under oath that he knows nothing about the rooster. Whereupon the plaintiff's claim is denied.

Hendrick Oloffsen, plaintiff, vs. Jan Andriessen from Barenborch, [1] defendant. Plaintiff says that he handed the defendant his goods at the South for safe-keeping, which the defendant denies. Ordered that the plaintiff produce proof that the defendant received the goods.

Jan Jacobsz from Haerlem, aged 30 years, declares that he heard Jan Jansen, [2] commissary at the South, and his wife and several other persons there say that Hendrick Olofsz at the South delivered some goods to Jan Andriesz, which he confirmed by oath.

---

[1] Barenburg, Hanover.
[2] Jan Jansen van Ilpendam.

Hans Nicola declares that he heard the wife of Albert Pitersz say that Jan Andriessen at the South sold a pack belonging to Hendrick Olofsz, which he confirmed by oath.

Ordered that Hendrick Olofsz by the first sloop that goes to Fort Nassau shall procure further information with full proof. Meanwhile, Jan Andriessen may not leave the country without bail.

Tomas Sael, plaintiff, vs. Jan Werrensz, defendant, about clapboards which the defendant is alleged to have stolen from the plaintiff. Plaintiff is ordered to bring proof tomorrow at 9 o'clock.

The 11th of March

Tomas Sael. plaintiff, vs. Jan Warrensen, defendant. Defendant is ordered to satisfy the plaintiff today. In default thereof, plaintiff may take back his own goods.

[186] On the 17th of March 1644

Piter Wyncoop, plaintiff, vs. the fiscal, defendant. Parties ordered to submit their complaints and answers in writing.

Andriaen Willemsen, plaintiff, vs. Andries, chief boatswain, defendant, alleging that the defendant said that the plaintiff informed the fiscal that there were dutiable goods in Mr. van Renselaer's ship. The chief boatswain says that Lubbert Jansen told him. Lubbert Jansen acknowledges in court that what he said at the tavern concerning the ship is not true, and that he has nothing to say of Andriaen Willemsen reflecting in any way on his honor and character, and that he is sorry for having said so, praying the plaintiff's forgiveness. Lubbert Jansen is condemned to pay the costs.

31st of March [1]

Whereas, the Indians, our enemies, daily commit much damage,
both to men and cattle, and it is to be apprehended that all of
the remaining cattle when it is driven out will be destroyed by
them, and many Christians who daily might go out to look up the
cattle will lose their lives; therefore, the director and council
have resolved to construct a fence, palisade, or enclosure, begin--
ning from the great bouwery to Emmanuel's plantation. Everyone
who owns cattle and shall desire to have them pastured within
this enclosure is notified to repair there with tools next Monday
morning, being the 4th of April, at 7 o'clock, in order to assist
in constructing the said fence and in default thereof he shall
be deprived of pasturing his cattle within the said enclosure.
Let everyone take notice hereof and communicate it to his neighbor.
Thus done and posted on the day aforesaid.

[2] Whereas Mamarranack, Wapgaurin, chiefs of Kichtawanck, and
Mongochkonnome, Pappennoharrow of Wiquaeskeck and Nochpeem, as
well as the Wappincx have come to Stamfoort, asking Captain
Onderhil to appeal to the governor of New Netherland for peace,
promising now and forever to refrain from doing harm to either
people, cattle, houses, or anything else within the territory of
New Netherland; also, that they will not come on the island of
Manhatans as long as we Netherlanders are at war with other
heathen, except in a [187] canoe before Fort Amsterdam; and whereas they likewise promise to do their best in looking up for us
Pacham;

---

[1] Revised from Laws and Ordinances of New Netherland, p. 37.
[2] Revised from Doc. Rel. Col. Hist. N.Y., 13:17-18.

Therefore, we promise not to molest them if the aforesaid chiefs and their people strictly observe what is hereinbefore written and they may cultivate their lands in peace as far as we are concerned. In confirmation whereof some of their prisoners are restored to them. Done in Fort Amsterdam in New Netherland, the 6th of April.

The 15th of April 1644

1 Appeared in council Gauwarowe, sachem of Matinneconck. speaking in the name of the adjoining villages of Indians, to wit, Matinnekonck, Marospinc and Siketeuhacky, who requested permission to plant [their land] in peace in his and the aforesaid villages; which is granted them on condition that they shall not attempt to do us any harm and shall not suffer the Indians of Reckonhacky, the bays, and Marechkawieck to come among them and shall keep away from them. And the same shall be announced to their sachems on the flat at Mr. Fordam's, so that in case they be attacked and killed among the said Indians or any of our enemies by the Dutch, we shall be guiltless thereof. Wherewith the chief Gauwarowe was very well satisfied and for confirmation hereof a present was given to him.

On the 10th of May 1644

Cornelis van[der] Hoykens, fiscal, plaintiff, vs. Tomas Bacxter, defendant, for escaping from his confinement and taking with him one, Mr. Roet, who had also been arrested. The fiscal demands that the defendant be condemned to pay the sum for which he had been arrested and. in addition a fine. The defendant is

---

1 Revised from Doc. Rel. Col. Hist. N.Y., 14:56.

condemned to haul a scow load of stone to the gate for the Company, out of which the fiscal shall be allowed 10 gl. by the aforesaid Company; also, to pay Philip, in the tavern, 16 gl. for Mr. Roet.

Cornelis Volckersz, plaintiff, vs. Adam Mat, [1] defendant, for payment of 4 schepels of rye for which he became surety. Parties are ordered to agree and defendant is condemned to pay the plaintiff.

[188] On the 17th of May 1644

Elsjen Jans, widow of Jan Pitersz, plaintiff, vs. Willem Harlo, defendant. Plaintiff produces a shilling in court which she says the defendant gave her as a pledge of his troth, which she confirms on oath. Ordered that the defendant shall prove within ten days that Elsjen has behaved improperly since he has been betrothed to her.

Jan Schepmoes, plaintiff, vs. Claes Calf, defendant, as husband of Brant Palen's daughter, defendant. Plaintiff demands in writing that Aeltje Claes, daughter of Marritjen Piters, be allowed her maintenance out of the estate of Brant Pelen, according to the marriage articles. As the defendant denies jurisdiction of the court and appeals to his competent judges of the colony of Mr. Renselaer, the case is referred to the court there and if no decision is rendered within two months in the aforesaid colony the case shall be argued here.

On the 25th of May 1644

Sybet Clasen, plaintiff, vs. Aeltjen Brackoenje about payment of six boards. Plaintiff having turned the work over to boss Jeuriaen, the latter is ordered to pay for the boards and the

---

[1] Adam Mott.

further claim of the half-barrel of beer is denied. If boss
Jeuriaen has any claim, he may institute his action against the
defendant.

On the petition of Philip Gerritsz the fiscal is ordered to
have Jan Onderhil give satisfaction to the petitioner and the
case is further adjourned until Onderhil shall have returned.

On the 1st of June 1643 [1]

Whereas we, the director and council of New Netherland,
have granted to Willem Albertsen Blauvelt a commission to go
privateering from here to the West Indies or the islands thereof
in the frigate La Garce, against the enemies of the High and
Mighty Lords the States General of the [189] United Netherlands,
and this especially in virtue of the charter granted by their
High Mightinesses to the honorable directors of the General
Chartered West India Company, the aforesaid Captain Blauvelt and
his accompanying crew, on the seventh of January last past, with
the help of God, by force of arms, captured a Spanish bark, laden
with sugar, tobacco and ebony wood, of which bark Franck Creolie
of Havana was captain and commander, coming from Santiago de Cuba
and intending to unload his cargo at Cartagena, which was his
destination. Also, on the eleventh of March following, the
aforesaid captain captured in the river of Matique bay a bark
laden with wines, the captain of which was Croisie of Biscaye,
coming from New Spain and destined to go to Witte Male, [2] which
above-mentioned barks were brought in and arrived here in New
Netherland on the 29th of May in company of the frigate La Garce;

---

[1] Intended for 1644.
[2] Guatemala.

Therefore, we, the director and council aforesaid, make known to all and every one who may show cause why the above mentioned brought-in barks should not be declared good prizes, to present themselves here in fort Amsterdam within a fortnight after the proclamation hereof or, in default thereof, we shall declare the above-mentioned captured barks good prizes at the demand of the fiscal, and they shall thereafter remain debarred from any action or claim which they might or could set up as owners. Thus published in fort Amsterdam in New Netherland, the day and year above written.

6 June, Monday

The fiscal, plaintiff, vs. Michiel Cristoffelsen, a prisoner, because he, the prisoner, wounded and stabbed the Negroes of the Company, according to the fiscal's complaint. The fiscal demands that the defendant receive corporal punishment and be put in the chain gang in the stead of the Negroes.

The defendant acknowledges voluntarily that he wantonly stabbed to death a goat belonging to Tryn Jonas and wilfully wounded two of the Company's Negroes, so that one of them apparently will remain maimed for life.

[190] Whereas Michiel Christoffelsen from Gottenborch [1] in Sweden, a former soldier, has heretofore repeatedly committed many acts of insolence, has wantonly stabbed to death a gravid goat of Tryn Jonas and, without knowledge or consent, has absented himself for a month and not rendered the Company any service and whereas, furthermore, the fiscal in his written complaint against the aforesaid Michiel Christoffelsen shows that

---

1 Göteborg, Sweden.

on last Sunday, being the 29th of May, without any reason or cause, he wilfully wounded two of the Company's Negroes who were sitting quietly, one in such a way that he is in danger of death and the other that he will remain maimed for life; all of which he, Michiel Christoffelsen, free from torture or irons, has voluntarily confessed;

Therefore, we, the director and high court martial of New Netherland, doing justice in the matter, condemn the delinquent, as we do hereby, to labor for twelve consecutive months for the Prince with the Company's Negroes and to be put in the chain gang, reserving his execution if the Negro come to die. Thus done the 6th of June 1644, in Fort Amsterdam.

6 June

Symon Pos, plaintiff, vs. Adriaen vander Donck, defendant, in a case of appeal. Having heard the demand and proposition of the plaintiff, it is resolved in council that he shall first protest before the colony of Renselaerswyc and in case he, the plaintiff, do not obtain justice there, he shall appeal to this court.

Cornelis Volckersen, plaintiff, vs. Jacob Wolphersz, defendant. Plaintiff demands of the defendant payment of fl. 12, due to him by balance of account from Jan Brent, which money was attached by the court messenger in the hands of the defendant and which fl. 12, in spite of the attachment, were paid by the latter to Jan Brent, which the defendant acknowledges. The defendant is condemned to pay the plaintiff fl. 12.

Henry Sately, plaintiff, vs. Adam Mat, defendant, for payment of fl. 50. Defendant says that he never received the lumber for

which the plaintiff claims fl. 50. Parties are referred to Jan
Onderhil, Bacxter and Mr. Smith, who are to settle their differences,
if possible.

Elsje Jans, widow of the late Jan Pitersz, plaintiff, vs.
Willem Harlo, defendant. 1st Default.

[191] 7 June 1644 [1]

Whereas the honorable director general and council of New
Netherland have observed that the soldiers and others residing
in Fort Amsterdam throw out ashes and other filth within the
fort; Therefore, we hereby make known to all and every one that
henceforth ashes and other filth must be carried outside the fort;
also, that no one is to make water within the fort. And if any
one be caught in the act by the sentinel, he shall pay to him or
the provost three stivers for each offense and, if he refuse to
pay, the sentinel or provost shall be empowered to levy execution
on the offenders.

On the 16th of June

Vroutjen, wife of Cosyn Gerritsen, defendant, vs. Tomas
Sandersz, plaintiff, for slander uttered by parties one against
the other. Parties are reconciled in court and declare that they
know nothing of each other but what is honorable and virtuous.

Hendrick Huwit, plaintiff, vs. Gerrit Jacobsz, defendant,
alleging that the defendant with an arrow shot out the plaintiff's
eye. Defendant says that other persons besides himself were
shooting arrows at the time. Ordered that the defendant prove
that other persons besides himself were shooting at the very
moment that the plaintiff was wounded.

---

[1] Revised from Laws and Ordinances of New Netherland, p. 38.

Philip Geraerdi, plaintiff, vs. Cornelis Arissen, defendant. Default.

Jan Eversen, plaintiff, vs. Marten Cruger, defendant. As the plaintiff does not appear, the defendant is discharged.

On June 30, 1644

Cornelio vander Hoykens, fiscal, plaintiff, vs. Laurens Cornelisen, defendant. Plaintiff, presenting his complaint in writing, demands justice. Defendant requests a copy of the complaint, in order to make proper answer thereto, which is granted him.

Hendrick Huwit, plaintiff, vs. Gerrit Jacobsz, defendant. Defendant says that Henry Willemsen and Puter Cock were shooting also. Being brought before the court, they confess that they were shooting, but declare that they did not hit the man, as he was lying asleep in the guardhouse.

[192] On July 6, 1644

At the request of the fiscal, Cosyn Barentsen, aged 21 years, declares in court that in company with Sergeant Hubert, Ambrosius Lonnen and some other Englishmen he was in a small clapboarded house, to which came Steven Stevensz, who, being drunk, made much noise. The sergeant went out and shut the door, asking Steven, "What do you want?" The deponent says that he did not hear what the answer was. The sergeant called the men to arms and ordered them to fire at Steven, whereupon the deponent immediately heard the report of a gun and an Englishman, named Willem, fell down dead in the aforesaid house, having been wounded in the head by two bullets. The deponent confirms this on oath.

Hendrick Hendricksen from Stambuit, in Friesland, aged 20
years, deposes at the request of the fiscal that Steven Stevensz
came with a gun on his arm, pulling the trigger three times.
Standing about 10 or 11 paces from Steven, the deponent saw the
sergeant come out of Ambrosius Lonnen's house, who called out,
"Shoot Steven!" Then he saw Tomas Mabs fire and noticed that the
bullets flew into Ambrosius Lonnen's house. The deponent confirms this on oath.

Gerrit Wolphersen, aged 34 years, declares at the request
of Steven Stevensz that he and Steven sat in his father's house,
taking a drink together. Steven, wanting to go to the deponent's
house to fetch his wife, took the gun of the servant, who took
out the bullets and threw the priming powder off the pan, so
that there was nothing but loose powder in the gun.

In court are exhibited several depositions in the English
lamguage, from which it appears that the commotion was caused
by Steven, but that the man was accidentally shot through [the
head] by Tomas Mabs.

The fiscal, in writing, demands justice and sentence against
Steven Stevensen and Tomas Mabs.

On July 7, 1644

The honorable director general and court martial have seen
the criminal charge of the fiscal against Steven Stevensz from
Rouwaen, [1] a soldier, and Tomas Mabs, as well as the sworn
depositions of divers witnesses, together with their own confessions and declarations made in court, without torture or
irons, from which it appears that the aforesaid Steven on the

---

[1] Rouen, France.

25th of June last [193] came to the house of Gerrit Wolphersen,
standing on the flat, in which a garrison is kept at present,
having in his hand a gun with which, the hammer being drawn back,
he several times took aim to shoot at one Tomas Cornil, but missed
each time; whereupon he, the delinquent, came within the stockade
which surrounds the house aforesaid, where he leveled his gun at
Tomas Mabs. The aforesaid Tomas Mabs, at a general alarm, seized
his gun and fired at Steven, so that the bullets passed through
Steven's waistcoat and shirt and further went through a clapboarded
house, where they killed Jan Windtwodt; which the aforesaid Tomas
Mabs, without torture or irons, has likewise confessed. And
whereas this crime, being mutiny and manslaughter, may not be
tolerated or suffered in countries where justice is maintained,
therefore, we, having invoked the name of God and doing justice,
condemn the aforesaid delinquents to be shot, as an example to
others like them.

Resolved in court to pardon them, this sentence having been
pronounced by way of example, for the good of the delinquents
and as a warning to others.

July 8, 1644

Piter Wolphersen, husband and guardian of Hester Symons,
plaintiff, vs. Tomas Sandersz, husband and guardian of Sara
Cornelis, defendant, for slander. Plaintiff produces a written
affidavit and therefore demands reparation of character, since
the defendant's wife declares that she has nothing to say against
Hester Symons and never perceived anything wrong about Hester
Symons and further begs the plaintiff's wife to forgive her if
she said anything to her discredit.

Whereas no one has come forward to show cause why the prizes brought in by Captain Blauvelt should not be declared good prizes and therefore no objection has been offered, we, the director and council, declare the same good prizes, inasmuch as they were captured by force of arms from the enemies of their High Mightinesses by the above named captain; therefore, all those who hereafter might claim any interest in them are hereby debarred from their right [to bring any action]. Thus done in court in Fort Amsterdam.

[194] On July 8th

Willem Kieft, director, plaintiff, vs. Jochim Pitersz, defendant, for payment of 500 and odd guilders. Defendant acknowledges the debt and says that he will bring in his counter-claim.

Jacob Elbersen from Cadoele, mate on the ship De Maecht van Enckhuysen, plaintiff, vs. Cornelis Groesen, defendant. Plaintiff demands that defendant prove that he treated him badly and ordered him ashore. Defendant affirms it and maintains that it happened. Jacob Elbersen and Cornelis Groesen forgive each other in court.

Mr. Moor, plaintiff, vs. Mr. Spyser, defendant, on account of attachment of the bark of Piter Lourensz and Mr. Trochmarten. Piter Lourensz is condemned to pay Mr. Spyser for the bark according to the power of attorney, provided that Mr. Spyser give security for the immediate return of the purchase money of the bark if Mr. Moore hereafter proves that the knight [1] is indebted to him.

---

[1] Sir Nicolas Throckmorton.

The fiscal, plaintiff, vs. Laurens Cornelisz, defendant. First default.

On July 14

The fiscal, plaintiff, vs. Laurens Cornelisz, defendant.

Having seen the written complaint of the fiscal against Laurens Cornelisz, skipper of the Maecht van Enckhuysen, setting forth that the aforesaid Laurens Cornelisz sold some pitch, train-oil and lace without having entered the same, we have duly considered the matter and observed that the goods that were sold are not worth more than fl. 300; also, that a skipper can not go on a voyage without taking something with him, as he does not know where he shall land and has many wants and that, if he had asked permission of the Company at Amsterdam to do so, such a little thing would not have been refused him; therefore, it is ordered that he, Laurens Cornelisz, shall pay a fine of one anker of wine for the benefit of the fiscal and his friends; wherewith he is discharged and the fiscal's complaint about the smuggling is dismissed.

This sentence is pronounced by Batiaen Jansz Crol, Willem Cornelisz Oldemarckt, and Captain Jan de Fries and Hendric van Dyc, ensign, who were requested by the honorable director provisionally to give their opinion regarding the offense committed by Laurens Cornelisz.

Absent: the honorable director and Mr. La Montangne, as being objected to.

[195] July 14, 1644

Laurens Cornelisz, in answer to the charge of the fiscal, denies having committed adultery with Hillegont Joris and requests time until the next court day to consider whether he shall take the oath.

It is ordered and adjudged by the court that on the next court day Laurens Cornelisz shall declare under oath that he has never had any carnal conversation with Hillegont Joris. In case he takes the oath, the further complaint of the fiscal shall be dismissed, and, in case of refusal, he shall pay a fine of one hundred and fifty guilders for the benefit of the fiscal and fifty guilders for the poor.

The fiscal demands that Laurens Cornelisz shall prove what he said of the honorable director.

He shall have to prove here what he said to the prejudice of the director, on pain of such punishment as is provided by law, both as to the box and the fl. 600, giving him eight days to do so.

All that was transacted in court on the 14th of July was ordered and adjudged by Bastiaen Jansen Crol, Willem Cornelisz Oldemarckt, Jan de Fries, captain, and Hendrick van Dyck.

On July 21, 1644

Whereas we have heretofore written to Holland for reinforcements in this our war with the Indians and whereas a goodly number of soldiers has arrived now by the Blauwen Haen, the question arises:

1. Whether it would not be advisable to keep all or some of them here, or [whether it would be best] to send them all on.

2. If any of them remain, where the means are to be procured to keep them and to provide clothing.

3. Also, who is to be in command of the militia, in order that no confusion occur.

Done by the honorable director, Bastiaen Crol, La Montangne, the fiscal, Captain de Fries and Captain Willem [Cornelissen], as councilors hereto invited.

Having duly considered the first article and taken into account that we have written to the honorable directors for reinforcements from the fatherland and that by the grace of God reinforcements have unexpectedly been sent here from Curaçao and have arrived here by the _Blauwen Haen_; also, that we are assured that the directors have been advised from the West Indies that reinforcements have been sent hither, for which reason it is believed here that the honorable directors will not incur any expense in Holland to assist us, since there are so many [196] soldiers here; therefore, it is finally resolved by the above named councilors for the general welfare and the best interests of the Company to keep here the company of Captain de Fries and to complete it with our former soldiers up to one hundred and fifty men and to discharge the English soldiers who still remain as civilly as possible according to their rank.

As to the second article, said friends advise to propose to the commonalty that each of them board some soldiers according to his means and circumstances, on condition that they be paid when the Company receives means in the country.

July 21

Mr. Crol, Captain Willem Cornelisen Oldemarckt and Captain de Fries, having looked over and examined the recusation presented by Laurens Cornelisz can to the best of their knowledge not find that any exception can be taken against the director and Councilor La Montangne in matters pertaining to the interests of the Company and the criminal case of the fiscal.

Resolved in court by the above named councilors that Laurens Cornelissen shall prove on the next court day what he has spoken in defamation of the honorable director, both as to the transportation of the box and the matter in which he alleges to have been defrauded, or, in default thereof, he shall suffer the penalty which according to imperial law shall be found proper.

Philip de Truy, plaintiff, vs. Antony Jansen of Sale, defendant, for damage by cattle. Plaintiff is ordered to prove that his fence was tight.

Isaac de Foreest, plaintiff, vs. Jan Detton, in a case of slander. Defendant declares that he knows nothing of the plaintiff and his wife but what is honorable and virtuous and is ordered to pay to the plaintiff within eight days fl. 5, which debt he acknowledges.

The fiscal, plaintiff, vs. Tomas Willit, defendant, for assault. Plaintiff, producing his complaint in writing, demands justice.

Ordered that the fiscal produce evidence of the assault.

[197]   July [28], 1644

The council (the honorable director exempted), to wit, Bastiaen Crol, Johannes La Montagne, Willem Cornelisz Oldemarokt and Captain Jan de Fries, having carefully weighed and with due deliberation examined the evidence as to the slander uttered by Laurens Cornelisz to the detriment of the honorable Director Willem Kieft, do find that inasmuch as Laurens Cornelissen persists in his statement that he received a box of pearls from the honorable director, but can not prove the same here, it is proper according to law that he, Laurens Cornelissen, shall in court beg forgiveness of God, the court and the aforesaid director, and acknowledge that he has spoken falsely; or, in case of refusal, he shall be banished from this country until he prove at Amsterdam that he brought over pearls for the honorable director. Having proved the same there, this sentence shall be annulled.

Laurens Cornelissen still persists in his statement and appeals from the sentence to Amsterdam, protesting against loss and damage.

The sentence shall remain intact, notwithstanding the appeal.

The above named council having seen the foregoing sentence provisionally pronounced by associates invited for the purpose in the matter of smuggling committed by Laurens Cornelisz, skipper of the Maecht van Enckhuysen;

Therefore, we order absolutely that the goods which are in the hands of the fiscal shall remain confiscated and that the defendant in addition shall pay a fine of fl. 20 in cash.

The fiscal, plaintiff, vs. Laurens Cornelisz, defendant, on account of adultery committed with Hillegont Joris.

Ordered that Laurens Cornelisz shall immediately take his oath that he is not guilty of adultery.

Laurens Cornelisz having taken the oath that he is not guilty, the complaint of the fiscal is dismissed.

August 2, 1644

I, Philip de Truy, court messenger of New Netherland, being authorized by the honorable director general and council of New Netherland, do summon you, Nicolaes Coorn, commander of Beeren Island, on behalf of Willem de Key, attorney for Govert Loockmans, to appear here in Fort Amsterdam six weeks from this date and

there to hear the complaint against you which Willem de Key, as
attorney of the aforesaid Loockmans, is to present to the court.
Done in Fort Amsterdam in New Netherland, the 2d of August 1644.
Thus sent and signed by the court messenger and the secretary by
order [of the court].

[198] On August 4 [1]

Whereas by this war which we have been obliged to wage and
still carry on against the Indians we find ourselves wholly without goods and effects and do not know wherewith to feed or to
maintain the soldiers, and whereas a goodly number of soldiers
have been sent to our assistance from Curaçao, we should indeed
have excused ourselves from accepting them, were it not that the
necessity of the country demanded their retention and the commonalty
insisted upon it. Therefore, it is deemed advisable to retain
a large number of them here and as it is impossible for the director
to provide them with clothing, the store being entirely empty
and the winter at hand, and as nothing can be effected with naked
men, who on the contrary are a heavy burden on us, no other means
are found available than to impose some excise on commodities
wherein those deal who only do business here, while others must
suffer serious loss.

Wherefore it is provisionally ordained (until help is
obtained from Holland) that each merchantable beaver being here
at the fort or brought to it shall pay fifteen stivers once for
all. And in order to prevent all frauds, all the beavers on which
the duty is paid shall be marked with the Company's mark by the

---

[1] Revised from Laws and Ordinances of New Netherland, pp.
40-41.

officer appointed thereto, and such beavers as three days after
the publication hereof shall be found to be unmarked shall be
confiscated. On leaving the country, the [merchants] will be
given a certificate that the duty has been paid to the Company.

Furthermore, henceforth there shall be paid on each barrel
of beer three guilders, payable by the brewer, on condition that
he shall be allowed to sell his beer to the tavern keepers at
fl. 22, and the tavern keepers [shall be allowed to sell the same]
again at nine stivers the half-gallon; and all the brewers shall
be bound to notify the receiver how many barrels they have brewed
each time, before it is removed from the premises. Thus done by
the honorable director, Johannes la Montagne, the honorable fiscal,
Captain Willem Cornelisz, Bastiaen Crol and Captain Jan de Fries,
and published the day and year above written.

The director and council have appointed Willem de Key
receiver of the duties on beavers and beer and allowed him as
compensation therefor five percent [of his receipts] over and
above his regular salary, on condition that he render a proper
and true account of everything, as he is bound to do according
to his oath of fidelity to the Company.

[199] August 8, 1644

Jan Jansen Schepmoes, guardian of the minor surviving
children of the late Marritjen Piters, plaintiff, vs. the heirs
of the late Brant Pelen, defendants.

Plaintiff says that some time ago he caused the defendants
to be summoned here before the supreme court of New Netherland
in order to claim all such inheritance as the surviving children
of Marritjen Piters, espoused wife (ondertrouwde vrouw) of the

late Brant Pelen, are entitled to according to the marriage contract entered into between the above named persons; and whereas
he, the plaintiff, on the court's refusal to hear the case, was
heretofore referred to the competent judges of said heirs in
Renselaerswyc, the said action, for failure of the court there
to render a decision within two months, should now be tried here.

Defendant says that he caused the plaintiff's attorney to
be summoned four times, although he himself should have been
summoned, but that said attorney never filed a complaint; that
it did not suit his convenience to wait any longer and that he
can not stay here any longer either, as the ship is ready to sail.

Parties being heard and it being found that the case is so
difficult that it can not be disposed of in so short a time without great detriment to the parties, and that the property is in
Holland whither defendant is going, therefore, parties are referred
to the honorable schepens at Amsterdam, on condition that the
money claimed as due to the heirs shall remain attached in the
hands of the heirs of Mr. Renselaer, deceased, until the case
shall be finally decided.

Piter Wolphersen complains to the court that Michiel
Cristoffelsz, Paulus Heyman and Huybert Jansen van Sprangh have
cut his wainscoting to pieces with cutlasses, which they confess.

Therefore, Paulus Heyman and Huybert Jansen are sentenced
to ride the wooden horse for three hours. And whereas Michiel
Cristoffelsz was put in chains for his former crimes and nevertheless has now committed this new offense, he is condemned to
stand for three hours under the gallows with a cutlass in his
hand.

On August 18

The fiscal, plaintiff, vs. the brewers residing about Fort Amsterdam. Plaintiff demands payment of the duty according to the ordinance. [The court having] noticed the unwillingness of the brewers, it is resolved that if they do not pay willingly, they shall be proceeded against with rigor of justice and be forced to pay.

[200]   August 25, 1644

The fiscal, plaintiff, vs. Philip Gerritsen, defendant, about attachment of beer. Plaintiff demands payment from the defendant, as the tavern keeper or the brewer must pay the excise according to the ordinance. Defendant is condemned to pay fl. 15, being the excise on five barrels of beer.

The fiscal, plaintiff, vs. Philip Gerritsen, on account of attachment [of beer], in the sum of fl. 9. He is condemned to pay according to the ordinance.

On August 18th last appeared the brewers residing about Fort Amsterdam and jointly declared that if they voluntarily paid the three guilders on each barrel of beer, they would have the Eight Men and the community about their ears.

The director and council of New Netherland make known to all persons that they shall not harbor nor give any food to Huybert Jansen and Michiel Cristoffelsen on pain of forfeiting one hundred guilders; and the aforesaid persons are summoned to appear within twenty-four hours to prove their innocence. This day, August 25, 1644. [1]

---

[1] Revised from *Laws and Ordinances of New Netherland*, p. 41.

On September 1, 1644

Frederick Lubbersen, plaintiff, vs. Laurens Cornelisz, defendant, for delivery of what belongs to the house which the plaintiff bought from the defendant.

Ordered that defendant produce satisfactory evidence of the purchase, or in default thereof make oath, and if he refuse to do so, plaintiff shall be allowed to make oath.

The fiscal, plaintiff, vs. Laurens Cornelisz, defendant, for fl. 20 fine. Defendant is condemned to pay.

Willem de Key, plaintiff, vs. Hendrick Kip's wife, for slander. 1st default.

September 2

Frederic Lubbersen, plaintiff, vs. Laurens Cornelisz, defendant. Skipper Laurens promises voluntarily to build the dike in front of Frederic's lot and his own, [1] provided the honorable director have the path leading to the secretary's house put in order once for all.

Defendant is discharged [from his obligation] with respect to the tuyn [2] and [plaintiff?] must recover damages from those who destroyed the tuyn.

[201] On September 2

Everardus Bogardus, minister, and Dirck Cornelisz are kindly requested by the honorable director and council of New Netherland to settle if possible the dispute between Fredrick Lubbersz and

---

[1] On April 14, 1643, Laurens Cornelissen sold to Frederick Lubbertsen a house and lot fronting on the East River and adjoining the path leading to the secretary's house, which corresponds to the present Maiden Lane in New York City.

[2] The meaning of the word tuyn in this connection is uncertain. The word may mean a garden, an enclosure, and also a framework of sticks and wattled twigs to retain the earth of the embankment along the river front.

Laurens Cornelisz respecting the delivery of the house sold by
Laurens Cornelisz to Fredrick Lubbertsz, because they have been
appointed thereto by parties and because the case was somewhat
known to them.

Laurens Cornelisz requests that the honorable director may
be pleased to remove the attachment against his money in Fredrick
Lubbersz's hands.

The director answers that he is ready to release Fredrick
Lubbersen's money, as soon as Laurens Cornelisz gives him security
that the beavers sent to Holland by his brother and consigned to
a stranger shall come into the hands of the right owners, Messrs.
de Visser and de Raet; also, that all the beavers which have been
handed to him by his brother shall be sent to Holland for the
account of said friends [and] delivered to the owners or to him;
furthermore that he proved the debt. The order which I have is
from Mr. de Raet, wherein he instructs me to see to it that
Laurens Cornelisz's brother makes a return.

September 8

Laurens Cornelisz requests that Elslandt and his wife shall
declare in what manner and at what price he sold the three pieces
of beaver, and six fishers.

Elslant's wife declares that her husband sold the beavers
and fishers to Laurens Cornelisz for fl. 30.

Willem de Key declares that Elslandt said to him that he
sold three beavers and six fishers to Laurens Cornelisz for
fl. 30, but counting the goods by the piece the amount should
have been at least fl. 36.

Laurens Cornelisz says in court that he received 25 beavers
from his brother and sent them over to his masters at Amsterdam
without anything more.

Willem de Key, plaintiff, vs. the wife of Philip Gerritsz
and Hendric Kip. Ordered that plaintiff shall produce his
witnesses on the next court day.

Tomas Hal, plaintiff, vs. Jan Damen, defendant, for payment
for posts and rails. Defendant says that the work was not
finished in time according to contract. Jan Damen is ordered
to pay the plaintiff, or to return the rails and posts to the
place from which they came.

[202] September 8, 1644

Piere Pia, plaintiff, vs. Piere Montfoort, defendant, for
60 lb. of tobacco for a gun. Plaintiff demands payment, or
restitution of the gun. Ordered that defendant satisfy the
plaintiff.

Cornelis Pitersz and Laurens Andrissz declare that last
Sunday they saw a Negro come with bow and arrow; also, that they
understood from a Negro woman that a man had been killed by the
Indians near Tomas Hal's house.

September 10

Jan Bridges and partners, plaintiffs, vs. Davit Abrahamsz
Sprinchaen, 1 defendant. Plaintiffs say that they sold to the
defendant their half-share in the bark.

The case is adjourned until the arrival of Claes de Ruyter
and Jan Pitersz, who were present at the sale and plaintiffs are
allowed to take their goods ashore.

September 15

Everardus Bogardus, minister, appearing for Tryn Jonas,
plaintiff, vs. Jacob Roy, defendant, regarding a dispute about
a small piece of ground situated between [the lots of] Tryn Jonas

---

1 Locust; apparently a nickname.

and Roy. Ordered that the place shall be inspected by the honorable director and council at two o'clock in the afternoon.

Willem de Key, plaintiff, vs. Hendrick Kip's wife, defendant. Ordered that the defendant be furnished with copies of the complaint and the affidavits.

Philip Gerritsz, plaintiff, vs. Jan Bridges and partners, defendants. Plaintiff demands fl. 25:5, for which their property was attached and which they paid to Samuel Schandelaer, [2] notwithstanding the attachment.

The defendant produces testimony that he paid on the 7th of this month, which according to his statement was before the attachment.

Ordered that the defendant prove that he paid before the attachment.

Cornelio vander Hoykens, fiscal, vs. Jan Sytjes, defendant, for drawing a knife.

Whereas the fiscal proves that the defendant drew a knife, he is condemned to pay the fine according to the ordinance.

[203] September 29, 1644

The fiscal, plaintiff, vs. Cornelis Pietersen and Laurens Andriesz, both soldiers, for assault committed on Sunday last, as appears from the fiscal's complaint and informations.

Having seen the complaint of the fiscal and the declarations of several witnesses and the dangerous consequence thereof; therefore, the court martial, administering justice, condemn Laurens Andriesz to pay one hundred guilders and Cornelis Pitersz fifty guilders, whereof fl. 75 shall be given for the benefit of

---

2 Samuel Chandler.

the wounded Robbert Pinoyer, on condition that he pay the surgeon
out of the fl. 75; fl. 50 to the fiscal and fl. 25 to the church.
Furthermore, the delinquents shall ride the wooden horse until
the parade is over and shall thence be conveyed to prison, or
else go immediately on board ship and not come on shore again
under penalty of forfeiture of their wages.

Michil Jansen, plaintiff, vs. Laurens Cornelisz, defendant.
Plaintiff demands payment of the money which Andries, his servant,
owed him, being fl. 90, because the defendant conveyed the
servant out of the colony without his consent.

Defendant answers that he did not know that the servant
was bound to service and only discovered this on the journey.

Plaintiff maintains that the defendant ought to have brought
the servant to the fiscal at the Manhatans and not elsewhere.

The court having considered the demand, the fact that the
defendant acknowledges that he knew on the way that the servant
was not free and that he did not deliver him here, it is ordered
that the defendant shall pay the plaintiff.

The wife of Cornelis Volckersz, plaintiff, vs. Tomas Sandersz,
defendant, for attachment of fl. 13:10. Ordered that the
defendant shall pay the plaintiff as much as he owes her before
he be allowed to draw out the money which was attached.

The fiscal, plaintiff, vs. Jan Wilcock, defendant. Ordered
that Wilcock shall give his answer in writing.

Willem de Key, plaintiff, vs. Hendrick Kip, defendant.
Plaintiff's demand and the affidavits having been examined, it
is order that next Thursday Hendrick Kip's wife shall acknowledge
in court that what she said to the prejudice of the plaintiff is

untrue, and she is forbidden to commit such an offense again, on pain of severer punishment.

[204] October 6, 1644, in Fort Amsterdam

Willem de Key, plaintiff, vs. Nicolaes Coorn, defendant, because Coorn, being appointed by Mr. Renselaer officer on Beren Island, fired with cannon at Loockman's vessel and disabled it. Defendant says that he was authorized to do so by Patroon Renselaer. Ordered that Coorn shall prove his statement by tomorrow. [1]

Antony Crol, plaintiff, vs. Gillis Pitersz, for payment of fl. 875 for account of Hendrick Jansen. Ordered that the bill of sale be carried out and the debt paid.

Jochim Kirsteede, plaintiff, vs. Isaack Allerton, defendant. Plaintiff demands an indenture of Luwis Hult's servant and is willing to pay fl. 50. Defendant asks eight days' time.

The fiscal, plaintiff, vs. Jan Wilckock, defendant, for slander. Plaintiff is ordered to submit his complaint in writing and he shall be answered to-morrow by defendant.

October 8, 1644

Symon Dircksen Pos, plaintiff, vs. Adriaen vander Donck, defendant, in a case of appeal from an interlocutory judgment pronounced by the court in Renselaerswyck.

The honorable director general and council of New Netherland having seen the proceedings in a case of slander and the judgment rendered by the above-named court between the aforesaid parties, having duly heard them and everything being fully considered, the honorable director and council find that the judgment is right and that there is no cause for appeal. They order that

---

1 Revised from Doc. Rel. Col. Hist. N.Y., 14:59.

the judgment shall have full effect and condemn the above-named
Symon Pos to pay the costs of the suit and besides a fine of
fl. 10 toward the building of the church.

[205] On October 8, 1644

The fiscal, plaintiff, vs. San Symonsen, skipper of the
Renselaer Wyck, defendant. Ordered that the fiscal furnish the
defendant with a copy of the complaint, in order that he may
make proper answer thereto.

Jochem Kiersteede, plaintiff, vs. Isaack Allerton, defendant.
Plaintiff [1] demands the freedom of Jems Bier. Allerton declares
that he promised Jochim Kiersteede to release him from Lamberton
if he paid £ 5 sterling, which he confirms on oath. Ordered that
Luwis Hulet shall prove that Jems Bier is his servant.

Willem de Key, attorney of Govert Loockmans, plaintiff, vs.
Nicolaes Coorn, officer of Renselaerswyck, defendant, for damage
done by defendant to Loockmans' sloop by firing, the fiscal
undertaking the prosecution of the case in the name of the
government of New Netherland.

Having seen the affidavits which were made and confirmed
on oath at the plaintiff's request, the affidavit of the defendant
and the conclusion of the fiscal, and taking into consideration
the protest and prohibition made to the defendant by the fiscal,
we condemn the defendant to pay the damage which he caused to
the plaintiff's sloop by firing, said damage to be assessed by
two arbitrators to be chosen for the purpose. We also forbid
him to do so again on pain of corporal punishment and order him
to produce within ten months the approval of his lord patroon,

---

[1] The original record has: ged[aegde], defendant.

confirmed by superior authority; in default whereof further steps
will be taken on the complaint of the fiscal; meanwhile, the
defendant shall not be permitted to leave the limits of New
Netherland. [1]

Symon Dircksz Pos, plaintiff, vs. Adriaen van[der] Donck,
defendant, in a case of attachment. Ordered that with respect
to the beavers Verdonck can claim no more than his interest
amounts to according to the judgment.

The fiscal is ordered to inquire into the contents of the
notice which Symon Pos posted at Fort Orange.

[206] October 20, 1644

Augustyn Heerman, plaintiff, vs. Philip Geraerdy, defendant,
regarding the purchase of wine. Plaintiff desires to make delivery
according to a verbal agreement of which he exhibits an affidavit.
The case is adjourned until the arrival of Isaack Abrahamsen, as
the defendant appeals to him.

Andries Hudden, plaintiff, vs. Jeuriaen Hendricksz, defendant.
Plaintiff demands that the defendant complete the job agreed upon
by day labor. Jeuriaen is ordered from this day on to finish
the little work which remains to be done.

Abraham Jacobsz from Steenwyck, plaintiff, vs. Andries
Hudden, defendant. 1st Default.

October 22

Whereas the director and council have thought fit to collect
here the duty on beavers, because the great need and the safety
of the country demand it; therefore, the said duty is also levied
on the goods laden in the ship Renselaer Wyck and said ship is

---

[1] Revised from Doc. Rel. Col. Hist. N.Y., 14:59.

forbidden to depart without having paid it, on pain of confiscation. Done in Fort Amsterdam in New Netherland, the 22d of October 1644.

The honorable director general and council of New Netherland, having seen the proceedings instituted at the request of Cornelis van[der] Hoykens, fiscal, plaintiff, vs. Piter Wyncoop, supercargo of the ship named Het Wapen van Rensselaers Wyck, defendant, in a case of smuggling committed by the same, from which proceedings it appears, both from the inspection by the fiscal and various other documents, that Piter Wyncoop smuggled guns and powder, yes, brought contraband goods into the country here, which is expressly forbidden; therefore, taking into consideration the petition presented by Arent van Curler, supercargo on the Wapen van Rensselaers Wyck, dated October 26 last, in which he requests that the case may be referred to the fatherland to be disposed of by the honorable directors and the honorable patroon and that because of the weakness of the ship, which apparently can not lay here over winter on account of its leaky condition, we do refer the case to the honorable directors to be decided there, in order to deprive the honorable patroon of all cause of complaint, on condition that [207] no goods shall be discharged from the ship until the directors have cognizance of the case, saving the interest of the honorable directors and the fiscal; nevertheless, all the goods which the fiscal seized and which were not included in the invoice are confiscated. This day, the 27th of October 1644, in Fort Amsterdam, New Netherland.

On November 3, 1644

The fiscal, plaintiff, vs. Symon Volckertsen from

De Streek, [1] a prisoner, on a charge of theft.

The aforesaid Symon Volckersz, aged 20 years, declares and voluntarily confesses that Antony Pietersz some time ago assisted him in stealing from Egbert van Borsum's sloop four beavers, which he wrapped in a woolen blanket, brought ashore and offered to sell to Marten Cregier, the criminal himself bringing them there. Not being able to sell them there, Antony, his accomplice, took the veavers and brought them to Schepmoes, where they were sold two for fl. 7:10 and one for fl. 2:10; he does not know how much Antony got for the fourth, having taken brandy in payment, which they drank together.

The honorable director general and council of New Netherland, having seen the complaint of Cornelio van[der] Hoykens, fiscal, against Symon Volckersz, born in De Streek, for theft committed by him in the sloop _Prins Willem_, on which he was a sailor; which delinquent voluntarily, without torture or irons, confessed that he stole four beavers belonging to the skipper, having previously committed other larcenies and having also been put ashore from the sloop _De Eendracht_ on suspicion of theft; all of which sets an evil example and tends to the corruption of an entire state and can not be tolerated in a place where justice is maintained; therefore, we, administering justice, condemn the delinquent to be taken to the place where it is customary to execute justice and there to be beaten with rods as an example to other such persons; furthermore, he is hereby banished beyond the limits of New Netherland for the period of six years. Done the 3d of November 1644.

---

[1] Literally, the streak, or region; the name of a row of seven villages between Hoorn and Enkhuizen, in the province of North Holland.

November 10

Jan Schepmors says that Antony Pitersz and Symon Woutersz sold two beavers at his house. Anthony said, "They are not my beavers, but they belong to Symon." The next day they brought another beaver to his house and sold that one too. Schepmoes declares that he did not know that the beavers were stolen, as such goods constitute the current medium of exchange in this country.

[208] November 10, 1644 [1]

Antony Pietersen, being heard in court, declares at the request of the fiscal that Symon Volckersz came to him on the strand and wanted to be taken on board, which deponent did. Having arrived there, said Symon took two beavers from his bunk and went ashore with them. Symon went ahead to Marten Crigier and offered to sell the beavers, which he refused to buy. Thence they went together to Schepmoes and there sold two beavers for fl. 7:10. The next day they again went on board, Symon saying that he wanted to get pease. Coming on board the sloop, Symon called to the aforesaid Antony to hold the bag and he saw that Symon pulled a veaver from under his mattress. The skipper said: "See that you take no more pease than belong to you!" They went ashore and sold the beaver likewise to Schepmoes. Symon said to the aforesaid Antony that he had earned two beavers by night watching at Fort Orange and that he had bought the other beaver.

November 15, 1644

Isaack Allerton, plaintiff, vs. Tomas Sandersz, defendant, in a case of attachment. Defendant says that he has not settled

---

[1] The original record has 1645.

properly with the plaintiff and that therefore he can not attach any definite sum. Plaintiff shows a written bond signed by the defendant.

It being observed that the defendant's helper earned fl. 46 and also caused the money to be attached, the director and council order that the man shall receive his earned wages and Isaac Allerton the remaining money which is due to the defendant from Blauvelt and others.

Antony Pietersen, prisoner, having been examined, is released in consideration of his long service to the Company, but in case he again be found guilty of any such offense, he shall be punished without mercy.

November 25

The fiscal, plaintiff, vs. Willem Wodheyt and Tomas Cornel, soldiers, at present prisoners. The fiscal, presenting his complaint in writing, demands punishment on account of the crimes committed by them, both in deserting their service and in stealing arms of the Company.

[209] November 25

Willem Wodtheyt from Yorkshire in old England, aged 22 years, acknowledges before the court martial that he deserted his service; also, that he took with him arms belonging to the Company and stole a pistol from his captain's room.

Tomas Cornel from Hartfoortschier [1] in old England, 24 or 25 years of age, acknowledges before the court martial that he, being a soldier, deserted the service of the Company.

---

[1] Probably intended for Hertfordshire, but possibly for Herefordshire, England.

The honorable director general and the court martial of
New Netherland, having seen the written criminal complaint of
the fiscal against Willem Wodtheyt from Yorkshire in old England,
at present a prisoner, wherein the fiscal charges him, the prisoner,
with having deserted his Company, taken with him arms belonging
to the Company, stolen a pistol from his captain's room and run
away from his master in Virginia, all of which he, the prisoner,
voluntarily, without torture or irons, acknowledged and admitted,
and which is in direct violations of the regulations of the
militia and consequently not to be tolerated or suffered in a
country where justice is administered; therefore, we, having
invoked the name of God and wishing to render a righteous judgment,
condemn the above named Willem Wodtheyt to be taken to the place
where it is customary to execute justice and there to be shot to
death as an example to all other transgressors. Thus done in
court martial, in Fort Amsterdam.

The honorable director and court martial of New Netherland,
having seen the criminal complaint of the fiscal against Tomas
Cornel from Hartfoortschier in old England, from which it
appears that the above mentioned prisoner, being a soldier,
deserted the service of the Company without pass or consent of
the honorable director or his captain, which he has acknowledged
free from shackles and which is a violations of the military
regulations; therefore, we, administering justice, condemn the
aforesaid delinquent to be taken to the place of execution and
there to be tied to a post and to have a bullet fired over his
head, as an example to others. Thus done in court martial, in
Fort Amsterdam in New Netherland.

[210] November 25, 1644

Hans Kiersteede, plaintiff, vs. Hendrick Jansen, defendant, for payment of fl. 84:12, which he had attached in the hands of De Caper. Defendant acknowledges the debt, wherefore it is ordered that the money shall be placed in the custody of the honorable director and council.

At the request of Cornelis Melyn there was heard in court Gerrit Hendricksz, aged between eleven and twelve years, who acknowledged that Jacob Melyn stood against the wall and made water, having a piece of bread in his hand and a dog with him. He threw a potsherd at the dog and accidentally hit Jacob Melyn in the eye. The boy had not spoken to him, Gerrit. He also says that Cornelia, Melyn's daughter, struck him, so that the neckerchief fell from her shoulders, he stepped on it, so that it tore.

December 1, 1644

Tomas Hal and Sybolt Classen, having a dispute about the building of a house, request the appointment of arbitrators to settle the case and choose Jeuriaen Hendricksz and Piter Cornelisz. The director and council order the arbitrators to reconcile the parties if possible; otherwise, to give us their opinion in writing. The cost shall be charged to the person whom the arbitrators shall think proper.

On December 7

Cornelio van[der] Hoykens, fiscal, plaintiff, vs. Jan Haes. 1st Default.

Cornelis Volckersen, plaintiff, vs. Hendrick Pietersz, defendant, because the defendant's dog bit a goat of the plaintiff

to death. Plaintiff demands payment for the goat, as he informed
the defendant several times that his dog bit goats. Ordered that
plaintiff prove that he warned the defendant that the dog was
dangerous.

December 15, 1644

Cornelio van[der] Hoykens, fiscal, plaintiff, vs. Symon
Jansz of Durikerdam, skipper and supercargo of the ship St. Piter,
defendant, for smuggling herring, brick, powder, guns, being
contraband goods. The plaintiff, presenting his complaint in
writing, demands confiscation of the ship and goods. The fiscal
is ordered to give the skipper copies of the complaint and
affidavits in the afternoon.

[211] December 17, 1644

Cornelio van[der] Hoykens, fiscal, plaintiff, vs. Symon
Jansen of Durikerdam, defendant, for smuggling. Defendant
answers in writing to the plaintiff's complaint. Plaintiff
replies in writing. Plaintiff demands that the defendant deliver
his masters' invoice. Defendant says that he has no invoice and
therefore can not deliver any.

At the request of the fiscal, Dirck Jacobsz, mate, aged 44
years, mate of the ship St. Piter, is asked whether he is aware
that six kegs of powder came on board at Durikerdam and whether
the same were unloaded here or elsewhere, or are still on board.
The mate answers that he did not know that six kegs of powder
were in the ship besides the ship's powder, which he confirmed
on oath in court.

Piter van[der] Bergh, supercargo, says that he saw that
off Durikerdam four ankers of distilled liquor and two half-aams
came on board and that he knows nothing about the rest.

Claes Clasen of Rarep, aged 21 years, cook on the ship St. Piter, is asked at the request of the fiscal whether off Durikerdam six kegs of powder did not come on board when the ship's crew were ashore; also, if small kegs were not being hidden away when the next day he came on board. He answers that he knows nothing about this; only, that it is known to him that there were three small kegs of ship's powder.

Claes Clasen aforesaid is asked whether on the voyage hither he cut the mark of the Company on a pair of bellows and went down into hold and marked three small kegs with the mark of the Company. He answers that he cut the mark for fun, but did not mark any kegs in the hold; also, that he does not know that kegs were marked by any one. Claes Clasen refuses to swear to this.

Arien Jansen of 't Ooch, [1] boatswain on the ship St. Piter, aged 24 or 25 years, being asked whether in addition to the ship's powder there had not come on board six kegs of powder and whether the same were unloaded elsewhere, says that he does not know anything about it and refuses to confirm the same on oath.

Symon Jansen, skipper of the ship St. Piter, being asked if he is willing to swear that besides the ship's powder he had no other powder on board, answers that he will take no oath.

The court orders that Gysbert de Witt shall swear to what he has testified.

[212] December 19, 1644

Jan Appelmint of Suffolk, about 58 years of age, declares at the request of Symon Jansen of Durickerdam, skipper of the

---

[1] Calandsoog, province of North Holland.

ship St. Piter, that Gysbert de Wit had in his bunk a spoon not
belonging to him and that said de Wit wanted to take away cheeses
belonging to the skipper, but did not succeed in doing so; furthermore, that before Durickerdam he saw a sloop alongside the ship
St. Piter from which some small kegs were brought on board, but
does not know what was in them.

Symon Jansen being asked in court if he has anything more
to say or to bring forward in vindication of himself, replies
that he has nothing to add to what is stated in his written
answer.

Cornelis van[der] Hoykens, fiscal, plaintiff, vs. Symon
Jansen of Durickerdam, defendant, in a case of violation of
contract.

The honorable director general and council of New Netherland, having seen the complaint of the fiscal against Symon
Jansen of Durickerdam, skipper and merchant on the ship St.
Piter, for violation of the charter-party signed by him, whereby
the defendant was bound to sail direct from Amsterdam to New
Netherland, on pain of forfeiture of ship and cargo if he did
otherwise; defendant's rejoinder to the plaintiff's reply, the
testimony of reliable witnesses and other evidence in the case,
from which it appears that at Durickerdam the defendant received
on board six kegs of powder without the knowledge and against
the orders of the directors; that he sailed from the Texel without letters, invoices or papers from the directors and without
having sent the supercargo ashore to get any; that contrary to
the orders of the directors he touched at the Bermudas, there
broke bulk and sold the greater part of his cargo for 500 hides

and a large number of pieces of eight; also, that in his ship
here articles of contraband were found [which were shipped] without the knowledge and consent of the directors, such as guns to
be sold to the Indians, and herring and brick [which were] not
entered; that defendant has refused to produced the invoice of
his own employers and also refused to confirm on oath his defense
against [the testimony of] the witnesses, as a part of his crew
have likewise refused to do; [213] all of which tends to the
great prejudice of the honorable directors and the complete
ruination of this country, which can not be tolerated or suffered
in a country where it is customary to maintain justice; therefore,
having duly considered the case, first called upon God and taken
notice of the fiscal's complaint, we find that according to
law the ship and cargo are subject to confiscation. Pronouncing
judgment in the matter, we therefore confiscate, as we do hereby,
the ship and goods belonging thereto for the benefit of the
honorable directors and those whom it may concern, except the
property belonging to the sailors on which they paid duty at
Amsterdam. We order that the arrears of wages due to the sailors
shall be paid out of the confiscated cargo and, inasmuch as they
can get at present no passage to Holland, they are allowed to
stay here in the service of the Company until they can leave
conveniently, each one keeping his wages and usual allowance for
board, on condition that they shall tell where the six kegs of
powder are or have been discharged; we also order the fiscal
to inquire where the powder is or who stored it. Thus done
in Fort Amsterdam, this 19th of December 1644.

[214] In the name of the Lord, Amen. Anno
1645, January 5

Isaac Allerton, plaintiff, vs. Sybolt Clasen, defendant,
for fl. 30. Plaintiff demands payment. Defendant is willing to
pay, provided that his groundbrief be delivered to him by the
plaintiff.

Augustyn Heerman, plaintiff, vs. Isaac Abrahamsz, defendant,
on account of attachment. Plaintiff offers to deliver the wines
sold [to the defendant] to Philip Geraerdy. Defendant acknowledges
that he purchased the wines in company with Philip Geraerdi.
Ordered that parties shall appear on the next court day.

Cornelis Volckersen, plaintiff, vs. Hendrick Pitersz,
defendant, it being alleged that the defendant's dog bit to
death a goat belonging to the plaintiff. Plaintiff produces one
witness, on whose sole testimony no judgment can be rendered.
It is therefore ordered that they settle with each other; otherwise the case is dismissed.

Catrina Trico, plaintiff, vs. Paulus van[der] Beeke, defendant,
for slander. Plaintiff complains that the defendant called her
a whore and a seawan thief. Ordered that written testimony be
produced.

The honorable director and council of New Netherland have
deemed it advisable to give G[e]orge Grace, residing in Virginia,
power of attorney to attach the property there of Jacob Gerritsen
Blenc for the account of the honorable directors, by virtue of
the judgment given against him.

On January 12

Catalyn Trico, plaintiff, vs. Pauwel van[der] Beeke,
defendant, for defamation. Plaintiff demands satisfaction for
the injury done to her [character], which she proves by two
witnesses. Defendant is ordered to prove what he said or, if he
can not do so, defendant shall acknowledge that he knows nothing
of the plaintiff that reflects on her honor or virtue. Defendant
declares that he can not prove the slanderous remarks made to
her and that he has nothing to say against her that reflects on
her honor or virtue. For the blow struck by the defendant he
shall pay fl. 2:10 and Pauwel is warned not to do so again on
pain of severer punishment.

[215] On January 12, 1645

Fredrick Lubbersen, plaintiff, vs. Jan Cornelisz, defendant.
Plaintiff demands payment for the posts which the defendant
received and claims [compensation for] the loss which he suffered
thereby.

Defendant acknowledges that he received a quantity of posts
and loaned 250 of them to Planck. Ordered that within a fortnight,
if not prevented by the ice, Jan Cornelisz shall in return deliver
posts of as good a quality as those which he received.

The honorable court martial having seen the complaint of the
fiscal and the defense of Barent Jorisz Tourbay, it is ordered
that he shall beg pardon of his captain, ensign and sergeant; he
is further condemned to be put on the wooden horse and if he
commit such offenses again, he shall be punished severely.

Whereas on the 27th of November 1642 Jan Jansen Schepmoes
was prosecuted by the fiscal of New Netherland before the director

and council for having purchased some beavers which had been
stolen by a soldier at Fort Orange, in consequence whereof he
got into trouble at the time, and whereas he, Jan Jansen Schepmoes,
as far as we know, has behaved himself well and decently in this
country and we are certain that he did not know that the said
beavers were stolen, we have acquitted him of the false charges
brought against him at the time by the fiscal. We also request
that no person molest the above named Schepmoes on that account.
This day, January 10, 1645, in Fort Amsterdam in New Netherland.

[signed] Willem Kieft

February 16

Barent Hendricksz, plaintiff, vs. Emanuel of Gerrit de Reus,
for payment of fl. 6 for wages. Defendant acknowledges the debt.
Defendant is condemned to pay [the amount] within eight days
with costs.

[1] Ordinance further prohibiting the sale of fire arms and
ammunition to the Indians

[216] On February 23, 1645

Whereas the director general and council of New Netherland
long ago noticed the dangerous practice of selling guns, powder
and lead to the Indians and at the time issued against it an
ordinance prohibiting the same on pain of death, some persons
have nevertheless dared to barter all sorts of ammunition among
the heathen, secretly purchasing the same here and then trans-
porting it up the river and elsewhere, to the great detriment
of this country, the strengthening of the Indians and the

---

[1] Revised from Laws and Ordinances of New Netherland, p. 47.

destruction of the Christians, as we are even now informed with
certainty that our enemies are better provided with powder than
we, which they manage to obtain from other barbarians, our friends.
Likewise, his Majesty of France has through his ambassador
seriously complained to the Lords States General of the selling
of arms to the Indians, which causes much harm to his subjects,
in consequence of which the Lords States General recommended to
the honorable directors to prevent and forbid the same and to
have the guilty parties rigorously punished, which, accordingly,
the honorable directors have earnestly ordered to do. Therefore,
we most expressly forbid, as we hereby do, all persons from this
time forth to venture to trade any munitions of war with the
Indians, or under any pretense whatsoever to transport the same
from here without express permission, on pain of being punished
with death and having the vessel confiscated in which the same
shall be found laden or to have been put on board. May this be
a warning to every one and may every one guard himself against
trouble.

March 9

Johan de Fries, captain, and Gysbert de Leuw, ensign, present
a petition praying that they may receive as much allowance for
board as they had in Brazil. Whereupon the following answer is
given them by way of apostil:

What the Company gives at other places we know not; here we
can not give more than the directors have ordered to give the
officers of this country. Referring the case to the honorable
directors, we are meanwhile ready to pay the ordinary amount.
As to your having come here pursuant to orders, we have up to the
present time not seen any such order, nor have we written for it.

[217]   March 9, 1645

Cornelio van[der] Hoykens, fiscal, plaintiff, vs. Piter van
[den] Berch, former supercargo on the ship St. Piter, and Willem
de Key, defendants, for not having properly performed their
duty. Defendants are examined in court.

On March 16

Abraham Pitersz, plaintiff, vs. Sybolt Clasen, defendant,
in a case of slander. Parties are ordered to produce proof at
the next session and Sybolt Clasen's wife is to appear personally.

Jan Reynsen, as attorney of Jan van Hardenberch, draper,
plaintiff, vs. Abraham Planck, defendant, for fl. 250:10, which
it is alleged Planck owes Hendrick Roesen. Abraham Planck denies
the debt and says that he paid Roesen, which he proves by
affidavit. Ordered that Abraham Planck shall be given a certificate
that he proved here that he paid Hendrick Roesen.

The fiscal, plaintiff, vs. Piter vanden Berch and Willem de
Key, defendants. Plaintiff presents his complaint in writing
and demands justice. Defendants demand copy of the fiscal's
complaint.

The fiscal, plaintiff, vs. Burgert Jorissen, defendant, for
having sold the mizzen mast of the ship St. Piter. Plaintiff
demands that the defendant shall prove how he got the sail,
claiming that the sail belongs to the Company, as the ship was
confiscated with the appurtenances thereof.

Ordered that the fiscal may attach all such goods as came
from the ship that were sold after the ship was confiscated,
provided that Borger retain the right to recover the amount
from the skipper.

Ritchert Gibbins, plaintiff, vs. Cornelis Melyn, defendant, for payment of fl. 24. Defendant demands restitution of fl. 24. Parties were led to agree in court that Gibbens shall receive fl. 22.

[218] March 21

Abraham Pitersen, miller, plaintiff, vs. Sybolt Clasen, defendant. Defendant and his wife declare that they know nothing of the plaintiff but what is honest and honorable.

Mary de Truy, plaintiff, vs. Cornelis Teunesen, defendant, because the defendant threatened the plaintiff with a hatchet and refused to pay for an adze which he received from her. Ordered that the defendant pay for the adze. As to the other matter, they must produce affidavits about it.

Arent Steffeniers, plaintiff, vs. Jan Snediger, defendant. Plaintiff demands fl. 15, which the defendant promised him for a blow. The defendant acknowledges that referees ordered that he was to pay fl. 15, whereupon he is condemned to pay.

George Homs, plaintiff, vs. Charles Morgen, defendant. for damages for physical injury. The case is referred to Captain Ondril, [1] Lieutenant Bacxter and Captain de Vries.

The honorable Director Willem Kieft, attorney for Messrs. Abraham de Visser and Elias de Raet, plaintiffs, vs. Evert Cornelisz. Whereas Evert Cornelisz has declared in court under oath that according to the answer he rendered a true and correct account to his brother Lourens Cornelisz, he is therefore discharged, provided that the aforesaid gentlemen retain the right

---

[1] John Underhill.

to recover the amount from his brother Lourens Cornelisz.

Ordered that Piter van[den] Berch shall have his answer
ready within eight days from this date.

March 23

The honorable Director Willem Kieft with the approval of
the council sent to the Reverend Bogardus an admonition in writing, dated March 23, which he would not receive, either open or
closed, and the said document is again sent by the court
messenger. [1]

The fiscal, plaintiff, vs. Piter van[den] Bergh and Willem
de Key, defendants. Defendants answer in writing to the complaint of the fiscal, who takes time till next session to reply.

[219] March [30], 1645

Cornelio van[der] Hoykens, fiscal, plaintiff, vs. Tobias
Esaias and Barent Jorisz **Tourbay**, defendants, for having taken
a wounded goat from the beach and eaten it. Defendants acknowledge
having taken and eaten the goat, but state that they did not know
to whom she belonged. They are condemned to ride the wooden
horse.

The fiscal, plaintiff, vs. Piter van[den] Berch, defendant.
Defendant denies having had 11 pieces of cloth. Ordered that the
plaintiff shall make inquiries about it.

Burger Jorisz, plaintiff vs. Jan Haes, defendant. 1 Default.

April 6

Having observed the unseaworthiness, age, etc. of the sloop
St. Marten; furthermore, that the sails, cordage and other

---

[1] Revised from Doc. Rel. Col. Hist. N. Y., 14:59.

appurtenances were worn out and that there are at present no
materials here to make her seaworthy; therefore, we have sold
the aforesaid sloop with her appurtenances to Eduwart Moor for
fl. 1300:-.

At the request of Cornelio van[der] Hoykens, fiscal, you,
Cornelis Melyn, are asked what goods you purchased in the year
1644 from Willem Cornelissen Oldemarckt, skipper of the Blauwe
Haen, [1] and what you gave in payment for them; also, whether you
know that said skipper or you made a present or gave some gold
coins to some one to keep the transaction secret. Cornelis Melyn
answers that on the next court day he will deliver a written
statement of what he bought of the said skipper and delivered
in return. He says further that he does not know that any
presents were given and never heard of it.

The fiscal, plaintiff, vs. Piter van[den] Berch, defendant.
Plaintiff replies in writing to defendant's answer. Defendant
requests a copy. Ordered that the plaintiff furnish the
defendant with a copy of his reply.

[220] April 8, anno 1645

Piter van[den] Berch presents a declaration in writing
regarding the smuggled pieces of cloth.

April 28

Master Johan Wilkock appeared in court and declared that
he was drunk when he stated that Jan Dollingh owed him fl. 1500.
He declares that this is not true and that he said so because he
was drunk.

---

[1] Literally: Blue Cock; but probably so named for Pieter
Jansen Blauhaen, one of the chief participants of the West India
Company, residing at Amsterdam, who represented the city of
Deventer in the Amsterdam chamber of the Company.

Jan de Vries, captain, plaintiff, vs. Jan Wilkock, defendant, because the defendant called the plaintiff a villain. The plaintiff produces two witnesses and demands reparation of honor.

Jan Wilcock declares in court in the presence of the ensign and the sergeants that he was drunk and does not know what he said; also, that he knows nothing of the captain but what is honest and honorable. He, Wilcock, begs the captain for forgiveness and acknowledges that he spoke falsely to the defamation of the captain. Therefore, the aforesaid Wilcock is condemned to pay a fine of fifty guilders, one-third for the fiscal and two thirds for the poor.

The fiscal, plaintiff, vs. Piter van[den] Berch and Willem de Key, defendants. The plaintiff requests that the trial may be expedited as the defendants have nothing more to say.

The director and council, in view of the small number of councilors, think it proper to engage Captain Johan de Fries, Ensign Gysbert de Leuw, and Commissaries Oloff Stevensen and Gysbert Opdyc to sit as councilors in this case.

Willem de Key challenges the captain, maintaining that he is a friend of his opponent and an enemy of his. Van[den] Bergh objects to Opdyck.

April 29

The fiscal is ordered to deliver to Cornelis Melyn an itemized account of the hides sold to him.

[221] May 2, 1645

Adam Brouwer, plaintiff, vs. Hendrick Jansen, locksmith, defendant, about the purchase of a house. Plaintiff demands delivery of the deed. Defendant is willing, provided the plaintiff

bind himself for the payment of the account rendered to him.
Ordered that in the deed the house be mortgaged until the defendant
shall be paid.

Gysbert Opdyck, plaintiff, vs. Teunes Cray's wife, defendant,
for slander. Defendant is ordered to produce proof.

Gysbert de Leuw, plaintiff, vs. Captain Johan de Fries,
defendant, for slander. Parties ordered to produce proof.

Borger Jorissen, plaintiff, vs. Jan Haes. 2d Default.

The fiscal, plaintiff, vs. Cornelis Melyn, defendant, for
payment of fl. 3307:10, for purchase of the confiscated hides
of the St. Piter. Melyn acknowledges that the account rendered
is correct. The fiscal demands payment. Defendant refuses to
pay, wherefore the fiscal is authorized to levy execution against
the defendant and in case the property of the principal be not
sufficient to sue the surety.

We, Willem Kieft, director general, and the council of New
Netherland, certify and declare that Jacob Jacobsz Roy, gunner
in Fort Amsterdam, on the 22d of April 1643 at our order and
command was to discharge three cannon in honor of the solemn
peace then concluded with the Indians, among which cannon was a
brass six-pounder, which burst and exploded, in consequence of
which the aforesaid Jacob Roy was severely wounded, so that for
a long time he was under the care of surgeon Hans Kierstede, who
with the help of God succeeded in restoring the said Jacob Roy
to health, but the said injury has left his right arm stiff, as
can be seen. Thus done, the 8th of May 1645, in Fort Amsterdam
in New Netherland.

[222] May 11, 1645

The fiscal, plaintiff, vs. Piter van[den] Bergh and Willem
de Key, defendants. Plaintiff requests a speedy trial.

In court appeared the invited councilors, Captain Johan de
Vries, Ensign Gysbert de Leuw, and Commissaries Oloff Stevensz
and Gysbert Opdyc.

Willem de Key still objects to Captain Johan de Vries and
gives reasons for the challenge. Piter van[den] Bergh is
satisfied to have Opdyck sit with the council. The fiscal is
ordered to inquire further where the cloth has gone and who
took it out of the cases.

Ritchert Cloff, plaintiff, vs. Philip Weyt, defendant, for
payment for 2200 lb. of pork. Defendant answers that he paid
Mr. Bosseroot in Virginia. Ordered that Ritchert Cloff give
security for the delivery of the bond and that the defendant
before he leaves here furnish surety for the payment of the
above named sum.

Gysbert Opdyck, plaintiff, vs. Tonis Cray's wife, defendant,
for slander. Whereas the defendant can not prove what she said,
it is ordered that she shall keep silence on pain of being
punished as she deserves.

Touchyn Briel, plaintiff, vs. Robbert Bottelaer, defendant.
1 Default.

The council having observed how much the Company needs a
carpenter here, Piter Cornelisz is engaged as house carpenter
at fl. 36 a month and fl. 100 a year for board.

[1] This day, being the 24th of May 1645, appeared here a chief named Witaneywen, sachem of Mochgonnekonc, lying on Long Island with 47 armed Indians, who offered his services to this country, whereupon the director convened these following persons: Fiscal van[der] Hoykens, Monsieur la Montangne, Captain Onderhill, Ensign de Leuw, Oloff Stevensen and Gysbert Opdyck, commissaries, Jan Eversen and Jacob Stoffelsen of the selectmen, to whom the said sachem submitted his proposition.

It is resolved that he shall embark in one of the sloops of the Company and sail to the [223] place where he is to put ashore his spies to discover the enemy, whose whereabouts they are to report to him, whereupon he is to endeavor to defeat them with all his force; and after the work is done he is to return here to be rewarded according to his deserts. The director is to provide them with the necessary food in the sloop, etc.

Before us, the director and council of New Netherland, appeared Wittaneywen, sachem of Mochgonnekonck, declaring that he is empowered by his bretheren named as follows, to wit: Rochkouw, the greatest sachem of Cotsjewaminck, Mamawichtouw, sachem of Catsjeyick, Weyrinteynich, sachem Mirrachtauhacky, and said as well in his own name as in that of his bretheren aforesaid that they had taken under their protection the villages called Onheywichkingh, Sichteyhacky, Sicketauhacky, Nisinckquehacky, at which place the Matinnekoncx are now living, and Reckouhacky. He asked to enter into a firm alliance of friendship with us

---

[1] Revised from Doc. Rel. Col. Hist. N. Y., 14:60.

and promised that nothing but friendship would be shown to the
Christians by him, his warriors, or any one in the above named
villages; and in order that his friendly feeling might appear he
offered to attack our enemies, which he did, bringing a head and
hands of the enemy. He agreed to help us henceforth against the
Indians, our enemies, which [offer] we accepted. In confirmation
of this agreement a present was given by us to the above named
chiefs, with promise not to molest them so long as he and the
villages aforesaid observe their duty, but to show them all
possible friendship. In testimony of the truth the original
hereof is signed by us, confirmed with our pendant seal and
handed to the chief, the 29th of May 1645, in Fort Amsterdam
in New Netherland.

[224] On June 8

The fiscal, plaintiff, vs. Piter vanden Berch and Willem
de Key, defendants. The fiscal once more requests in writing
despatch of justice.

The fiscal is ordered to number the papers and documents
properly and to make a list of them; then to deliver the documents
to us to be examined, in order that we may make an end of the
matter.

Lysbet Dirckx, plaintiff, vs. Jan Haes, defendant, in a case
of attachment. Ordered that Piter Breyley prove that he has a
one-third interest in the work. As Jan Haes acknowledges the
debt, plaintiff is to receive his one-third interest.

On June 10

Françoys Doutey, English clergyman, complains to the court
that Willem Gerritsz, an Englishman, wrote a scandalous song to
the detriment of the plaintiff and his daughter, which he
produces in court.

Having seen the complaint and the libelous song written by said Willem Gerritsz, as he acknowledges, it is ordered that he shall stand in the fort tied to the Maypole, with two rods around his neck and the said song over his head, and remain there as an example to others until the English service is over. Furthermore, if the song be again sung by him, he shall be flogged and banished from this country.

June 11

Arent Corsen, plaintiff, vs. Cristiaen Cristiaensz and Piter Pitersen, defendants. Plaintiff demands his one-third share of about 3200 lb. of pork, the three having jointly signed a bond therefor. Defendants say that more than Arent Corsen's one-third share was attached in their hands. Ordered that plaintiff shall receive and enjoy his one-third share of the pork, on condition that he give sufficient security here to indemnify the defendants; furtbhermore, that the defendants in return shall guarantee the plaintiff against any future claim by Jacob Blenck.

[225] June 16

Rouloff Jansen, plaintiff, vs. Jan Smeets, defendant, about the purchase of a house for fl. 400. Plaintiff demands that delivery be made according to the purchase. Defendant answers that he was drunk and that he does not know anything about the purchase. Plaintiff proves by two witnesses that the purchase was made. Parties request that Andries Hudden and Jacob Wolphersen be appointed referees to arbitrate the matter, whereupon the said persons are authorized by us to make the parties agree if possible.

Dirck Volckersz, plaintiff, vs. Jacob Stevensz, defendant, about the purchase of a gun. Ordered that parties bring proof at the next session.

Dirck Volckertsen, plaintiff, vs. Jacob Stevensen, defendant, about the purchase of a gun. Plaintiff demands delivery of the gun. Parties agree, on condition that defendant pay fl. 10 as an indemnity for non-delivery.

On June 23, 1645

Willem Bredenbent, plaintiff, vs. Gerrit the Moff, [1] defendant, for payment of fl. 35. Ordered that the case be postponed until the arrival of Lourens Duyts.

Dirck Volckersen, plaintiff, vs. Jacob Stevensen, defendant, about the purchase of a gun. 1 Default.

At a meeting of the court martial, the following persons were examined:

Andries Tummelyn, of Schweinfurt, 23 years of age, declares that yesterday evening between nine and ten, it being very dark and the weather rainy, he stood sentry on the main highway in front of Jan Damen's house, when some people came along. He called out, "Who goes there?" Received for answer: "Jonker Rascal;" "Boor!" and "Bumpkin!" One of them pointed his gun at him, whereupon he made a thrust at him with his half-pike; the others then ran away and he recognized them as being Paulus Heyman with his wife and Piere Malenfant. This day, June 20, 1645.

Liven Donck, of Caninghgom, in Flanders, 28 years of age, declares that yesterday evening, it being very dark and rainy,

---

[1] Moff is a Dutch nickname for a German.

lying in his bed at the house of Jan Damen, he heard the sentry
call out, "Who goes there?" to which some one answered, "Joncker"
and some other words which he could not understand very well on
account of the strong wind. Jumping out [of bed], he took his
cutlas and ran to the sentry and on coming outside saw Piere
Malenfant with a drawn rapier in his hand, who had been wounded
by the sentry, and Paulus Heyman, who had a gun in his hand; the
woman was crying loudly on the road to the fort, outside the
fence. All of which was sworn to by him this day, June 20, 1645.

[226]   June 20

Piere Malenfant, of Riennes, [1] in Brittany, 35 years of age,
declares that yesterday evening about nine o'clock, as it was
getting dark, he came from the farm in company with Paulus Heyman
and his wife, he carrying the child on his arm and the woman the
gun. Near Damen's house, the sentry, named Andries Tummelyn,
called out, "Who goes there?" He answered, "A friend." Paulus
Heyman said, "Good evening, Joncker Nobleman," to which the
sentry replied, "What do you want, Merchant?" Hyman retorted,
"Lick my a - e;" whereupon the sentry came out and he, the
deponent, seeing him coming, put down the child and drew his
sword. He then was stabbed through his arm and received another
stab in his thigh; all of which he confirms on oath.

Paulus Heyman, of Leyden, about 26 years of age, declares
in court that yesterday, it being dark and rainy, he came from
the farm with his wife and Piere Malenfant near Jan Damen's house,
where Andries Tumelyn stood sentry, who called out, "Who goes
there?" Piere answered, "Good friend" and "Joncker;" he, Paulus,

---

[1] Probably intended for Rennes.

said, "Nobleman," and walked on. Having gone on ahead, he heard
a noise and saw that the sentry and Piere Malenfant were fighting
on the road, on this side of the fence; all of which he confirms
on oath.

Tryntjen Barents, of Rotterdam, wife of Paulus Heyman, 29
years of age, declares that she came with her husband and Piere
Malenfant near Jan Damen's house, where the sentry called out,
"Who goes there?" Piere Malenfant answered, "Good evening,
Joncker," and Heyman answered, "Good evening, Nobleman." She
says further that she did not hear any more. The sentry came,
walking between Leendert and big Tryn. Seeing him coming, she
said, "Piter, there comes some one," and took her child from
Piere's arm. Malenfant went toward the sentry, who likewise
came toward him, whereupon he, Malenfant, was wounded. They
then went to the fort. This day, June 20, 1645.

On June 29, 1645

Willem Bredenbent, plaintiff, vs. Gerrit the Moff, defendant.
Ordered that Gerrit is condemned to pay if Aeltjen prove that
Gerrit desired her to have patience and [promised] that he would
then pay her; on the other hand, if he prove that Aeltjen
Brackonge's late husband released him from his obligation,
plaintiff's complaint is dismissed.

Having taken into consideration the complaint of the fiscal
against Piter van[den] Bergh and Willem de Key and the importance
thereof, the challenging of the judges, the secret intriguing
of some uneasy persons and the smallness of our number, since
only the two of us could sit as judges, we have thought fit to

postpone this case until the arrival of the new director (who is hourly expected), unless a ship sail from here to the fatherland before [his arrival]. Meanwhile, the fiscal is to use all diligence to see if he can obtain still further information and Piter van[den] Berch and Willem de Key are ordered not to leave the Manhatans meanwhile.

[227] On July 6, 1645

Jacob Stevensen, plaintiff, vs. Jan Snediger, defendant, in a case of attachment. Parties are agreed, so that plaintiff is to pay the defendant fl. 3.

Symon Dircksen Pos, plaintiff, vs. Adriaen vander Donck, defendant, in a case of appeal. Ordered that the papers shall be examined and the case brought to an end.

Marry Willems, widow of Willem Willemsz, plaintiff, vs. Jan Haes, defendant. The woman brings a child into court and says that defendant is its father. Defendant denies it and proves that she went with other men; wherefore it is ordered that said Marry shall depart from New Netherland and that the defendant shall make her a small present.

On Friday, being July 15

Ritchert Smit, plaintiff, vs. Jan Wilcock, defendant, because Wilcock traded at plaintiff's trading house contrary to contract, in support of which plaintiff exhibits two affidavits. Wilcock says that the house was sold and that the witnesses were not present. Ordered to produce proof within eight days.

Symon Pos, plaintiff, vs. Augustyn Heerman, defendant, because the defendant shipped plaintiff's beavers from above [1]

---

1 Fort Orange.

in the sloop <u>Renselaerswyck</u> without consent. Augustyn denies
that the beavers were shipped by his order and offers to prove
the contrary. Ordered that parties prove their contentions.

Philip Geraerdi and Ritchert Cloff, plaintiffs, vs. G[e]orge
Collen, defendant, for fl. 80 which it is alleged the defendant
owes Mr. Moor and for having run away. Defendant acknowledges
the debt, but says that he worked it out.

Tomas Bacxter, plaintiff, vs. Jan Pickes, defendant, because
he signed a bond for the purchase money of a bark, but has not
received the vessel. [Plaintiff] demands the return of his bond.

Mr. Gerrit Vastrick appeared in court and in the presence
of Cornelis Melyn reported that he had demanded payment of said
Melyn in virtue of a certain power of attorney given to him at
Amsterdam and that the said Melyn refused to make payment at the
time. Vastrich said, "If you do not pay me, I shall sue you at
law." Melyn answered, "I have nothing to do with the law; there
is no justice for me here," and abused him, Vastric, violently.
Therefore Vastric got two witnesses and went to said Melyn,
asking him whether he would repeat the preceding words, whereupon
Melyn said, "I have said nothing at all against the court or
against you; you are an honest man."

[228] July 20, anno 1645

Jan de Vries, plaintiff, vs. Gysbert de Leuw, ensign,
defendant, in a case of slander. They are given until next
Monday [for the defendant] to make answer in writing and parties
are ordered not to molest each other.

Jan de Vries, plaintiff, vs. Jan Alleman, defendant, for
having challenged the plaintiff to fight while he was lying on

his bed. Defendant acknowledges the charge, wherefore he shall be put on the wooden horse and be cashiered from now on.

Jacob Reynsen, agent of Jan van Hardenbergh, merchant at Amsterdam, plaintiff, vs. Jan Eversen Bout, defendant, for payment of 114 gl., 5 st., which, it is alleged, defendant owes Hendrick Roesen, deceased. Defendant swears in court that he does not owe the late Roesen anything. Plaintiff's demand is dismissed and the defendant discharged.

Augustyn Heerman, plaintiff, vs. Symon Pos, defendant, for payment of fl. 58:3. Defendant maintains that he is not bound to pay, as plaintiff without his consent brought down defendant's case of beavers which on the voyage hither from above was considerably damaged. Defendant is ordered to prove this.

Mr. Ritchert Smit, plaintiff, vs. Jan Wilcox, defendant. Parties are willing each to choose a referee to settle their dispute.

Jacob Reynsen, as attorney for Jan van Hardenbergh, plaintiff, vs. Abraham Planck, defendant, for payment of fl. 250:10, being the balance due to said Hardenbergh for the account of Hendrick Roesen, deceased. Defendant proves by affidavit that he paid, which he has confirmed on oath. Therefore, the plaintiff's case is dismissed and the defendant discharged.

Willem Bredenbent, plaintiff, vs. Gerrit the Moff, defendant. 1st Default.

Tonis Cray, plaintiff, vs. Piter van[der] Linden, defendant. 2d Default.

Adriaen vander Donc having presented a certain petition requesting restitution of the beavers seized by the fiscal, an apostil is entered thereon that final judgment has been rendered and that nothing more remains to be said here. Whereupon Verdonc takes exception, giving notice that he will proceed in the case when time and opportunity permit.

[229] The honorable fiscal, plaintiff, vs. Willem de Key, defendant. Having seen the proceedings of the fiscal of New Netherland against Willem de Key defendant, and duly considered the case, we have, in view of the importance thereof, sent over Willem de Key with the documents in the suit, in order that he may render an account of his actions to the honorable directors.

The honorable fiscal, plaintiff, vs. Piter van[den] Bergh, defendant. Having seen the proceedings of the fiscal against Piter van[den] Bergh and duly considered the case, we have, in view of the importance thereof, sent over Piter van[den] Bergh with the documents in the suit, in order that he may render an account of his actions to the honorable directors.

In court appeared Symen Pos, who said that Adriaen van[der] Donck was a dishonest man.

July 21, 1645 [1]

Symen Dircksen Pos, plaintiff, vs. Adriaen vander Donck, defendant, in a case of appeal.

Having seen the proceedings of the plaintiff as well as of the defendant and the judgment in the case rendered by the court of Renselaers Wyck, dated the 18th of November 1644, from which

---

[1] The original record was by mistake 1646.

the plaintiff appealed here, and having carefully weighed and considered everything, we, the director and council of New Netherland, decide that the judgment is well founded, but that the costs of the suit shall be assessed by us according to a properly itemized bill, without fine, as no demand on the part of any prosecuting officer appears, and the plaintiff is condemned in the costs of the appeal here.

Symon Dircksen Pos, plaintiff, vs. Augustyn Heerman, defendant, it being claimed that defendant, without the plaintiff's consent, has given orders to bring a case of beavers down [the river], which beavers were damaged. Having heard the complaint and the answer of both parties, it is ordered that Symon Pos shall prove that defendant gave orders to take the beavers down.

Augustyn Heerman, plaintiff, vs. Symon Pos, defendant, for payment of fl. 58. Defendant acknowledges the debt and is condemned to pay before plaintiff's departure, on condition that plaintiff give security for the judgment in the preceding action.

[230] On July 21, anno 1645

Whereas Governor La To[ur] has sent us seven soldiers, being the remainder of his entire force, and whereas we do not know what to do with the same and yet have to provide for them; therefore, it is resolved to take them into the service, as we intend to explore the mines and shall have need of our men, the more so as about forty soldiers have been discharged and have departed for Holland, in the expectation of peace, which as yet is not concluded.

July 27, 1645

Jan de Vries, plaintiff, vs. Gysbert de Leuw, defendant,
in a case of slander. Plaintiff complains of the abusive
language. Defendant presents his answer in writing. Ordered
that parties shall not offend each other on pain of dismissal
and forfeiture of monthly pay.

Jacob Roy, plaintiff, vs. Symon Groot, boatswain on the
Prins Maurits, defendant, about the purchase of the plaintiff's
house. The plaintiff proves that the purchase of the house for
fl. 1100 was absolute. Defendant is ordered to accept the house
according to the stipulated conditions, or to satisfy the plaintiff.

Gerrit Vastrick, attorney of Johan Roos, plaintiff, vs.
Cornelis Melyn, defendant, for payment of fl. 142. Defendant
promises to deliver to the plaintiff a bill of lading before
his departure and to send over goods by skipper Seger to
Mr. van[der] Voorde, in payment of Jan Roos, if he has not been
paid by any draft.

Tryn van Campen, plaintiff, vs. Piter van[der] Linden,
defendant, for payment of 5 schepels of corn. Defendant says
that the corn in his hands was attached by Tomas Hal. The
attachment is vacated and defendant is condemned to pay, with
costs.

Ritchert Smith, plaintiff, vs. Jan Wilcocx, defendant,
because defendant violated his contract in trading at Sloop's
Bay. Jan Wilcocx demands release from his suretyship for
fl. 400.

Whereas the case is very doubtful, Isaack Allerton and
Arent Corsz Stam are appointed arbitrators to reconcile the parties,
if possible, or else to give us their opinion in writing.

[231] July 27, 1645

Symon Dircksen Pos says in court that the council of the
colony is a false council.

The director general and council having examined the itemized
bill presented by Adriaen vander Donck for loss of time and
expenses, the amount is estimated at 70 days at fl. 4 a day and
fl. 20 to pay for the writing of the documents in the colony.

August 10, 1645

Piter van[der] Linden, plaintiff, vs. Jan Snediger, defendant,
for delivery of two beds. Symon Pos declares that he was present
when fl. 24 was promised for one bed and the best bolster with
two small pillows. Defendant is ordered to make delivery according to the deposition.

Cornelis Teunesz, attorney for Jan de Fries, plaintiff, vs.
Jan Wilcocx, defendant, regarding some dispute which Jan de Fries
and Wilcocx had on the road. Parties, making complaint and
answer, produce affidavits on both sides. Wilcocx exposes his
arm in court and says that the scar was left where the minister's
wife struck him with a stick.

Claes Jansen, baker, plaintiff, vs. Willem Bredenbent,
defendant. Plaintiff demands payment according to the contract.
Ordered that if Willem prove that Claes promised him something
aside from the contract, it shall be given to him.

Piter Cornelisz, plaintiff, vs. Tomas Sandersen, smith,
defendant. 1st Default.

August 25

Cristiaen Cristiaensen and Piter Pitersen, plaintiffs, vs.
Arent Corsen, defendant. Whereas they, the plaintiffs and the

defendant, by a bond dated November 10, 1645, are jointly bound
to pay Jacob Blenc in Virginia for pork, of which each of them
received his 1/3 share, plaintiffs demand that the defendant
make provision for the payment, as he remains here in the country
and they go to Virginia to pay there. Defendant says that his
money is ready; he desires security against all future demands
before he is willing to pay.

The court having seen the complaint and the answer, it is
ordered that the defendant shall hand to the plaintiffs his 1/3
of the payment and that they remain bound to pay Blenck and to
give a proper discharge here to the defendant, who is released
from all further demands on account of said bond.

[232]   August 30, 1645

Whereas there is a fair promise of obtaining a firm and
durable peace with the Indians, it is resolved and concluded in
council in Fort Amsterdam to order Philip de Truy, the court
messenger, to notify the burghers all around to come to the fort
when the flag shall be hoisted and the bell rung and there to
hear the terms which shall be agreed upon and, if any one should
have any good advice to offer, freely to express his opinion.

Philip de Truy, court messenger, having been ordered to
notify the burghers pursuant to the foregoing resolution, appears
and reports that he served on all the burghers round about on
the Manhatans, from the highest to the lowest, no one excepted,
the order which he received from the director and council to
appear in the fort and to hear the terms of peace and to be
pleased to offer to the aforesaid director and council their
good advice in the matter. He, the court messenger, says that

all the burghers gave them their kind attention and a favorable
answer, except one Hendrick Kip, tailor.

Articles of peace concluded in the presence of the Mohawks between
   the Dutch and the River Indians [1]

This day, being the 30th of August 1645, appeared before
the director and council in Fort Amsterdam, in the presence of
the entire community, the following sachems or chiefs of the
Indians, as well for themselves as in the capacity of attorneys
of the neighboring chiefs, to wit: Oratany, chief of Achkinckeshacky;
Sesekemu and Willem, chiefs of Tappaens and Rechgawawanck, Pacham
[and] Pennekeck having been here yesterday and empowered them to
act for them, and answering further for those of Onany and their
neighbors; Mayauwetinnemin, for those of Marechkawieck, Nayeck
and their neighbors; as also Aepjen personally, speaking for the
Wappincx, Wiquaeskeckx, Sintsings and Kichtawanghs.

1. They agree to and conclude a firm and inviolable peace
with us, which they promise, as we likewise do, to maintain and
nevermore to break.

2. If it happen, which God forbid, that any dispute should
arise between us and them, no war shall be commenced on that
account, but they shall come to our governor and we to their
sachems to make complaint and if any one be killed or murdered
the slayer shall be promptly brought to justice [233] and both
sides shall henceforth live together in amity.

3. They shall not be allowed to come with arms to the houses
of the Christians on this island of Manhatans; neither shall we

---

[1] Revised from <u>Doc</u>. <u>Rel</u>. <u>Col</u>. <u>Hist</u>. <u>N</u>. <u>Y</u>., 13:18.

come to them with guns, without being accompanied by an Indian
who can warn them.

4. Whereas there is still an English girl among them, whom
they promised to take to the English at Stamfort, they agree to
do so and, if she is not taken there, they promise to bring her
here and we shall pay them the ransom promised therefor by the
English.

We promise that all that is above written shall be strictly
observed throughout New Netherland. Thus done in the fort, under
the blue canopy of heaven, in the presence of the council of
New Netherland and the entire community called together for the
purpose, in the presence of the Maquas ambassadors, who were
requested to assist as mediators in this peace negotiation, and
of Cornelis Antonisen, their interpreter and co-mediator in this
matter. Dated as above. The original was signed with the mark
of Sisiadego, the mark of Claes Noorman, the mark of Oratamin,
the mark of Auronge, the mark of Sesekenins, the mark of Willem
of Tappaen, Willem Kieft, La Montangne, the mark of Jacob
Stoffelsen, Jan Onderhil, Francis Douthey, Go: Bacxter, Ritchert
Smith, Gysbert Opdyc; the mark of Aepjen, sachem of the Mahikans,
Jan Eversz Bout, Oloff Stevensz, Cornelio vander Hoykens; the
mark of Cornelis Tonisz. Below was written: Acknowledged before
me, and was signed, Cornelis van Tienhoven, secretary.

Proclamation ordering a day of thenskgiving to be observed [1]

On August 31

It is resolved in council to issue a proclamation for a day
of general thanksgiving, which thanksgiving shall take place on

---

[1] Revised from <u>Doc</u>. <u>Rel</u>. <u>Col</u>. <u>Hist</u>. <u>N</u>. <u>Y</u>., 13:19.

the sixth of September next in all the Dutch and English churches
within the limits of New Netherland. The proclamation reads as
follows:

Whereas it has pleased Almighty God in His infinite grace
and mercy, in addition to many previous blessings, to let us come
to a long desired peace with the Indians, it is deemed necessary
to send notice thereof to all the people of New Netherland, in
order that [234] in all the places in the aforesaid country where
Dutch and English churches are open to the public God Almighty
may be especially thanked, lauded and praised on Wednesday next,
being the 6th of September, in the forenoon, the text to be chosen
accordingly and the sermon to be applicable thereto. You will
please announce the same to the congregations next Sunday, in
order that they may be informed thereof; upon which we shall
rely.

Resolution to explore a mine in the Paritan country [1]

Whereas we have obtained from the Indians a few samples of
minerals which are considered by us to be valuable and we are
informed by the Indians that the hill from which they took the
aforesaid samples is situated inland near the Raretangs; Therefore, it is deemed by us to be to the best interest and advantage
of the honorable West India Company to use all diligence to
discover the aforesaid mine. If, upon being found, it proves
to be valuable, it is resolved to take possession thereof in the
name of the aforesaid Company and to build a fort there.

---

[1] Revised from Doc. Rel. Col. Hist. N. Y., 13:19.

Furthermore, whereas behind the Col, [2] in the colony of Meyndert Meyndersen van Keeren, some ironwork and ordnance has been sunk in the river by the Indians, it is resolved to raise the same if possible and, upon being recovered, to cause the same to be brought hither to the Manhatans.

On September 4, 1645

Claes Jansen from Emden, plaintiff, vs. Willem Bredenbent, defendant. Parties are ordered to bring proof on the next court day.

Jan Schepmoes, plaintiff, vs. Tryntjen Evers, defendant. Default.

The fiscal, plaintiff, vs. Jan Jansen Ilpendam, commissary at Fort Nassau, defendant, for having neglected to perform his duties properly. Ordered that the fiscal shall deliver to the defendant a copy of his complaint. [1]

[235] On September 7, 1645

Jems Bier says in court that Captain de Vries, without any reason, before Wilcocx had given any cause for it, called said Wilcocx a dog, a son of a bitch, and similar names, notwithstanding Domine Bogardus, his wife and a Dutchman (unknown to him) were standing in his doorway. Also, that Tomas Hal was present there, but that he does not know whether it was at the beginning or the end of the dispute when said Hal came there; which Jems Bier has confirmed on oath.

Captain Vries, plaintiff, vs. Jan Wilcocx, defendant. Case adjourned until the arrival of Tomas Hal.

---

[2] Achter Col.
[1] Revised from Doc. Rel. Col. Hist. N. Y., 12:25.

Claes Jansen, plaintiff, vs. Willem Bredenbent, defendant. Ordered that a copy of the complaint shall be delivered to the defendant.

September 21, 1645

Cornelis Antonisz, attorney for Jan de Fries, plaintiff, vs. Jan Wilcocx, defendant. Case adjourned until tomorrow morning, at eight o'clock sharp, to see whether the affidavits are rejectable.

Willem Bredenbent, plaintiff, vs. the heirs of Cornelis Lambersen Cool, defendants. The case is adjourned until Huych Aertsen comes down, as parties refer to him.

Piter Cornelissen, plaintiff, vs. Tomas Sandersen, defendant, because the defendant called the plaintiff an informer. Defendant acknowledges the slander. Ordered that defendant prove that the plaintiff called him a crazy devil.

In court appeared Gerrit Douman, sergeant, who produced three affidavits made in the presence of the fiscal, from which it would seem that he, Douman, was the heir of Jacob Naviere and whereas we, the director and council, have no objection thereto, he, Douman, is given permission to obtain a copy of the said Navier's account and to demand the earned wages due to him from the honorable directors at Amsterdam. The chest is provisionally turned over to him, under inventory.

[236] September [2]1, 1645

Mattys Gerbrantsen, plaintiff, vs. Cornelis Teunesen, defendant, for slander, for which plaintiff demands satisfaction. Defendant says that he knows nothing of the plaintiff but what is honest and honorable and that what happened was done in haste. As to the drawing of knives, parties may settle with the fiscal.

Cornelis Antonissen, plaintiff, vs. Claes Jansen Ruyter, defendant, for payment of seven beavers and fl. 98: 4:8, being the balance of an account of grain which plaintiff delivered to the defendant on his personal account and not for the patroon. Plaintiff confirms on oath that he loaned seven beaver skins to the defendant and that fl. 98: 4:8 are due to him on his own account.

The defendant shall deduct fl. 48 from the amount due to him by the plaintiff for his, the defendant's, two servants who helped the plaintiff in the harvest. Ordered also that the defendant retains his action against the colony on account of the grain.

Tonis Nyssen, plaintiff, vs. Ambrosius Lonnen, defendant, for payment of fl. 50. Plaintiff not being able to prove that fl. 50 are still due to him as heir of Jan Celes, the defendant declares on oath that he does not owe anything to Jan Celes, deceased. Therefore, the defendant is released from the plaintiff's demand.

Francis Wiecx, plaintiff, vs. Mr. Spyser, defendant, for loss of plaintiff's gun through Spyser's fault. As the plaintiff can not prove that he left the gun in the custody of the defendant, the defendant is released and the plaintiff's demand denied.

September 28

Jan Wilcocx, plaintiff, vs. Mr. Clercq, defendant, alleging that defendant fitted out a bark for privateering purposes, to

capture and make prize of plaintiff's [vessel]. Ordered that
Wilcocx shall prove his charges against Mr. Clercq next Monday,
on pain of Mr. Clercq being discharged, as he is about to depart.

[237] On October 11, 1645

Tomas Willit and Jeuriaen Blanck, plaintiffs, vs. Jochim
Kirstede, defendant, for damage which plaintiffs claim they
suffered through the defendant on the voyage to Rhode Island.

Ordered that Jacob Wolphersen and Gysbert Opdyck act as
arbitrators to reconcile the parties if possible, or, otherwise,
to give us their opinion in writing.

October 12

Claes Jansen and Elbert Elbertsen, plaintiffs, vs. Willem
Bredenbent, who married the widow of Cornelis Lambersz Cool,
defendant.

Parties on both sides having been heard, both as to the
complaint and the answer, and it being observed that the will
which the defendant produces is not legal, it is adjudged that
the contract made by Aeltjen Brackoengne, Gerrit Wolphersen and
Claes Jansen on January 5, 1645, shall remain intact and retain
its full force. Therefore, he, Willem Bredenbent, is condemned
to fulfil the aforesaid contract and to pay the money which the
above named Aeltjen Brackoengne promised to the aforesaid Ferrit
Wolpehersz and Claes Jansen as heirs of Cornelis Lambersz,
deceased, and if defendant claim anything outside the contract,
he may demand it.

Jan Jansen van Ilpendam, commissary at Fort Nassau, declares
in court that he took with him to the South some cloth, he does
not know how much, belonging to Marritjen Tymens. He promises

to tell tomorrow whether he delivered the cloth to Hendric Huygen, or sold it to some people elsewhere. He says that he received two bags of Haerlem cloth from Bogardus' wife, the same having been handed to him by Jochim Kirsteede, which bags were sold in his presence by Egbert van Borsum in the sloop _Prins Willem_ for two beavers; also, that he did not trade or sell any goods for Jan Jeuriaensen, [1] when the latter was there.

The fiscal, plaintiff, vs. Jan Jansen Ilpendam, defendant.

Having seen the fiscal's complaint against Jan Jansen for fraud committed by him in his office, also his accounts of many years, the declaration of the witnesses and Jan Jansen's own defense, it is after mature consideration of the case ordered that Andries Hudden shall provisionally be sent to Fort Nassau to make further inquiries there among the Company's servants and others about the defendant's trade, to take an inventory of all his and the Company's effects and to send hither whatever is not required there, and furthermore [238] to exercise command there as commissary until further order. The fiscal shall do the same here also and he, the defendant, shall bring in his answer to the points upon which he was questioned today. [1]

Whereas we have from time to time, after much trouble, expense and diligent inquiry received from the Indians a few specimens of a certain mineral which yielded gold and quicksilver; therefore, for the sake of the best interest and advantage of

---

[1] Jan Juriaensen Becker, afterwards a notary public at Albany. For a sketch of his career, see _Early Records of Albany_, 3:18-22.
[1] Revised from _Doc. Rel. Col. Hist. N. Y._, 12:25.

the Company we have thought it advisable to send thither thirty
soldiers with an officer to examine the hill from which these
specimens came and if possible to bring back a quantity of
specimens. [2]

On November 3, 1645

Piter Jacobsen, plaintiff, vs. Claes Jansen, defendant, for
payment of fl. 276:17. Plaintiff demands payment of the aforesaid sum. Defendant acknowledges the debt and says that it was
agreed between plaintiff and him, the defendant, that he was not
to pay until the arrival of ship of the Company from Holland,
or plaintiff's departure.

Jacob Stoffelsen, plaintiff, vs. Cornelis Melyn, defendant,
for payment of fl. 176. Defendant acknowledges the debt, wherefore Melyn is ordered to pay within one month from this date,
which he, the defendant, promises to do.

[239] On September 7 (say November 7), 1645

Hans Hansen, plaintiff, vs. Lambert Clomp, defendant, for
payment of fl. 225 for the purchase of a half-interest in a sloop.
Defendant acknowledges that he purchased the sloop, on condition
that it should be delivered tight and be made seaworthy.

Ordered, if the sellers can prove that the sloop was seaworthy when the purchase was made or afterwards and that Cornelis
Teunesz neglected or refused to fulfil his contract, defendant
is condemned to pay according to the agreement.

November 16

Hendrick Pitersen, plaintiff, vs. Jochim Kalder, defendant,
for fl. 195, arising from the purchase of land and a house. As

---

[2] Revised from Doc. Rel. Col. Hist. N. Y., 12:25.

no contract was made, nor any proof exists, the parties are
ordered to agree if possible.

Lysbet Tyssen, plaintiff, vs. Jan Forbus, defendant, for
payment of fl. 22:10 for house rent. Defendant acknowledges the
debt and is satisfied to have plaintiff receive the fl. 22:10
from Adriaen Dircksz in the inn. Defendant is condemned to pay
plaintiff in accordance with his acknowledgment and promise.

Jan Forbus, plaintiff, vs. Albert Jansen, defendant, for
payment of fl. 40. Defendant says that he promised to pay the
plaintiff fl. 40 out of the money which he was to receive for
Roelandt Hackwaert. Jan Forbus confirms on oath that the
defendant promised to pay for Roelandt Hackwaert. Defendant is
therefore condemned to pay.

Ordinance prohibiting the sale of intoxicating liquors to
Indians [1]

Whereas daily much strong liquor is sold to the Indians,
whereby heretofore serious troubles have arisen in this country
and, if no provision be made herein, it is to be feared that
further calamities may occur; Therefore, in order to prevent
the same, we, the director and council of New Netherland, do
forbid all tapsters and other inhabitants from this day forward
to sell, give, or trade to the Indians any wine, beer, or other
strong liquor, or, under any pretext whatsoever, to fetch it,
or to cause it to be fetched by the third or fourth hand, directly
or indirectly, from any houses, taverns, or elsewhere. If any

---

[1] Revised from Laws and Ordinances of New Netherland,
p. 52.

one, be he who he may, be found to have acted contrary hereto,
he shall for the first [240] offense forfeit five hundred guilders;
for the second offense forfeit double the amount, receive
arbitrary punishment and be banished from the country, and in
addition be held responsible for all the damage which may result
from the selling or giving of any liquor to the Indians. The
21st of November 1645. Published and posted at the usual places.

November 24, 1645

Jeuriaen Blanck and Tomas Willit, plaintiffs, vs. Jochim
Kirstede, defendant, for profit which they claim from the goods
sold by the defendant according to their agreement made with
him and which he, upon adjustment of accounts, offered to pay
them at Rhode Island, leaving the decision in the matter to the
oath of the defendant, or offering to take one themselves. The
defendant leaves it to the plaintiffs to take the oath, which is
done. Therefore, the defendant is condemned to pay them the
amount according to the adjustment of accounts.

On November 30, 1645, in Fort Amsterdam

Cornelis vander Hoykens, fiscal, plaintiff, vs. Jan Jansen
Ilpendam, defendant. The fiscal asks for speedy justice and
that Jan Jansen make written answer to the plaintiff's reply on
condition that the fiscal furnish him with copies of the
affidavits. Said Jan Jansen is ordered to answer by next
Thursday.

December 7, 1645

Jan Jansen is allowed time to see whether meanwhile he can
adduce evidence to overthrow the testimony.

Henry Breser, plaintiff, vs. Aert Willemsen, defendant, for
wages amounting to fl. 100. The defendant's wife, appearing for
the defendant, promises to pay this week as much as possible and
the remainder after Christmas, with which the plaintiff is
satisfied.

Lysbet Tyssen, plaintiff, vs. goodman Karreman, defendant,
about the purchase of a petticoat. Goodman Harck declares at
the request of goodman Karreman that when Karreman called him,
the deponent, Lysbet Tysen was standing in her doorway and
Roelant and Karreman were at the door on the road. Said Karreman
held up a woman's petticoat and asked what it was worth. Roelant
demanded four marks for the petticoat; it was a red petticoat,
lined with blue and bound with cord. The case is submitted to
referees, to wit: Mr. Ochden and Lieutenant Bacxter, to make
parties agree with each other.

[241] December 7, 1645

Tomas Willit, plaintiff, vs. Cornelis Tonisz, defendant,
for fl. 236, being the balance due for the purchase of a house.
Ordered that the defendant carry out and fulfil the contract made
and signed by him,

The fiscal, plaintiff, vs. Cornelis Melyn, defendant,
because the defendant violated the ordinance in selling wines
to the Indians. Ordered that the fiscal prove that the defendant
sold wines, or else that parties settle with each other.

Summons to the Rev. Everardus Bogardus to answer charges against
him and further proceedings [1]

[242] In the name of the Lord, Amen. Anno 1646 in New
Netherland.

The Honorable director and council to the Reverend Everardus
Bogardus, minister here.

Although we were informed of your proceedings in the time
of the Hon. Wouter van Twiller, the former director, and were
also warned to be on our guard, yet were we unwilling to pay any
attention thereto, believing that no man who preached the Word
of the Lord would so far forget himself, notwithstanding we have
letters in your own hand, among others one dated June 17, 1634,
wherein you do not appear to be moved by the spirit of the Lord,
but on the contrary by a feeling unbecoming heathens, let alone
Christians, much less a preacher of the Gospel. You there berate
your magistrate, placed over you by God, as an incarnate villain,
a child of the Devil, whose buck goats are better than he, and
promise him that you would so pitch into him from the pulpit on
the following Sunday that both you and his bulwarks would tremble.
And many other such like insults, which we refrain from mentioning, out of the respect we entertain for that gentleman.

You have indulged no less in scattering abuse during our
administration. Scarcely a person in the entire land have you
apared; not even your own wife, or her sister, particularly when
you were in good company and jolly. Still mixing up your human
passion with the chair of truth, which has continued from time
to time, you associated with the greatest criminals in the

---

[1] Revised from Doc. Rel. Col. Hist. N. Y., 14:69-71;
reprinted in Eccl. Rec. N. Y., 1:196-99.

country, taking their part and defending them. You refused to
obey the order to administer the Sacrament of the Lord and did
not dare to partake of it yourself. And in order that you may
not plead ignorance, a few out of many instances shall be cited
for you as follows:

On the 25th of September 1639, having celebrated the Lord's
supper, observing afterwards in the evening a bright fire in the
director's house, while you were at Jacob van Curler's, being
quite drunk, you grossly abused the director and Jochim Piterz,
with whom you were angry, because the director had asked something of you for said Jochim Pitersen, which you refused (according to the affidavit in our possession).

Since that time many acts have been committed by you, which
do not become a clergyman in the least. In the hope that you
would at least demean yourself in your office in a Christian-like
manner, we have overlooked those things until March 1643, when
one Maryn Adriansen came into the director's room with predetermined
purpose to murder him. He was prevented and put in irons. Taking
up the criminal's cause, you drew up his writings and defended
him. He, notwithstanding, was sent to Holland in chains against
your will. Whereupon you fulminated terribly for about fourteen
days and desecrated even the pulpit in your passion. In what
manner you conducted yourself every evening during this time is
known to those who were then your immediate neighbors. Finally,
you made up your quarrel with the director and things quieted
down somewhat.

In the year 1644, one Laureus Cornelisen being here — a man
who committed perjury; once openly took a false oath and was
guilty of theft - [243] he immediately found a patron in you,
because he bespattered the director with lies and you were daily
making good cheer with him. In the summer of the same year,
when minister Douthey administered the Lord's Supper in the
morning, you came drunk into the pulpit in the afternoon; also
on the Friday before Christmas of the same year, when you preached
the sermon calling to repentence.

In the beginning of the year 1645, being at supper at the
fiscal's, where you arrived drunk, you commenced as is your
custom to scold your deacons and the secretary, abusing among
the rest deacon Oloff Stevensz as a thief, although he did not
utter an ill word against you; whereupon the director, being
present, suggested to you in a kind manner that it was not the
place to use such language. As you did not desist, the director
finally said, that when you were drunk, you did nothing but abuse,
and that you had been drunk on Friday when you went into the
pulpit; that it did not become a minister to lead such a life
and to give scandal to the worthy congregation.

Some days after, the director not being able to attend church
in consequence of indisposition, to wit, on the 22d of January
1645, you abused him violently from the pulpit, saying "What
else are the greatest in the land but vessels of wrath and
fountains of evil, etc. Men aim at nothing but to rob one
another of his property, to dismiss, banish and transport." For
this reason the director absented himself from the church, in

order to avoid a greater scandal; as he will maintain that he
never coveted any man's property, or took it away, or acted
unjustly, or banished anyone who had not deserved three times
severer punishment. Whomever he dismissed was discharged because
such was his prerogative, and he will vindicate his act in the
proper quarter. It is none of your business.

On the 21st of March 1645, being at a wedding feast at Adam
Brouwer's and pretty drunk, you commenced scolding the fiscal
and the secretary then present, censuring also the director not
a little, giving as your reason that he had called your wife a
whore, though he says that it is not true and that he never
entertained such a thought and it never can be proved. Wherefore
on the 23d of March, we, being moved by motives of mercy and on
account of the respect attached to your office, instead of
prosecuting you, sent you a Christian admonition under seal,
which you twice refused to receive (according to the report of
the messenger).

You administered the Lord's Supper at Easter and Whitsuntide
without partaking of it yourself; furthermore setting yourself
up as a partisan; assuming that the director had sent the
Yoncker [1] and one Jottho, meaning Lysbet the midwife, to you in
order to seek a reconciliation, but that you would think twice
before making peace with him; using similar language also to the
Yoncker and Anthony de Hooges, as shall appear by credible
witnesses. At the making of the peace, many words and means
were used to break it off. Good effect was expected from the
order which was sent to you to offer up prayers to the Lord, but
instead of a prayer, people heard an invective, the tendency

---

[1] Adriaen van der Donck.

whereof was of dangerous consequence. Peace being concluded with the Indians, an extract from the order of the Lords States was sent to your Reverence, to return thanks to God on the 6th of September [244] therefor. Your Reverence preached indeed and gave a good sermon, but throughout not a word was uttered about the peace and, though the day was appointed specially for that purpose, you offered no thanks to God for it, as the other clergymen who dwell within our limits have done with great zeal. By this, people can estimate your disposition toward the Company, by whom you are paid, and the welfare of the country; which disposition is also manifested by favoring those who have grossly defrauded and injured the Company; the conventicles and gatherings held and still daily continued in reference thereto.

On the 22d of December, you said publicly, in the course of the sermon on repentance, that you have frequently administered the Lord's Supper without partaking of it yourself and wished that those who are the cause of the trouble were excluded, and that when families are visited, they can not give a reason why they absent themselves. Your bad tongue is, in our opinion, the sole cause, and your stiffneckedness and those who encourage you in your evil course the cause of its continuance. We know no one but only you who has refused to make peace. When you make a visitation you do not desire to know the reason, or are unwilling to ask it. We hold that men are bound to give a reason for such absence if it be demanded.

On the 24th of the same month, you remarked in your sermon that in Africa, in consequence of the excessive heat, different animals copulate together, whereby many monsters are generated.

But in this temperate climate you knew not, you said, whence
these monsters of men proceeded. They are the mighty but they
ought to be made unmighty, who have many fathers and place their
trust in the arm of the flesh, and not in the Lord. Children
can tell to whom you hereby allude. These and many similar
sermons which you have often preached have obliged us to
remain away from the church.

Seeing that all this tends to the general ruin of the land,
both in ecclesiastical and civil matters, to the disparagement
of the authorities whom your Reverence is bound by duty and also
by your oath to support; to the stirring up of a mutiny among the
people, already split into factions; to schism and contention in
the church, created by novel and unheard of customs, and to
rendering us contemptible in the eyes of our neighbors, which
things can not be tolerated where justice is accustomed to be
maintained; therefore, our bounden duty obliges us to provide
therein and by virtue of our commission from their High Mightinesses,
his Highness, and the honorable director of the Chartered West
India Company to proceed against you formally; and in order that
the same may be done more regularly, we have commanded that a
copy of these our charges be delivered to you, to be answered in
fourteen days, protesting that your Reverence shall be treated
in as Christian and civil a manner as our conscience and the
welfare of Church and State will permit. The 2d of January 1646.

[245] On the 4th of January

We have seen the writing, dated the third of January last,
sent us by Everardus Bogardus through the messenger, and found
it futile and absurd and not an answer to the extract, dated

2d of January 1646, sent to said Bogardus. It is therefore
ordered that said Borgardus shall give a pertinent answer to the
contents of said extract, either affirmatively or negatively within the time therein mentioned, on pain of being prosecuted as a
rebel and for contempt of court. Thus done in council at Fort
Amsterdam in New Netherland, on the date above written.

Jochim Kirstede, plaintiff, vs. Rem Jansen, defendant, for
payment of fl. 20 which defendant is alledged to have promised
to pay for Jan Haes. Defendant answers that he promised to pay
when the work would be completed by Jan Haes. Ordered that
defendant shall pay when the work is done.

Ordered by the director and council that Jan Jansen Ilpendam
shall appear next court day personally and either admit or refute
the testimony.

On January 7

Jan Jansen Ilpendam having been asked in court to bear
witness to the truth, as he is legally bound to do according to
his oath to the Company, he refuses to do so.

On January 18 [1]

Having seen a certain writing which Domine Bogardus has
sent us by the messenger, full of vain subterfuge, calumny,
insult and profanation of God's holy word, to the disparagement
of justice and his lawful superiors, which he uses according to
his custom to vent his passion and to cover up the truth and
does not serve as an answer to our charges and the order sent

---

[1] Revised from Doc. Rel. Col. Hist. N. Y., 14:71;
reprinted in Eccl. Rec. N. Y., 1:199.

him on the 2d and 4th of January last; therefore, we order him
for the second time to answer the same formally within 14 days,
either negatively or affirmatively, on pain as above.

January 25

Oloff Stevensen, plaintiff, vs. Everardus Bogardus, minister,
defendant, for slander. Defendant answers in writing.

Abraham Pitersen, miller, plaintiff, vs. Gysbert Opdyck,
commissary of provisions, defendant. Plaintiff complains of
slander. Defendant produces affidavits whereby he proves
plaintiff's dishonesty. Plaintiff demands copy of the affidavits.
Ordered that defendant furnish Abraham Pitersen with copies of
the affidavits to answer them.

[246] On February 1, anno 1646 [1]

Having seen the slanderous writing of Domine Bogardus,
purporting to be an answer to our charges, wherein he affirms
some and denies other points thereof and demands proof, it is
ordered that the fiscal shall give said Bogardus satisfaction
as his opponent.

Abraham Pitersen, plaintiff, vs. Gysbert Opdyck, defendant,
for slander. Parties present their demand and answer in writing.
Ordered that parties shall have their witnesses appear tomorrow.

February 2

Abraham Pitersen, plaintiff, vs. Gysbert Opdyck, defendant,
because the defendant called the plaintiff a grain thief.

---

[1] Revised from Doc. Rel. Col. Hist. N. Y., 14:72;
reprinted in Eccl. Rec. N. Y., 1:199.

Ordered that parties, if possible, shall settle their difference with each other; which was done in court, on condition that the documents in the suit shall remain in the hands of the honorable director and council. Furthermore, for weighty reasons, the aforesaid Abraham Pietersen is ordered hereafter, wind and weather permitting, to grind the Company's grain as far as it is possible before that of others and further so to conduct himself as a miller that no one will in the slightest degree have any ground for complaint against him. The said Abraham Pietersen shall not be allowed to brag, inveigh, or make use of any sharp words in any place whatsoever on account of this suit, and if hereafter he be found to have acted contrary hereto, the suit shall then be continued. Commissary Opdyck shall hereafter be allowed to weigh the grain when it is brought to the mill and when it comes back from there.

February 8

Hans Hansen, plaintiff, vs. Lambert Clomp, defendant, on account of the purchase of the sloop *Pharnambuco*. Having seen the suit between the plaintiff and the defendant regarding the sale of the aforesaid sloop, the parties are referred to arbitrators of their own choice, to wit, Fredrick Lubbersen and Jochim Kirstede, who by us are requested and authorized to act in that capacity.

Having seen the suit between the honorable fiscal Cornelio van[der] Hoykens, plaintiff, vs. Jan Jansen Ilpendam, commissary of Fort Nassau, defendant, the complaint, answer and sworn affidavits, from which it appears that the defendant grossly wronged the Company both in giving to the Indians more than the

ordinary rate of exchange and in other matters, as appears from
the complaint, the affidavits and his accounts, which makes it
impossible for us to audit or approve his accounts and to shoulder
another's fault; therefore, having maturely considered the matter,
we order, as we hereby do, that said defendant shall with all his
papers and the fiscal's complaint be sent to Amsterdam by the
first ship, to defend the case himself before the honorable
directors. [1]

[247] On February 15, 1646

Claes van Elslandt, attorney for Mr. Wolter van Twiller,
plaintiff, vs. Sybolt Clasen, who married the widow of the late
Aert Teunesen of Putten, defendant, for restitution of fl. 123
paid to Aert Teunesen. Plaintiff demands proof as to whom and
for what the money was disbursed. Defendant says that the fl. 123
were included in the item of fl. 273 adjusted with plaintiff, as
appears by plaintiff's own account, and that he can not furnish
any particulars now, as the person who expended it is dead and
he denies that he owes fl. 150.

The director and council having seen the written demand and
defendant's verbal answer and that the widow knows nothing of
this matter, it is therefore ordered that the account shall
remain unsettled until Mr. van Twiller furnish further explanation,
according to which the parties must regulate themselves.

Oloff Stevensen, plaintiff, vs. Everardus Bogardus, minister,
defendant. Default.

---

[1] Revised from Doc. Rel. Col. Hist. N. Y., 12:26.

February 22

Oloff Stevensen, plaintiff, vs. Everardus Bogardus, minister, defendant, for slander. Plaintiff demands proof of the charges brought against him in the answer delivered today and denies the same expressly. Ordered that the defendant prove the charges in eight days.

March 1, 1646

Tomas Becxter, plaintiff, vs. Jan Wilcocx, defendant, because Wilcocx accused the defendant of being a wood thief. Plaintiff demands reparation of character. Ordered that Wodtkock prove his charges in eight days, on pain of punishment.

Teunes Nysen, plaintiff, vs. Jeuriaen Fradell, for payment of the debt which his wife owed to Jan Celes, deceased. Parties agree, on condition that after a year from this date Jeuriaen Fradell shall turn over in payment his house and lot situated on the highway and a sound cow, whereupon Tonis Nyssen shall have no further claim.

Lambert Clomp, plaintiff, vs. Cornelis Teunesen, defendant. Ordered that the defendant appear in person.

[248] On March 8, 1646 [1]

The answer of Everardus Bogardus, minister, dated the 8th of March, having been read, it is ordered that if he has any further objections to make, either against the witnesses or otherwise against the proceedings, he must present the same within eight days and state the occasion which the honorable

---

[1] Revised from Doc. Rel. Col. Hist. N. Y., 14:72, reprinted in Eccl. Rec. N. Y., 1:199.

director and council have given him for abusing them from the chair of truth and for refusing to obey their order; in default whereof we shall proceed to pronounce judgment in the case, notwithstanding his subterfuges. This day, March 8, 1646.

Lambert Clomp, plaintiff, vs. Cornelis Tonisen, defendant, for delivery of the sloop Farnambuco. After examination of the documents and the acknowledgment of the defendant, it is ordered that the contract made in regard to the sloop shall remain in force and be carried out.

Oloff Stevensen, plaintiff, vs. Everardus Bogardus, defendant. The accusation of said defendant having been read, it is ordered that Oloff Stevensen shall make answer thereto in eight days.

March 9

Whereas the honorable Fiscal vander Hoykens has requested us, the director and council, that provisional curators might be appointed over the children and property left by the late Lyntjen Martens, wife of Adam Roelantsen, until the arrival of the father or definite news from him, we find the same to be highly necessary and can not select for the purpose any more fit persons than the four nearest neighbors, to wit: Philip Geraerdj, Hans Kirsteede, surgeon, Jan Stevensen, schoolmaster, and Oloff Stevensen, commissary in the store. Therefore, we have appointed the same, as we hereby do, curators of the children and property aforesaid until the above mentioned time. Thus done in our council in Fort Amsterdam, the 9th of March 1646.

Robbert Coppingh, plaintiff, vs. Claes Jansen, defendant. Plaintiff represents in writing that defendant, together with

Roelandt Hackwaert, bound himself as surety and co-principal to pay him, plaintiff, the sum of three hundred guilders, as appears from the signature of the above named Claes Jansen. He therefore demands payment of the aforesaid sum. Defendant denies that he signed as surety or principal and says that he was deceived and that [the value of] his signature does not extend beyond that of a witness, the more so as the writing was not read to him when the signing took place; which he offers to confirm on oath.

The honorable director general and council of New Netherland having seen the complaint and written document of the plaintiff, together with the defendant's denial and offer to take an oath, it is ordered that Robbert Coppingh shall bring a sworn certificate from Robbert Dunsterre and Willem Durant, or one of them, that the aforesaid bond was word for word read to Claes Jansen before he signed it and that he signed it, not as a witness, but as a surety and co-principal; and when this is proved, Robbert Coppin shall receive justice as is proper.

[249] Lambert Clomp, plaintiff, vs. Cornelis Teunesen, defendant, demanding that the defendant shall accept the sloop according to the agreement signed by him. Defendant denies that he signed the contract produced by the plaintiff and says that he was not here when the contract was made.

Ordered that the defendant prove that he was not here when the signing took place.

Tonis Nyssen, plaintiff, vs. Jeuriaen Fradel, who married the widow of the late Hendrick de Boer, defendant, for payment of fl. 1500. Ordered that Tonis prove the claim and that

Jeuriaen give evidence of what óld Jan, after he was wounded, said about what old Jan had received from Hendrick de Boer.

Oloff Stevensen, plaintiff, vs. Everardus Bogardus, defendant, for slander. Plaintiff demands proof of what the defendant lays to his charge in his answer dated the 22d of February, denying the same firmly. Ordered that the defendant prove the same in eight days.

[1] Whereas Domine Bogardus has thus far not answered the papers sent him on the 8th of February, he is hereby ordered to answer them on the next court day and to give the reason why he calumniated the magistrate from the chair of truth and in his writings.

Claes van Elslandt, plaintiff, vs. Sybolt Clasen, defendant. Plaintiff demands security for the claim which he makes on the part of Mr. van Twiller. Ordered that the defendant give security, and if the debt be found just, the defendant is to pay interest on the money.

March 15

Oloff Stevensen, plaintiff, vs. Everardus Bogardus, minister, defendant, for slander. Defendant makes written answer to plaintiff's denial and accuses him, plaintiff, anew of having threatened the honorable directors, as stated in defendant's writing of March 15. Plaintiff accuses defendant as previously of slander and defamation and maintains that he is not worthy to be a minister, inasmuch as he fails to prove that plaintiff

---

[1] Revised from Doc. Rel. Col. Hist. N. Y., 14:72; reprinted in Eccl. Rec. N. Y., 1:199.

enriched himself with his master's goods, which is the first
point to be proved. As to the other charge in his answer, he
protests that it is false until it is absolutely proved and
asks prompt judgment. Ordered for the second time that defendant
must prove his allegations in the space of eight days.

[250] March 15, 16[46] [1]

The court having examined the document dated March 15, 1646,
delivered by the messenger on the part of Everardus Bogardus,
minister, it is ordered for the second time that defendant declare
at the next session whether he has any further objections against
the witnesses or other points in the proceedings and, if he has
none, to state the reasons which moved him to slander the director
and council from the chair of truth and to disobey their order.
In default whereof the case shall be adjudged.

Tonis Nyssen, plaintiff, vs. Jacob Stevensen, defendant,
for payment of fl. 26:6. Plaintiff demands payment of fl. 26:6.
Defendant acknowledges the debt. Ordered that defendant is to
pay within six weeks, in default whereof the garment may be sold.

March 22, 1646

Oloff Stevensen, plaintiff, vs. Everardus Bogardus, minister,
defendant. Defendant produces written interrogatories and
depositions. Ordered that the deponents swear to the depositions
before the director and council.

[1] Everardus Bogardus, minister, has delivered in court an
answer to the resolution of the 15th of March and previous dates,
wherein he declares that for the present he will not enter

[1] Revised from Doc. Rel. Col. Hist. N. Y., 14:72;
reprinted in Eccl. Rec. N. Y., 1:199.

further or deeper into the matter, neither as to the evidence or the rest of the proceedings, and whereas he, Bogardus, has rejected the director and council as judges, although we, by virtue of the commission grantedtto us by their High Mightinesses, his Highness and the honorable directors, are qualified to decide the case without hesitation, as it concerns our office and through us the authority of our superiors, yet, in order to obviate all occasion for criticism, we are content to place our case in the hands of impartial judges of the Reformed religion, such as Domine Johannes Megapolensis, Mr. Douthy, both ministers, and three impartial [church] members of this province, provided that Bogardus shall submit his case, as we do, to their judgment and that in the meanwhile he shall not privately or publicly, directly or indirectly, by abuse or calumny offend the director and council; and if meanwhile another director and other councilors arrive here, we are content to place the matter in their hands. On which he is ordered to communicate his resolution on the 12th of April next. This day, the 22d of March 1646, in council in New Amsterdam.

[251]   April 12, anno 1646 [1]

Having seen the answer of Everardus Bogardus, minister, delivered in writing on the 12th of April, whereby he refuses the civil offer made to him by the director and council on the 22d of March last, to leave the [decision of the] suit against him in the hands of two Reformed ministers and some impartial [church] members of this country, but appeals to the coming of

---

[1] Revised from Doc. Rel. Col. Hist. N. Y., 14:72-73; reprinted in Eccl. Rec. N. Y., 1:199-200.

a new director and council, and whereas we are uncertain as to
the time when a new director may arrive, we can not neglect to
put a stop to the disorders and scandals which have prevailed
hitherto, but are resolved to proceed with the suit. We therefore order that an answer to his last writing delivered to us
shall be sent to him, Domine Bogardus, within eight days, to be
replied to by him for the last time on the 26th of this month,
in default whereof the case shall be decided.

Jan Onderhil, plaintiff, vs. Jan Joons, [1] defendant.
Plaintiff says that defendant entered into a contract to serve
him until after haying time and produces various depositions to
that effect. Defendant asks copies of the depositions, which
are allowed him on condition that he make answer hereto in eight
days, on pain of having judgment given against him.

Jan Onderhil, plaintiff, vs. Sergeant Huybert, defendant.
Plaintiff complains that defendant hired his servant without his
consent. Ordered that plaintiff prove his assertion.

Joris Wolsie, appearing for Tomas Willit, plaintiff, vs.
Cornelis Tonisen, defendant, for the balance of the purchase
money of a house. Ordered that defendant may not sell the
house until Tomas Willit's wife is paid.

Barent Jacobsen, plaintiff, vs. Jan Joons, defendant, for
fl. 25:18. Defendant denies the debt and asks proof.

Creupel Bos, [2] plaintiff, vs. Piter Cornelissen, defendant,
for rent of a certain parcel of land. Defendant promises to
keep his agreement.

---

[1] John Jones.
[2] Literally: Cripple Bush.

Oloff Stevensen, plaintiff, vs. Everardus Bogardus, minister, defendant. Default.

Ordered, as before, that the defendant shall cause his witnesses to appear personally in court and shall further bring in such evidence as he can produce to prove his accusations against the plaintiff.

[252] On April [19 anno] 1646, New Amsterdam

Oloff Stevensen, plaintiff, vs. Everardus Bogardus, defendant. Bogardus produces two witnesses against Oloff Stevensen in the case of slander.

The fiscal, plaintiff, vs. Borger Jorisen, defendant, alleging that the defendant tapped without having paid the excise on beer. Ordered that the fiscal prove in eight days that Borger tapped beer. As to the road which has been made in front of his door, he [the defendant] must rail or fence it off, so that no persons can fall into [the water] and see to it that there be a good wagon road.

Willem Goulder, plaintiff, vs. Tomas Gridj, defendant. 1st default.

On April 26, 1646

The fiscal, plaintiff, vs. Borger Jorisen, defendant, because the defendant tapped beer at his house and sold it by the can without having paid the excise.

Having seen the fiscal's complaint against Borger Jorisen on account of smuggled beer which he tapped at his house, retailed by the can and sold at eight stivers the vaen; [1] the

---

[1] One vaen equals 5.12 quarts.

defendant's confession that he and some company drank three half-barrels in his house which had not been entered and that he retailed in his house four vanen by the can, and that he is not willing to swear that he did not sell any more beer for money without having entered it; all of which tends to the prejudice of the Company; therefore, we condemn the defendant, as we do hereby, to pay a fine of fl. 25, for such benefit as may be proper; and if he commit a similar offense again, said Borger shall forfeit fl. 300.

The fiscal, plaintiff, vs. Maria de Truy, defendant, for having tapped to the Indians contrary to the ordinance. Ordered that the fiscal prove his charge.

Willem Gouder, plaintiff, vs. Tomas Gridj, defendant. 1st default.

The answer having been read of Domine Bogardus, sent by the messenger on the 26th of April, wherein, as in his preceding [answer], he persists [in his charges], with many idle threatening words, it is ordered that the case shall be decided on the available documents, etc.

Oloff Stevensen, plaintiff, vs. Everardus Bogardus, minister, defendant, who sent a written answer by the messenger. Whereas Domine Bogardus says that he has still other things to say against Oloff Stevensen, it is ordered that he, the defendant, shall personally appear on the next court day and present his charges with the evidence in support thereof, in default whereof the defendant shall be debarred from all exceptions and judgment shall be given on the basis of the available documents. Furthermore, the plaintiff shall show cause why the evidence should be rejected.

[253]   May 1, 1646

Jan de Fries, plaintiff, vs. Tobias Esaias and Doom
Hendricksen, defendants. Plaintiff says that the testimony
given by the defendants on July 27, 1645, at the request of
Gysbert de Leuw, is untrue. Ordered that de Fries prove that
defendants testified falsely.

May 3, 1646

Cornelis Teunesen, plaintiff, vs. Cornelis Mauritsen,
defendant, for payment of fl. 77. Parties on both sides having
been heard, as well as the arbitrators who made the agreement
and who declare that the defendant was promised fl. 77 at once
if the plaintiff sold the house for cash payment, or else, if
he sold it on credit, after two months, it is ordered that the
decision of the arbitrators shall be carried out and that the
money shall remain in Mr. Wilcocx's hands until Cornelis Mauritsz
shall have been paid by the plaintiff or Wilcocx.

Jan Damen, plaintiff, vs. Jan Wilcocx, defendant. Plaintiff
says that under an agreement with Wilcocx he was to receive for
one hundred guilders of loose seawan whole beavers at market
price. Ordered that Jan Damen shall retain possession of his
money until Wilcocx obtain beavers here, when he shall have to
pay promptly.

Everardus Bogardus appeared in court and produced
interrogatories on which Jacob Wolphersen and Hendrick Kip are
to be examined. They request time. Ordered here that they
shall answer yes or no next Tuesday, at ten o'clock.

Jan de Fries, plaintiff, vs. Gysbert de Leuw, defendant, for slander. Default.

Willem Goulder, plaintiff, vs. Tomas Gridj, defendant. 3d default. Three defaults having been entered for non-appearance, the defendant is condemned to pay fl. 20.

La Violette, plaintiff, vs. Michiel Piket, defendant. 1st default.

May 8

Hans Tymonsen, gunner of the ship T'Amandere, plaintiff, vs. Jan Snediger, defendant, alleging that the defendant called him a branded thief. The defendant says that he knows nothing of the plaintiff but what is honest and honorable and that in using the opprobious words he did not mean the plaintiff.

The fiscal, plaintiff, vs. Borger Jorisen, defendant, for slander which the defendant uttered to the defamation of the fiscal. The defendant acknowledges his fault, begs the fiscal's pardon and promises not to repeat the offense. As to the fine, it is ordered that the parties shall choose two referees.

[254] May 18, 1646

Hendrick Hendrickssen from Doesborgh, plaintiff, vs. Annitjen, wife of Arent Steffeniersen, defendant, because she, the defendant, accused the plaintiff of having eaten pork which looked like hers. The defendant declares that she knows nothing of the plaintiff but what is honest and honorable and if she said anything, she is sorry for it. Whereupon the defendant is ordered to keep silence in the future; the parties are dismissed and the case is definitely closed.

May 26

At the request of the honorable fiscal Sent Nannincksen,
gunner's mate of the ship _Tamandere_, Hendrick Antonissen, steward,
and Hans Tymonsen from Ditmersen, gunner, have been examined
respecting powder and lead belonging to the ship, which one of
them is alleged to have sold, as appears more at large from the
interrogatories.

May 31

Whereas Cornelis Melyn, an inhabitant here, sowed and
fenced in a certain piece of land lying north of the Company's
garden, taking more land than belongs to him, sweeping away with
a curve behind the said garden, and making use of the earth and
sods of the Company's land and the common road to inclose the
said land; therefore, on complaint of the fiscal, the court
inspected the land on the 31st of May and found the situation
to be as above described. And although this is a criminal
offense and of grave consequence, according to the Imperial
statutes, chapter xxxvij, page 23, the director and council have
nevertheless consented that said Melyn shall cut his grain and
then without further delay deliver up the Company's land in the
same condition as it was in the spring, which he promises to do
and for which he will sign an agreement; and if any damage should
occur through rain storm or other cause, the same must be made
good by him.

Jan Damen, plaintiff, vs. Evert Pels, defendant, about
freight of 76 schepels of wheat. It is decided that the
plaintiff is to receive the grain free of charge at the Manhatans.

Hillegont Joris, plaintiff, vs. Piter Wyncoop, defendant.
Plaintiff demands the reason why defendant keeps her husband
under arrest in the colony. Defendant answers for debt and if
she, plaintiff, is willing to pay, he promises to release her
husband. Ordered, that as the case is pending in Rensselaerswyck
it must be decided there, unless the parties now agree here.

Piter Jacobsen, plaintiff, vs. Mr. Dollingh, defendant, for
payment of a pipe of wine which is said to belong to Seger
Teunesen and which pipe of wine Dirck Jacobsen, mate of the
St. Pieter, was to receive from Dollingh in Madera. Dollingh
produces a receipt showing that he paid Dirck Jacobsen according
to the order. Defendant is given a fortnight in which to make
his defense.

[255] May 31, 1646

Dirck Clasen, plaintiff, vs. Jan Teunesen, defendant, on
account of the purchase of a coat of fl. 54. Defendant says
that he owes only fl. 42. A bond is produced which, after
deduction [of the payments made on it], is found to amount to
not more than fl. 3:7, which will be deducted from the coat
aforesaid. Ordered that Jan Teunesen must discharge Dirck Clasen
or pay the costs of the suit.

The fiscal, plaintiff, vs. Borger Jorisen, defendant, in a
case of slander. Ordered that defendant settle with the fiscal
if possible; otherwise, if the case come again before us, it
shall be disposed of.

The fiscal, plaintiff, vs. Jorse Wolsy, defendant. Plaintiff,
having seized some powder which was not entered, demands its

confiscation. Defendant says that it belongs to Allerton, his master, and requests delay until his master shall have come back from New England; which is granted him.

June 1, 1646

Pater Vaer, plaintiff, vs. Jan Wilcocx, defendant, regarding the purchase of a Negro woman. Plaintiff demands delivery. Defendant is willing to make delivery. Ordered that the defendant satisfy the Swedish governor and Pater Vaer.

The fiscal, plaintiff, vs. Hans Tymonsen from Ditmersen, gunner of the ship **Tamandere**. The gunner is asked in court where he sold the Company's powder which he poured from the cartouches [1] into a pail. As the defendant remains obstinate, it is ordered that he be imprisoned and next put to torture if in the meantime he makes no confession.

The fiscal, plaintiff, vs. Borger Jorisen. 1 default.

June 7

Nicolaes Coorn, sheriff of the colony of Renselaerswyck, plaintiff, vs. Antony de Hooges, secretary of the colony aforesaid. Plaintiff presents his complaint in writing. Defendant asks copy in order to answer to-morrow.

Nicolaes Coorn, plaintiff, vs. Sybolt Clasen, defendant, for payment of fl. 120 for delivery of tiles. Defendant acknowledges the debt and offers to pay, provided he may have an extension of time.

---

[1] Cardoesen; large cartridges fired from cannon.

Piter Wyncoop, plaintiff, vs. Antony de Hooges, defendant, because de Hooges attempted to arrest Piter Wyncoop while in bed. Plaintiff wants to know the reason. Defendant is to answer to-morrow.

Ensign Gysbert de Leuw, plaintiff, vs. Luycas Elbertsen, defendant, defendant having said that plaintiff was challenged by Gysbert Cornelisen to fight with the sword. Defendant denies that he said so and declares that he knows nothing that reflects on the ensign's honor and character. He is to pay the costs of the suit.

[256] On June 7, 1646

Cors Pitersen, plaintiff, vs. Jan Lichtvoet, defendant, for payment of 40s. English for freight. Ordered, that plaintiff prove the justice of his claim.

Cornelio van[der] Hoykens, fiscal, plaintiff, vs. Borger Jorisen, for slander and threats. The plaintiff, presenting his complaint in writing, shows by depositions that the defendant abused the plaintiff as a villain and threatened to take some of his flesh yet before he, the plaintiff, left the country. And whereas he, the defendant, acknowledged it and begged for pardon, he was allowed to make satisfaction to the fiscal according to the award of referees, but when they met, he made fun of them, so that the fiscal, ex-officio, was obliged to summon the defendant to appear in court for the third time. We therefore condemn the defendant, as we do hereby, to pay a fine of sixty guilders, with costs, and to remain in prison until he has paid the said 60 guilders. And whereas he, the condemned, while

sentence was being pronounced by us, said with threatening language:
"That will do; only give me papers to that effect;" he shall,
after paying, remain confined in chains in the said prison for
another twenty-four hours, on pain of arbitrary correction if
hereafter he be found to have done or spoken anything to the
prejudice of the Company or its honorable officers.

Lysbet Tyssen, plaintiff, vs. Tomas Bacxter, defendant,
for payment of fl. 75. Defendant acknowledges that he received
fl. 50 and two hides, so that the entire sum ammounts to fl. 63:10.
He is condemned to pay.

Piter Jacobsen, plaintiff, vs. Tomas Bacxter, defendant,
for payment of fl. 253, on which fl. 5 are paid. Defendant
acknowledges the debt. He is condemned to pay at **plaintiff's**
discretion.

Joris Dircksen, plaintiff, vs. Jan de Cuyper, [1] defendant,
for defendant having drawn his knife on him, plaintiff. Ordered
that the fiscal make inquiry.

June 8

Cors Pitersen, plaintiff, vs. Jan Lichtvoet, defendant.
Plaintiff demands payment and submits the matter to the
discretion of Jacob Wolphersen.

Dirck Volckersen, plaintiff, **vs.** Antony de Hooges, defendant,
for damages suffered through defendant's detention of the sloop
Renselaerswyck. The complaint and the answer of parties having
been read, de Hooges is discharged and plaintiff ordered to
institute his action against Nicolaes Coorn.

---

[1] Jan, the cooper.

Piter Wyncoop, plaintiff, vs. Antony de Hooges, defendant.
Parties have settled in court.

[257]   June 8, 1646

Piter Wyncoop, plaintiff, vs. Jan Cornelisen, defendant,
for payment of fl. [149:18]. [1] As defendant acknowledges part
of the debt, he is ordered to pay now as much as he acknowledges
and to prove through Piter Hertgers that he paid the balance,
as he claims.

Piter Wyncoop, plaintiff, vs. Adriaen van[der] Donck,
defendant, for payment of fl. 134:[8], as appears by a certain
bond signed by Antony de Hooges. Whereas said de Hooges
acknowledges the debt and promises to pay Piter Wyncoop in
current seawan within six weeks from this date in the colony of
Renselaer[swyck], said de Hooges is condemned to fulfil his
promise in the time aforesaid.

Nicolaes Coorn, sheriff of the colony of Renselaerswyck,
plaintiff, vs. Antony de Hooges, chief commissary, defendant,on
account of a certain dispute between parties about the sloop
Renselaerswyck and other matters. As the action is instituted
above, in the colony, and as ship are daily expected with which
apparently other orders [for the government] of the colony are
to come, we have sent back the case, in order that the parties
may get ready to prosecute the suit at that time.

Jacob Hendricksen, soldier, is commanded not to trespass
any more on the lot of Dirck Volckersen and not to molest Dirck
any more, on pain of punishment.

---

[1] Original figures destroyed. The amount inserted is taken
from O'Callaghan's translation.

11 June [1]

Whereas Oloff Stevensen, deacon and commissary of merchandise and the store, has presented to us a petition wherein he requests that four referees may be appointed to us to settle the difficulty which he has with Domine Everardus Bogardus, minister here, to which said Bogardus also consents, according to his own writing delivered to us by him, Oloff; therefore, we do not object to do so and hereby appoint the persons of Domine Megapolensis, Mr. de Hooges, Jonker Adriaen Verdonck and Laurens van Heusden, commissary, whom we kindly request and also authorize and fully empower to decide and settle the aforesaid question as far as their honors shall be able to do so, reserving the action which the honorable fiscal may have against Oloff Stevensz. Thus done in Fort Amsterdam, the 11th of June anno 1646.

The honorable director and council to you, Rev. Bogardus, minister here: [1]

Although the offer we made your Reverence to submit our case to the judgment of impartial men, as you requested, sufficiently proves the justice of our proceedings and the inclination we have for peace, just as your refusal proves the contrary, nevertheless, the respect we bear the dignity of the ministry and the desire for your Reverence's welfare prompt us once more, seeing that the opportunity therefor now presents itself, to try to submit the case to those whom we had nominated thereto, namely, the ministers Domine Johannes Megapolensis and

---

[1] Revised from Doc. Rel. Col. Hist. N. Y., 14:73.

Mr. Douthey and such other impartial members as you yourself
will be willing to select; protesting in case of refusal that
we shall proceed to judgment. And in order that we may with
more fervor pray God in the midst of the congregation that He
would dispose your and our hearts to a Christian concord, we
request that Domine Megapolensis may preach next Sunday, as has
always been his custom and, being here, make us partakers of the
gifts which God has granted him. Your Reverence will be pleased
to gratify us in this matter to the extent that we may hear him
on that occasion. Relying hereon and not doubting that your
Reverence will have no objection to it, seeing the justice of
our request, we shall await your Reverence's answer thereto today
and to the preceding matter next Thursday, being the 14th of
June.

[258] Whereas we, the under signed, are authorized by the
honorable director and council of New Netherland as far as
possible to settle the question between Domine Bogardus and Oloff
Stevensen, we have examined and considered all the documents in
the proceedings and find that Oloff Stevensen is not guilty
according to the commission granted to him by the honorable
commander and that Domine Bogardus said that had he known of it
or the same been shown to him he should never have had such
intentions; Therefore, we have unanimously decided and concluded
that the question between the aforesaid persons regarding the
indigo, beavers and whatever else may appertain thereto shall be
from now on finally settled, disposed of and extinguished, without hereafter being in any way revived on either side. And in

regard to the complaints which may be made and instituted in
consequence of this case against Domine Bogardus, these shall
be void and not tend to his prejudice at any future time.

Done at Manhattan this 11th of June anno 1646. The original
was signed by Johannes Megapolensis, ecclesiastic in Renselaerswyck,
Antony de Hooges, Laurens van Heusden and Adriaen van[der] Donck.

Here follows the approval of the honorable director general
and council of New Netherland.

Whereas a certain suit has for a long time been pending
before us between Oloff Stevensen, deacon and commissary of
merchandise and the store of the West India Company, plaintiff
in a case of slander, and Domine Everardus Bogardus, minister,
defendant, in which after long litigation, the defendant failing
to produce proof, we were ready to pronounce judgment, the parties
respectively requested us to order and authorize four referees
to decide the case, which, in consideration of the standing of
the persons, was done and authorized.

The said [referees] having decided the question to the
satisfaction of the parties, they have requested that the same
be approved and confirmed by us, as we do hereby approve and
confirm the same to be firm and binding as if the decision were
pronounced by ourselves. Thus done in council in Fort Amsterdam
in New Netherland, the 12th of June anno 1646.

[258] Ordinance establishing a court of justice in
Breuckelen [1]

We, Willem Kieft, director general, and the council residing
in New Netherland on behalf of the High and Mighty Lords the

---

[1] Revised from Laws and Ordinances of New Netherland, pp. 58-59.

States General, his Highness of Orange and the honorable directors
of the General Chartered West India Company,

To all those who shall see these presents or hear them
read, Greeting.

Whereas on the 21st of May last, by the proprietors of
Breuckelen, situated on Long Island, Jan Eversen Bout and Huych
Aertsen were unanimously chosen as schepens to decide all questions
which may arise as they shall deem proper, according to the
Exemptions of New Netherland granted to particular colonies,
which election is subscribed by them, with express stipulation
that if any one refuses to submit in the matter aforesaid to said
Jan Eversen and Huych Aertsen, he shall forfeit the right which
he claims to the land in the allotment of Breuckelen; Therefore,
in order that everything may be done with greater authority, we,
the director and council aforesaid have authorized and appointed,
and hereby do authorize the said Jan Eversen and Huych Aertsen
to be schepens of Breuckelen. And in case Jan Eversen and Huych
Aertsen do hereafter find the labor too burdensome, they shall
be at liberty to select from among the inhabitants of Breuckelen
and to adjoin to themselves two more [schepens].

We charge and command every inhabitant of Breuckelen to
acknowledge and respect the abovenamed Jan Eversen and Huych
Aertsen as their schepens, and whoever shall be found to show
himself refractory toward them shall forfeit his share as above
stated. Thus done in council in Fort Amsterdam in New Netherland.

Ordinance providing for the proper drawing up of legal instruments [1]

[259] June 12, 1646

Whereas it is daily learned that, contrary to the good faith
and the orders of the honorable States General and our ordinance
published in the year 16[ ], [2] grave mistakes occur in the
writing and drawing up of evidence of the truth by private
individuals who are neither bound thereto by oath, nor called
thereto by authority, whereby often many things are written to
the advantage of those who have the affidavits drawn up, interspersed with sinister, obscure and dubious words, oftentimes
contrary to the meaning of the affiants, to the great prejudice
and damage of the parties; Therefore, in order to prevent this
result, dangerous in a republic, and to promote the knowledge
of the truth necessary in all courts, we annul and declare
invalid, as we do hereby annul and declare invalid, all affidavits,
interrogatories and other instruments serving as evidence which
are written by private individuals and not confirmed by oath
before the court here or other magistrates, as we also from
henceforth annul all affidavits which hereafter are not written
by the secretary or other duly authorized person, likewise all
contracts, wills, agreements and other important documents,
unless, through necessity, it should be impossible to call on
such person. This day, the 12th of June 1646.

---

[1] Revised from Laws and Ordinances of New Netherland,
p. 59.

[2] Date left blank. See Ordinances of Aug. 19, 1638, and
Aug. 9, 1640.

[260] 14th of June

Cornelio van[der] Hoykens, fiscal, plaintiff, vs. Rem
Jansen, [1] chief boatswain of the ship T'Amandere, prisoner,
defendant. Plaintiff presents his complaint in writing and
demands justice. Defendant admits that he knew that the former
skipper had stolen three Negro women from the said ship and that
he, the prisoner, received three pieces of eight from the proceeds, but says that he gave the skipper something else in return.
Ordered that the fiscal make further inquiry before the next
court day.

Cornelio van[der] Hoykens, fiscal, plaintiff, vs.
Hendrick Antonisen, steward of the ship T'Amandere, prisoner.
Plaintiff in writing demands sentence of the prisoner for neglect
of duty in remaining on shore during the night without leave.
Defendant demands copy of the complaint, which shall be given
him.

Isaack Allerton, plaintiff, vs. the honorable fiscal,
defendant, for powder seized by defendant. Whereas the plaintiff
has offered to confirm by oath that the aforesaid powder was
received at his house by his servant during his absence and
without his knowledge, the fiscal is ordered to restore the
aforesaid powder, provided the servant pay a fine of fl. 25.

The honorable fiscal, plaintiff, vs. Jan de Vries, defendant,
for slander and scandalous remarks against the honorable
director and his commission. Ordered that a copy of the affidavit
shall be delivered to the defendant.

---

[1] Under date of June 17, 1646, given as Rem Dircksen.

Tomas Bacxter, plaintiff, vs. Willem Bredenbent, defendant, for payment of fl. 50. The court having heard the demand and the answer, the defendant is condemned to pay fl. 25.

Tomas Bacxter, plaintiff, vs. Teunes Tomassen, defendant, for payment of fl. 36. As the defendant admits the debt he is condemned to pay.

[1]7th of June

The fiscal, plaintiff, vs. Rem Dircksz, chief boatswain of the ship T'Amandere, a prisoner. Having seen the complaint and the affidavits which the fiscal produces, whereby it appears that he, [the prisoner], struck the supercargo van Heusden on board and threatened him with a knife; having also heard said prisoner's defense and his acknowledgment that he knew that 3 Negroes had gone secretly on shore at the Barbadoes without the supercargo's knowledge and that the former skipper who had stolen them presented him with pieces of eight; also, that contrary to the ordinance he has remained on shore at night; all of which are matters of grave consequence and tend to the serious prejudice of the honorable West India Company, we, therefore, condemn, as we hereby do, the aforesaid Rem Dircksen to leap three times from the yard arm, to be flogged by all the members of the crew and further to be immediately dismissed from the ship and to forfeit three months' wages for the benefit of the fiscal.

[261] The 17th of June 1646

The honorable fiscal, plaintiff, vs. Hendrick Antonisen, steward of the ship T'Amandere a prisoner. Having seen the complaint of the fiscal against Hendrick Antonisen, a prisoner, and

the latter's defense, by which it appears that at divers times
he remained on shore at night without leave, neglected the
honorable Company's provisions on board, concealed a portion of
them and did not report what was in the ship, also brought on
shore and sold sweet oil, secretly took on board two barrels of
sugar at the Reciff without entering them and brought them here,
which are matters of grave consequences and prejudice to the
honorable West India Company; therefore, we condemn, as we hereby
do, the said steward to leap three times from the yard arm and
to be flogged by all the ship's crew; the sugar to be confiscated
and the prisoner to be permanently dismissed from the ship.

24th of June 1646

Fredrick Lubbersen, plaintiff, vs. Dirck Volckersen, defendant,
for [payment of] stipulated freight. Parties agree in court to
submit their case to arbitrators.

The wife of Mr. Pauwel, plaintiff, vs. the wife of Jan Lichtvoet,
defendant, for slander. Ordered that the fiscal shall take charge
of the case.

The wife of Jeuriaen Blanck, plaintiff, vs. Symon Joosten,
defendant, for purchase of two beaver coats. Parties agree that
the defendant shall give a beaver to boot.

Lambert Clomp, plaintiff, vs. Cornelis Teunesen, defendant,
for payment of fl. 50. Defendant admits the debt and promises
to pay on his return from the South with Jeuriaen Blanck.

Jacob Stoffelsen, plaintiff, vs. Piter Wolphersen, defendant,
for hire of a horse. Defendant declares on oath that he is not
indebted to the plaintiff. Therefore, plaintiff's suit is
dismissed.

Isaack Abrahamsen, plaintiff, vs. Mr. Dollingh, defendant,
[for money due] in chartering plaintiff's sloop. Whereas the
plaintiff went with his sloop to the Manhatans instead of to
Stamfoort, plaintiff is ordered to seek his remedy against those
who employed him.

Jan Heyn, plaintiff, vs. Mr. Dollingh, defendant. Ordered
that plaintiff shall wait until Mr. Wytingh shall again pass
through here.

The honorable fiscal, plaintiff, vs. Jan de Fries, defendant.
Ordered that defendant shall deliver a copy of his statement.

Anthony Jansen, plaintiff, vs. Hendrick Smith, defendant,
as to a difference about their lot. Ordered that the place shall
be inspected.

Abigael Cleer, plaintiff, vs. Willem Goulder's wife, defendant,
for slander. Whereas the plaintiff produces witnesses to prove
the slander and the defendant does not maintain his charges, he
is condemned to pay the costs and ordered to let said Abigael
alone in peace.

[262]   [25th of June 1646]

The honorable director general and council of New Netherland,
having seen the criminal charges of the fiscal against Jan Creoly,
Negro slave of the honorable Company, from which it appears that
Jan Creoly aforesaid is accused by some Negroes of having committed
sodomy by force with a boy of about ten years, named Manuel
Congo, also a Negro, whereupon the said Jan Creoly was placed in
confinement and examined in the presence of the aforesaid boy,
who without being threatened in any way confessed to the deed in

the presence of the prisoner. After the previous examination
the aforesaid Jan Creoly, at present a prisoner, has without
torture and while free from irons confessed having committed
sodomy with the aforesaid boy and that he had also committed
the said heinous and abominable crime on the island of Curaçao,
on account of which sins God Almighty overthrew Sodom and Gamorrah
of the plain and exterminated the inhabitants from the earth.
(Genesis, ch. 19. See also God's covenant, Leviticus, ch. 18,
v. 22; and in the same chapter, v. 29, God says: "For whosoever
shall commit any of these abominations, even the souls that commit
them shall be cut off from among their people.") For which
reason such a man is not worthy to associate with mankind and
the crime on account of its heinousness may not be tolerated or
suffered, in order that the wrath of God may not descend upon
us as it did upon Sodom. Therefore, having invoked the name of
God so as to pass a just judgment and wishing to do justice, we
condemn the said Jan Creoly, as we do hereby, to be brought to
the place of justice to be strangled there to death and his
body to be burned to ashes, as an example to others. This day,
the 25th of June 1646.

The honorable director general and council of New Netherland
having examined Manual Congo, aged about ten years, regarding
the crime committed on him by Jan Creoly, Negro, he confesses
that the same was committed by force and violence, as those who
were present declared and which in view of the abomination is
not described here, the said Creoly having likewise confessed
that he committed the crime by force, without the consent of

the boy. And although according to law a person with whom
sodomy has been committed deserves to be put to death, yet, in
view of the innocence and youth of the boy, we have ordered that
he be brought to the place where Jan Creoly shall be executed
and that he be tied to a post, with wood piled around him, and
be made to view the execution and be beaten with rods. This
day, the 25th of June 1646, this sentence was executed.

[263] June [28], 1646

Joris Homs, plaintiff, vs. Tonis Nyssen, defendant, for
payment of fl. 40. The defendant acknowledges the debt and
says that he must pay the child of the said Homs here first
when a ship of the Company arrives, and this not in money, but
in clothes. Ordered that the defendant shall promptly fulfil
this obligation.

On this day the court messenger has delivered in court a
lampoon signed by Jan de Fries, serving as a rebuttal to the
reply of the fiscal, entitled: "To the honorable Council of
Justice in Fort Amsterdam." And whereas this is contrary to
the usual custom and the order of the honorable gentlemen and
tends to the disparagement of the honorable director and council
of New Netherland, it is ordered that the same shall be ignored
and be returned by the messenger, with order to summon the said
de Vries to appear in person on next Thursday, being the 5th of
July, on pain of being placed in confinement.

5th of July 1646

The fiscal, plaintiff, vs. Jan de Vries, defendant. Case
is put over until the next court day and parties are ordered

meanwhile to make everything ready that is needed or serviceable for their prosecution or defense.

The fiscal, plaintiff, vs. Jan Snediger, defendant, for selling a gun that did not belong to him. Defendant admits having sold to Piter Wolphersen a gun which had long stood in his house without his knowing to whom it belonged. Case put over until the next court day to examine the witnesses.

Examination in court of Tomas Gridj, at present a prisoner, aged 60 years, from Devenschier in old England, charged by Jan Joons with and suspected of having stolen silverware and other goods and having tried to induce the said Joons and others to commit theft also. Which is partly admitted by said Gridj, except that he says that he has not stolen any silverware, whereupon it is ordered that he shall be again placed under arrest and that the fiscal shall secure further evidence.

Maria Robberts, wife of Tomas Gridj, declares in court that Jan Joons in the winter, about Christmas, the exact date she does not remember, in the evening, when the candle was lit, brought to her house the shirts of Spyser, which she well knew were stolen and that the same were put away by her husband.

6th of July

Tomas Gridj, a prisoner, admits that he has had and kept stolen goods in his house and that the goods which were stolen at different times last winter were taken out of his house; he also acknowledges that he solicited Spyser's nephew, a young man of about 18 years, to steal his uncle's grain, lead and whatever else he could lay his hands on and bring them to him, which the aforesaid young man has also declared to be so, and

whereas Gridj remains obstinate in denying that he stole silverware, notwithstanding, the strong indications we have against
him, it is ordered that he be put to the torture.

[264] 10th of July

The honorable director general and council of New Netherland
having seen the criminal charges of Fiscal vander Hoykens against
Tomas Gridj, who, while free from torture and irons, has confessed that he had concealed stolen goods, well knowing that
they were stolen; also that he converted the stolen goods to
his own use, which is directly contrary to law and order and
tends to very grave consequences and cannot be tolerated; therefore, we, administering justice, have condemned, as we do hereby
condemn, the said Gridj to be brought to the place where justice
is usually executed and there to be flogged with rods; and,
furthermore, to be forever banished beyond the limits of New
Netherland. This 10th of July 1646 in Fort Amsterdam.

26th of July anno 1646

The honorable fiscal, plaintiff, vs. Adam Roelantsen,
defendant, for having been to the warehouse without the knowledge
of the fiscal and there taken some linen out of his chest before
the chest had been inspected. The fiscal demands that the
defendant shall replace the linen in the warehouse. Defendant
answers that the linen was taken from him by the soldiers.

Adam Roelantsen being summoned to court for slander which
he is alleged to have uttered at Amsterdam, the defendant
declares under oath that he said nothing to the sister of Aeltjen
Douwens but "Go to New Netherland and save your sister, the whore,

who in the Bermudas was threatened by the director of New
Netherland to be put in irons."

Symon Pos, plaintiff, vs. Augustyn Heerman, defendant.
Ordered that the defendant shall personally appear next week
and bring with him all his papers serving for his defense.

Cornelis Teunesen, plaintiff, vs. Jan Wilcocx, defendant,
for the balance due to plaintiff for services rendered to
defendant on the South river. Ordered that as soon as Wilcocx
be paid by the Swedish governor by bill of exchange or in beavers,
he shall satisfy and pay the plaintiff.

The fiscal, plaintiff, vs. Jan de Fries, defendant.
Defendant is asked if he has anything more to say. Answers,
that he persists in his testimony and has nothing more to say.
Ordered that the papers in the suit shall be brought in and
then judgment shall be rendered.

The fiscal, plaintiff, vs. Jan Snediger, defendant, for
selling a gun. Case is adjourned until the next court day.

Symon Josten, plaintiff, vs. Piter Wolphersen, defendant,
for payment of fl. 204:16. Defendant admits the debt and is
ordered to pay the claim.

[265] Whereas the fiscal of New Netherland, plaintiff,
against Johan de Fries, late captain, had complained that the
defendant since his arrival here has cultivated the friendship
and society of some dangerous persons, enemies of the Company's
welfare and of this country and defamers of their authorities
notwithstanding the warning given him by the director; furthermore,
that he is leading a scandalous life, highly dangerous in this

infant republic; that he has also with unbearable arrogance
called the director a liar in the presence of the entire council,
taking hold of his Polish casse-tête with the intention of striking him, had he not been prevented; and that a few days later,
meeting Councilor La Montangne, he called him many vile names,
for which he was finally cashiered, being expressly forbidden to
give offense to any one on pain of forfeiture of all his wages,
notwithstanding which, on the 7th of June 1646, being in a tavern,
he is said in the presence of several persons to have made many
contemptuous remarks about the director and to have maintained
that the director had no power to grant commissions or to make
captains, according to the depositions of five witnesses, adding
this impudent and infamous statement, "I don't care a damn for
the firector's commission," as appears by two credible witnesses,
which induced the fiscal to bring the said de Vries before the
court. In the course of these proceedings de Vries has presented
a certain written rejoinder, changing the ordinary style of
address, full of facetious statements and not fit to be presented
to any court, tending to undermine justice, which is the foundation
of the republic; all of which are matters which can not be
tolerated in a place where it is customary to administer justice.
Nevertheless, inasmuch as de Fries, following therein the foot-
steps of some others, appears to consider us as being partial,
therefore, in order to demonstrate the justice of our proceedings
and that they are devoid of passion, we have referred the case,
as we do hereby refer the same, to the honorable directors, to
dispose thereof as their honors shall see fit. Furthermore, we

order that de Fries shall appear before their honors to defend
his case and purge himself before them, to which end he is to
depart in the first ship, direct to Holland. In addition thereto
he is expressly forbidden to return here to New Netherland until
he shall have cleared himself, without this being counted a
sentence of banishment against him or other infamous punishment.
Thus done in council in Fort Amsterdam, the 2d of August
anno 1646.

[266] 2d of August

Whereas a certain suit has been pending before us between
Johan de Fries, late captain, plaintiff, in a case of slander,
and Gysb[ert] de Leuw, defendant, wherein said defendant tried
to maintain that Elary, a certain Negro woman, who the plaintiff
claimed to be his, belongs to the Company, having been the slave
of one Juan Antonio, Portuguese, who is said to have been imprisoned
at Marinhan for treason and therefore could not dispose of his
property; all of which, he, the defendant, proves by various
depositions of persons then residing at Marinhan, to which the
plaintiff replies that he bought said Negro woman from the aforesaid Portuguese according to a certain bill of sale thereof in
his possession, maintaining furthermore that said Portugese was
not in prison for treason, but had sought refuge in Marinhan and
consequently could dispose of his property, in regard to which
matter we cannot come to an absolute decision here, and whereas
the book of resolutions of Marinhan is apparently in possession
of the honorable directors, from which it can be seen whether
the said Juan Antonio was confined for treason or not; therefore,

we refer this case to their honors to be decided by them as their
honors shall see fit. Thus done in council in Fort Amsterdam,
the 2d of August anno 1646.

Jan Damen, plaintiff, vs. Jan Dollingh, defendant, for
payment of 40 gl., being the balance of a bill of exchange for
2,040 gl. of which Mr. Jan Evence received 2,000 gl. The statements of the plaintiff and the defendant having been heard, it
is ordered that Jan Dollingh shall bring proof from Onckewey
and Jan Evens.

Ambrosius Lonnen, plaintiff, vs. Tonis Nysen, heir of Jan
Celes, defendant, for payment of 14 gl. Ordered that plaintiff
shall prove by witnesses or in writing that Jan Celes owed him
for 14 gl.

Symon Joosten, plaintiff, vs. Augustyn Heerman, defendant,
for 21 gl. which plaintiff claims he paid to the defendant on
account of Pater Vaer. Defendant says that Pater Vaer was never
indebted to him and therefore he did not receive anything on
Pater's account and offers to prove this by his book and by
Jacob Reynsen. Ordered that defendant shall prove it when he
shall have received his book.

Symon Pos, plaintiff, vs. Augustyn Heerman, defendant.
Ordered that the case be closed and that parties on both sides
shall hand in their proofs.

Jan Heyn and Evert Cornelisen, plaintiffs, vs. Jan Dollingh,
as surety for Mr. Wytingh, defendant. Plaintiffs demand from
defendant as surety the sum of 57 gl. and 12 st., for the reason
that Mr. Wytingh charged them fl. 9:12 for 36 beaver skins which
they bought at 8 gl. apiece.

The honorable director and council having seen the certificate
confirmed by oath by Davit Provoost, commissary, and the plaintiffs' own declarations, also confirmed by oath, whereby it
appears that Wytingh charged them 1 gl. and 12 st. more for each
beaver skin than they were sold for; we, therefore, condemn, as
we hereby do condemn Mr. Dollingh, as Mr. Wytingh's surety, to
tender and pay the plaintiffs the aforesaid sum of 57 gl. and
12 st., with the costs incurred, provided always that Jan Dollingh
shall have the right to recover the amount from Mr. Wytingh.

[267] Whereas, we, Willem Kieft, director general, and the
council of New Netherland, granted a commission to Willem
Albertsen Blauvelt to go privateering from here to the West
Indies or the islands thereof against the enemies of their High
Mightinesses the Lords States General of the United Netherlands
and especially within the limits of the charter granted by their
High Mightinesses to the General Chartered West India Company,
the above named captain Blauvelt and his accompanying crew did
on the 7th of May of this year with the help of God capture by
force of arms the bark St. Antonio de la Havana, laden with sugar
and tobacco, coming from Havana and bound for Campeche, which
bark was brought to New Netherland on the 8th of July last.
Therefore, after three previous proclamations between the 8th of
July last. Therefore, after three previous proclamations between
the 8th of July and this date, in which time no one has come
forward to make any objections, we, the director and council,
declare the said bark and lading a good prize, all claims which
any one hereafter may set up to the said bark and lading being

henceforth debarred. Thus done the 2d of August anno 1646, at
New Amsterdam.

On the 6th of August anno 1646

Ambrosius Lonnen, plaintiff, vs. Jan Onderhil, defendant,
for payment of 30 gl. for herding cattle. Defendant denies the
debt. Ordered that Plaintiff prove his claim.

The honorable fiscal, plaintiff, vs. Jan Snediger, defendant,
for having sold a gun which did not belong to him. Defendant
is ordered to cause Jan Eversen to be summoned to learn from
him the truth of the matter.

Haye Jansen, plaintiff, vs. Haye Jansen, that is to say,
Hendrick Jansen, defendant, for freightage due him. Defendant
promises to pay plaintiff in beavers as much as two referees
shall judge proper. At the request of the parties Jacob
Wolphersen and Oloff Stevensen are requested to inspect the
beavers which are to be given in payment, to see whether the
same are merchantable or not.

The 16th of August 1646

Jan Onderhil, plaintiff, vs. Isaack Allerton, defendant,
alleging that the defendant before his arrival here promised
the plaintiff that he, the plaintiff, would receive higher wages
from the commonalty than from the Company. Defendant denies
having made such promise and demands proof. Jan Onderhil promises
in court that he or his heirs shall nevermore trouble or molest
the defendant on account of this matter.

Jan Evance, merchant at New Haven, plaintiff, vs. Jan
Wilcocx, [defendant]. First default.

[268] On the 17th of August anno 1646

Jan Evance, merchant at New Haven, plaintiff, vs. Jan Wilcocx, defendant, for purchase of the ship <u>Abigael</u>. Plaintiff demands delivery according to the contract of sale. Defendant says that he is ready, provided a definite time is set when he is to receive his payment. Ordered that the ship shall be delivered to the purchasers and that the purchasers shall cause Governor Johan Prints to state in writing that the bond dated the 6th of July 1646, old style, shall be paid by said governor in the month of September or October; or else, that at the same time a bill of exchange for the amount of the bond must be delivered to the seller. In default thereof the purchasers shall pay interest on the money and, if the seller fail to make delivery, he shall be condemned to make good all damage, loss and interest and also pay the costs of the suit.

On the 23d of August

Dirck Volckertsen, plaintiff, vs. Laurens Pietersen, defendant, for the payment of about 150 gl. Defendant admits that he owes something. Ordered that the attachment shall remain in force and that meanwhile parties shall reach an agreement.

Claes Pietersen, plaintiff, vs. Jan Jansen from Hoorn, defendant, for attaching two shirts which the defendant claims resemble his own shirts, which are brought into court. The court never discovered any fault in Claes Pietersen to this date and order the defendant to remain silent if he can not prove that the shirts belong to him and when Seger Teunesen comes, to whom he appeals, he can then speak or hereafter keep silent.

At the request of Cosyn Gerritsen it is ordered that Hans
Hansen shall prove this day week that the rapier sold by him to
the plaintiff belonged to him and that no one has any claim to
it. In default thereof the attachment shall be vacated.

[269] On the 30th of August anno 1646, in New Amsterdam

The honorable fiscal, plaintiff, vs. Jan Wilcocx, defendant.
First default.

La Valee, plaintiff, vs. Jan Wilcocx, defendant. Parties
consent to settle through arbitrators, which they are allowed
to do.

Hans Hansen, plaintiff, vs. Cosyn Gerritsen, defendant,
for payment for the rapier. The court having heard the plea
and answer, Cosyn Gerritsen is condemned to pay for the rapier,
or to prove as he says that the rapier belonged to the Company.

Haye Jansen, plaintiff, vs. Hendrick Jansen Cool, defendant.
Plaintiff demands payment of 611 gl. for freight. Defendant
answers that if he is forced to pay the entire freight the
skipper ought to compensate him for the cheeses lost in the
ship and for the half-aam of brandy which leaked out or was
tapped, as may be suspected from the plugs which are stuck in
the cask. Ordered that defendant prove by certificate of the
skipper that the cheeses were in the ship and that the half-aam
was tapped by the crew.

Jan Haes is ordered in court to complete the work he is
bound to do for Borger Jorissen, the more so, as he admits his
obligation; or, in default thereof, he shall be placed under
arrest.

Tomas Stevensen, plaintiff, vs. Elias Perckman, defendant, for a two-thirds interest in the ship. Parties are requested on the part of Wilcocx and Mr. Smith to submit the case to arbitrators, permission for which is granted to them.

On the 6th of September anno 1646

The director and council of New Netherland having observed the scarcity of money for the support of the Company's servants and this country and that several persons owe the Company considerable sums, among them Hendric Jansen, the smith, who, instead of paying, even insults the honorable fiscal; therefore, the honorable fiscal is hereby ordered and authorized to force said Hendrick Jansen to pay by means of legal proceedings and to have him return the Company's tools of which he has had the use for a long time.

[270] 10th of September 1646

Whereas the sentence and the account of Jan de Fries are sent to his house and the ship De Jager lies at present ready to sail for the fatherland, you, Jan de Fries, are hereby commanded to repair this week on board said ship in order to proceed in her to Holland. Done in council, the day and year aforesaid.

On the 13th of September

Jan Jansen from Hoorm, plaintiff, vs. Claes Pietersen from Purmerent, defendant. Plaintiff lost some shirts on the voyage from Holland hither and as the defendant has sold here some shirts like them, plaintiff wants to know where the defendant got them. Defendant answers that he bought the shirts at

Amsterdam, without being able to say in what street. The
director and council, having heard the plaintiff, find not a
particle of guilt in the defendant, wherefore the plaintiff is
ordered to keep silent on condition that the defendant, when he
goes to Holland and shall have arrived at Amsterdam, is bound
to point out the shop where he bought the shirts.

Sybolt Classen, plaintiff, vs. Rouloff Jansen, defendant,
as surety for Jan Haes. The plaintiff demands payment from the
surety. Defendant answers that he paid Jan Haes. Ordered that
parties shall prove their assertions.

Whereas the honorable director general and council of New
Netherland have been reliably informed that Jacob Eversen
Sandelyn, skipper of the ship Den Schotsen Duytsman, [1] without
order or commission from the Chartered West India Company, chamber
of Amsterdam, has come into the South river of New Netherland
with the aforesaid ship and there sold a quantity of duffel
cloth and other goods to the Swedish governor, for which he
received from the aforesaid governor a bill of exchange amounting
to the sum of 2,050 gl., which bill of exchange and letter of
advice have been handed by Laurens Laurensen from Vleckeren to
Everardus Bogardus, minister here, to be transmitted to Holland;
and whereas this tends to the great prejudice of the Company and
the serious detriment of this country; therefore, we hereby order
said Bogardus to deliver immediately into [271] our hands the
above mentioned bill handed him by Laurens Laurensen, or to
declare into whose hands he has delivered it. In default thereof,

---

[1] The Scotch Dutchman.

the aforesaid Bogardus shall be responsible for all damage and loss which the honorable Company shall suffer thereby and be considered an accessory of those who endeavor to rob the honorable Company of its revenue and seek to ruin the country. Thus done in council in Fort Amsterdam in New Netherland, the 21st of September anno 1646.

We, the undersigned, declare that by order of the court in New Netherland we have this day read the aforesaid order to Domine Bogardus, who gave the honorable fiscal for answer that it was not enough for the sheriff or fiscal to make some assertions, but that he must prove his above written complaint. The fiscal asked Bogardus, "Did you not have the bill of Sandelyn?", whereupon the minister answered, "I did not say that." All of which we declare took place in our presence at the house of Bogardus, the 21st of September 1646, in New Amsterdam.

The original was signed, Cornelio van[der] Hoykens, fiscal, Evert Duykingh. Below was written; Acknowledged before me, and was signed, Cornelis van Tienhoven, secretary.

In council in Fort Amsterdam, at the request of the honorable fiscal, Laurens Laurensen from Vleckeren was asked this day whether he had received any letters from Jacob Sandelyn to be delivered to Everardus Bogardus, with request from said Sandelyn that Bogardus should forward the letters to Holland, and whether there was not a bill of exchange among them from the Swedish governor. Laurens Laurensen says that he received a package of letters from the aforesaid Sandelyn, among which letters there were also some from the Swedish governor, and delivered them here to Everardus Bogardus. Done the 21st of September anno 1646. Was signed by Willem Kieft, director, and Cornelio van[der] Hoykens, fiscal. Below was written: Acknowledged before me, Cornelis van Tienhoven, secretary.

The 27th of September

At the request of the Reverend and very learned Domine Johannes Megapolensis, minister in the colony of Renselaerswyck, and in accordance with the promise heretofore made by our predecessors to Jan Francisco, junior, a Negro, in view of the long and faithful service rendered by him, the same is hereby manumitted and given his freedom, provided that during the remainder of his life he shall pay yearly as an acknowledgment for his freedom 10 schepels of wheat or the value thereof.

[272] [4]th of October anno 1646

Mr. Arnoldus van Hardenbergh, plaintiff, vs. Haye Jansen, defendant, regarding a gun. Plaintiff declares under oath in court that the defendant said to him: "Take my gun and keep it until I return yours." Therefore, the defendant is ordered to deliver the said gun to the plaintiff and to leave it in his hands.

Having seen the petition which has been presented to us by Mr. Arnoldus van Hardenbergh, who has power of attorney from his brother, Mr. Johan van Hardenbergh, dated the 7th of September 1645, praying for the return of 4 cases of duffel cloth, properly marked Nos. 2, 3, 4 and 5, which his brother is said to have shipped in the ship St. Piter, Symon Jansen from Durigerdam, skipper, addressed to Symon Dircksen Pos and confiscated here with the aforesaid ship, as also an insurance policy from which it appears that said Hardenbergh insured his consignment in the aforesaid ship St. Piter for 6,000 gl.; and having seen also the interrogatives of Piter Barentsen, bookkeeper of the honorable West India Company; two bills of lading, both dated August 24th 1644, signed by Symon Jansen, one for 4 cases of duffel cloth, marked Nos. 2, 3, 4, and 5, consigned to Symon Dircksen Pos, marked S. I., and the other for 4 cases, Nos. 6, 7, 8 and 9, duffel cloth, marked I. R., consigned to Jacob Jansen and Jacob Reyntjes; the affidavits of Jan Ibesen and Symon Jansen, skipper; the answer of the fiscal of New Netherland, the replication of the plaintiff and other documents to the same purpose;

Therefore, we order, as we do hereby, that the plaintiff, Mr. Johan van Hardenbergh, shall be obliged to declare under oath before competent judges in Holland, first, that the 4 cases, Nos. 2, 3, 4 and 5, belonged directly to him and that he has not turned them over to the skipper, Symon Jansen, or anyone else on bottomry, half-profit, or on any other condition; secondly, that the mark of Symon Jansen was placed upon them by mistake; thirdly, that he consigned the said cases to Symon Dircksen Pos, advised him by letter and sent him bills of lading; fourthly, that the two **dozen pieces of cloth** found in case No. 3 did not belong to him. Which being done, the 4 cases of duffel will be restored to him. Thus done in council in Fort Amsterdam in New Netherland, the 4th of October anno 1646, new style.

[273] Haye Jansen, plaintiff, vs. Jan Laurensen, defendant, for the balance of freight and other charges which plaintiff and defendant are claiming from each other.

Seger Tonissen and Jan Jansen Schepmoes, together with
Mr. Isaack Allerton, are ordered and requested by the honorable
director general and council of New Netherland to examine as
referees the writings and other matters on both sides and if
possible to make parties come to an amicable agreement, or to
report to us their opinion in writing.

Jan Jansen, plaintiff, vs. Haye Jansen, defendant, for the
delivery of an aam of caraway [seed]. Ordered that the defendant
shall prove that the aam was put ashore, or, in default thereof,
that he shall satisfy the plaintiff. In regard to the anker,
plaintiff shall prove to whom he delivered it.

Arnoldus van Hardenbergh has declared under oath before
the council that Haye Jansen said to him: "Take my gun and keep
it until I return yours." Whereupon, said Haye is condemned to
restore the gun.

11th of October

The wife of Jan Eversen Bout, plaintiff, vs. Marry de Truy,
the wife of Cornelis Volckertsen, defendant, about the purchase
of boards sold by Cornelis Volckertsen. Defendant acknowledges
that the boards were sold by her husband to the plaintiff and
says that she has boards enough to satisfy both the plaintiff
and Rouloff Jansen, who afterward bought the said boards from
her. Ordered by the director general and council that the first
sale to the plaintiff shall take effect, the defendant being
ordered to deliver the boards which Cornelis Volckersz sold and
to deliver to Rouloff Jansen the boards which she sold to him,
unless the defendant's husband considers his wife incompetent

in his absence to make any purchases or sales. Done in Fort
Amsterdam in New Netherland, on the day above written.

18th of October 1646

Adam Roelantsen, plaintiff, vs. Jan Jansen from Hoorn,
defendant, about the purchase of a cask of anise water containing
9 ankers. Jan Jansen promises to deliver 3 ankers immediately
and one half-aam when Seger Tonisz arrives.

Govert Aertsen, plaintiff, vs. Jan Jansen from Hoorn,
defendant, about a claim of 32 cheeses. Ordered, if Govert
can prove that the cheeses were taken by his mate from a barrel
in the ship and put into a canoe and that they were discharged
by Jan Jansen, that Jan Jansen shall pay for them or restore
them.

[274] On the 18th of October 1646

Antony Jansen, plaintiff, vs. Edman Adley, defendant, for
damage which the defendant is said to have done to cattle.
Ordered that the plaintiff shall prove that the defendant does
not take proper care of his cattle and farm, for which purpose
the magistrates of Breuckelen are requested by the parties and
Jan Eversen and Huych Aertsen are authorized and requested by
us to inspect the farm and cattle of Antony Jansen, to judge
whether Adley does as a lessee should. The parties shall satisfy
the said referees and if it be found that Adley has been
neglectful, he shall leave the farm, or give security.

Adriaen Dircksen, plaintiff, vs. Marten Arentsen, defendant.
Third default.

Whereas the defendant has allowed the third default to be
entered against him, he is condemned to satisfy the plaintiff;

in default whereof, the plaintiff shall have the right to have the defendant put in debtors' prison at his expense.

Tonis Nyssen, plaintiff, vs. Mr. Stikley, defendant, in a case of appeal. Plaintiff demands his sow and the increase thereof. Parties having been heard in court, the plaintiff refuses to swear that the sow belonged to him and the defendant swears that the sow which Tonis claims belongs to him and that he bought her from Willem Washbandt. Willem Wasbandt likewise declares that he sold the sow to Mr. Stickli and that she was raised by him. Whereupon the plaintiff's demand is denied and he is ordered to pay the costs of the trial. Thus done in Fort Amsterdam in New Netherland, the 18th of October 1646.

To Cornelis Groesen, supercargo of the ship St. Jacob:

Whereas since the departure of the ship St. Jacob we have been reliably informed that the skipper, Haye Jansen, tried to sell here about 4000 pounds of lead, for which purpose he spent here several days on shore with his mate, leaving his ship off Staten Island; and whereas by a careful watch which we caused to be kept there we have not been able to learn that the said lead was landed, consequently, that it must still be on board the ship, and whereas the ship has departed from here and the said lead was not found by our men who went on board, owing to the quantity of ballast, water, wood, etc., with which the ship was encumbered; therefore, we hereby order and recommend to you to pay all possible attention to this in Virginia and to remember the oath which you took to the honorable directors; also, that the opinion which people here have of you, that you

connived with the skipper, may thereby be found to be untrue.
Sent on board the 24th of October anno 1646.

[275] On the 2d of November 1646

Jan Dollingh, plaintiff, vs. Michiel Tamtor, supercargo on
the bark of Mr. Wytingh, in a case of attachment. Whereas he,
the plaintiff, according to the judgment of the 2d of August
last, as surety for Mr. Wytingh, has paid Jan Heyn and Evert
Cornelissen, the defendant is condemned to reimburse Jan Dollingh
and to pay the costs of the trial.

8th of November 1646

Augustyn Heerman, as attorney for Haye Jansen, skipper of
the ship St. Jacob, plaintiff, vs. Marten Arentsen, defendant,
for passage money and board. Marten Arentsen proves by two
witnesses that during the voyage hither he did his work as a
carpenter and sailor. The defendant also declares under oath
that Haye Jansen promised him at Amsterdam that if he performed
work as other sailors he would have his passage free. The director
and council having heard the testimony of two witnesses and
declarations of the defendant confirmed by oath, the plaintiff's
claim is denied and the defendant is acquitted.

15th of November

The fiscal, plaintiff, vs. Tryntje Kip, defendant, for
slander. Second default.

Augustyn Heerman, plaintiff, vs. Adam Roelantsen, defendant,
for board and board for himself and his son. The director general
and council having heard the declaration of Seger Tonissen, who
declares that skipper Haye agreed with Adam Roelantsen at Amsterdam that he would have free board and free transportation of his

chest provided he worked like a sailor on the ship, [and having
also heard] the declaration of Teunes Dircxsz, formerly chief
boatswain, that the skipper said on the ship that he did not
wish to take any money for Adam's son's board because he read
the prayers; therefore, the plaintiff's claim is denied and the
defendant acquitted.

[276] On the 30th of November anno 1646

Jan Jacobsen from Haerlem, plaintiff, vs. Aeltjen Douwens,
defendant, for slander. Aeltjen Douwens declares that she knows
nothing about the wife of Jan Jacobsen that reflects on her honor
or virtue. Ordered that Aeltjen Douwens shall not offend the
wife of Jan Jacobsen any more; likewise, her opponent shall
keep quiet.

Sybolt Claessen, plaintiff, vs. Jan Haes, defendant, for
damage to clapboards. Jan Haes promises to deliver the clapboards
to Sybolt Claessen before the next court day, which he is ordered
to do on pain of imprisonment.

Dirck Volckertsz, plaintiff, vs. Jan Haes, defendant for
damage done to plaintiff's house. Defendant says if plaintiff
can prove that he knocked down any part of the framework of the
roof of the house, he will build the same up again. Ordered that
plaintiff shall prove his charge.

Joris Batselaer, plaintiff, vs. Jan Haes, defendant. Ordered
that plaintiff shall prove his charges.

Having seen the petition of the schepens of Breuckelen,
stating that it is impossible for them to take care of all the
suits that occur there, especially as regards crimes of violence,
or those concerning the impounding of cattle and other matters

appertaining thereto which frequently occur in connection with
farming, and that in order to prevent all disorder it would be
necessary to appoint a sheriff (schout), for which office they
propose the person of Jan Teunesen; therefore, we grant their
request and authorize, as we do hereby, the person of Jan
Teunesen to perform the duties of sheriff, to arrest delinquents
with the advice of the schepens, to supervise the pound, to
impound cattle, to collect fines and to do all that a faithful
sheriff is bound to do. Whereupon, he has taken the oath before
us and the honorable fiscal, to whom he shall be especially
responsible, as in Holland the deputy-sheriffs are responsible
to the sheriffs and the sheriffs to the bailiffs or marshals;
and we hereby order and command all those who reside in the
jurisdiction of Breuckelen to acknowledge the said Jan Teunesen
as sheriff. Thus done in our council in Fort Amsterdam in New
Netherland, the 1st of December anno 1646.

[277] On the 13th of December 1646

Adriaen vander Donck, plaintiff, vs. Philip Jansen,
defendant, for the sum of fl. 80, being the balance of wages
due for hauling two masts. The complaint and answer of the
parties having been heard, the defendant is condemned to pay the
true value of the masts, according to the judgment of two
impartial men, provided that the plaintiff give security for the
refunding of the money if Antony Crol should hereafter be able
to prove that payment was made before this date.

Oloff Stevensen, as attorney for Mr. Wolter van Twiller,
plaintiff, vs. Claes van Eslandt, defendant. Plaintiff demands

that the defendant render an accounting of Mr. Wolter van Twiller's effects here in this country. Ordered that defendant shall render an account between now and Christmas.

Tomas Hal, plaintiff, vs. Jan Laurensen, defendant. Plaintiff says that he came 8½ yards short on 4 pieces of duffel which Jan Laurensen sold to him, the plaintiff. Ordered that the plaintiff shall prove his statement.

The honorable fiscal, van[der] Hoykens, plaintiff, vs. Adam Roelantsen, defendant, charging defendant with having tried to violate the wife of Harck Syboltsz in her house, about which the said Harck Syboltsen's wife and her mother, appearing in court, complain and for which they demand justice. The defendant admitted in court having touched the naked breasts of Weyntjen Teunes, for which reason the defendant is placed in confinement.

December 17

The honorable director general and council of New Netherland having seen the criminal proceedings begun at the demand of the honorable fiscal, plaintiff, against Adam Roelantsz, at present a prisoner, on account of force and violence committed against Weyntjen Teunes, wife of Harck Syboltsen, at her house, which the said Weyntjen declares on oath to have occurred, to wit, that Adam Roelantssen by force tried to have intercourse with her at her house and also immodestly attacked her, of which the marks are said to be still visible on her body, having also considered the written complaint of the fiscal and the serious consequence thereof which in a land where it is customary to maintain justice can not be tolerated or suffered; Therefore, we condemn the aforesaid Adam Roelantsen to be brought to the place where it is customary to execute justice and there to be flogged and furthermore to be banished from this country as an example to others. Thus done in Fort Amsterdam in New Netherland, the 17th of December 1646.

In consideration of the fact that the aforesaid delinquent is burdened with four small motherless children and that the cold winter is approaching, the honorable director and council have postponed the execution to a more suitable opportunity when the delinquent shall be able to depart. Dated as above.

[278] Jellitjen, wife of Gerrit Douman, complains in court that Elke Jansen has stolen her money that was in the cradle, inasmuch as Elke remained in her house while she and her husband went to church and that on coming home from church, Elke Jansen being still in her house, she immediately missed the money. Elke denies having stolen the money and says that she never saw it. Case adjourned until tomorrow to secure further evidence.

Gerrit Seers, soldier, aged about 26 years, declares at the request of Gerrit Douman that Elken said to him yesterday, "If the sergeant has again sent out a spy, I have two attorneys who will see the matter through for me, if I only stick to the words which the attorneys tell me to say." The aforesaid Elke Jansen is provisionally released on her promise to answer at any time the charges brought against her by the sergeant.

The fiscal, plaintiff, vs. the wife of Hendrick Kip, defendant, alleging that said Kip's wife said that the honorable director and council were false judges and that the honorable fiscal was a false fiscal.

Hendrick Kip appearing with his wife makes answer that his wife received such a shock at the time that Maryn Andriaensen attempted to murder the honorable director in his room that she has never been well since and that, when she experiences the least excitement, the woman does not know what she is doing. The wife of Hendrick Kip declares that she never said that the honorable director and council were false judges, or that the fiscal was a false fiscal.

The plaintiff's complaint and the answer of the defendant and her husband being heard, the defendant is ordered to prove that she has not said anything to the detriment of the honorable director and council or the fiscal. The fiscal is ordered to prove his charges on the next court day, or to compound with his opponent.

Jan Onderhill, plaintiff, vs. Jan Hadduwe, defendant, for having slandered plaintiff's daughter. Jan Hadduwe declares in court that he has nothing to say that in anyway reflects on the honor and virtue of his daughter. Ordered by the honorable director general and council that Jan Hadduwe in the presence of Debora, daughter of Jan Onderhill, shall acknowledge having done wrong and to pray her for forgiveness.

Jan Hadduwe prays Jan Onderhill for forgiveness and is therefore condemned to pay the costs of the trial.

Tomas Spyser, plaintiff, vs. Tomas Sandersen, defendant. Plaintiff complains that the defendant keeps him off his land, assaults him, calls him a rogue and a rascal and has shot dead one of his goats. Ordered that the first time defendant gives offense to Tomas Spyser [279] or anyone of the neighbors he

shall be banished from the plain. As to the goat and damage to
the cabbage, parties shall each select two of their neighbors to
decide the matter as arbitrators and Tomas shall now take his
produce from the land and deliver it to Spyser.

Jonas Wodt, plaintiff, vs. Pietertje, wife of Claes Jansen,
for balance due for two cows. Plaintiff is condemned to pay
12 gl., on condition that the defendant shall give security to
repay the money if defendant's husband can prove that the
plaintiff kept the cows six or seven weeks longer than was
agreed upon.

On the 28th of December anno 1646

Jellitjen, wife of Gerrit Douman, says in court that last
Sunday she went to church with her husband, leaving at her house
her young daughter with Elke Jansen and Jan de Voocht. The aforesaid woman says that she left money in a cradle at her house and
that when she came home the money was no longer in the cradle.
Jan de Voocht, being drunk, lay asleep, therefore, she says Elke
must have stolen the money. Elcke Jansen says that she never
knew of the money, let alone stealing it.

Jan Pitersen from Amsterdam, jailer, declares at the request
of Elcke Jansen that the eldest daughter of Douman, being
questioned, said that her mother had taken the money out of the
cradle and mislaid it. Case is adjourned until tomorrow in
order meanwhile to prove the accusations and to give the accused
an opportunity formally to establish her innocence.

Gerrit Segers, soldier, aged about 26 years, declares in
court at the request of Gerrit Douman that Elcke Jansen said to
him yesterday, "If sergeant Douman has sent out a spy, I have

two attorneys who will see me through, if I only stick to what
my attorneys tell me to say." Gerrit Segers has confirmed this
on oath before the honorable director general and council.

[280] In the year after the birth of our Lord and Savior Jesus
          Christ, one thousand six hundred and forty-seven.

                    This day the 10th of January

Paul Heyman, heretofore cadet, is appointed in council
superintendent of the honorable Company's Negroes at 25 gl. a
month and 100 gl. a year for board.

          Symon Dircksen Pos was asked in court what payment he promised
to make to Mr. Augustyn Herman as surety for Cornelis Maessen.
Symon Pos answers that he was bound to pay in seawan, silver coin,
or beavers, and that in the colony of Renselaerswyck he had
offered silver money in payment to Mr. Augustyn, except that it
fell a little short of the full payment. Augustyn Heerman says
that he must have beavers, and not seawan or silver money; also,
that Pos offered silver money at a much higher than the current
rate. Ordered that parties shall prove their statements.

          Whereas some difficulty has arisen between Jan Teunesen,
schout, and Jan Eversen, magistrate of Breukelen, about slander,
and the difference is of little moment and it would be of
dangerous consequence should the court in their own locality
remain divided, parties are therefore reconciled before the
court here, promising by clasping of hands that each will
respect the other in the office to which he has been called.

                    [281] 16th of January 1647

          Symon Dircksen Pos, plaintiff, vs. Augustyn Heerman,
defendant, for compensation for loss suffered by him on some

beavers sent to him from Fort Orange by Harmanus Bogardus in the yacht <u>Renselaerswyck</u>.

The documents produced by the parties having been examined and the parties respectively having been heard, it appears that the defendant at the request of the plaintiff paid and delivered to Cornelis Maessen, in Holland money and cloth, the sum of fifty-eight guilders and three stivers, on condition that the plaintiff should deliver therefor to him at Fort Orange good merchantable beavers, such as he, the plaintiff, according to his own confession, received from said Maessen. The plaintiff failing to make such delivery to the defendant, the latter wished to place him under [civil] arrest, and to prevent this Harmanus Bogardus became surety for the plaintiff, who promised to pay at the first opportunity. This not taking place, the defendant approached the plaintiff here in New Amsterdam for payment, and after much argument was offered by him half-beavers and <u>drielingen</u>, [1] which the defendant refused, on account of the loss he would suffer thereby. He threatened him that he was going to Fort Orange for the last time and that he would there have one of the plaintiff's cases opened to get his pay out of it. Arriving there, he went, accompanied by two councilors of the colony of Renselaerswyck, to the house of the surety, Harmanus Bogardus, demanding his pay or that he should open one of the plaintiff's cases and pay from it what was due him. Said Bogardus refused to do this, but upon the advice of the above mentioned councilors it was resolved to send a case of beavers hither to the plaintiff, who could himself pay out of it. This

---

[1] One <u>drieling</u> = 2/3 beaver. See <u>Doc</u>. <u>Hist</u>. <u>N</u>. <u>Y</u>., 1:64.

was done, after the defendant had left, in the yacht <u>Renselaerswyck</u>, on board of which, during the voyage, some beavers in the case were damaged, which damage is estimated at two hundred guilders.

Having duly considered everything, we declare, as we do declare hereby, the defendant not liable for the damage to the beavers that has been sustained, seeing that he did not request the case to be sent down, but only that it be opened in order that he might obtain his pay, and this by order and with the knowledge of the court. The plaintiff is to recover his loss from Harmanus Bogardus or in whichever way he shall see fit. Thus done in Fort Amsterdam in New Netherland, the 16th of January 1647.

[282] Sybolt Claessen, plaintiff, vs. Cornelis Tonissen, defendant, for payment of fl. 150. The wife of the plaintiff, appearing, admits the debt and requests time. Defendant is ordered to pay one-half now and the remainder next Easter.

Jan Laurensen,[1] plaintiff, vs. Adriaen van[der] Donck, defendant, because the defendant, while being officer of the colony of Renselaerswyck, attached and kept three pieces of duffel which are alleged to belong to Coster.[2] Defendant answers that he does not know of any cloth belonging to Coster. Ordered that parties shall submit their complaint and answer in writing.

---

[1] Jan Laurensen Appel.
[2] Willem Coster.

Cornelis Volckersen, plaintiff, vs. Adriaen van[der] Donck, defendant, about some debt due to the plaintiff by Hans Fomer. The defendant promises to pay when the accounts between him and Hans Fomer shall have been settled.

Whereas by order of the honorable director general and council of New Netherland notices have been posted regarding the leasing of the ferry, house and effects of Cornelis Melyn and these notices have been torn down by some malicious persons to us unknown, notwithstanding they were affixed at the usual places, such as the fort, the warehouse and the tavern, and whereas this is a matter of grave consequence which can not be tolerated; therefore, the honorable director and council aforesaid hereby promise to give a reward of one hundred guilders to whoever shall be able to report who tore off the above mentioned notices, and in addition [they promise] to conceal the name of the informer. Thus done in council in Fort Amsterdam in New Netherland, the 29th of January 1647.

The last of January

Elke Jansen, plaintiff, vs. Gerrit Douman, defendant, for accusing her of theft, for which plaintiff demands reparation. Ordered that Douman's wife shall prove that Elke said that Douman himself stole the money and that Gerrit Se[g]ers committed perjury.

[283] The 7th of February 1647

Andries Roulofsz, plaintiff, vs. Harmen Bastia[ensen], defendant, for [the return of] fl. 16 in seawan and 6 beavers loaned by the plaintiff to the defendant. The defendant

acknowledges the receipt of the aforesaid amount. The defendant
is condemned to pay the six beavers and is to retain the
remainder until the return of the sailmaker. The crew of the
T'Amandare, plaintiffs, vs. Jan Dollingh, defendant, for payment
of 40 gl. Jan Dollingh answers that the crew has not performed
the work they undertook to do. Jan Dollinc is ordered to pay
20 gl.

Huych Aertsen, plaintiff, vs. Willem Goulder, defendant,
for purchase of a house and plantation with grain for the sum
of 200 gl. Ordered that Huych Aertsen shall prove that he sold
the house and grain and that Goulder's wife received the grain
and that when Huych asked her on losing her husband, Smith, if
she kept to her bargain, she took it ill.

Mr. Ritchert Smith and Willem Smith, plaintiffs, vs.
Françoys Douthey, minister, defendant. Plaintiffs demand that
Mr. Douthey shall declare in writing who are his associates,
in order to make answer thereto on the next court day; which is
ordered.

Hendrick Jansen, smith, plaintiff, vs. Jan Jansen, cooper,
defendant for the payment of fl. 170:10. Defendant admits the
debt [and promises] to pay.

[Elcke] Jansen, plaintiff, vs. Gerrit Douman, sergeant,
defendant. Defendant [proves that the plaintiff said] that his
father and mother had robbed one another and that the sergeant
might also have stolen the money from his wife. Case is
adjourned and plaintiff is ordered not to speak any more of the
matter.

Jan Appel, plaintiff, vs. Adriaen van[der] Donck, defendant.
First default.

14th of February

Jan Lourensen Appel, plaintiff, vs. Adriaen vander Donck, defendant, for the return of 117 **yards** of duffel, consisting of 3 pieces belonging to Willem Coster. Plaintiff presents his claim in writing and is ordered to deliver the defendant a copy to answer it.

Tomas Sael, plaintiff, vs. Willem Harck, defendant. Willem Harck and Willem Lourens promise to haul all the timber for Tomas Sael according to contract, provided that they be released from the previous contract and that when the work is finished they shall be paid as arbitrators shall judge fair.

[284] [21st of February]

The honorable fiscal, plaintiff, vs. Hans Reyger and Dirck Zieken, soldiers, prisoners. The fiscal presents his complaint in writing and demands justice. Defendants admit in court that they committed what the fiscal charges them with.

The honorable director general and members of the Court Martial having seen the criminal charges of the fiscal against Dirck Sieken and Hans Reyger from Norenborch, soldiers, at present prisoners for very insolent behavior by the aforesaid prisoners on the public street, pointing their guns and threatening to shoot people, Hans Reyger having drawn a bare knife against his superior officer and wrestled with him and Dirck Sieken having struck the captain of the guard, in the fort; all of which they, the prisoners, in the Court Martial have voluntarily, without torture or irons, admitted having done and committed; all of which is directly contrary to the military regulations.

Therefore, we, wishing to do justice, condemn the above delinquents to be taken to the place of public execution and there to be harquebused according to military law.

Thus done in the Court Martial, on the 21st of February 1647, in New Amsterdam.

The last of February

[Peter Ebel, heretofore] a soldier, [appeared] before the council and was appointed [by the director and council provost marshal] at [24 gl. a month and 100 gl. a year for board].

7th of March 1647

Gabriel Martensen, plaintiff, vs. Jan Huybersz, defendant, for payment of fl. 10:16 st. Defendant admits the debt and is condemned to pay.

Claes Cornelissen Meutelaer, plaintiff, vs. Cornelis Teunesen, defendant, for purchase of land to be paid for in 3 instalments, twice in the month of May. Is ordered to produce proof.

Mr. Ritchert Smith requests that the question between him and Mr. Douthey may be terminated. The honorable director and council therefore order that parties shall submit their case on the next court day, when sentence shall be pronounced. This day, the 7th of March anno 1647.

14th of March

Whereas Symon Root, native of [blank] on the [blank], being in the great tavern on the island of Manhatans in New Netherland, quarreled with one Piter Ebel, provost, it finally happened, after the aforesaid persons had fought together, that a piece of Symon Root's ear was cut off with a cutlass, whereof the aforesaid Symon Root in council demands a certificate in due form, in order that in the future, if necessary, he may make use thereof. Therefore, we, the director and council of New Netherland, [285] [hereby certify that the ear was cut off with the] cutlass in question in the place aforesaid. We request all those to whom this certificate may be shown to give full credence thereto. In token of the truth we have signed this and confirmed it with our pendent seal in red wax, this 14th of March, to wit, the certificate given to Symon Root.

Whereas Mr. Arnoldus van Hardenberch, attorney of Mr. Johan van Hardenberch here requests compensation for 20 pieces of duffel cloth which he claims are not subject to confiscation inasmuch as they belong to his brother and not to the skipper of the ship St. Piter; therefore, it is ordered that said Mr. Johan van Hardenberch shall confirm on oath several points in controversy before the authorities in Holland and that then the duffel or the value thereof shall be returned to him, together with the interest thereon. Meanwhile, we consent that the account of duties on exported beavers which said Arnoldus has with the Company shall remain open until advice is received from the fatherland in regard to the declaration of Mr. Johan van Hardenbergh, it being well understood that said advice must be sent here by the first opportunity and that said Arnoldus shall furnish sufficient security that in case his brother remains in default, whatever duties he owes shall be paid here out of what is confiscated. Thus done in council the 11th of March anno 1647, in New Amsterdam.

[Whereas the honorable director general and council of] New
Netherland have deemed it most serviceable and expedient in the
interests of the honorable Chartered West India Company to select
a fit person to collect and receive the duty on beer and liquors
here in New Netherland; therefore, the honorable director and
council aforesaid appoint and commission as receiver of said
imposts the person of Rouloff Jansen Haes, and we therefore
order and command all and singular to acknowledge the aforesaid
Rouloff Jansen as our appointed receiver of the duty aforesaid,
and those who owe anything on that account are promptly to pay
the amount to the receiver aforesaid without any gainsay. Thus
done in Fort Amsterdam in New Netherland, the 11th of March
anno 1647.

Adam Roelantsz, plaintiff, vs. Jan Teunessen, schout at
Breukelen, for payment of [   ]. Defendant admits the debt
and requests time. Defendant is condemned to pay the amount
and the costs of the summons.

Jan [   ], plaintiff, vs. [   ], wife
of Arent Corsen, defendant, [   ]. Defendant
says that she has no knowledge thereof.

[286] [Whereas] the late Jan [   ] debts amount
to more than the value of the estate and it nevertheless is a
Christian duty to place the said [children and property] under
supervision; therefore we, the director general and council of
New Netherland, hereby authorize Jan Jansz Damen, Oloff Stevensz
and Cornelis van Tienhoven provisionally to take proper charge
of the children aforesaid and of the property left behind, provided that they shall not have to concern themselves with the
debts and assets of the estate.

Agrees [with the original, the] 11th of March 1647

[287] In the name of the Lord, Amen

In the year 1647

Whereas the honorable Petrus Stuyvesant, director general of New Netherland, Curaçao and the islands thereof, and the honorable council have considered it necessary and expedient for the best interests of the directors of the Chartered West India Company to appoint and commission a fit and experienced person as commander over all large and small vessels that are at present here or that may hereafter be sent hither, in order, in the absence of the aforesaid honorable general, to command the ships, officers and crews, both on land and water, and to exercise authority and command during all expeditions and exploits, all in conformity with the instructions to be furnished him to that end, in order to prevent all confusion and disorder; [therefore,] the person of Jelmer Tomassen is at present [appointed thereto, being] judged competent for the said office. Thus done in council in Fort Amsterdam in New Netherland, the 27th of May 1647. Was signed: P. Stuyvesant, Willem Kieft, L: van Dincklaghe. La Montagne.

The honorable general and council of New Netherland, Curaçao, etc., deem it highly necessary for the best interests of the honorable West India Company that a faithful person be appointed in this country superintendent of equipments to look after and exercise proper supervision over all large and small vessels, skippers, sailors and workmen in the service of the Company, and over all other property of the Company and whatever else may appertain thereto. Therefore, the aforesaid general

and council have engaged Paulus Leendersz, at present captain
of the Groote Gerrit, as superintendent of equipments, who promises
to conduct himself diligently and faithfully in the aforesaid
office. This 27th day of May anno 1647, in Fort Amsterdam. Was
signed: P. Stuyvesant, Willem Kieft, [L: van Dincklaghe], La
Montangne.

Whereas, Jan Claesen Bol, captain of the ship Swol, requests
leave to depart for the fatherland with the ship De Princes,
his request is granted and the honorable general and council
have engaged Hans Wyer as captain of the ship Swol at fl. [   ]
per month. This 27th day of May anno 1647.

[288] Willem Kieft, late director, requests that some persons
may be examined in council, to which end they have been legally
summoned. It having thereupon been taken into consideration
whether the said summoned persons should be examined by the
whole board or by a committee appointed for that purpose, the
honorable director and council have unanimously decided that
they shall be heard and examined in full council.

Jan Eversz Bout having been legally summoned to appear before
the council to testify to the truth, at the request of the
honorable Director Willem Kieft, which he has obstinately refused
to do, it is resolved and decided to place him under arrest.

Paulus Leendersz, superintendent of equipments, is ordered
in council to take measures that the ships Groote Gerrit,
De Kath and De Liefde be made ready to go to sea at the earliest
possible opportunity, in order to cruise against our common
enemy, the Spaniard, in the West Indies and the islands thereof,

to the best advantage and profit of the honorable directors. In
Fort Amsterdam in New Netherland, the 6th of June anno 1647.

Whereas Commissary Davidt Provoost has come from the Fresh
river of New Netherland and requests his discharge, reporting
that the house De Hoop, situated on said river, is in great need
of repair and requires more attention than it has hitherto received,
especially as said house De Hoop is one of the farthest outposts
of New Netherland to the north and the possession of the Fresh
river has been preserved thereby up to this time; and whereas,
in case said house De Hoop, which is a heavy burden to the
honorable directors, were abandoned, the English, who have usurped
there our purchased and paid-for ground, would immediately annex
the place, whereby the possession of the aforesaid river, the
farthest boundary, would come into the hands of the English,
which would tend greatly to the disparagement and discredit of
their High Mightinesses and the honorable West India Company;

Therefore, all things being well weighed, it is after mature
deliberation in council resolved and concluded to maintain the
house out of respect for their High Mightinesses and the honorable
directors and to that end to send thither again a proper person
in the stead of the former commissary.

Thus done and ratified in council in Fort Amsterdam of New
Netherland, the 6th of June anno 1647.

[289] It being considered and duly weighed in council that
the seafaring persons assigned in this country to the honorable
Company's ships can not be provided according to the ordinary
list of ship's rations, as some provisions are wanting here
which are usually distributed on shipboard; it is therefore

resolved by the honorable council to distribute to each man
(those in the cabin excepted) on board the Company's ships and
assigned to this jurisdiction, the following weekly rations:

Stew according to circumstances
3½ pounds of hard tack
1½ gills of vinegar ⎫ per week
1 pound of dried fish
2½ pounds of pork or beef

Thus done in council in Fort Amsterdam in New Netherland,
the 6th of June anno 1647.

[Ordinance against selling liquor during divine service on the
    Sabbath and against drawing knives] [1]

Petrus Stuyvesant, director general of New Netherland,
Curaçao and the islands thereof, commander in chief of the
Company's ships and yachts cruising in the West Indies;

To all those who shall see these presents or hear them
read, Greeting:

Whereas we see and observe by experience the great disorders
in which some of our inhabitants indulge in drinking to excess,
quarreling, fighting and beating, even on the Lord's day of rest,
whereof, God help us!, we have seen and heard sorrowful instances
only last Sunday, to the disparagement of the court of justice,
to the reproach and censure of ourselves and our office, to the
scandal of our neighbors and finally in disregard, yea contempt,
of God's holy laws and ordinances, which command us to sanctify
this His rest and Sabbath day to His honor, forbidding all wounding, slaying and the means and occasions whereby the same might
arise;

---

[1] Revised from Laws and Ordinances of New Netherland,
pp. 60-62.

Therefore, we, with the advice of the late honorable director
general and our appointed council, in order as much as it is
practicable and possible for us to provide herein and to prevent
the curse, instead of the blessing, of God falling upon us and
our good inhabitants, do hereby order and command that none of
the brewers, tapsters and tavern-keepers shall on the Lord's day
of rest, by us called Sunday, before two o'clock when there is
no sermon or otherwise before four o'clock in the afternoon, set
before, tap or serve any people any wine, beer or strong liquors
of whatever sort or under any pretext whatsoever— travelers and
daily boarders alone excepted, who may be provided therewith for
their necessity in their lodgings— on pain of forfeiting their
licenses and in addition being fined six Carolus guilders for
every person who is found in their house at that time partaking
of any wine or beer. And in like manner we forbid all tavern-
keepers, retailers and tapsters on that day and all other days
in the week, in the evening after the ringing of the bell, which
will be at about nine o'clock, to have any more common tippling
[209] or to tap or serve any wine, beer, or strong liquors, except
to their own families, travelers and boarders, under the same
penalty.

And in order to prevent the too rash drawing of knives,
fighting, wounding and accidents resulting therefrom, we, therefore, pursuant to the laudable ordinances of the most wise and
worshipful council of the city of Amsterdam, do hereby enact
and ordain that whoever shall in passion or anger or cause to
be drawn any knife or dagger against another shall forthwith
incur a fine of one hundred Carolus guilders, or, in case he

fail to pay the money, be punished by being put for half a year
at hard labor on bread and water; and if he wound any one therewith, three hundred guilders, or to spend a year and a half at
the aforesaid labor. And we also charge and command our fiscal,
lieutenants, sergeants, corporals, as well burghers and inhabitants
as soldiers, at every opportunity to exert due diligence in visiting such places and without any dissimulation to attack and
apprehend all contraveners hereof, in order that they may be
prosecuted according to law.

Thus done in Fort Amsterdam in New Netherland, the 31st of
May A°. 1647.

Whereas Michiel Piquet, now that the deponents who testified
against him at the request of the fiscal have sworn to their
declarations, remains headstrong and obstinately refuses to confess the truth, it is after mature deliberation resolved and
concluded in council to subject him to torture and that he shall
be notified thereof, giving him until 7 o'clock in the morning
of the 15th of June to reconsider. This day, the 13th of
June 1647.

The Honorable Petrus Stuyvesant, director general of New
Netherland, Curaçao and the islands appertaining thereto, and
the honorable council, having seen and examined the charge and
complaint brought by the fiscal against Cornelis Symonsz and
Gerrit Philipsz, both sailors under the flag of the honorable
general above mentioned, whereby the fiscal ex-officio shows and
proves that the aforesaid persons, at present prisoners, in contempt of the aforesaid director's placard and ordinance affixed

to the main mast of the ships and yachts, providing that no one
may go ashore without special leave of the captain and in no
case may remain over night, have, notwithstanding, violated
[291] his aforesaid ordinance and placard, not only once or
twice, but repeatedly, one of them, to wit, Cornelis Symonsz
alias de Boer, having been arbitrarily punished therefor and
the other, to wit, Gerrit Philipsz, having at the time incurred
the same punishment and in addition broken out of the honorable
directors' prison on the island of Curaçao by striking with his
fist a certain woman prisoner; and whereas they, the prisoners,
after having committed one fault and another, have once more
misbehaved themselves, remaining several days and nights ashore,
to the serious inconvenience of the Company and the delay of the
ship's necessary work, contempt of justice and violation of the
aforesaid director's ordinance and command, which, being matters
of evil consequence, neither can nor ought to be tolerated in a
country under a well regulated government where military and
naval discipline prevails, but ought to be punished as an example
to others;

Therefore, the valiant and honorable Petrus Stuyvesandt,
with the advice of his military and naval council, administering
justice in the name and on behalf of the High and Mighty lords
the States General, his Highness the Prince of Orange and the
honorable directors of the Chartered West India Company, have
sentenced and condemned the aforesaid prisoners, as they hereby
do sentence and condemn the same, as an example to others to be
chained for three consecutive months to a wheelbarrow or a hand-
barrow and put to the hardest labor, strictly on bread and water,

without wages. They deny the fiscal's further demand. Thus done
and sentenced in council in Fort Amsterdam in New Netherland,
the 13th of June A°. 1647.

To the honorable commissioners ordered to investigate the differences between the Hon. Mr. Kieft and Jochim Pietersz
and Cornelis Melyn

Honorable Gentlemen:

The petition of Jochom Pieters and Cornelis Melyn, together
with the draft of the interrogatives, whereupon were to be
examined all the former counselors with the exception of the
honorable director, which were placed in our hands at the close
of the session of our council, have been read and considered only
by us privately, however not without considering and reflecting
upon the consequences which might result and arise therefrom.
I therefore request that your honors first be pleased to consider
them and communicate your advice thereon to us.

1. Was it ever heard or seen in any republic that
vassals and subjects did without authority from their
superiors, conceive, draft and submit to their magistrates
self-devised interrogatives to have them examined thereon?

[292] 2. Whether it will not be a matter of very bad
consequence and prepare the way for worse things to have
two malignant private subjects arrogate to themselves the
right and presume to subscribe for the entire council interrogatory articles on which to examine the former board,
without being authorized thereto by their superiors or
orders of the commonalty? I say malignant subjects, in
view of the animosity between them and the late director

and council, by whom they were held and proved to be disturbers of the public peace, as also in view of the opinion
and decision of the honorable directors themselves, by whom
they were declared to be men unworthy of being trusted or
being promoted to any station or office.

3. Whether, if this right be granted to these cunning
fellows, they will on account thereof hereafter not assume
and arrogate to themselves greater authority against us
and the appointed councilors, to usurp similar, yes,
greater power in opposition to us, should our administration
not suit their whims?

4. If the honorable directors should have written anything to the honorable director and council on the subject
of deriving some revenue from the Indians, (of which I have
some recollection) in case it could be affected without
creating trouble, c.n their secretary, to whom such secrets
are entrusted, be questioned by two private individuals and
have we power to oblige him to give such information in
case he refuse?

The honorable councilors and appointed commissioners having
given their opinion thereupon I shall also add mine in writing,
in order that we may arrive at a justifiable decision as to what
we ought to do in such a dangerous conjuncture. Done in Fort
Amsterdam in New Netherland, the 14th of June, 1647. Was signed:
P. Stuyvesant.

Opinion of the honorable general on the preceding proposed
   articles

To the first proposition, I answer that I never saw, heard
or read of the like. To the second, that it is of dangerous consequence to yield so much to persons of such bad reputation.
To the third, that it is to be supposed that they will hereafter
put the same or even worse in practice against us, but that I
have little fear on that score. To the fourth, I answer absolutely,
No. Was signed: P. Stuyvesandt.

   [293] Opinion of the honorable Mr. Dincklagen

According to civil or military law it is not practical for
subjects or vassals to submit or draw up interrogatories relating
to public or other affairs without permission, authority or
power from their superiors.

To the first he says, No; and if it happens it is contrary
to practice and a species of opposition. To the second says,
Yes; and that no malignant persons, if their malignancy is
proved, can be allowed to have any voice in public affairs. To
the third says, that such may indeed happen. To the fourth says,
No. Was signed: L: van Dincklaghe.

                Opinion of Fiscal Van Dyck

To the first article, the fiscal says that it does not
become vassals or subjects to prescribe laws, especially when
they are not duly authorized thereto by the sovereign power; he
is therefore of the opinion that no action should be taken in
regard to the interrogatories, but on the contrary that they
should be punished as disturbers of the peace and declared to
be incompetent. To the second article; the fiscal says, Yes,

as they are acting as disturbers of the peace without any order
of the commonalty and therefore no notice can be taken of the
interrogatories. To the third, Yes. To the fourth, No, as
otherwise the secretary would bear his name in vain or improperly.
Was signed: H. Van Dyck, fiscal.

Lieutenant Nuton's answers to the proposed articles

To the first, that he has never heard of or seen such a
thing; also, in his opinion subjects are not allowed to do so
without authority or order from their superiors. To the second
answers, that evil consequences may follow, and answers, yes.
To the third article answers, Yes. To the fourth article
answers, Absolutely no. Was signed: Brian Nuton.

Opinion of Commander Looper

To the first answers, No, and that such neither can be nor
ought to be tolerated. To the second answers, Yes. To the third,
Yes. To the fourth, No. Was signed: Jacob Looper.

[294] Opinion of Commander Jelmer Tomasz

To the first, says that what such subjects had to offer in
their defense ought to have been submitted by consent and not as
a right by way of interrogatories. To the second, if they be
allowed to do this, it will be a matter of evil consequence. To
the third, says, if they be permitted to do this, they will
hereafter show greater boldness. To the fourth, that it is not
lawful for private individuals to question the secretary without
consent from those in authority. Was signed: Jelmer Thomas.
The opinion of Paulus Leendersz, Superintendent of Equipments

To the first, answers no subject can make laws, much less
interrogate the former council concerning public affairs, without

authority from the superior power and that on the contrary they
are liable to punishment for so doing. To the second, Yes. To
the third answers, Yes, for should things hereafter not go to
their liking they would then indeed wish to be master; wherefore
it is his opinion that they ought to be decidedly punished as
examples to others. To the fourth article, Poulus Leendersz
expressly answers, No; also, that no member of the late council
can be interrogated by private persons without authority. Was
signed: **Pouwelis Lendersz van die Grift.**

Opinion of Jan Claesz Bol, captain of the ship De Princes

To the first answers, that, as Jan Claesz Bol understands
it, it is without any foundation in law that subjects without
authority from above should interrogate their superior officers.
To the second, that it is a matter of very grave consequence and
richly deserves punishment. To the third, Yes. To the fourth,
No. Was signed: Jan Claessen Bol.

But in order that these petitioners, Jochim Pietersz Kuyter
and Melyn, may receive full measure, that our supreme and sovereign
government and the honorable directors may be furnished more
light and information as to the cause of the war, and that we
be safeguarded against complaints and all reproach of passion
and partiality, whereof the petitioners in their petition seem
to suspect us and the council, stating N.B. in plain words that
their honors should herein for the time being set aside all distinction in rank between persons and persons; it is and remains
our opinion, under correction, that the honorable commissaries,
pursuant to the request of the petitioners, should hear the
summoned persons [295] on interrogatories and report their

answers, in order to transmit these under cover to the honorable
directors, without returning and showing them to the petitioners,
unless they first make and prove some definite statements,
squaring with their first petition and the apostil thereon, to
wit, that they state categorically the motives and the causes of
the war and give the names of those who have been the first
authors and instruments thereof; furthermore, that they produce
power of attorney from the honorable Lord of Nederhorst, whose
name they use in their petition; also authority and power from
the commonalty to remove the responsibility for the war from the
latter, as they presume to do in their first petition. This being
done and proved, a copy of the opinions of the honorable council
may with the approval of the honorable council be granted them,
provided they first show power and instructions from the honorable
directors and the supreme and sovereign government and from the
inhabitants of this country to procure any evidence respecting
the war. And in default of sufficient documents and proof [it
is our opinion] that they, together with the accused, [should]
be sent to the fatherland to defend and substantiate their accusations and complaints before the supreme and sovereign government,
as we are not commanded either by instructions from the honorable
directors or orders from the supreme and sovereign authority to
institute any inquiry therein, much less to pronounce definite
judgment in the premises against the director and council or
anyone else. Thus done in council at Fort Amsterdam in New
Netherland, the 14th of June anno 1647. Was signed:
P. Stuyvesant, L: van Dincklaghe, H: van Dyck, fiscal, Jacob
Loper, Jelmer Thomas, Pouwelis Lenders van de Grift and
Jan Claesz Boll.

Teunis Andriesz from Amsterdam appeared before the council and requested an increase of his monthly pay, as he is now serving as pilot on De Liefde. Therefore, the honorable general and council allow him 26 guilders per month as wages, on condition that the increase shall commence when his term of service expires and if he binds himself then to serve again as pilot for two years for the aforesaid wages. The 14th of June anno 1647.

The chief pilot on board De Cat is allowed by the council 26 guilders a month, commencing [blank].

Whereas at present there is no provost and it is necessary to appoint a person to that office; therefore, Adam Roelantsz appeared before the council and requested the said appointment. To which office we, the director general and council appoint him hereby and order and command every one to leave him free and unmolested in the performance of his duties, for which service he, Adam Roelantsz, shall receive as wages 26 guilders and 100 guilders a year for board. The 14th of June 1647.

[296] Whereas the honorable director general and council have been reliably informed that several private traders, sailing to the south and who are under the jurisdiction of this government, go into the interior toward the Minquas country with cargoes of cloth, seawant and other articles, whereby not only trade is spoiled, but the traders who remain with their sloops at the usual trading posts sustain great loss and damage; and whereas, furthermore, the Indians might be tempted thereby to murder or kill such persons in order to obtain their goods, whereby this country might again be involved in trouble and war;

Therefore, for the best interest and advantage of the West India Company and this country, we forbid and prohibit, as we do hereby, henceforth all and every one of our inhabitants from going into the interior with trading goods or any other commodities and command them to wait at the usual trading posts for trade. Thus done in Fort Amsterdam in New Netherland, the 18th of June anno 1647.

The honorable general and council having seen the written petition of the late Honorable Director Willem Kieft, and the same being duly weighed and considered by us, Jochim Pietersz and Cornelis Melyn are ordered to substantiate by satisfactory impartial testimony the opinions submitted to the council by Mr. Kieft and to produce in council the letter sent by the Blaeuw Haen, not the same, but the original draft or authentic copy thereof; in default whereof the fiscal may institute an action for slander against them. Thus done and ordered in council in Fort Amsterdam in New Netherland, the 18th of June anno 1647.

Whereas for the maintenance of the house The Hope, situated on the Fresh river of New Netherland and within the limits of this province, it was resolved and concluded on the 6th of June last to send a fit and faithful person thither in the stead of Commissary Davidt Provoost; therefore, we have resolved and concluded to send thither Gysbert op Dyck, former commissary of provisions, who served as commissary there for the honorable directors and therefore is acquainted with all the circumstances; which said Op Dyck shall provisionally reside there, in order to take care and have proper supervision of everything. This 20th day of June anno 1647, in New Amsterdam.

[297] Whereas many matters of moment, both legal and otherwise, occur here daily in New Netherland with those of the
English nation within the jurisdiction of said province and also
many English letters come from various places from the neighboring
governors of New England, which mostly treat of and relate to
matters of state; and whereas none of the Company's officers here
can readily read and write English and we have great need of a
person somewhat conversant with law in order to serve us on all
occasions and also to write necessary English letters; therefore,
it is resolved and concluded to engage G[e]orge Bacxter as ensign,
provided that he shall be employed in the matters aforesaid; for
which service he is allowed 42 guilders a month for himself and
his boy and 200 guilders a year for board. The 28th of June 1647.

The honorable general and council having considered the
necessity of repairing the ship Swol, which is old and unseaworthy,
for which purpose the necessary materials are not on hand nor
procurable here at present, and whereas said ship would lie here
at great expense to the honorable directors, it being impossible
to send her to sea in her present condition and she must therefore
as a wreck be hauled ashore; therefore, it is unanimously resolved
in council to sell the aforesaid ship to the best advantage and
profit of the aforesaid directors if a purchaser can be found at
the highest and best price practicable and possible, the more so
as the above named ship has heretofore been condemned at Curaçao.
This 20th of June anno 1647, in New Amsterdam in New Netherland.

It is considered expedient and proper for the best advantage
and profit of the honorable directors of the Chartered West

India Company to send the ship <u>Groote</u> <u>Gerrit</u>, of which Jelmer
Tomasen is commander, to Boston, in New England, laden with
lumber, to sell the same there for the highest price possible
and in return to take in as many provisions as can be procured
there and to sail thence direct to Bonayre, all according to the
special instructions relating thereto. And if God grant the ship
a safe voyage, he is to deliver the cargo of provisions to the
hands of the honorable Vice-Director Roodeborgh and after unloading again to take in logs and after having completed his lading
to prosecute his voyage to New Netherland, until he arrive before
Fort Amsterdam. Thus done in Fort Amsterdam in New Netherland,
the 20th of June 1647.

[298] In the interest of the honorable directors it is considered in council expedient and proper for the increase of trade
and commerce of this country to equip, fit out and send to sea
the yachts named <u>De Liefde</u> and <u>De Kath</u>, to cruise against our
enemies the Spaniards and their adherents, within the limits of
the charter. Done in Fort Amsterdam in New Netherland, the
20th of June anno 1647.

Jan Seno de St. Germain, at present a prisoner, being
questioned at the requisition of Fiscal Van Dyck, declares that
he received from the wife of Michiel Piquet two beavers, about
15 ells of white linen, 4 ells of cambric, two bunches of black
and white strung seawan, one half an arm long and about as thick
as a man's arm; also a black bag of loose seawan, about half an
ell long; which articles were buried and delivered (after being
prohibited from doing so) by him, the prisoner, to one Gascon,
to be handed to the runaway Piket. This 24th of June anno 1647,
in Fort Amsterdam.

Jochim Pietersz appeared in council and answered in writing
the complaint of the late director, Willem Kieft, and said that
they had more evidence from the three men who signed the petition
than they had as yet exhibited to the honorable director general
and council and that they would lay it before their High
Mightinesses upon their arrival in Holland and there show the
cause of the war.

At the request of Willem d'Key, as attorney of the honorable
directors, Jan Dollingh declares in court, with offer and promise
of solemn oath, that he, the deponent, did in the year 1644 sell
to Willem Cornelisz Oldemerckt in New Netherland the accounts of
what he and Isaack Boevees had earned in Curaçao, for which
accounts he declares that he received in payment from the above
named Oldemerckt 18 snaphances, declaring further that he has
not traded or made any further bargain with the aforesaid Willem
Cornelisz, nor received any other merchandise from him. The
deponent says that Willem Cornelisz made him a present of a keg
of about 40 pounds of powder, but that he did not give or pay
anything for it, and after he, the deponent, had received the
guns, he gave the said snaphances to Seger Tonisz; "So help him
God Almighty." The 24th of June anno 1647.

[1] [299] Whereas large quantities of strong liquors are
daily sold to the Indians, whereby heretofore serious difficulties
have arisen in this country, so that it is necessary to make
timely provision therein;

Therefore, we, the director general and council of New
Netherland, forbid all tapsters and other inhabitants henceforth

---

[1] Revised from Laws and Ordinances of New Netherland, pp. 64-65.

to sell, give or trade in any manner or under pretext whatsoever
any beer or strong liquor to the Indians, or to have it fetched
by the pail and thus to hand it the Indians by the third or fourth
hand, directly or indirectly, prohibiting them from doing so
under penalty of five hundred Carolus guilders, and of being in
addition responsible for the damage which might result therefrom.

Also, every one is warned and forbidden to do any damage
to farms, orchards, or gardens, either to the fences or fruits,
and whoever shall be found to do any damage either to the fences
or fruits of any farms, gardens, or orchards, shall pay a fine
of one hundred guilders and in addition be subject to arbitrary
correction.

Also, all inhabitants of New Netherland are charged and
commanded properly to fence off their lands so that cattle may
not commit any damage therein, which cattle, whether horses or
cows, and especially goats and hogs, must be herded or otherwise
placed where they can do no harm, to which end Fiscal van Dyck
shall erect a pound (schut huys), in which he may detain the
cattle until the damage be made good and the fine be paid. Let
every one be warned and guard himself against loss.

Done in Fort Amsterdam in New Netherland, the 1st of July
[anno 1647]. Present: the honorable general, the late director,
Kieft, Mr. Dincklaghe, Mons. La Montangne, Captain Lieutenant
Nuton, Paul Leende[rsen], Jacob Loper, Jelmer Tomasz and Jan
Claesz Bol.

Copy

Monsieur Sergeant Litschoe: You will do well not to allow
any goods to be landed except on our signed order or that of

Secretary van Tienhoven, written by our order, and meanwhile to keep the fiscal's order and hand it to us. Done in Fort Amsterdam, this 28th of June anno 1647. Was signed: P. Stuyvesandt.

The sergeant is ordered not to obstruct the bearer hereof, Willem Tomasz, master of De Valckenier, in discharging his vessel, but to afford him all possible assistance, taking care only that no goods be discharged or landed that are contraband, such as guns, powder, lead and other munitions of war, or anything that is not marked with the Company's mark. He shall therefore, with the supercargo, keep a perfect record of the goods that are shipped in the boat or any other craft and send us a list thereof with every boat. Done in Fort Amsterdam on the Manhatans, this 3d of July 1647. The original hereof was signed: P. Stuyvesandt.

[300] The honorable director general and council of New Netherland, having seen the criminal charges of the fiscal against Jan Seno de St. Germain, at present a prisoner, which charges the fiscal supports by affidavits; and having also heard the prisoner's confession that contrary to the injunction served by the fiscal in the presence of the witnesses, he removed seawan and other goods from the house of Michiel Piquet, who was arrested for a crime committed by him, broke jail and escaped from prison; therefore, the aforesaid case having been duly considered and it having been found that the same tends greatly to the contempt of justice, the aforesaid Germain is ordered to beg pardon of God and of the court and to acknowledge that he did wrong; furthermore, he is condemned to work with others six weeks at the fort when said Germain is restored to his previous health.

Thus done and sentenced in court. Present: the honorable director general, the late director, Willem Kieft, Mr. Dincklaghe, Captain Lieutenant Nuton, Mons. La Montange, Commander Jacob Looper, Paulus Leendersz and Jan Claesz Bol. The 3d of July anno 1647, in New Amsterdam.

[1] Petrus Stuyvesant, director general of New Netherland, Curaçao and the islands thereof, and the honorable council;

To all those who shall see these presents or hear them read, Greeting:

Whereas we by daily experience find, see and observe the frauds, abuses and smuggling which our people as well as those of other nations daily commit in the exportation of beavers, otters, bear skins, elk hides and other peltries which, without being entered and consequently without paying any impost or duty, are shipped or sent away beyond this our jurisdiction and government to New England, Virginia and other regions, whereby the granted concessions and revenues of our honorable directors are seriously impaired; as also in the importation of some English goods and merchandise in return, which often are entered at half the value, whereby we, and through us the honorable directors, are not only defrauded of the import duties on the English goods and merchandise and the export duties of the beavers and peltries, but also the goods and merchandise of our good and loyal inhabitants, merchants, factors and traders who pay or have paid just and proper duties thereon in the fatherland or here at our custom house are greatly depreciated, trade and

---

[1] Revised from Laws and Ordinances of New Netherland, pp. 65-68.

commerce corrupted and we deprived and defrauded of our income
and revenues.

Therefore, being desirous to prevent the same as far as it
is feasible and possible for us, we, the above mentioned director
general and council, do most emphatically ordain, order and command both our own subjects and strangers and foreigners that no
one of them shall presume to sell, barter, trade, or remove, or
ship, or export, directly or indirectly, any wares or merchandise
of whatever nature or quality they may be within our government,
as well here in New Netherland as at the island of Curaçao and
elsewhere, without due entry being first made of such merchandise
and the quantity, quality and value of the same being presented
to us or our agents; which being done it shall be lawful for
each and every one, both strangers and inhabitants, to dispose
of, sell and barter their wares and merchandise in the usual
course of trade to anyone according as it shall be expedient or
profitable to the owners or sellers; provided that the seller
remain bound, whenever it pleases us, to show by his books or
accounts to whom they have been sold or what goods have been
bartered for them, so that after delivery and receipt the proper
duties and impost may be faithfully paid and received before
he leaves the country, under penalty of confiscation and forfeiture
of all concealed goods that may be found in the first instance
or afterwards and in addition a fine of five hundred Carolus
guilders.

We likewise ordain, interdict and forbid all persons, of
whatever nation or quality they may be, any elk hides, bear

skins, otters, beavers or other peltries to remove, exchange, export, transship or to transfer from one vessel into another or to land the same, directly or indirectly, under any pretext whatsoever, unless first of all such elk skins, bear skins, otters, beavers or other peltries are entered with us or our deputy, without fraud or delay, as to their quantity, either here at the Manhatans, or at the places where they have been bartered, negotiated or traded, or at least at the nearest place where we have stationed our commissary, resident, or deputy, on pain of confiscation and forfeiture of all the peltries and accompanying goods and merchandise which afterwards shall be found smuggled or concealed. And in order that all frauds and smuggling may be for once stopped and prevented, it is further by us, the director general and council, ordained, enacted and decreed as we hereby do ordain and enact and decree, that henceforth, or at least after the sending away of the beavers and peltries on the ship De Princes, elk hides, bear skins, otters, beavers and all other furs shall be marked and stamped with a certain mark thereto ordered or yet to be ordered by some person here in New Amsterdam, to be sworn for that purpose on behalf of the honorable directors, in order that at the proper time a regular duty may be received or caused to be received on such bear skins, elk hides, deer skins, otters, beavers and other peltries, so that they may be shipped or sent beyond or within the limits of our government to New England, or to the Swedes in the south, to Virginia, or to the fatherland, under penalty of confiscation of all beavers, otters, bear skins, elk hides, deer and fox skins, which shall be found here or hereafter in the fatherland unmarked and not stamped.

Moreover, for the further prevention of all sorts of smuggling, inasmuch as the duty is not and cannot be immediately paid in beavers, all merchants, factors, peddlers, traders and other commercial persons, whether inhabitants or foreigners, are warned and commanded by us to show clearly, whenever it shall be our pleasure, by their accounts and books to whom they have bartered and traded such marked and stamped beavers, otters, bear skins, deer skins and other peltries, under a penalty of payment by the last receiver or purchaser thereof who remains in default or neglect of a double duty on the furs which are missed and not entered on his books; and within three days after the departure of the ship De Princes all merchants, traders and inhabitants at the Manhatans shall duly enter their beavers, otters, and other peltries and have them marked, on pain of confiscation and fine as aforesaid. Thus done and enacted in council at Fort Amsterdam in New Netherland, the 4th of July anno 1647, New Style. Present: the honorable director general, Mr. Dincklagen, the honorable ex-director, La Montange, Captain Lieutenant Nuton, Commander Looper, Jan Claesz Bol, captain of the Princes, and the superintendent of naval equipments Mr. Poulus Leendersz. [1]

[302] The honorable director general and council having heard the signed and written criminal complaint against Michiel Piquet, born in Rouen, and made an examination of the inter-rogatives whereby it appears that the above named Michiel Piquet

---

[1] The preceding law was disapproved in Holland, as shown by extracts from letters of the directors of the West India Company, dated Jan. 27, 1649, and Feb. 16, 1650, cited by E. B. O'Callaghan in Laws and Ordinances of New Netherland, pp. 68-69.

has most foully slandered with his tongue the late director,
Kieft, calling his honor a betrayer, a villain and a traitor,
also saying if no one would shoot him, he, Piquet, would do it
himself; that his legs would not carry him out of the country
and that within a short time a great shedding of blood would
occur at the place where the former director transferred his
authority to General Petrus Stuyvesant and that Cornelis Melyn
had fully one hundred men on his side; also if the Honorable
Petrus Stuyvesandt did not behave himself better than the former
director, he too would have to pay the penalty, striking under
his arm; all of which more fully appears by divers depositions
of creditable witnesses; wherefore he was arrested by the fiscal
and brought before the court for that scandalous and godless
act. He, the culprit, has dared to break jail and to escape
from imprisonment and although he has been three times summoned
by the ringing of the bell to come and defend his case and to
hear all such charges as the fiscal should ex-officio bring
against him, he has failed to appear. Therefore, then, after
invoking God's holy name, having duly considered and found it
to be a matter of grave consequence which cannot be tolerated
in a well ordered republic where it is customary to maintain
justice, we declare the said Michiel Piquet, as he has not
appeared on the third summons, to be debarred from all exceptions,
defenses and pleas of which he might make use in this case, and
condemn the said culprit to be banished for the rest of his life
from the province of New Netherland, with confiscation of all
his property, from which what is due to the honorable Company

shall first be deducted, one-third to be applied to the honorable
Company, one-third to the church and one-third to the benefit
of the honorable fiscal, and in addition his name is to be affixed
to the gallows as an example to other such turbulent persons.

Thus done in council in the presence of the Honorable
P. Stuyvesandtt, the honorable ex-director, Willem Kieft,
Mr. Dincklagen, Mr. La Montangne, Captain Lieutenant Nuton,
Paulus Leendersz, Jan Claesz Bol and Jacob Looper, the 4th of
July anno 1647, in Fort Amsterdam in New Netherland.
Ordinance imposing an excise on wines and spirituous liquors [1]

[303] Petrus Stuyvesant, director general of New Netherland,
Curaçao and the islands thereof, and the honorable council, to
all those who shall see these presents or hear them read, Greeting:

Whereas the fortress of New Amsterdam now some time ago,
during the war, fell into great decay, so that the walls are
daily overrun and more and more trampled down by men and beasts,
which tends not only to the disrepute of our sovereign and supreme
authorities and the disrespect, yes, contempt for this state
among our neighbors, whether English, French or Swedes, yes,
even among the Indians and heathen, but also reflects on ourselves and our good inhabitants and is most perilous and dangerous
in time of attack and defense against all enemies from outside;
therefore, we, the director general and council, pursuant to
the order of the honorable directors, intend to put the fort
into proper repair, to complete the church, as we are already

---

[1] Revised from *Laws and Ordinances of New Netherland*,
pp. 69-71.

busy doing, to order a pier built for the convenience of the
traders and burghers, and to construct a sheet-piling to prevent
the erosion by the river in front of this city of Amsterdam,
all of which are very proper and highly necessary public works
which will require a considerable amount of money, both to procure the materials and to pay the workmen; therefore, to facilitate
and render more easy the raising of said money, we have resolved
to ordain and establish a reasonable excise and impost on wines,
brandy and liquors which are imported from abroad. Accordingly,
we do hereby ordain and enact that all tavern-keepers and tapsters
shall pay an excise on Spanish wine, brandy and liquors of two
stivers per quart and on French wine of one stiver; that is to
say, on each anker of Spanish wine, brandy and liquors three
guilders and four stivers and on French wine one guilder and
twelve stivers, and on larger vessels in proportion. Likewise,
all skippers, factors and peddlers who wish to transport or sell
such wine, brandy or liquors elsewhere within our government
shall pay the same excise; with the understanding nevertheless
that the merchant, burgher, farmer and others of our good
inhabitants (tapsters and retailers by the large and small
measure alone excepted) shall be at liberty to lay in a stock
in their houses, dwellings and places of abode by the large and
small cask for their private consumption on the same terms as
those who purchase from the merchant, factor or trader in the
first place, provided only that the burgher and other good
inhabitants remain bound to obtain a permit from our appointed
officer, receiver or collector before he lay in or store the
wine in the cellar and to pay therefor 6 stivers per anker of

French wine and 12 stivers per anker of brandy or Spanish wine, larger casks in proportion.

In order to prevent all fraud and smuggling, the seller shall be bound to enter with the receiver-general or collector the quantity and quality of the sold wines and liquors before delivery. In like manner the purchaser is ordered and commanded not to receive, ship, export or store any wines without having first obtained a proper excise receipt from the receiver or collector, and exhibiting it to the officer, on pain of forfeiting such wines and of paying five hundred guilders additional, to be applied, one-third for the Company, one-third for the Church and one-third for the fiscal or the informer who shall make the complaint.

Thus done and enacted in council in Fort Amsterdam. Present: the honorable General P. Stuyvesant, the late director, Mr. Willem Kieft, Mr. Dincklagen, Mons. La Montangne, Captain Lieutenant Neuwton, Commander Jochim Loper, Paulus Leendersz, Commissary of Naval Stores, and Jan Claesz Bol. The 4th of July anno 1647.

[304] Ordinance respecting large and small vessels and smuggling [1]

The honorable director general and council of New Netherland, Curaçao and the islands thereof, residing in New Netherland on behalf of the High and Mighty Lords the States General of the United Netherlands, his Highness of Orange and the honorable directors of the Chartered West India Company, do hereby ordain and enact:

---

[1] Revised from Laws and Ordinances of New Netherland, pp. 71-72.

1. That all private yachts, barks, ketches, sloops and boats under fifty lasts, [2] whether Dutch, English, French, Swedish or others, desiring to anchor under the Manhatans, shall not seek nor have any other roadstead than in front of the city of New Amsterdam, between Capsken's Hoeck and the finger-post near the City Tavern, under penalty of fifty Carolus guilders for the first time after they have been warned; and the large ships may anchor between the said Hoeck and the second finger-post, standing on the way down toward the Smits Valey, under penalty of the like fine.

2. No skippers, merchants or traders, nor any ships on their first arrival, may land, remove, transport or transship any merchandise or wares on shore until the arrived ships are inspected and the goods entered with the honorable general or his honor's deputy.

3. After sunset and before sunrise no ships are allowed to discharge or load, or to send off or receive any boats with goods or merchandise, or for any other purpose, except to convey one of the officers on board or ashore, which must be done in the evening before the ringing of the rogues' bell and in the morning after reveille, and from no other place than forward of and about the sailors' quarters, on pain of forfeiting all goods and merchandise then found in the boat and one pound Flemish in addition.

---

[2] One last = 2½ tons burden.

4. No ships, large or small, shall be allowed to depart without being first inspected and without having given twelve hours' previous notice and received proper clearance from the honorable general or his deputy, under a penalty of one hundred guilders.

5. No skippers, traders or any one on board the ships shall be permitted to conceal, carry away or transport out of the district of our government any of the Company's servants, free traders or inhabitants of New Netherland, of whatever nation or quality they may be, without a proper pass or permit signed by the director or his deputy, under a penalty of six hundred guilders.

Thus done in council in Fort Amsterdam. Present: the Hon. General Petrus Stuyvesant, the former Hon. Director Willem Kieft, Mr. Dincklagen, Mr. La Montange, Capt. Lieut. Nuton, Jacob Loper, naval storekeeper Paulus Leendersz, and Jan Claesz Bol, captain on the _Princes_, the 4th of July anno 1647, in New Netherland.

[305] Having heard the complaint of the fiscal against Jochom Pietersz and Cornelis Melyn, he is ordered to formulate his complaint against the parties more distinctly and to institute his action against each one separately with proofs as to what the parties have done severally and also jointly. Meanwhile he is authorized to confine the aforesaid Jochim Pietersz and Cornelis Melyn each in his own house until further orders. Thus decreed in council. Present: the honorable general, Mr. Dincklagen, the Captain Lieutenant, Commissary Paulus Leendersz, and Jan Claesz Bol. The 4th of July anno 1647.

All the farmers who have cultivated and occupied their lands for more than ten years are summoned before the council in Fort Amsterdam and informed that they are liable to pay the honorable West India Company the tenth of their crops; which aforesaid farmers answer and acknowledge that the time had expired and that they were truly obliged to pay the tenth; but inasmuch as they had suffered great damage on their lands and otherwise in consequence of the war which God had inflicted upon them, they prayed that they might be spared for that reason this year, being willing to pay their honors their just due next year.

All of which being taken into consideration by the director general and council and that the people had only recently returned to their lands, it is deemed highly necessary and advisable to release the farmers this year from the tithes which shall be collected next year, when it is hoped that they will amount to something more. Thus done in council. Present: the honorable General P. Stuyvesant, the late director, Willem Kieft, Mr. Dincklagen, Lieutenant Nuton, Mr. La Montange, Paulus Leendersz, commissary of stores, Mr. Jacob Looper and Jan Claesz Bol. The 6th of July anno 1647, in Amsterdam of New Netherland.

Whereas four letters are brought to the council by skipper Willem Tomasz, addressed to Seger Tonisz, and whereas he is dead and goods have been sent to him, it is resolved that the letters shall be opened by Secretary Tienhoven on behalf of the honorable Company, the administrators of the estate of Seger Tonisz and Mr. Augustyn Herman, who shall jointly report to us if there be anything therein in which the honorable Company is interested.

Mr. Augustyn Heerman shall receive the private goods addressed to Seger Tonisz by the ship De Valckenier as per invoice and dispose of them for the benefit of the owners, on condition of receiving a commission of 10 percent. Thus done. Present: the honorable general, the late director, Mr. Kieft, Mr. Dincklagen, Mr. La Montangne, Captain Lieutenant Nuton, Commander Loper, the commissary of naval stores and Mr. Jan Claesz Bol. The 11th of July anno 1647.

[306] Whereas the sailors of the ship De Vackenier show before the council that they jointly took on board the said ship as boatswain's perquisites 20 ankers of brandy and liquors without having entered the same and humbly request that they may keep said brandy and liquors and dispose thereof to their benefit, it is the opinion of the council that such a small matter ought not to be refused to an entire ship's crew. Therefore, their request is granted, on condition that they pay the duty on the return goods. Done in the presence of the honorable General P. Stuyvesant, the late director, Mr. Kieft, Mr. Dincklagen, Mr. La Montange, Lieutenant Neuton, Jacob Loper, Paulus Leendersz and Jan Claesz Bol, the 11th of July anno 1647.

On the 16th of July 1647

Cornelis Melyn appeared before the council and on the requisition of the honorable Fiscal van Dyck declared and acknowledged as follows:

1. That when the honorable Fiscal van[der] Hoykens came with the secretary and the deputy sheriff to levy on his property on account of the debt arising from the purchase of confiscated

hides, he asked him if he had any warrant to execute him. Whereupon Fiscal van[der] Hoykens answered that he had been ordered
to do so. To which Melyn says he replied: "Let him who gave
you orders see to it that he does not come to the gallows or
the wheel."

2. He denies that he said that he was not subject to the
jurisdiction of the honorable director, which is proved by
three witnesses.

3. Melyn confesses that two of his servants asked him for
permission to get maize belonging to the Indians on Long Island
and states that they went without his permission and stole the
maize from the pits of the Indians, who fell upon them and shot
one Englishman dead. Also, that he did not inform the late
director, Mr. Kieft, of the circumstances.

4. Answers that he never took or extorted any venison
from the Indians.

Cornelis Melyn requests a copy of the charges against him.

Fiscal van Dyck, on the other side, demands that the aforesaid Melyn be first committed to prison before a copy be
furnished him.

The above written declaration and confession of Cornelis
Melyn was made in the presence of the honorable General Petrus
Stuyvesant, Mr. Dincklagen, Captain Lieutenant Nuton, Paulus
Leendersz, commissary of naval stores, and Jan Claesz Boll.

[307] The 16th of July 1647

Jochom Pietersz Kuyter appeared in council and declared
and acknowledged as follows:

1. Jochom Pietersz denies that he taunted Director Kieft with being a "Saul," but says that he heard several others call him that.

2. Says that in the course of conversation which took place at the house of the late Bronck, when peace was made with the Wisquaeskex, which negotiations were protracted by the slowness of the Indians, he made the remark "How we could make the Indians pay now for what they have done to us and put them in the cellar."

3. Says: When the Eight Men were met about the excise and some few words passed, the honorable Director Kieft interrupted and said: "There are some among you who say that I have as much money in my house as four horses could draw away from it; others, again, intend to say wonderful things when I arrive in Holland." Whereupon he, Jochom Pietersz, becoming annoyed, said: "Sir, to what purpose are those words? We are here on public, not on private business." He said further: "If one were to repeat all the words which his honor has uttered here and there, there would be no end to it, but this may be done when his honor has taken off the coat with which the lords, his masters, have invested him".

The director, becoming angry, left the room and said "You ungrateful rascal".

4. In regard to mortgaging the country, he says that he requested this by petition and as it was taken into further consideration by the honorable director and council nothing had come of it. The declaration is made in the presence of the honorable director general, Mr. Dincklagen, Captain Lieutenant Nuton, Paulus Leendersz, commissary of naval stores, and Jan Claesz Boll.

The criminal complaint of the fiscal against Jochom Pietersz and Cornelis Melyn, defendants, being read and heard in council, plaintiff demands that the case be expedited and sentence pronounced.

The papers in the case being examined by the director general and council and read to the parties, they are _ex_ _superabundantia_ commanded on the next court day to establish by sufficient impartial testimony the slander contained in their letter to the honorable directors; in default whereof we shall proceed to pronounce sentence according to law. We order that meanwhile they shall remain under arrest. Present: the honorable general, Mr. Dincklagen, Captain Lieutenant Nuton, Paulus Leendersz, commissary of naval stores, and Jan Claesz Bol. Thus done in Fort Amsterdam in New Netherland.

[308] On the 4th of this month, in his action against Jochom Pietersz and Cornelis Melyn, Fiscal van Dyck was instructed and ordered by us and the honorable council to institute his action more clearly against each party individually and to support its justice by valid documents at the next session of the court, to be held on the 9th and 11th following, for the reason that many charges are brought against them jointly of which they were not both guilty and which had no connection with each other, so that they can not be included in one and the same complaint and sentence. As may be seen from his second bill of complaint this has been and still is neglected by the said fiscal, either from wilful disobedience, incompetency, or ignorance in his office. It is therefore necessary, in order that we may render a riper and better founded decision in the case, that I, myself, and the

honorable council be first informed of the exact charges which
are brought against each party in particular and what the documents are in the case.

Cornelis Melyn is accused:

1. Of having insulted the late Director Kieft, then his
lawful governor and commander, in his official capacity and
threatened him with the wheel and gallows, according to affidavits
signed by three witnesses, namely, Fiscal van[der] Houkens,
Secretary Tienhoven and Deputy Sheriff Bredenbent.

2. Of having in fact opposed the order issued by the
director and plainly said that he was not subject to the
director, although he was then a burgher and inhabitant of the
Manhatens. The opposition appears from the protest made against
him, Melyn, by the fiscal for that opposition. That he uttered
the actual words is attested by the three officers aforesaid.

3. The sworn affidavit of Pieter van[der] Linden, a man
of about 50 years of age, partly confirms the foregoing. The
actual words, though spoken elsewhere and on another occasion,
are: "What have we to do with that devil's head? Let him rule
the Company's servants;" and other mutinous and seditious words.

4. This is further confirmed by the declaration made by
Gerrit Vastrich, a free trader, before the director and council
in Melyn's presence, that he said: "I have nothing to do with
the court; there is no justice for me here."

5. Said Melyn is accused of the fact that his servants at
his command had stolen the maize belonging to the Indians. This
is shown and proved by two witnesses, both being soldiers.

6. Said Melyn is accused of having long before the war taken away from the Indians part of the game which the Indians hunted on Staten Island. This is testified only by one person and maintained by the Indians who are still available.

[309] Jochim Pietersen Kuyter is accused:

1. Of having compared Director Kieft to "Saul," and one Augustyn Herman to "David", who sometimes soothed his anger by playing. But one witness.

2. Of having proposed at Bronck's house during the peace conference with the Indians to throw the Sachems into the cellar and to fire on the rest. For this there are two witnesses, to wit, Jan Damen and Secretary Tienhoven, but they are not positive that they heard him say so.

3. Of having ordinarily treated the Indians ill and threatened to nip them with a pair of red hot tongs and after he had given them a drubbing in his house causing his servants to chase them as far as La Montange's farm. Only one witness.

4. Of having in the presence of the Eight Men or some of them, when assembled as a board, threatened the director with strange things when he laid down his office. This the director declares; also Mr. Allerton on our requisition.

5. Of having tried to induce Director Kieft to mortgage the Manhatans to the English, according to his petition and deposition. This concerns the accusation of each individually and the proofs thereof.

Now follows what they jointly are accused of:

1. That they have written libelous and slanderous letters against and to the prejudice of the honorable director. Among

others, one dated the 28th of October 1644, wherein they accuse the director, as is to be seen and read in the copy of the original, the substance whereof is briefly as follows:

2. They stated that on the arrival of the ship De Blaeuwe Haen the director could have put 40 men in the field and accused him of having then neglected the opportunity to defeat the Indians within a radius of twenty miles.

3. That the people no longer take any interest in the country or public affairs, but waste their time in private disputes and quarrels.

4. That the director usurps princely power over them, Montangne maintaining that the director was his Highness' lieutenant here and possessed more power than even the Company.

5. That the Eight Men when assembled were always met with foul and taunting words.

6. That the treatise about the war sent to the directors contained as many lies as lines.

7. That 2500 pounds of gunpowder were confiscated and put in the powder cellar and that not 500 pounds were used or consumed in the war.

8. That the Indians had heretofore always lived like lambs with us and our nation, but the director was seized with a reckless desire for war and by an accursed order caused the Indians to be murdered.

9. That the high station and authority of the director had hindered and prevented skipper Laurens from defending his case; and many other things, as are to be seen and read in the original.

All of which points, Director Kieft and the former officers declare and prove by counter evidence to be false and malicious lies.

[310] It is further charged against them:

1. That the aforesaid letter was indeed written in the name of the Eight Men, but that not all that is written in it was read to the Eight Men.

2. That the Eight Men were never assembled as a board, either before the letter was written to prepare the draft thereof, or during the drafting of the letter, or after the letter had been written, or even at the signing of the letter, but that the same was signed *precario*.

3. That they sought and endeavored in the name of the lord of Nederhorst and the commonalty to make Director Kieft responsible for the cause and beginning of the war, without however having or being able to produce any authority or power of attorney from the honorable lord of Nederhorst and the commonalty here.

4. That in their second petition to us and the honorable council, requesting *Litis decisio*, they appear to suspect the council of passion and partiality, requesting that for the time being they might be pleased to set aside all distinction in rank between persons and persons, according to their own petition.

Finally, refusing us and the council sufficient documents and proofs, giving for answer that they had indeed more proofs in regard to the petition of the three men, but that they would exhibit them in the fatherland before the honorable States, thus repudiating the new council.

With reference to these accusations, the fiscal, in his first conclusion, presented on the 4th of July, demands that they both, without distinction, be punished by being put to death; and in his second conclusion, presented on the 11th of July, that they be both banished from the country and each fined one thousand guilders, according to the original.

The honorable councilors, having now this day heard the defendants' replication and answer and seen the counter evidence, are pleased [to promise] to have ready at the next session their judgment and opinion regarding the punishment demanded and the faults committed. We shall add ours thereto in writing. This day, the 18th of July 1647.

Opinion of Mr. Dincklagen

Having seen the letter sent to the fatherland by Cornelis Melyn and Jochom Pietersz Kuyter, without their signatures or those of their associates, touching public affairs and the government, it being no duty and business of theirs to attend to the general affairs of the country, much less to write about them, but said letter being a way and means of exciting the commonalty against Mr. Kieft, their director and commander; also, having seen the depositions in this case made against them by some persons, setting forth various calumnious statements and crimes, I am of the opinion, according to written law and customs, that Cornelis Melyn is liable to perpetual banishment beyond the jurisdiction of New Netherland and Jochom Pietersz to banishment for a certain length of time. This day, the 18th of July 1647, in New Netherland.

[311] Opinion of Briant Nuton, Lieutenant

Having heard on the 4th of July last in full council Cornelis
Melyn, accused by Fiscal van Dyck of mutiny and opposition to
justice, committed during the administration and against the
person of the late honorable director general, Willem Kieft,
then his lawfully appointed governor, in proof of which accusation
various affidavits have been submitted and read to Melyn, who
also signed with his own hand the slanderous letter which was
sent to the honorable directors, not a particle of which letter
has been proved up to this date, but on the contrary appears to
be untrue by the declarations of various inhabitants, which con-
stitutes falseness and calumny involving life and honor; therefore, I, Brian Nuton, am of the opinion that the aforesaid Melyn
deserves to be banished forever and be declared a forger and be
compelled to ask God and the court for forgiveness, leaving the
fine to the discretion of the honorable general and council.
This day, the 18th of July anno 1647.

The opinion of Brian Nuton, Lieutenant

Jochim Pietersen having threatened the late director, being
his lawful commander, that when he had laid down the cloak with
which he was invested by the lords his masters, he should then
have him, and many other things, as appears by the fiscal's
accusation; also having in company with Cornelis Melyn written
calumniously against the late honorable director, which involves
not only honor but life, to prove which, time enough has been
allowed him, but he has failed to prove the calumnies written
by him and Melyn and proof to the contrary having been shown;
therefore, Brian Nuton finds it to be consistent with law and

conscience that the above named Jochom Pietersz be declared a
forger and be banished for seven years from the jurisdiction of
New Netherland and pay such fine as the council shall deem proper.
This day, the 18th of July anno 1647, in New Amsterdam.

Opinion of Paulus Leendersen, commissary of naval stores,
in regard to Cornelis Melyn

Cornelis Melyn deserves in his opinion to be forever banished
and never more to be allowed to come within the limits of New
Netherland; also, to be fined 500 guilders and to beg pardon of
God and the court.

Opinion of Paulus Leendersen in regard to the offenses of
Jochim Pietersen

Jochim Pietersen shall be sent to the fatherland to defend
his conduct and shall not be at liberty to come within the limits
of New Netherland before and until he shall have done so, and in
addition forfeit 300 guilders; and in case he return here, he
shall be obliged to bring a valid certificate from the full board
of the honorable directors and the gentlemen before whom the case
may be tried. He shall also beg pardon of God and the court and,
if he refuses, he shall be fined as punishment therefor 100
guilders and forthwith be sent on board ship, without being at
liberty to return here on shore. This 18th of July anno 1647,
in Fort Amsterdam in New Netherland.

The opinion of Jan Claesen Bol, master of the ship De Princesse.

Whereas I have well examined and considered the case of
Cornelis Melyn and Jochim Pietersen, I find that it is a matter
of very evil consequence which ought not to go unpunished, but
on the contrary ought to be punished as an example to others.

Cornelis Melyn

Therefore, Cornelis Melyn ought in my opinion to be perpetually banished from New Netherland as a false liar and seditious person and in addition be fined 500 Carolus guilders.

Jochim Pietersz Kuyter

The person of Jochim Pietersz Kuyter ought to be banished from New Netherland until he shall have proved before the directors the lies and statements which he has falsely made against the honorable General Kieft and be fined 200 guilders. This 18th of July anno 1647.

The opinion delivered by the honorable Director General Petrus Stuyvesandt in the case of Fiscal van Dyck against Jochom Pietersen and Melyn.

1. Both complaints of the fiscal are dubious, unfounded and not consistent with the forms of law, inasmuch as no laws or legal authorities are cited therein by which it is proved or conclusively shown that defendants can be punished by death, or with banishment, or by fine, which are three distinctive punishments, it not being enough to demand a man's life, money or banishment, unless it be shown upon what law such demand is based.

[312] 2. The charges on which the demand is founded are not sufficiently proved by the fiscal, especially as regards the person of Jochim Pi[etersen], whose offenses have no connection with those of Melyn. Therefore, in my humble opinion they cannot be included in one and the same complaint, much less punished in the same manner.

3. The modification of the demand tends to show that it is not well founded, nor consistent with legal form; the more so,

as he communicated with the parties, as the fiscal declared of
his own accord in full council. I cannot, therefore, come to
any conclusion on the joint complaint, but only on the offenses
and accusation as far as they are proved against each of the
defendants separately.

First, against the defendant, Cornelis Melyn, of whom it
is said and proved by three creditable witnesses:

1. That he threatened the late director, Willem Kieft, his
chief and commander, with the gallows and wheel.

2. That he opposed the exercise of justice.

3. That he defied the law.

4. That he sought to stir up mutiny and sedition. Proved
by two witnesses.

5. That his servants endeavored to steal maize belonging
to the Indians, which he declared occurred without his knowledge
and against his wishes. The claim, however, is unfounded, as
he made no complaint or accusation in the matter.

6. That he took by force a portion of the game of the
Indians. Proved by one witness and more clearly indicated by
the circumstances.

7. That he concocted or helped to concoct a false and
slanderous letter against the honorable General Kieft, which is
here refuted, disproved and shown to be quite contrary to the
facts.

On the first four counts he could according to divine and
human law be charged with having committed crimen laesae majestatis
and thus be held to have forfeited his life and property. "Thou

shalt not revile the gods, nor curse the ruler of thy people."
Exod. 22:28. "Curse not the king, no not even in thy thought."
Eccl. 10:20. "Be subject unto the higher powers." Rom. 13:1.
To speak evil of one's superiors is one of the greatest offenses
one can commit against one's government, says Bernardinus
Muscatellus in Praxis Criminalibus. Whoever censures the
government of his supreme authorities ought not to remain
unpunished, since, in fact, he commits crimen laesae majestatis,
says plainly Lodovic[us] in Tractatus de Injuriis.

Injuries committed by deed or in writing against any
officer, any of the magistrates, or any member of the council
are more heinous and may be brought to the attention of the
court by any one, for it is a capital offense which according
to law deserves capital punishment. Damhouder, in Criminalibus.
To utter words tending to mutiny and rebellion demands capital
punishment, according to the sworn Articles of War.

[314] The fifth and sixth charges are not sustained by
sufficient evidence, otherwise he would be punishable as one
who usurped one of the functions of sovereignty, or who had
committed theft, force, extortion and violence. On this point,
Damhouder, in Criminalibus, fol. 22, says: "Whoever imposes
needless tolls, tributes, imposts, excise taxes, or other contributions, however they may be called, without authority of the
Prince, and exacts and levies these by force, constraining the
people thereto, commits public violence and is to be punished
capitally. If he does it without force or any one's objection,
it is private violence and punishable by a fine of 50 pounds of

gold, or otherwise at the discretion of the judge. In like manner
are to be punished such person's agents, factors or servants,
in so far as they carry out their master's crimes and misdeeds,
in which case the matter ought to be further investigated and
his servants rigidly examined regarding it.

As to the seventh charge, he is convicted of having committed falsety, defamation and slander in writing against his
lawful superior, for which he is equally punishable with his
accomplice, Jochim Pietersz Kuyter, who purges himself of the
other above mentioned crimes, so that they can not be included
in the same accusation and condemnation. Therefore, it is my
opinion that by virtue of the laws aforesaid Cornelis Melyn
ought to be punished with death and confiscation of all his
property. This 18th of July anno 1647. Was signed: P. Stuyvesandt.

**Opinion delivered by the honorable General P. Stuyvesandt in
the case of Fiscal van Dyck against Jochem Pietersen**

In regard to the accusation and charges brought against
Jochim Pietersz Kuyter, he purges himself. In my opinion the
charges are also not clearly proven or of little consequence.
The first, alleged by one witness, is doubtful, without proof
that by Saul he meant the director.

There is no categorical declaration as to his proposition
at Bronck's house, either that he uttered the words, or that he
spoke them with the meaning attached to them. Furthermore, the
matter has had no effect. He, himself, declares that the words
were spoken conditionally, to wit, that if we should treat the
Indians as they would treat us under similar circumstances, we

could throw the sachems into the cellar and massacre the rest,
without he or anyone else proposing that such should be done;
a poss ad esse nulla datur consequentia. The most that can be
deducted from this would be that he admitted the justice and
lawfulness of the war, which he and his accomplice now deny and
of which they now accuse the director of having been the causa
movens. [315] It is said that he originally treated the Indians
ill but this is not sufficiently proved. He acknowledges that
he has treated them according to their deeds and no one proves
the contrary.

2. As to the charge that he endeavored to induce the director
to mortgage New Netherland, he says that this was done with good
intention and as a member of the council, agreeable to the best
of his judgment, and that he left it to the director's discretion
as the result proves, and is therefore excusable.

That he insulted the director in the presence of the Eight
Men and threatened him with the finger is a matter of more
serious consequence than all the foregoing, being an offense
against his person and dignity and in his person against the
supreme sovereign authorities. The Articles of War say and
declare on this point: "Whoever shall say anything to spite or
ridicule his superiors shall be punished by loss of limb or
life." This is military law and customary in that service. It
is also reasonable, for he who does not hesitate to give utterance
to the evil thoughts in his mind against his lawful superiors,
what mischief would he not be capable of committing if he had
the power and the opportunity? Herewith agrees what Johannes
Bernardinus Muscatellus says in Praxis Criminalibus: "To speak

evil of one superiors is one of the greatest offenses one can commit against one's government. Whoever slanders God, his authorities, or his parents shall be stoned to death according to divine law."

But on this point also a distinction is made by many imperial statutes and jurisconsults, as Macrobius relates of Emperor Augustus, that he stood more abusive language from others than he applied to others. And Albricus says : "If any one speaks ill of his rulers, as far as their person is concerned, he should not be punished therefor, that is to say, with loss of life, but should he speak disparagingly of their administration, he must not go unpunished, because he thereby in fact commits crimen laesae majestatis." So that according to this rule it should first be investigated and determined to what end and purpose these slanderous words were spoken. The defendant does not absolutely deny them, but says that as one of the Eight Chosen Men, assembled in council, he had, in connection with some debatable question, said to the director that people would be able to bring many charges against him, the director, as soon as he had laid down the cloak with which the honorable directors had invested him, which, in our opinion, applies only to the director's person, and not to his office. The witness, Mr. Allerton, also simply declares that he merely heard such or similar words; nevertheless, in so far as he committed offenses against his general and superior, the defendant is liable to punishment therefor, as Damhouder says in regard to injuries by word or threat: "He commits an injury who threatens another by gesture — as was done in this instance by the finger and words —

and the injury is the greater or the more serious when committed
against a member of the council, an officer, or an ecclesiastical
person and in a public place, as the honorable director was then
at the meeting of the Eight Men, which time and place aggravate
the offense, so that in my opinion he ought to be punished by a
fine of 300 guilders and reparation of the injury, that is, to
acknowledge before God and the court that he spoke evil. Was
signed: P. Stuyvesandt.

[316] Mr. Johannes La Montangne appears in council and
requests permission to marry Angeneta Gillis t'Waert, widow of
the late Arent Corsen. As we are sufficiently assured that he
perished and the honorable directors themselves write that they
have made inquiries about the aforesaid Arent Corsen and have
learned nothing of him; therefore, as the above named La Montangne
and she, Angeneta, declare that they have no scruples about it,
they are permitted to enter into the married state with each
other. This 18th of July anno 1647.

On the 22d of July 1647

Whereas Cornelis Melyn thus far fails to pay what he owes
to the West India Company, notwithstanding sufficient time has
been allowed him; therefore, the above named Melyn is ordered to
pay within twenty-four hours his debt which is due the aforesaid
Company, or, in default thereof, execution may issue against the
aforesaid Melyn and his sureties.

Cornelis Melyn appeared in court and declared that Hans
Jansen and big Barent, residing in Breuckelen, carried away
without his consent the maize belonging to the Indians on Long
Island, wherefore Fiscal Hendrick van Dyck is authorized to place

them in confinement, in order to inquire further into the matter. This 22d of July 1647.

Whereas it is highly desirable that the church begun in Fort Amsterdam be completed and made tight before the coming winter, it is thought necessary, in order to have the work on the church progress, to provide materials and to keep proper accounts thereof, to appoint church wardens to have proper supervision of the church and all that is required thereto. Therefore, the honorable General Petrus Stuyvesandt, Jacob Wolphersen and Jan Jansen Damen are unanimously chosen and elected by the council church wardens. This 22d of July anno 1647.

Whereas the honorable director general and council have considered and judged it necessary to appoint and choose surveyors to take care that all houses here in this city of New Amsterdam be placed in proper alinement; also to straighten all fences, etc. not standing here as they should; therefore, Mr. L: van Dincklagen, Paulus Leendersz commissary of naval stores, and Secretary van Tienhoven are appointed and commissioned to said office. This 22d of July anno 1647.

Whereas Domine Everardus Bogardus, until this time minister here, has requested by petition his dismissal and leave to go to the fatherland and the honorable director general has considered it highly necessary that the community of Jesus Christ should be provided with a pastor and teacher, to which their honors have invited Domine Johannes Backerius, who has accepted; therefore he, Domine Johannes Backerius, is allowed 100 guilders per month salary, commencing from the expiration of the term of his engagement, and 200 guilders annually for board, with firewood free. We have promised him to write to the honorable directors for another clergyman in his place, or, if their honors do not send one, to allow him an increase of board money. Thus done in council; present: the honorable General P. Stuyvesant, the late director, W: Kieft, Mr. Dincklagen, Captain Lieutenant Nuton, La Montange, Paulus Leendersz, commissary of naval stores, and Jan Claesz Bol, Captain of the ship De Princesse. The 22d of July anno 1647.

Jochim Pietersz and Cornelis Melyn being asked in council if they have any additional or further proofs touching the letter sent by them to the honorable directors, they gave for answer, No.

What the honorable Director General P. Stuyvesandt has proposed to the council we consider being highly necessary, to wit, that Mr. Dincklagen preside over the ordinary court and there represent the person of the honorable general; also, that in addition to the present councilors some of the Company's principal officers be called as such and that by this council in the name of the honorable general shall be definitely decided all questions; that they shall in matters of importance ask his honor's advice and that he shall also preside over them whenever he pleases. Thus resolved in council.

[318] As to the slanderous letter, the defendants, Melyn and Jochim Pietersen Kuyter, are equally guilty. The accusation on that point is clearer and of greater consequence and from their own confession and the testimony of others it is as clear as the sun at midday that:

1. Both have been the principal authors and instigators
who conceived, drafted and signed the said letter and, notwithstanding the probability that it was composed and put in final
shape by Minister Bogardus, it is nevertheless true that they,
as principals, had said letter copied, collated and authenticated
by a subordinate and minor clerk or boy in the secretary's office,
as appears by the transmitted copy of the original, the same being
signed by both of them and certified as agreeing with the original.
Which contains this falsehood that the original was not yet
signed by all of the Eight Men when the copy thereof was dispatched
according to the declaration of Melyn and Allerton and that it
says: "Was signed, Jacob Stoffelsz, Barent Dircksz and Gerrit
Wolphersz," whereas they can not write and therefore all had
made their marks, instead of signing their names.

2. It is clearly enough shown and proved that this letter,
written behind the director's back, is in most points and as
regards the principal accusations false and untrue, according
to the defense of the director and the declaration of the commonalty in general, the principal burghers being heard in turba,
and also according to the voluntary confessions of the co-signers,
who during the interrogatory answered that they did not know, nor
had read or heard, that such complaints against the director
were set forth in the letter; which falseness and untruthfulness
can also be deducted from the substance of the confessions of
the defendants and from their own unfounded arguments.

3. It is clearly enough proved by their own confessions
and the confessions of the co-signers that the letter was not

framed by the Eight Men in session, or that any orders thereto
were given; also, that it was not signed in their board meeting,
but by proxy, whereby the falsety becomes the more apparent and
the probability may be presumed and inferred that the entire
contents of the letter were not read to the co-signers, or that
it was erased and altered after it had been read to them, or
that the other plain and simple men, who can not read or write,
were grossly misled by the defendants, for Tomas Hal declares
that Jochim Pietersz said: "We shall be responsible for that,"
or "Leave that to us to attend to," while the letter was signed
now by one and then by another.

Therefore, if the defendants remain in default of proving
and making good the calumnious aspersions and defamations
written behind the back of their lawful commander, who super-
abundantly proves the contrary, the defendants can, in my opinion,
be accused and condemned:

[319] In the penalty for false accusation by deed or in
writing, the penalty for slander and defamation, and the penalty
for conspiracy and sedition, which are provided by law and also
mentioned in God's word.

Damhouder, in Criminalibus, fol. 270, says, "If any one
accuse another of any crime which he can nor prove, he is to be
condemned to make restitution and reparation of loss and damage,
not only to the accused, but also to the treasury. The Articles
of War punish by loss of limb or life whoever makes, dictates or
copies fraudulent letters or statements, or commits any similar
act whereby the truth is hidden. See fol. 51, where many legal
authorities are cited.

Herein, however, jurists distinguish, as when no one suffers loss by the committed falsehood; in that case the punishment is not death, but extraordinem. Falsehood and bearing false witness are forbidden by the word of God, Exod. 20:16; Deut. 5:26, and in Deut. 19:19, 20, 21, it is commanded that the false witness shall be punished poena talionis, that is, by such punishment as he sought to inflict on the innocent. Now, in case the accusation and testimony adduced in the letter against the honorable Director Kieft, in which he is accused of extortion, tyranny, murder, robbery, etc., were true and clear, he would run the risk of losing honor, life and property. This agrees also with other laws and statutes. A distinction, however, is made by Godefrid[us] a [   ], in Tractatu rea tuum, question 7, to wit: "If the accused or innocent person be not condemned on the testimony of the witnesses, then the witnesses may not be punished by death either, the intention being that only in the first case poena talionis may apply and that in the other case the falsehood be punished extraordinem." To which opinion I am inclined also.

To compose, draft or make a fair copy of false instruments, etc., this sort of forgery, Damhouder, fol. 270, says is punishable by perpetual and irrevocable banishment, not by cutting off the hand and confiscation of property. I have already commented on injuries by writing, etc. Damhouder says, that it is a capital offense and may be punished capitally and that the place, time and person increase the punishment.

Seditious and unlawful meetings are punished according to their nature. As a rule all seditious, illegal assemblies and conspiracies are forbidden and included under poena crimen

laesae majestatis, but seeing that these at that time were of
the Eight chosen men, it was lawful for them to hold a meeting,
but not without the previous knowledge of their superior; therefore, in this case they are not wholly excusable.

Regardless, therefore, of the preceding, the defendants can
be justly condemned in the confiscation of their properties and
claims and be perpetually banished, provided they be declared
infamous and as forgers unable to give further evidence to the
truth; [320] all who have signed the letter being likewise
deserving with them of punishment, but of a less degree. However, as to the punishment that the defendants deserve it is to
be observed that the writing of the letter jointly does not
excuse Melyn from the judgment and decision rendered by me
against him individually on the 18th of July, which is hereby
still further confirmed. Done in Fort Amsterdam in New Netherland, the 22d of July anno 1647.

Gentlemen, we have extended our decision and judgment to
somewhat greater length and supported the same by authorities
and law, but without partiality, simply to afford the council
more light in case hereafter such arguments and accusations be
brought against us, the more so as the fiscal in his conclusion
did not introduce a single legal authority to prove that the
defendants may be punished with death or banishment. However,
we leave each of the honorable members of the council at liberty
to use his own judgment and the right to decide as in his conscience he shall see fit. The 22d of July anno 1647.

Whereas for some years past all free traders here in New
Netherland have paid duty on all peltries purchased and bartered
by them here and exported to the fatherland by every opportunity
of ships, the council have therefore considered it highly necessary
to establish a fixed duty, in order that each person may know
what impost he has to pay. Therefore, it is resolved that the
duty shall be computed as follows:

On every exported merchantable beaver skin shall be paid
15 stivers, two halves being counted as one whole and three
drielings as two whole beavers; on each other and bear skin
15 stivers; on each elk hide 15 stivers, and on the other furs
of less value according to circumstances. Thus done in council.
Present: the honorable Director P. Stuyvesant, the honorable
Willem Kieft, late director; Mr. Dincklagen, Mr. La Montagne,
Lieutenant Nuton, Paulus Leenersz, commissary of naval stores,
and Jan Claesz Bol. The 23d of July anno 1647.

[321] On the 23d of July anno 1647

Jan Dollingh from Bristol, aged about 32 years, being
legally summoned to court, declares that when Mr. Bratton's
bark a short time ago was about to sail, it was found that
Mr. Bratton aforesaid must pay 50 Carolus guilders duty on the
goods which were sold by him here. Fiscal van Dyck came and
demanded the aforesaid duty and said to Mr. Bratton: "Fifty
fuilders is too much for the honorable Company; give the
Company 30 guilders and me ten guilders." The deponent
declares that he paid the said ten guilders to the fiscal in
seawan in the Great Tavern and handed him a note for 30 guilders

for the Company in payment of the duty. The deponent declares
that he heard from Joris Wolsey and Ritchert Clof that Mr. Tomas
Willet made the above named fiscal a present of a veaver on condition that he should not inspect his bark. Thus done in council
in Fort Amsterdam, dated as above.

Ritchert Clof from Manchester, aged 40 years, being legally
summoned to court, declares that he heard Mr. Willet say that
the honorable fiscal came to inspect the bark of the said Willet.
The aforesaid Willet said in the deponent's presence in the house
of Isaack Allerton that he said to Fiscal van Dyck when he came
on board to make his inspection that it was too much trouble to
open the hold and to overhaul things and that in doing so he
would lose much time. He promised to give Fiscal van Dyck a
beaver if he would not inspect. Deponent further declares that
G[e]orge Wolsey carried a veaver. The deponent asked where he
was going with it. Wolsey answered, he was going to take the
beaver to Fiscal van Dyck. July 23, 1647.

Sentence pronounced on Cornelis Melyn [1]

Whereas Cornelis Melyn, born at Antwerp, aged about forty-
five years, inhabitant and burgher of the city of New Amsterdam
in New Netherland, has been pleased (according to the trustworthy
and sworn affidavits thereof), on the 2d of May 1645, to oppose
and obstruct the execution of Justice, threatening the Hon.
Director Kieft, at that time his lawful governor and superior,
with the gallows and the wheel, or, as the delinquent, according
to his own confession, without torture or irons twisted the words

---

[1] Revised from Doc. Rel. Col. Hist. N. Y., 1:349-50.

of the fiscal and others ordered to execute judgment and said:
"Let those who have given you orders see to it that they do not
reach the gallows and the wheel," [322] and has further resisted
justice and the order of the Hon. Director Kieft aforesaid, so
that the fiscal was obliged to enter a protest of contumacy and
opposition against him, Melyn, as likewise, according to divers
other affidavits taken the sworn to at various times, he, Melyn,
stands convicted of having slandered justice and the court here,
saying that there was no justice here; that he was not subject
to the jurisdiction of the honorable director; that the honorable
director might occupy himself with the Company's servants; that
he was a headstrong fool (een duyvels Cop), with many mutinous
and seditious words uttered against this one and that, as well
soldiers as freemen, advising the Company's servants to leave
its service, as they would receive neither money nor pay; that
the director, like the biggest liar in the country, gave fair
words and plenty of promises, which bore no fruit, &c.; in order
to instigate the freemen not to pay anything, as is apparent to
us by divers collected affidavits and credible testimonies, with
name and surname, duly read in his, Melyn's, presence; also,
that he, by his servants, endeavored, even before, or in the
beginning of the war, to purloin either secretly or forcibly,
the maize belonging to the Indians of Long Island at that time
not yet at war with our nation, for which they even killed an
Englishman; whereof, contrary to two witnesses, he denies. It
appears, however, by his own confession made in our presence,
on the 16th of July of this year, without torture or irons,

that he had a knowledge thereof; confessing that his servants
with soldiers had attempted to do so, but contrary to his order
and command, whereof he, however, has neither before nor since
complained nor given any information, which is proof enough that
he connived at and silently assented to it. Moreover, that he
exacted and took by force from the Indians, when they were hunting on Staten Island, a portion of their game, according to the
sworn affidavit dated the last of July anno 1645; all of which
are matters of very dangerous consequence, tending to mutiny,
defamation of justice and supreme authority, to force, violence
and exaction. To this is also to be added that he, Melyn, with
one Jochom Pietersz Kuyter forged, conceived, drafted and wrote
on the 28th of October 1644, in the name of the Eight Selectmen,
a most false and calumnious letter and caused it to be transcribed
and sent to the honorable directors of the Chamber at Amsterdam,
thereby clandestinely and most scandalously charging, defaming,
criminating and accusing the Hon. Director Kieft, then in loco
their governor and superior, of divers grave and criminal errors,
as is and can be further seen and read at length in the original
and in the authentic copy thereof.

Which having been investigated and inquired into by us and
our council at the request of said Director Kieft, said calumnious
letter has been found to consist in many points of false and
defamatory lies, as is apparent and proved by our own experience,
by the testimony of others heard to the number of fifteen, and
also by the declaration and answers of the co-signers.

Whereupon the fiscal instituting criminal action and suit, charged, accused and convicted said Melyn of having here committed in writing against the honorable director general [323] and justice the crimes of insult, defamation and falsehood, and consequently is declared guilty of laesae majestatis.

Which documents and proofs having been examined, investigated and inquired into by the honorable director general and council, and everything material having been duly weighed, the case was found to be of very bad consequence and ought and cannot be tolerated in a law abiding and well regulated government, but must be punished as an example to others.

Wherefore, the Hon. Director General Petrus Stuyvesant, with the advice of his council, administering justice in the name of the High and Mighty Lords The States General, his Serene Highness the Prince of Orange, and the honorable directors of the General Chartered West India Company, has sentenced and condemned, as he does hereby sentence and condemn, the aforesaid Cornelis Melyn to be banished for seven years from the district and jurisdiction of New Netherland and also to depart by the first ship, revoking all previous granted benefits, rights and pretensions which he may have obtained, or yet claims from the honorable directors and, moreover, to pay a fine of three hundred Carolus guilders, to be applied, one-third for the poor, one-third for the fiscal, and one-third for the church; dismissing the fiscal's further demand.

Thus done and enacted in council, in Fort Amsterdam in New Netherland, the 25th of July A⁰. 1647. Was signed: P. Stuyvesandt, L. van Dincklaghe, Brian Newton, Poulus Leendersz van die Grift, and Jan Claesen Boll.

Ordinance regulating the erection of buildings in
New Amsterdam [1]

Whereas by experience we notice and observe the irregularities
hereto and still daily practised by the inhabitants in building
and erecting houses, in extending their lots far beyond the
survey line, in putting up hog pens and privies on the public
roads and streets, and in neglecting and omitting properly to
build on the lots granted and given to them, the Hon. Director
General Petrus Stuyvesandt and the honorable council, in order
to prevent the same in the future, have thought fit to appoint
three street surveyors (Roy meesters), to wit: the Hon. Lubbert
van Dincklage, Paulus Leendersen, naval store keeper, and
Secretary Cornelis van Tienhoven, whom we hereby authorize and
empower to condemn and in the future to prevent [the erection
of] all unsightly and irregular buildings, fences, palisades,
posts, rails, etc. Therefore, we order and warn all and every
one of our subjects who hereafter may be inclined to build, or
to fence in gardens or lots, within or near the city of New
Amsterdam, not to venture to do so or to undertake the same
without having previously notified, spoken to and obtained the
consent of the aforesaid appointed surveyors, under penalty of
a fine of 25 Carolus guilders and the condemnation of what they
have built or set up. Likewise it is also our intention that
one and all of those who heretofore have obtained any lots shall
consider themselves warned and notified that within nine months
from this date they must properly build on said lots good and

_____

[1] Revised from Laws and Ordinances of New Netherland,
pp. 74-75.

substantial houses according to the ordinance, or, in default
thereof, such unimproved lots shall again revert to the patroon
or lord proprietor, or be conveyed to others, as he pleases.
Thus done in council in Fort Amsterdam. Present: the Hon.
Director Kieft, ^{2} Mr. Dincklage, Mr. La Montagne, Lieutenant
Nuton, Paulus Leendersen, naval store keeper, and Jan Claesz
Boll. 25 July A^o. 1647.

The honorable Petrus Stuyvesandt, director general of New
Netherland, Curaçao and the islands depending thereon, and the
honorable council, having seen and examined the demand and complaint instituted by the fiscal against Willem Pietersz from
Bolsaert, mason; having also seen the information secured to
that end by the fiscal and heard the verbal defense and acknowl-
edgement made in court by him, Willem Pietersen, at present a
prisoner, that he on divers occasions and days, forgetting his
duty and oath, has neglected his work as a mason by drinking,
for which he heretofore has been repeatedly committed to jail;
and whereas the aforesaid prisoner has now, nevertheless, again
dared to neglect his work by drinking, whereby the honorable
Company suffers loss and damage, as he draws his pay without
rendering any service in return, and, being arrested therefor
has, while in prison, undertaken to break the lock with a bolt
of the stocks and with the aid of Jan Albertsz, smith, with a
bar broken open the door of the prison; all of which, to wit,
to neglect his contracted service by drunkeness [326] and being
in prison on that account to break open the same, are matters of

---

^{2} Thus in the record.

grave consequence, which can not be tolerated or suffered, but deserve to be punished as an example to others;

Therefore the valiant and honorable Petrus Stuyvesant, with the advice of the honorable council, administering justice in the name of their High Mightinesses, the Lords States General, his Serene Highness, the Prince of Orange, and the honorable directors of the West India Company, have sentenced and condemned, as they do hereby sentence and condemn, the above mentioned delinquent to work six consecutive months with the Negroes and to pay a fine of three months' wages, one-third for the Company, one-third for the church and one-third for the fiscal, as an example to others. Thus done in council. Present: the honorable General Petrus Stuyvesant, the late director, Willem Kieft, Mr. Dincklagen, Johannes La Montangne, Lieutenant Nuton, Paulus Leendersen, commissary of naval stores, and Jan Claesz Bol, captain of the ship De Princesse. The 25th of July anno 1647.

The honorable Director Petrus Stuyvesant, director general of New Netherland, Curaçao and the islands thereof, and the honorable council, having seen the charge of Fiscal van Dyck against Jan Albertsz, smith, and the information secured by the fiscal and heard the confession of Jan Albertsz, from [   ], smith, in the service of the Chartered West India Company, at present a prisoner, who, forgetting his oath and duty, has dared to neglect his work through drunkenness, thus dishonestly drawing his pay, for which he was put in prison, and having at the request of Willem Pietersz loaned his knife to pick the lock of the stocks in which they were both confined, which could not be done, and after Willem Pietersz, mason, had broken the lock with a bolt he, the prisoner, undertook to break open the public jail, assisting Willem Pietersz aforesaid to break open the door of the prison with an iron bar, which is a matter that cannot be tolerated in countries where it is customary to administer and maintain justice and must be punished as an example to others;

Therefore the valiant and honorable Petrus Stuyvesant, with the advice of the honorable council, administering justice in the name of the high and mighty Lords the States General, his Serene Highness, the Prince of Orange, and the honorable directors of the West India [327] Company have sentenced and condemned, as we do hereby sentence and condemn, the above named delinquent to be locked for three months to an anvil and in addition to forfeit three months' wages, one-third for the honorable Company, one-third for the church and one-third for the fiscal, as an example to others. Thus done in council. Present: the honorable P. Stuyvesant, the late honorable director, Kieft; Mr. Dincklagen, Lieutenant Nuton, Paulus Leendersen, commissary of naval stores, and Jan Claesen Bol, captain of the ship De Princesse, the 25th of July anno 1647, in New Netherland.

On the 11th of August

Hendrick van Dyck, fiscal, plaintiff, vs. Jan Dollingh, defendant. The written complaint of the fiscal having been examined, it is ordered that Jan Dollingh shall be provisionally released on his promise, confirmed by clasping of hands, to appear on the first court day. He is also expressly forbidden to enter the house of Sara Willet or to molest her pending the

suit and the fiscal is ordered provisionally to produce his
witnesses at the next session of the court.

[Resolution to send Secretary van Tienhoven to Hemstead to
      inquire into the truth of a report of Indian troubles
      there] [1]

23d of August, A°. 1647

This day appeared in council certain deputies from the
village of Heemsteede, situated on Long Island, who report
verbally and in writing that they had been reliably informed by
two Indians (one named Adam) that Mayawetinnemin or, as he is
now called, Antinome, son of the chief Mecohgawodt, had by seawan
invited and thereby excited some Indians to war against the
Dutch and English, and that it is certain that the Indians were
resolved to kill the English at Heemsteede, under the jurisdiction
of this government, in the field when they were harvesting their
grain and hay, and then cut off their entire village, to which
wicked plot the chief of Catsjajock and his brethren at the east
end of Long Island had agreed. And whereas this is a matter of
very great importance and we very much suspect that this report
is invented by the English, as they have long coveted the above
named Antinomy's land, it is unanimously resolved to send
Secretary van Tienhoven, who understands [328] the Indian
language, with one or two of those of Heemsteede, equally conversant with the Indian tongue, to the east end of Long Island
in a sloop to enquire of the chief and his brethren, who were
always friends of and offered their service to our nation,
whether the above report be true or not, and the reason which

---

[1] Revised from Doc. Rel. Col. Hist. N. Y., 14:79.

induced them to undertake such mischief against us. It is also resolved and concluded that the said chief of Catsjajock and his brethren shall be presented with three cloth coats and some trifles in the name of the honorable Company, with an offer of our friendship, which the late Director Willem Kieft had formerly promised them when peace was concluded. All of which being done and investigated, this matter shall be disposed of as the exigency and circumstances of the case shall demand. Thus done the 23d of August A⁰. 1647, in Fort Amsterdam in New Netherland. Was signed: P. Stuyvesandt, L. van Dincklage, La Montagne, Briant Nuton, Poulus Leenders van die Grift.

26th of August anno 1647

Honorable Gentlemen: We are ordered and instructed by the honorable Company to fortify and repair in a proper manner the dilapidated fortress of New Amsterdam and for the lessening of the expense to induce the commonalty to lend a helping hand thereto; also to encourage the soldiers by a small compensation and reward to assist. And now being ready to make a beginning therewith the question is: "How is the fort to be repaired?" With sods or, as the directors order, with stones, as it was first begun? And how to induce the community to lend a helping hand.

Secondly, we are daily informed and understand from the reports of the commonalty in general as well as by the Indians that at the making of the truce the Indians were promised presents — some of our Dutch people say several hundred fathoms of seawan; the Indians say a parcel of cloth and a bag full of seawan, in compensation of their blood which had been shed. Daily experience shows that they are restless and dissatisfied.

Some of the most prominent citizens have repeatedly been to see us; they dread a new war in case the Indians are not made content by presents, for which purpose we are not provided either with money or goods. Further, if we allow the uneasiness of the Indians and the counsel and advice of the commonalty to go unheeded and we be now or hereafter involved in a new war with the natives who are little to be trusted, the fickle commonalty will lay the blame on us because we have not provided in time against it when the Indians could and ought to have been pacified by the presents which have been promised them.

[329] Thirdly, as some apply to us for the little red-wood [1] that remains, what is the honorable council's advice? Shall we sell it or keep it for the Company for some future occasion, as I have also advised them?

The honorable director general and council having considered and debated the aforesaid propositions and paid attention to everything connected therewith, the result is: If the fort is to be repaired and rebuilt as it ought to be, that is, all around with stones laid in mortar, by which means alone it can be hereafter maintained, the soil hereabout not being suitable for building up the fortress here with sods, unless every year new and nearly as large sums be expended thereon, it will require a considerable sum of money in wages alone, both in laying and hauling the stone and burning the lime, for which the honorable directors command us to request the commonalty to lend us a helping hand who, in consequence of the loss suffered by the

---

[1] Stockvisch hout, or logwood, from the West-Indian islands, used as a dyestuff, to produce dark red colors.

war, are also not sufficiently prosperous to be [compelled]
thereto by our authority. We find it advisable, however, to
submit the proposition to them in general and to hear their
answer thereto, but as it is difficult to bring so many heads
under one hood or so many different votes to unanimity, we deem
it expedient and wise to propose to them to elect from among
themselves the double number of nine of the most respectable and
experienced persons as select men and their representatives to
confer, speak and consult with us on these and other burdens
which concern the commonalty; from which double number of nine
persons we shall select a single number, who shall always in the
future, whenever invited to, assist in seeking and promoting
with us the interest of the country in general in matters of
like character; provided, nevertheless, that they shall not
have power of their own authority to constitute or convene any
assembly, but must wait until they are summoned by us and the
honorable council, as is customary in our dear fatherland and
elsewhere.

2. As to the troubles and difficulties with the Indians,
we deem it necessary to observe the orders of the honorable
directors to prevent by all means in our power that on our part
no cause be given them for any discontent or for a new war,
which, should it again break out, would utterly ruin the farmers
just beginning. The last would be worse than the first and
destroy all hope of those who should come after them. We consider it therefore advisable and necessary to confirm the peace
formerly concluded by a present to the Indian sachems, but in

no wise to offer it to them as a bounded duty, much less by
virtue of a previous promise, as they together claim that in
making the peace the promise of compensation for bloodshed was
made to them which according to their demand would mean entirely
too much. We advise, therefore, that this present be offered
to them as being sent by the honorable directors as a renewal
and continuation of the ancient alliance and friendship and
that they be told at the same time that we are not responsible
for the last war which the old Sachem who has gone away may have
caused; also, that we have no desire for new trouble and war,
but wish to live with them in peaceful alliance and as good
neighbors; in token and in confirmation of which we offer them
this present.

[330] As to the third and last point, concerning the sale
of the remaining red-wood, we consider it not only advisable,
but highly necessary, to obtain certain means, as well for the
construction of the fortress and houses that have fallen into
decay and for the payment and discharge of the debts that were
left and have already been incurred, as for using a portion
thereof for the present to be offered to the Indians; all of
which the commonalty, which scarcely begins to recover its
breath, cannot contribute. And as we have little or nothing on
hand and hardly anything is to be expected from the fatherland
as long as the Company remains in its present condition, we are
against our will and inclination urged and obliged to effect
this sale to place ourselves on a firm basis and to restore
this province. We also find it necessary to retain half the

proceeds of the red-wood for the repair of the fort, without using it for any other purpose, and the remaining half for the incurred debts.

Thus done in council in Fort Amsterdam in New Netherland, the 27th of August 1647. Was signed: P. Stuyvesant, L. van Dincklagen, La Montangne, Brian Newton and A. Keyser. In the margin was written: Present, the honorable general, the honorable Dincklagen, Lieutenant Nuton, Mr. La Montangne, Paulus Leendersz, commissary of naval stores, and Commissary d'Keyser.

Proposition submitted by the honorable Director General Petrus Stuyvesandt to the honorable council in session on the 20th of September anno 1647

1. The report of Secretary Tienhoven and Commissary van Bruggen, respecting their mission to the east end of Long Island and the passage of an authentic document on the subject.

2. Their report concerning the ship Beninjo, or Hercules, which they say sailed from the chamber of North Holland or Medenblick and comes to trade within the limits and territory of our jurisdiction, to the prejudice of our merchants here who have paid the proper duty. The aforesaid secretary and commissary declare on this point that the skipper and merchants of said ship had requested them to urge us to grant them permission to trade here, on condition of paying the proper duty on their cargo and returns, from which it sufficiently appears that they are smugglers and therefore that their ship and cargo are liable to confiscation if they can be reached, of which in my opinion there is little chance and expectation, as they are on guard and well armed, to wit, with 10 guns and 27 men, and as there is no vessel ready to reduce them. Furthermore, they would in advance

be informed by some one or other of our designs and run away and
probably likewise they would be aided by the English of New Haven,
where the merchants have their store on land, so that it ought
to be well and carefully considered what is to be done in the
matter. [331] I understand that fraud has been committed therein
and that therefore the ship and cargo would be subject to confiscation if here, but I fear that he, [the skipper], would slip
away, as heretofore Symon Jansz did, and that meanwhile most of
the goods would be sold here in this country under the name of
English merchandise, which would then greatly prejudice our
traders, who are already complaining of the matter. I think it
would not be unwise to admit the merchandise, provided they
oblige themselves over their signatures to pay proper duty on
the whole capital, as it is customary in the fatherland and pro
rata of the cargo.

3. As to the ship Swol, which is laid up at great expense
and cost to the Company and at the same time more and more
deteriorates as to its standing and running rigging, it was
heretofore resolved to sell it to the best advantage of the
Company, which I still consider to be most advantageous for it.
Now, we are offered 9000 guilders, payable in produce of this
country, to wit, provisions and seawan, for said ship with twenty
iron pedreros, four of which are lying among the ballast and
are unsuitable for said ship, with an old set of sails, running
and standing rigging, anchors and cordage as per inventory.
This, in my opinion, is 1000 to 1500 guilders too low, but as
no higher price and bid can be obtained and it is to be feared

that if the ship lie over next winter the rigging, cordage and other effects will receive still further damage and injury, the question is, shall we let her go at that price or haul her on shore and as occasion offers sell the top-hamper or salvage the same for our sloops and burn the hull for the iron work?, it being necessary that one of the two courses be adopted before winter.

4. Govert Aertsen requests permission to go to New Haven to purchase some goods from the ship that has arrived there and to sell them here, on which he promises to pay 16 per cent. Shall he be allowed to do so?

5. An end ought to be put to the criminal proceedings against Mich[iel] Piquet which have now been pending for nearly five or six weeks and are not carried on by the fiscal. As regards my opinion of his previous crimes and sentences, I have granted him pardon by the advice of the council. What has occurred since or between the two concerns me most as an individual, to wit, being threatened to be shot between this place and my Bouwery, as the complaint alleges. Therefore, being a party to the case, I scruple to assist in pronouncing judgment and sentence. I therefore request the council to be pleased to pronounce a proper judgment according to law and equity and to terminate the case, inclining, if proper and allowable, more toward mercy than to the rigor of the law; the more so as the prisoner, whilst holding my pass and pardon, has been de novo placed under arrest, from which he would otherwise apparently have escaped.

6. To propose whether Andries Hudden shall continue on
the South river or who else to send there, as it is highly
necessary that a proper person be stationed there. Was signed:
P. Stuyvesandt.

[322] The 20th of September 1647

Whereas the ship named St. Beninjo, or Harcules, which
sailed from Medenblick, has arrived at what the English call
New Haven, situated in New England, of which vessel Cornelis
Claesen Snoo is master and Mr. Willem Westerhuysen and Samuel
van Goedenhuysen merchants, who have caused application to be
made to the honorable director general and council here for
permission to trade in this province, offering to pay here in
New Netherland the duty on imported and exported goods and
returns; therefore, the honorable director and council, having
duly weighed and considered the impossibility of having said
vessel by force brought here and fearing also that if any preparation were made to that end here, it would immediately become
rumored about and said ship, which lies always prepared and ready
to sail, would thus slip away from us, have for the best advantage
of the honorable Company and the benefit of the inhabitants here
resolved and unanimously concluded to grant freedom of trade to
the above named merchants with their ship and goods, on condition
of paying the honorable Company here the proper duties. Thus
done in council on the date above written. Was signed:
P. Stuyvesant, L. Dinckaghe, La Montangne, Brian Newton and
A. Keyser. In the margin was written: Present, the honorable
general, Mr. Dincklaghe, Mr. La Montangne, Lieutenant Nuton,
Paulus Leendersz, commissary of naval stores, and Commissary
Keyser.

In council at Fort Amsterdam it is resolved and concluded
for the best advantage and interest of the Chartered West India
Company to sell the ship Swol to Mr. Goudjer, who offers 9000
guilders for said ship with twenty iron guns, or 7000 guilders
with ten iron guns and what is specified in the inventory and
to let her go at that price if no more can be obtained, for in
case said ship be not sold she will lie here to rot and decay
to the great loss and damage of the Company. Done as above.
Was signed: P. Stuyvesantt, L. van Dincklagen, La Montangne,
Brian Newton and A. Keyser. In the margin was written:
Present, the honorable general, Mr. Dincklagen, Mr. La Montangne,
Lieutenant Newton, Paulus Leendersz and Commissary Keyser.

[333] The honorable director general and council having
observed the fitness of Commissary Andries Hudden have unanimously
resolved and concluded to continue him in the service of the
Chartered West India Company as Commissary at Fort Nassauw on
the South river of New Netherland, which Hudden shall be given
the same allowance and salary as shall be granted to other commissaries stationed at distant outlying posts.

Done the 20th of September anno 1647. Was signed:
P. Stuyvesant, La Montange, Brian Newton, A. Keyser. In the
margin was written: Present, the honorable general, Mr. Dincklagen,
Mr. La Montangne, Lieutenant Nuton, Paulus Leendersz and
Commissary Keyser.

Being informed and advised on the 17th of September, upon
the return of Secretary Tienhoven and Commissary van Bruggen,
among other reports, that they fell in with and found in front

of the place called by the English, New Haven, within the limits
of our jurisdiction and government, a certain ship called Beninjo
which sailed with consent and commission from Medenblick, the
master and merchants of which had earnestly prayed and requested
of them to procure from us and our council permission to go with
their ship, persons, merchants and goods in front of our capital
and residence of New Amsterdam on the Manhatans and there, on
paying to the government the customary duties on the imported
goods and exported returns, to enjoy the same trading privileges,
exemptions and power to trade and do business as we were
accustomed to confer on other of our traders and merchants,
which being communicated to us and our council by our secretary
and commissary, we, not doubting the correctness of their reports
or the sincerity of the applicants, have consented, granted and
allowed, as we on their application do hereby consent, grant and
allow the skipper, Cornelis Claesen Snoo; the merchants, Mr.
Willem Westerhuysen and Samuel van Goedenhuysen, and the sailors
of said ship Beninjo to come and go with their persons, ships,
goods and merchandise, without let or hindrance at the very first
opportunity, to trade and transact business the same as our own
subjects, on condition that they pay to us or to the honorable
directors the customary duties on the imported merchandise and
exported returns, as others of our merchants and traders are
wont to do, without our being obliged, however, in virtue thereof,
to grant them like priveleges hereafter.

Done at Fort Amsterdam, on the Manhatans in New Netherland,
and for further security signed with our own hand and sealed with

our usual seal, this 22d of September anno 1647. Was signed:
P. Stuyvesant, L. van Dincklaghe, La Montangne, Brian Newton,
Pouwelis Leendersz van die Grift and A. Keyser.

[Ordinance establishing a board of Nine Men] [1]

[334] Petrus Stuyvesant, on behalf of the High and Mighty
Lords the States General, his Serene Highness the Prince of
Orange, and the honorable directors of the General Chartered
West India Company of the United Netherlands, director general
of New Netherland and the Curaçao islands, captain and commander
in chief of the said Company's ships and yachts in these northern
part of America; together with the honorable council;

To all those who shall see or hear these presents read,
Greeting!

Whereas in accordance with our commission and general
instructions we have no other aim, wish or desire but that this
province of New Netherland entrusted to us and especially this
our capital and residence of New Amsterdam may grow and increase
in good order, justice, government, population, prosperity and
mutual peace and improvement, and be provided with and aided in
the upkeep of a strong and substantial fort, a school, church,
sheet piling, pier and similar highly necessary public works
and common buildings, whereto we according to the instructions
given to us are ordered to solicit the cooperation of the commonalty, as this tends mostly to their own welfare and protection
and is customary in all well administered government, colonies
and places; yet, we are disinclined by virtue of our granted

---

[1] Revised from *Laws* *and* *Ordinances* *of* *New* *Netherland*,
pp. 75-78.

commission and instructions to burden and oppress the good and
peaceable commonalty, our dear vassals and subjects by means of
exactions, imposts and intolerable taxes, but wish in the most
reasonable manner to request their consent thereto and to induce
them to lend a helping hand in undertaking such honorable and
most necessary works. And whereas it is difficult to bring so
many heads under one capuche, or to reduce so many votes to one
voice, we have, with the advice of our council, heretofore proposed and submitted to the commonalty that they, without passion,
hatred or envy, select a double number of nine persons from the
most notable, most reasonable, most honorable and most prominent
of our subjects, in order that from them a single number of nine
persons may be chosen and appointed as Selectmen to confer with
us and our council about such consent and assistance and to the
best of their knowledge and information to help forward and
promote the welfare of the commonalty as well as of the common-
wealth. For which purpose then, a double number having on the
day aforesaid been selected by the good commonalty, our dear
subjects, the following are chosen therefrom by us and our
council, to wit:

From the merchants — Augustyn Heerman, Arnoldus van
Hardenberch and Govert Loockemans;

From the burghers — Jan Jansz Damen, Jacob Wolphertsz
and Hendrick Kip;

From the farmers — Machiel Jansz, Jan Evertsen Bout and
Tomas Hall;

As spokesmen for the commonalty, who, having taken the oath
of fidelity to us and the honorable council to regulate and
govern themselves in conformity to the orders and instructions
already given or yet to be given, are hereby confirmed in their
aforesaid capacity, under the following rules:

First. That as good and faithful spokesmen and agents of
the commonalty they shall strive for and as far as lies in their
power help to promote the honor of God and the welfare of our
dear fatherland, the greatest advantage of the Company and the
prosperity of the worthy commonalty here, and the advancement
of the pure Reformed [335] religion, as taught at this day in
the churches here and in the Netherlands.

Second. That they shall not set up and hold any private
conventicles and meetings, much less hold any consultations and
pass resolutions, without the knowledge and consent of the
director general and council, or without his special and particular
order, except only that, when legally convened and having heard
the proposals of the honorable director general and council,
they may adjourn and take a recess in order to confer with each
other and consider such proposals and thereafter report thereon;
provided, nevertheless, that the director general retains the
power to appoint either himself or some one of the council to
act as president at such consultations and deliberations, to
collect the votes and to make a report to the council.

Third. Whereas in consequence of the increase of the
population lawsuits and disputes which parties bring against
each other are multiplied, as well as many questions and quarrels

of trifling moment which can be determined and disposed of by
arbitrators, whereby matters of greater importance are frequently
held up and remain undecided, to the prejudice and injury of
this place and the good inhabitants thereof and also to the
great expense, loss of time and vexation of the contending
parties, three of the delegates shall once a week, on Thursday,
the usual civil court day, have access to our general council,
as long as civil cases are being tried, in order to obtain a
knowledge of the cases of parties who may be referred to them
as arbitrators and referees, to wit, one from the merchants,
one from the burghers and one from the farmers, who shall rotate
in regular order once a month. And if any one of them be
indisposed or absent, he may substitute another of the delegates
in his place. Furthermore, the parties who by the council are
referred to them as arbitrators and referees shall, upon being
judged, remain bound to submit themselves without opposition to
the pronounced decision, or, in default thereof, be fined one
pound Flemish for the first time, to be paid before the com-
plainant can appeal or obtain a hearing before our council from
the decision of the referees.

Fourth. The number of the Nine elected Selectmen shall
continue until further order and circumstances, provided that
annually six shall retire and that 12 shall be nominated from
the most qualified inhabitants, whose names shall be returned
to us by the Nine Men in meeting assembled, without it being
necessary hereafter to convene the entire commonalty for that
purpose, which meeting shall take place on the last of December
following the next New Year's day and so every year successively.

Thus done and enacted in council, the 25th of September A⁰.
1647. Was signed: P. Stuyvesant, L. van Dincklaghe, La Montagne,
Brian Newton, Poulus Leendersz van die Grift and A. Keyser.
[Propositions made by Director Stuyvesant concerning claims on
    Long Island made by the Earl of Sterling] [1]

[336] Propositions submitted by the honorable director
general to the council in session, the 28th of September A⁰.
1647.

The day before yesterday I was informed by Mr. Harck,
sheriff of Vlissingen, [2] that a certain Scotchman named Forrester
had come there to Vlissingen with commission to take possession
as governor of Long Island and of all the islands situated within
five miles thereabouts; that said Forrester had spent two nights
at Heemsteede and one night at Vlissingen with our vassals and
subjects there and had exhibited to them his commission. He
came here on his way to Gravesande and Amersfoort, there to
exhibit his commission to the English residing under our allegiance
and government. As nothing is to be expected from this but
mischief and further encroachment on the Company's lands granted
them by charter from their High Mightinesses, our Sovereigns,
we have requested the said governor to show his commission and
instructions and asked him by what authority he came within our
limits. To which he gave for answer that he came here to demand
my commission and authority. Wherefore I had him taken into
custody and on the next day placed under arrest at the City
Tavern at the Company's expense, and having demanded his commission found one with an old seal depending, but not signed with

---

[1] Revised from Doc. Rel. Col. Hist. N.Y., 14:79-80.
[2] Flushing, L. I.

any name and, besides, a power of attorney signed by Marry
Sterlingx, accompanied by a pass from Parliament, and nothing
more.

The further question is, What shall be done with said
pretended governor?

Thirdly, that the commissioners be pleased to make a final
disposition of the criminals in prison, particularly Picquet.

[1] Fourthly, as Commissary Hudde has returned in consequence
of contrary winds and weather and in his absence was accused by
Mr. Dincklagen of unfaithfulness toward the Company and his own
cousin, this, being proved, unfits him in my opinion for the
charge on the South river. Meanwhile, I ask of the council a
proper certificate that, according to my bounden duty, I first,
on the 20th instant, on the regular court day, proposed to the
council whether Commissary Hudde should be sent again to the
South river, or whether another should be sent in his place.
Nothing was then alleged against his person; he was therefore
continued by a unanimous vote of all the members of the council.
Neither was anything said against him at the following meeting,
being the 26th, when the previous resolution was to be recon-
sidered and signed. Was signed: P. Stuyvesandt.

[337] The 28th of September anno 1647 [2]

The proposition of the honorable director general respecting the pretended governor of Long Island and the neighboring
islands being heard in council, it was unanimously considered
highly necessary by the honorable director general and council

---

[1] Revised from <u>Doc</u>. <u>Rel</u>. <u>Col</u>. <u>Hist</u>. <u>N</u>. <u>Y</u>., 12:42.
[2] Revised from <u>Doc</u>. <u>Rel</u>. <u>Col</u>. <u>Hist</u>. <u>N</u>. <u>Y</u>., 14:80-81.

to hear the aforesaid pretended governor, named Forrester, personally in council, in the presence of two or three impartial witnesses, and to examine his commission, in order to ascertain by whose authority he, Forrester, lays claim to the government of Long Island and the islands situated thereabouts. Was signed: P. Stuyvesandt, L. van Dincklaghe, La Montagne, Brian Newton, Poulus Leendersz van die Grift and A. Keyser.

Andreas Forrester, born at a place called Dondey [1] in Scotland, appeared in council, in the presence of Carel van Bruggen, Adriaen van [der] Donck and Philip Geraerdy, impartial witnesses, all understanding the English language. Being asked, who had given him commission to take possession of Long Island and the neighboring Islands as governor and where said commission was, said Forrester exhibited a large parchment, covered with writing, in the form of a commission, to which hung an old broken seal; having no name subscribed, nor any place designated where the commission was issued; also, a power of attorney signed by Marry Steerlings.

The honorable director and council asked said Forrester why the commission was not duly signed? To which he gave for answer, it was not customary and that the seal alone was sufficient.

Said Forrester was further asked if he had no other, or better, commission than the one he now produced and what authority he had to demand the general's commission? To which he gave for answer, he had no other commission at present and therefore could not produce any other.

------

[1] Dundee.

Said Forrester was also asked in council if their High Mightinesses' ambassador had said in England that he, on behalf of the Lords States, relinquished those parts of New Netherland. Andru Forrester answered that such had been said in the lifetime of Mylord Steerlings.

[338] The 28th of September 1647

In council in Fort Amsterdam. Present: The Hon. Director General, Mr. Dincklagen, Mons. La Montangne, Lieutenant Nuton, Paulus Leendersz and Commissary de Keyser. All that is material in regard to the commission and claim of Andru Forester, the pretended governor of Long Island etc., was after mature deliberation well weighed and considered.

First, seeing an unsigned written parchment in the form of a commission, from which depended an old broken seal.

Secondly, that said Forrester had exhibited on Long Island, to the English residing under the allegiance and obedience of the Lords States, his commission, and thus induced the simple farmers to believe many things, whence further encroachments on this jurisdiction are to be feared and expected; in order to prevent such and similar mischiefs, it is unanimously resolved and concluded in council, for the sake of our Sovereigns' reputation, the Company's interest, and the prosperity of our nation in these parts, to send the pretended governor a prisoner to Holland by the ship De Valckenier, to vindicate his commission before their High Mightinesses. Was signed: P. Stuyvesant, L. van Dincklaghe, La Montangne, Brian Nuton, Poulus Leendersz van die Grift and A. Keyser.

[1] Appeared in council, Andries Hudden, commissary on the South river, and demanded proof of Mr. Dincklagen wherein he had defrauded any person, or whom and where he had robbed any one of anything, and what induced Mr. Dincklagen to utter such slanders against the above named Hudden.

Whereas it is highly necessary for the preservation of the Company's guns, muskets, and other munitions of war to appoint a captain at arms to have proper supervision over the soldiers and means of defense; therefore, the honorable director general and council have considered Hans Wever a proper person, who is this day appointed captain at arms at 16 guilders per month. Was signed: P. Stuyvesant, L: van Dincklaghe, La Montangne, Brian Newton, Poulus Leendersz van die Grift and A: Keyser.

[339] The 30th of September 1647

In council was examined the person of Michiel Piquet, at present a prisoner regarding the accusation made by the fiscal that the prisoner intended to shoot the honorable Director General Stuyvesant between his farm and the Manhatans when his honor rode to his farm, which four witnesses swear he did say. Therefore, he, Piquet, was asked whether he had anything to say in his defense; if so, to say and produce it now; also, if he had anything to say against the sitnesses, who confirmed their testimony on oath in his presence, why they should not be believed. Michiel Piquet gives for answer that the deponents stole watermelons and some boards and were, therefore, unworthy of belief. Being asked if he could prove it, he says that ne has no proof, but that God was his witness.

---

[1] Revised from Doc. Rel. Col. Hist. N. Y., 12:42.

Opinion of the honorable General Petrus Stuyvesandt

Having seen the sworn affidavits and testimony of four persons, who were not challenged or objected to by the accused, nor held by us as being anything but honest persons and therefore worthy of belief, and who moreover have taken the proper oath; therefore, it is my opinion that proper sentence may be pronounced upon the evidence without its being necessary to subject the prisoner to torture. The reasons are:

First — According to God's word as a general basis of law, all truth shall be established by the testimony of two or three witnesses. Hare there are four and in addition we have their oath.

Second — The Imperial statutes of Charles the Fifth, which are in force in our country, state in Tractatu Crim. chap. 21, fl. 12, "when a judge is to pronounce sentence involving a man's blood, life or limb, he is to observe this rule, that he sentence or condemn no man to so dire a punishment unless the guilty person, that is the evil-doer, be convicted of the crime with which he is charged, either on his own confession or the corroborating testimony of his accomplices, or other striking proof as clear as day." A majore ad minus valet consequentia: If he may without his own confession be punished or put to death on the sole sworn testimony of his accomplices who are accessory to the crime, how much the more so on the sworn affidavits and testimony of persons, who up to that time were acknowledged as men of probity, whom the accused himself does not challenge except by general denial. With this agrees Damhouder, in Tractatu Criminalibus, chapter 49, fo. 88. "Two competent, irreproachable

and unobjectionable witnesses, giving direct testimony to the
fact, either from what they have seen or of which they have
certain knowledge, constitute proof, the same as the confession
of the criminal or the acknowledgment of parties in court,
voluntarily, without torture."

Third — Independent of the evidence the case is clearly
enough proved by the circumstances.

[340] Fourth — The delinquent, having suffered torture,
would according to legal opinions be free from punishment and
have the right to institute an action for slander or defamation
against the four witnesses for having unjustly accused him out
of hatred, and who therefore, according to the Imperial ordinances,
quoted above in Tractatu Criminalibus, chap. 15, fo. 15, would
be liable to the penalty which the delinquent or accused would
have incurred.

I, therefore, conclude that where there are three witnesses,
no further proof or certitude is required to arrive at a definite
judgment, although the accused has not confessed the deed, of
which opinion I remain, until I am better informed either from
God's word or the Imperial statutes. This 30th day of September
1647. Was signed: P. Stuyvesant.

Opinion of Mr. Dincklagen

If Michiel Piquet is to be punished as he deserves it must
be on his own confession, either voluntarily or by torture, as
he is accused by four witnesses of having said that he would
shoot the honorable director and the fiscal. Nemo in auditus
et sine propria confessione facile condemnatur. This 30th of
September 1647. Was signed: L. van Dincklaghe.

Opinion of Lieutenant Briant Nuton

Lieutenant Nuton says that the offender, Michiel Piquet, to the best of his knowledge, may be sentenced to be punished by the court on the testimony of four witnesses, who at the request of the fiscal have testified against him, in such manner as the crime shall demand according to law, provided that the witnesses are irreproachable. Was signed: Brian Newton.

[341] Opinion of Paulus Leendersz, commissary of naval stores

Having heard the fiscal's demand, it can in my opinion not be allowed, unless he be first brought to the rack and make his own confession; or else, in my judgment, he cannot be put to death. But if he be not subject to capital punishment, then there is no need of the rack, for on the evidence of these four persons he can be banished from the country and punished corporally. The last of September 1647. Was signed: Pouwelis Lendersz van die Grift.

Opinion of Commissary de Keyser

Having heard the complaint of Fiscal Hendrick van Dyck, concerning the offense committed by Michiel Piquet in threatening the honorable director general and the honorable Mr. Kieft, it is my opinion that the offender should first be tortured, because the threat is clearly proved by four witnesses, who attest the fact; and when he confesses he ought to be condemned, and if he does not confess he may for his former crimes be banished from the country. Done at Manhatans, this last of September 1647. Was signed: A. Keyser.

Resolved in council that the honorable director and each of the councilors shall separately give his advice and vote how each of them individually thinks the offender, Michiel Piquet, ought and deserves to be punished according to God's word, the written law, his conscience and the best of his knowledge, and that as the majority of votes shall agree the sentence shall be rendered and pronounced.

The honorable Director General Petrus Stuyvesandt judges that Michiel Piquet deserves to be put to death. Was signed: P. Stuyvesant.

Mr. Dincklagen says that Michiel Piquet should forever be banished from this country and in addition be confined for 25 years in the house of correction. Was signed: L. van Dincklaghe.

Briant Newton says that the delinquent should be sent to Holland and be confined for ten years in the house of correction at Amsterdam.

La Montangne says that Michiel Piquet should be confined for ten years in the house of correction. Was signed: La Montagne.

[342] Paulus Leendersz says that Michiel Piquet should be confined for 25 years in the house of correction at Amsterdam and be banished forever from New Netherland. Was signed: Pauwelis Leendersz van die Grift.

Andriaen de Keyser says his advice is that Michiel Piquet be banished forever from New Netherland and be confined for twelve years in the house of correction. Was signed: A: Keyser.

Whereas Michiel Piquet, a native of Rouen in France, has
on the [   ] of June, at the house of one Pieter Montfoort,
allowed himself to be induced to slander the former director
general, Mr. Kieft, with his tongue and to call him a traitor,
rascal, and a betrayer, at the same time threatening the said
honorable director that his legs would not carry him out of the
country; and also his successor, the Honorable Pieter Stuyvesant,
unless he behaved better, as by the informations and sworn testimony
more fully and clearly appears. And whereas the aforesaid Piquet,
at present a prisoner, at the time obstinately denied and refused
to admit this, it is nevertheless, aside from the sworn testimony
and depositions, sufficiently verified and proved by his flight,
violation and breaking out of prison, notwithstanding he was
cited and summoned on three successive court days to defend his
case and to hear all such charges as the fiscal in his official
capacity was instituting against him, for which grave and criminal
offenses and crimes, he, Piquet, having been banished by the
director and council from this government and jurisdiction of
New Netherland, was afterwards, on his own humble petition and
that of other our dear subjects, graciously pardoned and granted
remission of the aforesaid banishment, only with this reservation
that henceforth he was to conduct himself honestly and to absent
himself from the island of the Manhatans and our capital and
place of residence, New Amsterdam. Not being satisfied and contented herewith, he has afterwards de novo threatened to shoot
the new director general, Petrus Stuyvesant, between Fort New
Amsterdam and his farm and also Fiscal van Dyck and, after

having committed the deed, to go to the savages, or natives, of
this country and territory, to offer himself to be their captain
and war chief against the Dutch nation; also, to murder and slay
the former director, Willem Kieft, in whatever land he should
find him, whether in Holland, France, or elsewhere, the prisoner
being sorry that he had not bought the pistol which he saw in
Jan Botser's sloop in order therewith to shoot the fiscal, as
more fully appears by the repeated and sworn depositions of
four, as far as we [343] know and it does appear, honest and
credible witnesses, entered in the record of Fiscal Van Dyck.
All of which acts and threats, although not carried into effect,
are of evil consequence and cannot be tolerated in a land of
justice. Therefore, the honorable Petrus Stuyvesant, director
general of New Netherland, Curaçao, etc., administering justice
with the advice of the honorable council in the name of the
High and Mighty Lords the States General, his Serene Highness
the Prince of Orange, and the honorable directors of the General
Chartered West India Company of the United Netherlands, have
condemned and sentenced, as we do hereby sentence and condemn,
the aforesaid Michiel Piquet, at present a prisoner, to perpetual
banishment from this their government of New Netherland, to be
sent in the ship De Valckenier to the most wise and honorable
council of the city of Amsterdam, in order with their consent
for the term of eighteen consecutive years to earn his living
and passage money by rasping in their work house, or otherwise
according to their honors' pleasure, dismissing the fiscal's
further demand. Thus resolved by a majority of votes in our

council at New Amsterdam in New Netherland, the 4th of October
1647. Was signed: P. Stuyvesant, L: van Dincklaghe, La Montangne,
Brian Newton, Pouwelis Leendersz van die Grift and A. Keyser.

Whereas there lately arrived from New Haven, situated within
the limits of New Netherland, a ship named St. Beninjo, of which
Cornelis Claesen Snoy is master, Mr. Willem Westerhuysen merchant
and owner, and the merchant named Samuel van Goedenhuysen a
passenger, who through Commissary Carel van Bruggen and Secretary
Tienhoven made a verbal request to us, the director general and
council, for permission to come personally to the Manhatans with
their ship and cargo, offering to pay the honorable Company here
the regular duty, this was granted to them on the [   ], as
can be more fully seen by the entry in the Resolution Book. Said
permission was handed to them by Govert Aertsz at New Haven,
whereupon the above named Goedenhuysen came here at the first
opportunity with the said Govert Aertsen, arriving at this place
with his sloop on the [   ], without bringing hither a penny's
worth of his, the skipper's, or said Westerhuysen's goods, or
paying any duty, or bringing with him any invoices or writings.
The said Goedenhuysen also reported that the ship Beninjo lay
ready to sail for Virginia, from which we, the director and
council, see, perceive and notice their deceitfulness and false
pretense, and whereas the opportunity now presents itself to
capture the said ship Beninjo without arousing suspicion as to
our intention, inasmuch as the ship Swol, being sold, must be
conveyed to New Haven; therefore, it is unanimously resolved
and concluded in council to provide the ship Swol with men and

ammunition and to instruct and command Paulus Leendersz, the
commissary of naval stores, to bring the ship hither if possible,
either voluntarily or by force, in order that proper proceedings
may be instituted against said skipper and those whom it may concern, all according to the order and instruction of the honorable
directors. Thus done in council in Fort Amsterdam in New
Netherland, the first of October 1647. Was signed: P. Stuyvesant,
L: van Dincklaghe, la Montangne, Brian Newton, Poulus L: van
die Grift and A. Keyser.

[344] Proposition of the honorable Director General Petrus Stuyvesandt

With the advice of the council we brought away the ship
St. Beninjo from the Rooberch, otherwise called New Haven by the
English, and on last Friday, being the 11th instant, examined
the skipper, pilot, supercargo Goedenhuysen and all his officers,
in presence of us and the council, on the interrogatories prepared
for that purpose, all of which were distinctly read to them and
also answered by them.

First, that the ship sailed from Patria for New Netherland
without commission from the Prince or the States, and without
proper authority from the Chartered West India Company, chamber
at Amsterdam, or any others, save only a commission from the
chamber of the North Quarter to get a cargo of salt within the
limits of the charter, [in] the West Indies, from the Orinoco
or westward to the coast of Florida, without leave to break bulk
elsewhere than therein specified; which commission and authority
he clearly exceeded, voluntarily and deliberately setting his
course straight towards New Netherland, where he not only broke
bulk before New Haven, but almost completely discharged his ship
of all its cargo.

Second. It appears by the confession of his crew and of Samuel van Goedenhuysen that on the merchandise brought with them they nowhere paid any duty or customs.

Third. That articles of contraband were brought in the ship and landed, among others 300 pounds of powder and ten guns, packed in a cask marked R. X. P; also that there are still about 400 or 500 pounds of powder in said ship, brought along with no other intent than to trade them in this country according to the declaration of the owners themselves.

Fourth. It appears that the skipper had already planned in the fatherland to defraud the Company, as he had engaged his crew to go to the English Virginia and thence to New Netherland, as they declared; or, as the charter reads, to all free and unfree places.

Fifth. Their deceit and guilt is manifest from their own confession and declaration, which is confirmed by the affidavits of Secretary Tienhoven and Carel van Bruggen, whom the supercargo and skipper requested to secure from us and the council permission to come here unmolested, pay the lord his due, and to cry _Pater pecavi_.

Sixth. It is shown by their own confession and proved by the circumstances that as they cheated and defrauded the honorable directors in the fatherland, so did they intend to do here, petitioning by their agents and offering to acknowledge their fault and pay the regular duty, which they did not intend to do, only to gain time and delay. This is proved by their own statement and declaration and by the case itself. Their declaration, that of Supercargo van Goedenhuysen as well as that of the skipper, pilot and the common sailors, is a [lie], for that they were ready to sail, not to come here, but to go to the English Virginis, is confirmed by the circumstances and the case itself, because up to this moment they had not sent or entered one piece of goods, or paid one farthing of duty, which is proof enough that the ship going empty to the Virginis would have sought there nothing else than a cargo of tobacco and not paid us or the Company a doit, either on the merchandise or the return cargo.

[345] Seventh. The unfree nature of the ship and goods appears by the action of the English nation, who first endeavored by persuasion and afterward by force to recover the ship from us, as the commissary of naval stores, Paulus Leendersz, Carel van Bruggen and all the soldiers and sailors can attest.

Therefore, the opinion of the council is asked, what is to be done with said ship and whether it is not subject to confiscation, as we think it is, with all its appurtenances. This 15th day of October 1647. Was signed: P. Stuyvesant, L: van Dincklaghe, la Montagne, Brian Newton, Powelis Leendersz van die Grift and A: Keyser.

On the 16th of october 1647

Cornelis Claesen Snoy, master of the ship St. Beninjo, being legally summoned, appeared before the council, where he was asked if he, the skipper, had any other or better papers or commission than he had delivered or exhibited up to this time. Furthermore, [he was told] that if he had anything more to

produce for the release of himself and his ship, he must do it
now. The said Cornelis Claesz Snoy gave for answer that he had
no other or better commission or papers than those which he had
exhibited and, therefore, that for the present he had nothing
more to produce for the release of his ship and the cargo. He
requests that the director general and council may not proceed
against him with the utmost rigor of the law and he acknowledges
that he did wrong.

The honorable Petrus Stuyvesandt, director General of New
Netherland, Curaçao, and the islands thereof, and the honorable
council, having examined and heard Cornelis Claesz Snoy, skipper
of the ship St. Beninio, and the pilot, Jan Tepjes, and all of
the ship's officers and sailors, as is more fully to be seen
and read in the interrogatories to that end prepared, in which
it is admitted that the said skipper engaged his crew to sail
to the English Virginia, to stop at 99 places and not to pass
the hundredth, both free and unfree, according to the agreement
made with the crew; [it appears] that he set his course straight
toward New Netherland, arriving at the Roodeberch, by the English
called New Haven, in New Netherland, [346] and came there, into
the district and limits of New Netherland, without commission
from the Prince or the States, or consent of the honorable
directors of the West India Company, chamber at Amsterdam, much
less paying duty to the same, and broke bulk and discharged and
landed all his goods and merchandise at New Haven aforesaid,
except some ropes and a few other goods, as by the inventory more
fully appears. Furthermore, it appears by a declaration of the
ship's crew that contraband goods, such as powder and guns, were
landed from said ship and that at present, exclusive of the ship's

powder, between three hundred and four hundred pounds of gun powder are still found in said ship in brandy kegs. The skipper himself also acknowledges the crime and fault which he has committed, which appears by the interrogatories of the 11th of October, and on the 16th instant admitted that he had done wrong, and therefore requests moderation of justice, declaring also that he could not produce any further or better commission, or papers, or documents, than those which he had already submitted for defense of his ship and goods. It also appears by the confession of said skipper and the crew that they did not mean or intend, according to their promise and request, to sail toward the Manhatans in front of the city of New Amsterdam, which was graciously permitted them on paying the regular duty, but on the contrary that they lay with their sails set ready to sail to the English Virginia with the first fair wind that God would vouchsafe them. From this it is manifest that their request had no other object than to deceive the honorable director general here, as they did deceive the honorable directors in the fatherland, more especially, as after the receipt of the permit several sloops came here from New Haven, but with no goods of the skipper Westerhuysen, or Samuel van Goedenhuysen, and it does not appear that they attempted to pay one farthing. All of which aforesaid matters greatly tend not only to the injury and damage of the honorable directors, who were thus wickedly defrauded of their duties, revenues, and rights, which were granted them by their High Mightinesses in consideration of their great and excessive burdens they have to bear, but also to the ruin of this province

and the other merchants, who honestly pay the duty, and all other
inhabitants in general, as well as to the ruination of the trade
in this country. All of which having been duly weighed and considered and regard having been had as to all that is to be done
and observed in this matter, after having invoked God's holy name,
we find this to be of very grave consequence and to tend not
only to the great loss and damage of the honorable directors of
the Chartered West India Company, chamber at Amsterdam, but also
to the ruin of all merchants and inhabitants who honestly pay
duty and whom these smugglers and defrauders of the public duties
undersell, and also especially to the utter ruin and destruction
of the trade with the Indians, which by such persons, God help
them, is almost totally ruined; and in order to prevent such
fraud in the future, we, Petrus Stuyvesant, director general of
New Netherland, Curaçao, and the islands thereof, and the council,
administering justice, as we do hereby, in the name of [347]
their High Mightinesses, the Lords States General of the United
Netherlands, his Highness of Orange, and the honorable directors
of the Chartered West India Company, for the reasons and causes
aforesaid, do declare the aforesaid ship St. Beninjo, with all
the goods now laden therein, subject to confiscation; wherefore,
then, we confiscate, as we do hereby confiscate, the said ship
and goods to the behoof of the honorable directors, save that
public notice shall be given on three consecutive court days,
so that any one who has any claim may within that time show cause
why the ship and goods should not be subject to confiscation.
Thus done in council at Fort Amsterdam in New Netherland, where

were present, the honorable general, Mr. Dincklagen, La Montagne, Briant Newton, Paulus Leendersz and Adriaen Keyser, the 16th of October anno 1647. Was signed: P. Stuyvesant, L. van Dincklaghen, La Montangne, Brian Newton, Poulus Leendersz van die Grift and Adriaen Keyser.

In the margin was written: Nothing having appeared to this date when the last proclamation was made in defense of said skipper, except what has already been mentioned in the judgment and appears more fully by the documents, therefore, we hold the aforesaid judgment concerning the confiscation of the ship valid and, therefore, we do confiscate, absolutely and without further appeal, said ship and her appurtinances to the benefit of the Company. Thus done in council at Fort Amsterdam in New Netherland, the 21st of February anno 1648, in New Netherland.

[1] Whereas the commissary of Fort Orange (which is a place of much consequence to the honorable directors, both with regard to the extension of their limits and the trade) has absconded from there upon the report of a certain infamous and scandalous crime which it was said he had committed, and therefore, said place is vacant and it is highly necessary that it be again supplied with a good, honest and suitable person; therefore, the honorable general requests the members of the council that each of them would please to give his opinion and vote for whom, in this country, he thinks to be the fittest for said charge, in the best interest and for the service and advantage of the honorable Company.

---

[1] Other translation in Doc. Rel. Col. Hist. N. Y., 14:81.

The honorable director general votes that Michiel Jansen shall be offered the commissaryship of Fort Orange and, in case he should refuse such offer, then to send thither Carel van Bruggen, late commissary at Curaçao, and in case he refuse, said van Bruggen must quit the Company's service.

[348] Mr. Lubbert van Dincklagen votes for Michiel Jansen.

Mr. La Montangne says that as Carel van Bruggen has served the honorable Company for many years, honestly and faithfully, he is entitled to the place before any others.

Brian Newton, lieutenant, says that Carel van Bruggen ought to be commissary of the honorable Company at Fort Orange, as he has served the Company for many years.

Paulus Leendersz is of the opinion that Carel van Bruggen, being an old Company's servant, is next in line for the commissaryship.

Adriaen de Keyser, commissary, votes for Carel van Bruggen and thinks that the commissaryship ought to be given to him before others.

The honorable director general and council, having seen the plurality of votes and observed further the long and faithful service Carel van Bruggen has rendered the Company, find him fit to fill for the present time the office of commissary at Fort Orange, wherefore, he is appointed in council commissary at Fort Orange. Done the 6th of November anno 1647, in New Amsterdam. Was signed: P. Stuyvesant, L: van Dincklage, La Montangne, Brian Newton, Poulus Leendersz van die Grift and A: Keyser.

Whereas the honorable director general and council of New
Netherland have seen the criminal complaint of Fiscal van Dyck
against Andries Trompetter, at present a prisoner, who at divers
times has conducted himself very unruly and disobediently, both
at Curaçao and here in New Netherland, daily wasting his time
in drunkenness, neglecting the Company's service and, in addition,
refusing to obey the order of the officers placed over him, as
when recently the delinquent, being drunk on the ship St. Beninjo,
refused to carry out the orders of the commissary of naval stores,
who struck him twice with a cane, whereupon he, Andries, threatened
the said commissary, saying, if he had with him what he had not,
the naval officer would not again do that; all of which is a
matter of great moment and grave consequence, which cannot be
tolerated in a land where justice is maintained; Therefore,
having attended to everything which is to be done and observed
herein, the honorable Petrus Stuyvesant, director general of New
Netherland, Curaçao, and the islands thereof, and the honorable
council, administering justice in the name of their High
Mightinesses, the Lords States General, his Highness of Orange,
and the honorable directors of the Chartered West India Company,
chamber at Amsterdam, have condemned the above named Andries
Trompetter to jump three times from the yardarm and to receive
from the crew of the ship St. Beninjo one hundred lashes before
the mast on his breeches while yet wet. Thus done in council
at Fort Amsterdam in New Netherland, the 5th of November anno
1647. Was signed: P. Stuyvesant, L. van Dincklagen, La Montagne,
Brian Newton, P. Leendersz van die Grift and A: Keyser.

[349] Proposition submitted to the Council by the Honorable
Petrus Stuyvesant, Director General

1.   In a case where a
soldier commits a crime
of a purely military na-
ture, should not the en-
sign and sergeant be ad-
joined [to the court],
agreeably to the instruc-
tions of the honorable
directors?

Resolved in council, whereas
the case is military, the ensign
and sergeant should be adjoined
according to the order, and [the
council should; then cause the
crime to be punished.

2.   What order is to be
made on the petition of
those of Flushing; also,
in regard to what we have
been told, that those of
Flushing have never taken
the oath of allegiance to
the High and Mighty Lords,
the States General, or to
his Highness, or to the
Company, or to the governor,
as the sheriff and one
Thomas Newton himself have
reported to me.

Resolved that the honorable
general go thither with one or
two of the council to put everything in proper order, as according to circumstances shall
be best and most advantageous
for the security of this province.

3. What answer shall be
returned to the letter from
New Haven, and who shall be
sent after the runaways and
prisoners?

Resolved that the prisoners
shall be demanded in a friendly
manner, as of neighbors and
friends, leaving the question of
territory to our superiors.

4. What provision is to
be made to prevent fire,
as the place consists for
the greater part of wooden
houses, thatched with reed,
and we therefore consider
it too dangerous in case
a fire should occur, as
recently happened?

Resolved, as this point
mostly concerns the community,
that it be referred to the
nine selectmen, in order that
provision may be made herein
in the most suitable manner
to the least cost to the
inhabitants.

5. As school has not
been held for three months
for lack of a proper place,
whereby the youth grows up
wild, where is school to be
held so as to keep the youth
off the street, and bring
them under discipline?

Resolved, as above set
forth in the 4th article.

6.   Who shall be sent to
New Haven to collect our
debts and to fetch the
prisoners from there? Was
signed: P. Stuyvesant.

Resolved that Adriaen
d'Keyser shall be sent
thither.

Thus done in council, the 11th of November anno 1647,
in New Amsterdam.

Written proposition submitted by the
Honorable General to the Honorable Council

Honorable Officers and Councilors:

A painful accident prevents me from assisting this time at
your honors' deliberations. Meanwhile, I would earnestly recommend to your honors to expedite the criminal proceedings against
the present prisoner, as your honors shall find consistent with
the merits of the case.

[350] Secondly, in regard to the seized brandy, consisting
of 17 ankers, which came from the north, not knowing from whom
or for whose account, it is my opinion, if they are duly entered,
that they may pass on payment of the proper duty, as is usual
in the fatherland, without our having any further claim thereto,
and this in conformity with the license granted them by us with
your honors' advice in regard to merchandise which they voluntarily
bring hither. Meanwhile, the fiscal's complaint and demand may
be heard, whereupon your honors can render judgment.

Thirdly, I submit to your honors' consideration the accompanying letter from Antony de Hooges regarding the Negro sent here yesterday from Fort Orange and recommend that he may be promptly and rigorously examined.

Fourthly, if the Nine Men be convened this afternoon according to the last issued order, I recommend that some one of the council be ordered to attend their deliberations and proceedings. This 14th of November anno 1647, in New Amsterdam in New Netherland. Was signed: P. Stuyvesandt.

To the Selectmen representing the Commonalty of
the Manhatans, Breuckelen, Amersfoort and Pavonia
Kind Friends:

A sudden and unfortunate accident and the consequent pain prevent my presence and the verbal presentation of what I have thought necessary to communicate to you in order that you may enact what is best for the public good and of the least burden to our dear subjects and the worthy commonalty.

The first thing that concerns us is our design, if God spare our life and health, to build up and repair in the spring our fortress of New Amsterdam, in order to have a sure and safe retreat for our dear subjects' persons and goods in case of need of defense against foreign enemies, whereto some preparation ought to be made in time. And being ordered and commanded by instructions from the honorable States General and the Company to request the commonalty to lend a helping hand in accomplishing such a worthy and highly necessary undertaking, as appears by the accompanying extract, I have thought it necessary to

communicate with you as interlocutors and spokesmen for the
commonalty and to ask your advice as to the means by which this
may be effected at the least expense and with the least trouble
to the community.

Secondly, regarding the completion and the maintenance of
the church, toward which I have already advanced something and
for which still more is required, how is this to be collected
from the community? The best plan, in the opinion of the
churchwardens, would be for one of the churchwardens, accompanied
by one of the Nine Men, to go around and make a monthly collection from door to door.

[351] Thirdly, no less needed than the preceding is the
erection of a new school house and schoolmaster's dwelling for
the convenience of the community and the proper education of
the children. We are willing, individually and for the Company,
to contribute reasonably thereto and to continue to lend a
helping hand to this laudable work. In the meanwhile, we shall
take steps to provide a proper place during the coming winter,
either in the kitchen of the fiscal, which seems most suitable
to me, or some other locality inspected by the churchwarden.

Finally, to enact a good ordinance against fires, which
may occur here as in other places, and such at the least expense
and loss to our good citizens. On these points you will, as
representatives and spokesmen of the commonalty, be pleased to
communicate your opinion and best advice to us and the council.
This 14th of November anno 1647.

Below was written:

Yours and the commonalty's well-disposed and most willing servant,

Was signed: P. Stuyvesant

Below was written: Agrees with the original, Cor: van Tienhoven.

Whereas Jones Jonassen from Utrecht, a soldier, has lately dared, in company of one Gerrit Segersen, also a soldier, at present a fugitive, to steal fowls by night from the hennery of Cornelis Volckersz, bringing them by night into his quarters in the fort, where they were found the next day behind a chest; also stuck with his cutlass, as he acknowledges, flinging it at a hog on the premises of Cornelis Volckersz aforesaid, so that it died of the wound, which a soldier, who has taken the oath to their High Mightinesses, the Lords States General, his Highness of Orange, and the honorable directors of the Chartered West India Company, has no right to do, being on the contrary in duty bound to prevent all mischief and disturbances of the public peace by reason of his being in the public service; and in order that such crimes be not committed again by him, the delinquent, and others, and that the people may possess their property in peace, therefore, we, wishing, on the requisition of the fiscal, to administer justice, as we do hereby in the name of their High Mightinesses, the Lords States General of the United Netherlands, his Highness of Orange, and the honorable directors of the Chartered West India Company, have condemned the said Jonas Jonasz to ride a wooden horse for three consecutive days from two o'clock in the afternoon until the close of the parade, with a fifteen pound weight attached to each foot. Thus done in New Amsterdam, the 15th of November anno 1647.

Was signed: L. van Dincklaghe, La Montangne, Brian Newton,
Poulus L: van die Grift and A: Keyser.

In the margin was written: Present, the honorable
Mr. Dincklagen, President, Mr. La Montangne, Brian Newton,
Lieutenant Paulus Leendersz. In my presence, C: v: Tienhoven,
Secretary.

[352] The 22nd of November anno 1647

Abraham Willemsz, from Amsterdam, requests by petition to
be dismissed from his service as seaman, which is granted him
by the honorable director general and council with permission
to earn his living here as other subjects.

[1] Whereas Fort New Amsterdam is entirely out of repair and
it is highly necessary that it be put at the earliest and most
convenient opportunity in a thorough and complete state of
defense; Therefore, in order that this noble work, which not
only tends to the reputation of this province, but also affords
a safe refuge to the inhabitants of this place in time of danger,
which God avert, may be more speedily and diligently completed,
we, the director general and council of New Netherland, have
deemed it proper and highly necessary, in pursuance also of the
order of the honorable directors, to request the commonalty to
lend a helping hand to this laudable work, prized by all nations;
and in order that the commonalty may not be burdened with heavy
and intolerable charges we have judged it to be the best plan

---

[1] Other translation in Laws and Ordinances of New Netherland, p. 79.

of all that every male person, from 16 to 60 years, shall each
for himself work 12 days in the year at the said fort, and that
whoever finds it inconvenient to perform such labor himself
shall be exempt therefrom upon payment of two guilders for each
day.

The last of November

[1] Resolved and concluded in council at Fort Amsterdam that
until further order and more opportune time the loose seawan
shall continue current and in circulation; only that in the
meanwhile all imperfect and broken and unperforated beads which
are declared bullion may be picked out and shall meanwhile be
received at the Company's office as heretofore, provided that
the Company, or any one on its part, shall in return be at
liberty to trade therewith among the merchants or other
inhabitants, unless for large quantities it be otherwise agreed
upon or stipulated by any individual or on behalf of the Company.
Thus done the day and year aforesaid.

[353] The director general and council of New Netherland,
to all those who shall see these or hear them read, greeting!
Be it known that we by friendly letters and earnest protests
have requisitioned and requested from the governor and magistrates
of New Haven, situated within the limits of the province of New
Netherland, [the surrender of] three runaways, to wit: Jan Claesz
from Bellekum, ship carpenter, Bastiaen Symonsz Root, sail maker,
and Meyndert Gerritsz, house carpenter, all three bound by oath

---

[1] Other translation in Laws and Ordinances of New
Netherland, p. 80.

to the service of the General Chartered West Indies Company, from
which they ran away secretly and fled to New Haven aforesaid,
where they were for a time kept in detention by Governor Eton
and the Magistrates and afterwards discharged, and since that
time, contrary to all neighborly duty and intercourse, have
been and still are employed in their own service and work,
without sending back to us the said fugitives (who fled now ten
or twelve weeks ago), notwithstanding we have several times, in
all friendship, requested and written for this to be done, yes,
have twice sent a yacht for that purpose with an offer of like
friendship, neighborly duty and payment of all expenses incurred.
Besides the aforesaid three, also two others, to wit: Willem
Westerhuysen and Samuel van Goedenhuysen, both bound by oath,
allegiance and burgheright to the world renowned commercial city
of Amsterdam and consequently subjects and vassals of our free
Netherlandisch state, and therefore accountable to the free,
sovereign government thereof, or their representatives here;
which persons, Westerhuysen and Goedenhuysen, who sailed as con-
trabandists, smugglers and defrauders of the obligatory customs
and regular duty, without a proper commission or license, were
not only admitted by the aforesaid governor and magistrates to
New Haven against our friendly request and earnest protest, but
also maintained there, whereby we were prevented from proceedings
against our own nation and countrymen without prejudice according
to law and in such manner as we as competent judges are bound to
answer for before our and their sovereigns, the High and Mighty
Lords the States General, by which act of refusal the aforesaid

governor and magistrates have violated and broken the previously
observed neighborly correspondence and maintenance of justice.
Wherefore we, the director general and council, contrary to
nature, expectation and intention, are obliged lege talionis,
to have recourse to the same weight and measure and hereby do
give notice that all persons, whether noble or ignoble, free or
bound to service, debtor or creditor, servant or master, down to
the least prisoner, of what nation, age or quality they may be,
coming henceforth from the colony of New Haven to us or any
place within our government, shall be at liberty and free to
come and go, remain, move about and depart without being by any
one molested on account of their flight, much less sent back,
and shall absolutely enjoy the same liberty and freedom that is
granted and given to our own nation here, on condition only of
taking the proper oath of allegiance and thenceforth comporting
themselves as honest servants and vassals. In order that no
man may plead ignorance [354] or extend these beyond our intent
or meaning, we most expressly give notice that we remain inclined
and obliged faithfully to observe our ancient and unbroken
neighborly correspondence with all other English colonies,
governors and magistrates, both in and beyond our limits, those
of New Haven only excepted, in apprehending and sending back
all persons, fugitives and runaways. Therefore, we command all
of our officers, magistrates and constables to publish, post and
obey these in all the places of our government exclusively
toward those who come over to them from the New Haven colony,
on pain of our displeasure and arbitrary correction. Thus done
and resolved in our council on the 4th and published on the 5th
of December anno 1647, in New Amsterdam in New Netherland.

[355] Anno 1648 in Fort Amsterdam in New Netherland

1 Resolved in council that for the best interest and advantage of the honorable directors all the effects which the late Director Kieft turned over by inventory, but which were loaned by him to divers persons shall be recalled for the use of the honorable Company. Should any of them not be on hand or forthcoming, those who have them shall be made to pay for them. This 12th of January anno 1648.

2 The honorable director general and council having seen that the confiscated sloop, formerly commanded by Seger Tonisz, deceased, lies here against the shore and decays more and more and, furthermore, is greatly out of repair and would cost much before it could be made seaworthy again; and having likewise considered the little service this small sloop could render the honorable Company, it is judged for the best advantage of the honorable Company to sell the said sloop publicly to the highest bidder. This 12th day of January anno 1648.

3 Whereas the sawmill standing on Nooten Island [4] is wholly decayed and in ruins and to all appearance can not be repaired by the carpenters who are now here, and the iron work which is still on it is daily disappearing; therefore, it is for the best advantage of the honorable West India Company considered advisable and unanimously resolved in council to take down said mill if possible, or otherwise to burn it, in order to salvage the iron work, which shall be used to the best advantage of the

---

1 Other translation in Doc. Rel. Col. Hist. N. Y., 14:81.
2 Other translation in Doc. Rel. Col. Hist. N. Y., 14:81-82.
3 Other translation in Doc. Rel. Col. Hist. N. Y., 14:82.
4 Nut Island.

honorable Company. Thus done and resolved in council at Fort Amsterdam in New Netherland, the 12th of January 1648.

[1] [356] The director general and council of New Netherland having observed that in and around the city of New Amsterdam there are brewers who tap and sell by retail, whence it may happen and occur that the beer thus brewed and retailed be not properly entered and the legal excise thereon paid; therefore, the said director general and council, in conformity with the rule and customs of Holland, forbid, as they do hereby, all those who brew in and around this city to tap, entertain parties, or sell beer by the can; also, no tapsters shall be allowed to brew, or to have others brew for them; all this on pain of forfeiting all such beer as shall be found on such brewers' or tapsters' premises, and in addition of being prohibited from doing business for the space of [   ] months. Thus done the 12th of January anno 1648.

Whereas one Jan Tonsen, Eduwart Tomas Styls, Jan Laurensz and Jan Hick, inhabitants of Flushing in New Netherland, are with others the principal opponents to the general vote and decision of their neighbors in contributing toward the support of a Christian and godly Reformed minister and to the nomination of a schout, wishing, contrary to the custom of the fatherland, to nominate and elect but one person only and request the honorable general and council to confirm the same; it is resolved for the best interest, advantage and peace of this province to have the said person summoned to appear on the 23d

---

[1] Other translation in *Laws and Ordinances of New Netherland*, pp. 80-81.

of January before the honorable director and council and, in
case of refusal or declining to appear, said person may be
arrested by the fiscal to be proceeded against as the case may
require.

Furthermore it is resolved to write to the inhabitants of
Flushing to obey the already issued orders by nominating three
persons for the election of a schout, and that Schout Harck
shall continue until said order be obeyed and the appointment
be made by us. This 17th day of January anno 1648, in New
Amsterdam.

[Ordinance prohibiting wooden chimneys and appointing fire-
wardens in New Amsterdam] [1]

[357] Whereas the honorable director general of New Netherland, Curaçao and the islands thereof, and the honorable council,
have by experience seen and observed that some careless people
neglect to keep their chimneys clean by sweeping and do not pay
attention to their fires, whereby recently fire broke out in
two houses and greater damage is to be expected in the future
by fire, the more so as houses here in New Amsterdam are for the
most part built of wood and thatched with reed, besides which
the chimneys of some of the houses are of wood, which is most
dangerous; therefore, the honorable general and council have
considered it advisable and most expedient to provide herein.
Wherefore the said honorable general and council ordain, enact
and command, as they hereby do, that henceforth no chimney shall
be built of wood or lath and plaster in any house between the
fort and the Freshwater, but those already erected may remain

---

[1] Other translation in Laws and Ordinances of New
Netherland, pp. 82-83.

until further order and pleasure of the fire-wardens. And in
order that the foregoing shall be well observed, the following
are appointed fire-wardens: from the honorable council, Commissary Adriaen d'Keyser, and from the commonalty, Tomas Hall,
Martin Cregier and Gorger Wolsey, with power at their pleasure
to inspect the chimneys of all houses situated and standing
within this city between this fort and the Freshwater, to see
if they are kept well cleaned by sweeping. And if any one be
found negligent, he shall, every time the aforesaid fire-wardens
make an inspection and find the chimneys foul, pay them forthwith,
without any contradiction, a fine of three guilders for every
flue found on examination to be dirty, to be applied to the
maintenance of fire ladders, hooks and buckets, which shall be
procured and provided at the earliest and most convenient opportunity, and if any one's house be burned or be the cause of fire,
either through negligence or his own fire, he shall forfeit
twenty-five guilders, to be applied as above. Thus done and
enacted at Fort Amsterdam in New Netherland, and published the
23d of January.

23d January 1648

Whereas the honorable general and council of New Netherland
find it highly necessary for the service of the honorable
directors to engage a pilot on the ship _Beninjo_, and whereas
Jan Tepjes van Schellingen at present requests by petition to
serve the Company as pilot on the said ship, he is appointed
pilot on the ship _Beninjo_ by the honorable director and council
at 34 guilders per month, commencing the first of January
anno 1648.

[358] The honorable director general of New Netherland, Curaçao and the islands thereof, and the honorable council, having seen the complaint of the fiscal against Roulof Cornelisz, a soldier, at present a prisoner, who recently, in the morning of the first of January, among other insolent acts, while intoxicated, made bold to inflict, without provocation, according to the affidavits, five wounds on Corporal Jacob Luersen, when said corporal endeavored to separate said Roelof Cornelisz and Casper Steenmetsel, [1] who were quarreling with each other, so as to prevent further injury and mishap, as more fully appears by the affidavits; which is not only a direct violation of the 32d article of the sworn military regulations, but also contrary to the ordinance published on the last day of May 1647; therefore, Petrus Stuyvesant, director general of New Netherland, etc., and the honorable council, in the name of their High Mightinesses, the honorable States General, his Highness of Orange, and the honorable directors of the Chartered West India Company, wishing to do justice, as they do hereby, condemn the said Roelof Cornelisz to ride the wooden horse with a ten pound weight to each foot for three consecutive days, for two hours each day, and in addition to forfeit six months' pay, to be applied, one-third for the poor, one-third for the church and one-third for the fiscal, besides paying the injured and wounded man for his pain, loss of time and the surgeon's fee, as an example to other such turbulent persons. Thus done and executed, the 28th of January, at Fort Amsterdam in New Netherland.

---

[1] Caspar Steinmets.

Willem Gilfoordt, an Englishman, at present a prisoner and charged with having willfully ravaged a young girl of about ten years of age.

The said prisoner being closely examined in court denies everything and says that being drunk he signed a bond in favor of Ritchert Clof, without owing him anything, as he was told some time after the signing took place by Jan Hadduwe, he having, owing to his drunkeness, no knowledge thereof and having forgotten the same.

[1] [359] For the best interest and service of the honorable Company and for the better prevention of smuggling it is unanimously considered in council to be advisable and profitable to mark the beavers, bearskins, otters and elkhides with the Company's mark as soon as they are brought here from other places, provided that whoever shall have the beavers stamped shall be responsible for the duty.

Likewise, all merchants and traders shall remain bound to enter all peltries, bartered, exchanged or purchased either from the heathen or Christians, with the commissaries of the Company at or about Fort Orange, Fort Nassau, or the House the Hope, and to bring with them a certificate thereof signed by the commissary. Furthermore, all other peltries which may be traded or bought on the way hither, between Fort Orange or the South River [and the Manhatans], or elsewhere where there are no commissaries of the Company, must be entered by the owner immediately on arriving in the roadstead here before the fort;

---

[1] Other translation in Laws and Ordinances of New Netherland, pp. 83-84.

and if any one shall be found to have acted contrary hereto, the peltries which may then be discovered shall be held and declared subject to confiscation. The traders shall enter with the receiver the peltries which are procured on the island of Manhatans or elsewhere in this vicinity from the natives or others within three days after he has traded or bartered them, on pain of confiscation.

There must be paid from this day forward and until further order or circumstances, at the Company's counting house, as duty on every whole beaver, 15 stivers; on one otter, 15 stivers; on one bearskin, 15 stivers; on one elkhide, 15 stivers; on each deerskin, 5 stivers; on a coat of raccoon, wild cat, or fisher's skins, 15 stivers; on ten separate skins counted as one coat, also 15 stivers; and all this on the peltries which are entered for exportation. Thus done and enacted, the 29th of January anno 1648, in New Amsterdam.

Resolved unanimously in council that Roulof Jansz Haes, receiver of the Company's revenues in New Netherland, shall be paid a salary of 480 guilders a year, and shall be at his own expense as to board and lodging, provided that he be obliged to do all that he is ordered to do as receiver of the Company. Said receiver shall also be bound to assist in the marking of beavers and other peltries, for which he shall be allowed an assistant. For marking said peltries he shall receive for each whole skin, eight pence, and for the others in proportion, to be divided between him and his mate, provided that they shall diligently

assist in inspecting and see to it that no fraud be committed.
Thus done, the 29th of January anno 1648, in New Amsterdam.

[360] [1] On the first of February 1648

Willem Harck, schout of Vlissingen, [2] and his associates
appeared in council and requested that the honorable director
general and council would provide them with a pious, learned
and Reformed minister and then order that each inhabitant of
Vlissingen must contribute to the support of such godly work
according to his ability, and that thus an end may be put to the
present differences, which will tend to promote quietness, peace
and harmony in the said village and enable them to live together
as subjects under the protection of their High Mightinesses, his
Highness of Orange, the honorable directors and the present
administration here.

Tomas Sael, Jan Laurens and Willem Turner, of the opposite
party, delegated thereto by the remaining persons on their side,
request the same as the schout and his associates have asked.

The aforesaid parties having been heard in council and
the justice of their request being acknowledged, it is resolved
by the honorable director and council to issue such order on
their application and request as in their opinion may serve to
promote peace, harmony and tranquility both in ecclesiastical
and political affairs.

Whereas a letter has been sent from the colony of Rensselaerswyck by an Indian, wherein they relate the sad and miserable

---

[1] Revised from Doc. Rel. Col. Hist. N. Y., 14:82.
[2] Flushing, L. I.

death and end of Harman Meyndersz, late commissary of Fort
Orange, who, being reputed to have committed sodomy, absconded
and, being pursued by justice, was caught by an officer of the
court [1] there in an Indian house in the interior of the country;
and [whereas] in defending himself he set said house on fire,
whereby not only all the provisions of the Indians for the
winter, but also all their seawan and peltries were burned, for
which they demanded satisfaction of said colony, which was granted
to them on account of the serious consequences;

Therefore, it is unanimously resolved in council to be
for the best interest and advantage of this country to sell the
garden of said Harmanus, in order to satisfy the Indians from
the proceeds as far as the money permits and, if this be not
sufficient, to make up the balance on behalf of the Company,
inasmuch as he, Harmen Meyndersz, was a servant of the Company
and had no other means to pay for the damage. This 8th of
February 1648, in New Amsterdam.

[361] The 11th of February anno 1648, in New Amsterdam

The council, [being met] in plenary session to consider
the information taken about sodomy alleged to have been committed
by Harman Meyndersz vanden Bogaert with one Tobias, a Negro boy
slave of the honorable Company at Fort Orange, they have, [at
the request] of the honorable director general to take the
matter of this heinous crime into further consideration,
unanimously thought it advisable to delay the sentence until
spring, when further information can be secured from Fort Orange.

---

[1] Hans Vos. See _Minutes of the Court of Rensselaerswyck,
1648-52_, p. 105.

The 18th of February

The council having heard the complaint of the fiscal against Willem Gilfoort, at present a prisoner, about violation and rape of a young girl named Maria Barents and having seen the information secured by the commissaries appointed for that purpose, it is ordered that the midwives and some reputable women shall examine the said girl, now about eleven years old, and make a proper report of their examination, whereupon the matter shall be disposed of by definite sentence.

A certain petition of the selectmen being presented to the council, the director and council note in the margin that they approve for the present of what the selectmen propose from a sense of well meant duty and, as they claim, for the promotion of the public interest, and will take the same into further consideration and make and issue such order thereon as they shall consider to be to the public benefit and advantage, consistent with their commission and instructions. Meanwhile, they wish to warn the selectmen in the future to keep within the bounds of their commission, to hold no meeting or assembly except with the knowledge and consent of the director, and not to draw up any propositions, much less to pass any resolutions, except in the presence of and before a deputy from the honorable council; [362] also, that in their future petitions they must observe more respect in submitting their requests, that is, that they must not presume to dictate to the director and council what they ought to do. Thus done and noted in the margin of their petition, the 18th of February A°. 1648, in New Amsterdam.

Whereas Willem Gilfoort of Westcontrey, aged 30 years, at present a prisoner, has been pleased in May last, at the house of Isaack Allerton, by force and violence to uncover a girl named Maria Barents, aged eleven years, to throw her down in the cellar and, having untied his breeches, to place himself on the said girl, attempting for about a quarter of an hour to have carnal conversation with her, but, as the girl was too young, was unable to accomplish his evil purpose, as will more fully appear from the information thereof and as has also been confessed by the said prisoner without torture or irons; and whereas this is a matter of very serious consequence, which in a country where justice prevails can not be suffered or tolerated, but ought to be severely punished, in order that the children of honest people may not be dishonored and led away from the path of virtue by such [evildoers]; Therefore, Petrus Stuyvesant, director general, and the honorable council administering justice in the name of their High Mightinesses the lords States General of the United Netherlands, his Highness of Orange, and the honorable directors, condemn the aforesaid Willem Gilfordt, as they do hereby, to be brought to the place where it is customary to execute justice, to be severely flogged there with rods and thereafter to be banished forever from this jurisdiction, as an example to others. The delinquent deserves greater and severer punishment, but in consideration of the fact that it has appeared to the director and council that shortly after the said crime one Willem Gerritsz Wesselsz with the will and consent of the said Maria Barents has had conversation with her, the delinquent

is freed therefrom, provided that he is to suffer the above
mentioned punishment and banishment. This day, the 24th of
February A⁰. 1648.

[363] Whereas Jonas Jonassen from Utrecht has at divers
times not only behaved in a very insolent manner, but also dared
to go out of the fort by night after the watch had been set, to
break open the hen houses and to steal fowls, as he did at
Cornelis Volckertsz's, and moreover killed a hog with his cutlass,
for which offenses he, Jonas Jonasz, was placed on the wooden
horse and mildly punished in the hope of amendment, he, the
prisoner, nevertheless, persists in his evil ways, neglects his
watch, absents himself from the guardhouse when his turn comes
and runs around drinking, thus neglecting his duty and bounden
service. Furthermore, he, Jonas Jonasz, has twice, while drunk,
been pleased to chase Indians and to beat them with his naked
sword and also by force to take away and steal their seawan
which they were carrying in their pouches, which is a matter of
very serious consequence and importance which might furnish the
Indians with a pretext for avenging themselves in return on men
or cattle or otherwise, and thus bring dreadful misfortune on
this province and its inhabitants. The honorable director and
council considering it highly necessary to provide herein and
being therefore compelled to do right and justice, as they do
hereby in the name of the High and Mighty lords the States
General of the United Netherlands, his Highness of Orange, and
the honorable directors of the Chartered West India Company,
they have condemned, as they hereby do condemn, the aforesaid
Jonas Jonasz to be stripped of his arms and then to be taken to

the place where justice is generally executed and to be flogged
with rods, which being done, he shall be chained to a wheelbarrow
to work and labor with it as long as the honorable director and
council shall see fit, as an example to such evil doers and
highway robbers. Thus sentenced and executed the 3d of March
anno 1648, in Fort Amsterdam in New Netherland.

Whereas Jems Hallet, an Englishman, at present a prisoner,
has ventured not only to run away from the jurisdiction of New
Netherland without a proper pass but also to carry out of her
bounden service a young girl who was in the employ of Adriaen
Dircksz, tavern keeper here, and moreover has stolen at Greenwich
in New Netherland divers articles, though of little value;
therefore, the honorable director general and council, administering justice, have condemned said Jems Hallet to be brought to
the place where justice is usually executed, [364] there to
witness the punishment which shall there be inflicted, and in
addition to saw during one whole year for the Company, the stolen
goods to be paid for out of his earnings, and if he work diligently
he shall earn fair wages at the discretion of the honorable
director and council, and every evening after having finished
his work he shall be placed in confinement, unless he give
security that he will not run away. Thus done the 3d of March
anno 1648, in New Amsterdam.

Whereas the honorable director general and council on this
day have heard the excuses offered by Willem Gerritsz, [1] an
Englishman, for the carnal conversation had by him with Maria
Barentsz and have likewise seen the petition and promises of the
said Willem Gerritsz, who offers to serve the honorable Company

---

[1] William Guilfort.

in all such work as he may be employed in; therefore, the said honorable director general and council, having taken into consideration the demand of the fiscal, the excuses of Willem Gerritsz and his offers and promises of good and honorable conduct, have graciously pardoned him, provided that he shall serve the honorable Company for one year in sawing all sorts of lumber, for which at the expiration of the year he shall be paid as much as according to his diligent and faithful labor he shall deserve. Thus done the 3d of March anno 1648, in New Amsterdam.

Whereas Egbert van Borsum, by petition, has requested to be discharged from the command of the sloop Prins Willem, which is granted, the director general and council have considered it necessary for the service of the honorable Chartered West India Company to provide said sloop again with a faithful and experienced person. Therefore, the said director general and council have commissioned and appointed, as they hereby do commission and appoint, Sinneken Jacobs master of the said sloop, for which service he shall receive the sum of 18 guilders a month and 100 guilders a year for board, commencing this 5th day of March anno 1648, in New Amsterdam.

[365] Whereas Elisabet Feax, on account of adultery committed by her, was before our arrival legally divorced from her husband Robbert Feax by the former honorable director general and council, but since that time has lived and kept company with her lover, the adulterer, and, as the witnesses declare, has also had carnal conversation with him, contrary to all good laws and the order issued by us, and furthermore with his has also attempted to

alienate, sell and dispose of the lands, cattle, furniture and
other effects left by her former husband Robbert Feex to his
four children, even to others who reside outside of our jurisdiction, whereby the children would be impoverished and become
a charge either on the Company or on the community, which in a
good and well regulated government neither can nor ought to be
tolerated and suffered; therefore, both for the maintenance of
justice and the preservation of the minor children and fatherless
orphans, we hereby declare the aforesaid Elisabet Feax incompetent
and powerless to dispose of any property, whether belonging to
her former husband or her children, much less to alienate, estrange
or sell the same, and, although she deserves a much heavier
penalty and punishment, we nevertheless, out of special favor
and for a private reason us thereunto moving, consent that with
her children she may dwell and live at Groenwits, [1] under such
curators as we have already appointed, or may hereafter appoint
for the benefit of her children, and be supported out of the
property left behind and still available, provided that she
remain separated both as to bed and board and common intercourse
from her lover, Willem Hallet, and abstains from keeping company
with him, on pain of corporal punishment; as we hereby sentence
and condemn the adulterer, Willem Hallet, to remain banished
from our jurisdiction and the government entrusted to us and to
leave the same within one month from the date hereof and not to
trouble or molest any one within our jurisdiction on pain of
corporal punishment, declaring further his pretended effects

---

[1] Greenwich.

confiscated for the benefit and advantage of his child procurated
by her, provided that a sum for traveling expenses at the discretion of the director and council be allowed him and that in
addition he pay the costs of these proceedings. Thus done in
council in Fort Amsterdam in New Netherland, the 9th of March
anno 1649.

[Ordinance against goats and hogs running at large in New
    Amsterdam] [1]

[366] Whereas it is daily seen and observed by the honorable
director general and council of New Netherland that the goats
and hogs here around Fort Amsterdam daily commit great damage
in orchards, gardens and other improvements, in consequence of
which not only the propagations of beautiful orchards and gardens
is prevented, but considerable loss is caused to individuals;
therefore, the honorable director general and council, wishing
to provide herein, do from this time forward ordain and enact
that no goats or hogs shall be pastured or kept between the
fortification of New Amsterdam (or its vicinity) and the Fresh
Water, except within each person's own enclosure, and that built
in such a way that the goats can not leap over and cause damage
to any person's property. Also, goats beyond the Fresh Water
shall not be pastured without a herdsman or keeper, on pain of
having the goats found at large on this side of the Fresh Water
or beyond it without a herdsman or keeper taken up by the fiscal

---

[1] Revised from Laws and Ordinances of New Netherland.
p. 85. The same ordinance is entered on page 372, with the
statement: Thus passed the 10th of March and published the
16th of March anno 1648, in New Netherland.

and declared forfeit by the honorable director general and council.
May everyone be warned hereby and guard himself against loss.
Thus done in council at Fort Amsterdam in New Netherland, the
10th of March anno 1648.

[Ordinance for the regulation of trade and navigation, etc.] [1]

Petrus Stuyvesant, on behalf of the High and Mighty lords
the States General of the United Netherlands, his Highness [the
Prince] of Orange, and the honorable directors of the Chartered
West India Company, director general of New Netherland, Curaçao
and the islands thereof, together with the honorable council;

To all those who shall see these presents or hear them
read, Greeting.

Whereas, pursuant to the good intention and order of the
aforesaid High and Mighty lords the States General, his Serene
Highness and the honorable directors, we should like nothing
better than to witness and promote the flourishing increase in
wealth and population of this province of New Netherland and the
general welfare and prosperity of its good inhabitants, whereto
first of all are required good order and regulation in matters
of trade, navigation and edification, as well as in government
and legislation, we have taken, and are still taking, more
closely into consideration and deliberation the petition and
written remonstrance of the nine elected selectmen, our good
and dear subjects, wherein they represent and by sad experience
prove the daily decline and encroachment of [367] trade and
navigation, proceeding for the most part from the underselling,

---

[1] Revised from Laws and Ordinances of New Netherland,
pp. 86-92.

frauds and smuggling perpetrated by one person against another,
chiefly by those who take little or no interest in this new and
growing province and feel little love or concern for its flourishing state and welfare and therefore do not benefit it either by
laying out farms or putting up buildings, but solely apply themselves, with small capital and little merchandise (for which for
a brief period they only hire a room or house) to the beaver and
fur trade and, having traded and bartered said peltries from the
inhabitants or the natives at the highest price, sufficiently
above their value, resort to one method or another, by night
and at unseasonable hours, to convey them secretly out of the
country or to the north, without paying the proper duty thereon
and, having enriched themselves by these and other illicit
practices and means, they take their departure and go home again
without conferring or bestowing any benefit on this province or
the inhabitants thereof. By this underselling and fraudulent
trade, the wares and merchandise of others, who by means of
farms or honest buildings which add to the importance of this
place interest themselves in the country, are depreciated and
remain unsold to their great loss and damage. Wishing, as far
as lies within our power, to remedy and prevent the same, for
the sake of the establishment of a more stable course of commerce and mutual trade, as also for the greater benefit and
profit of the oldest and interested inhabitants and the promotion of the prosperity and growth of this place, New Amsterdam,
we, the above mentioned director and council, do therefore
hereby ordain and enact on the subject of trade as follows:

That henceforward no person shall be allowed to keep a
public or private store on shore, in cellar or garret, or to
carry on trade by the small weight and measure within our
jurisdiction in this province of New Netherland, except our
good and dear inhabitants who first have taken the oath of
allegiance, own real estate of the value of at least two or
three thousand guilders, and also promise to reside, or at least
to keep fire and light, in their own house here in this country
within this province for four consecutive years; with this
exception and reservation, however, that those who are already
sworn and faithful subjects, although not interested to that
extent in the country or owning real estate to the above amount,
may continue their undertaken trade and business for the support
of their house and family and purchase wares and merchandise in
large or small quantities, each according to his circumstances
and means, from the wholesale merchants and traders, in order to
retail them again by the pound and small measure, provided they
promise and engage to remain for four consecutive years within
this jurisdiction, or not to depart out of it without the knowledge
and special consent of the director general in loco; also not to
make use, in buying and selling, of any other ell, weight or
measure, than the legal ell, weight and measure of our name-giver,
Old Amsterdam, hitherto in general use here, on pain of suspension of business and, in addition, a fine of twenty-five
guilders.

Item. In order to preserve and maintain trade and commerce
with all new comers, whether merchants, factors or scotchmen from
the fatherland and elsewhere; also, with our neighbors of Virginia

and New England, &c. and to prevent all monopoly, and the better
to accomodate the inhabitants, it is permitted and allowed to
those persons to supply daily, Sundays excepted, the burghers,
inhabitants and strangers with goods in large and small quantities
[368] from their ships, yachts and sloops, provided that the
goods and merchandise are in the first instance properly entered
and the previously enacted and customary duties on what is sold
correctly paid at the office of the receiver, and that in the
buying and selling no other weight, measure or ell be used than
that in use here, on the penalty aforesaid.

In like manner, also, are hereby given and granted to the
strangers and inhabitants a weekly market-day, to wit Monday,
and annually a free market for ten consecutive days, which shall
begin on the first Monday after Bartholomew's day, [1] new style,
corresponding to the legal Amsterdam Fair, on which weekly and
annual days the neighbors and strangers, as well as the inhabitants,
are allowed and permitted to supply the purchaser from a booth,
by the ell, weight and measure, wholesale and retail, according
to the demand and circumstances of each, in conformity to the
weight, ell and measure as aforesaid, and no other.

With regard to the navigation, which is the chief means
whereby commerce, trade and traffic are preserved and sustained,
the director general and council are informed and see by
experience that considerable fraud, smuggling, abuses and
illegalities have for some time past crept in and are taking
deeper root daily, through the illicit gain by which many, being
misled, abandon their usual business, occupation, employment and

---

1 The 24th of August.

trade, and invest all their means in one vessel or another, in
which they not only lodge and board, without conferring any
benefit on this place or country, but, under pretext of procuring
maize or other grain, corrupt, defraud and ruin the trade both
in seawan and peltries with the natives, to the great loss and
damage of the honest traders, merchants and inhabitants of this
place. For the redress and prevention thereof the honorable
director general and council do hereby ordain and enact, that
no person shall henceforth be at liberty to frequent, navigate,
or trade at the South or the North River, or in any bays, kills
and creeks situated at and between them, except only the burghers
and inhabitants of this city who possess real estate therein to
the aforesaid amount of two or three thousand guilders, whereunto, however, they, pursuant to an old ordinance and custom,
shall previously week and obtain from the director general a
certificate and commission and at each voyage a clearance, to
be exhibited to the commissary and officer there, and apply to
him again for another to be shown to us or our deputy here, on
which shall appear and be entered the correct quantity and
quality of the shipments, wares and merchandise and returns,
without concealing anything in the least thereof, on pain of
confiscation of all concealed merchandises and peltries in said
ship, yacht or sloop, whether they be shipped and conveyed on
private account or on freight. We likewise order our fiscal
here, and commissaries, officers and servants residing at Fort
Orange, Fort Nassau, and elsewhere, to pay strict and close
attention to drawing up, examining and exacting of such clearances,
on pain of dismissal.

Item. In order that the intent of these presents be the better understood and cleared of all cavil and obscurities, the director and council aforesaid reserve to themselves the power to grant at their discretion and pleasure, for a few months, commission to trade at said rivers, streams and trading posts, but only to such as are actually sworn inhabitants and vassals in this place, having taken the oath of allegiance and entered into bonds to continue under our government for four consecutive years, although [369] they have not in fact invested the aforesaid sum nor own a domicile in the country; provided that they promise and engage, in the meantime, to adorn this place with a decent and burgherlike building and invest in the country according to their rank and means; but no other person shall be permitted or allowed to have built or to buy new yachts, sloops or vessels, unless he own real estate in the aforesaid city of New Amsterdam, below the Fresh Water.

Item. They reserve to themselves, in order to promote greater intercourse and mutual commerce both between the colony of Renselaerswyck and other places annexed and subject to this government, to admit such colony into these civil exemptions and privileges for one, two or three vessels, according to circumstances and the exigencies of the case, provided that the persons own real estate there or here to the amount aforesaid, and remain subject to the regulations previously made or hereafter to be enacted in the matter.

The navigation of the East River, toward this place as well as to our neighbors and allies and to English Virginia, is left open and free as heretofore to all persons of whatever quality or nation they may be, on condition that all our inhabitants, whether of this or other places under our government, shall apply for and obtain a new commission and permit and correctly enter with the fiscal, or in his absence at the office of the receiver, the goods and merchandise which they transport hither and thither; and such persons are hereby warned that all merchandise, goods and returns, with the exception of firewood, clapboards, lime and stone, which are not entered, shall be liable to confiscation, together with the boats, barks, lighters and canoes in which the same may be found.

We ordain and enact that the previous ordinance and regulation respecting the anchoring of large and small vessels, being published and posted anew, shall be strictly enforced, respected and obeyed; to wit, that no yachts shall be allowed to anchor except at the appointed anchorage and shall not remove thence until, having been inspected by the fiscal, they have received from the director, or, in his absence, from the fiscal, a written permit to discharge elsewhere.

We also ordain and enact, for the prevention of scandalous smuggling, that no boats, barges, yawls or canoes shall, in the evening after sunset and in the morning before sunrise, board or leave any vessel, or discharge or land any goods or merchandise, under a penalty of one pound Flemish and forfeiture of all goods and merchandise found in them, unless, on account of great haste and hurry or some pressing circumstance, a special permit be previously asked for and obtained from the honorable director, or, in his absence, from the vice-director or fiscal.

We also command our fiscal strictly to enforce and execute this our regulation and ordinance together with the other, after the publication and posting thereof, and to proceed against the contraveners thereof without any exception, according to the tenor of these presents.

Thus done in council, the 10th of March, anno 1648, in New Amsterdam in New Netherland.

[Ordinance regulating taverns in New Amsterdam] [1]

[370] Petrus Stuyvesant, director general of New Netherland, Curacao, etc., and the honorable council,

To all those who shall see these presents or hear them read, Greeting.

Whereas we see and experience that our former edict enacted against unseasonable drinking to excess, both at night and on the Sabbath of the Lord, to the scandal and shame of ourselves and our nation, is not observed and obeyed according to our intent and meaning, we hereby renew the same and do ordain and enact, that it shall henceforth be maintained and executed in stricter observance and enforcement pursuant to the tenor and provisions therein set forth.

Meanwhile, the reason and cause why this our good edict and well meant ordinance is not obeyed according to the tenor and purport thereof are, that this sort of business and the profit easily accruing therefrom divert and lead many from their original and primitive calling, occupation and business to resort to tavern-keeping, so that nearly the just fourth of the

---

[1] Revised from Laws and Ordinances of New Netherland. pp. 93-96.

city of New Amsterdam consists of brandy shops, tobacco or beer
houses, by the multitude whereof not only are more honorable
trades and occupations neglected and disregarded, but even the
common people and the Company's servants seriously debauched;
and what is still worse, the youth, seeing and following, as
from their very childhood, this improper example of their parents,
are drawn from the path of virtue and into all sorts of irregu-
larity. Hence, also, proceed cheating, smuggling, and frauds
and the clandestine sale of beer and brandy to the Indians and
natives, as daily experience, God help us! shows, from which
nothing but new difficulties between us and them are to be
apprehended; and, moreover, decent taverns established and
licensed for the use and accomodations of travelers, strangers
and inhabitants which honorably and honestly pay their taxes
and excise and own or lease suitable houses, sitting under heavier
expenses, are seriously injured in their licensed and lawful
business by these clandestine groggeries.. Being willing to provide therein according to the exigency of the case, the circumstances of the time and our ability, therefore we, the director
general and council aforesaid, on the subject of the tapsters
and tavern-keepers do ordain and enact the following regulation
and ordinance;

1.

First, henceforward no new ale-houses, taverns, nor tippling
places shall be opened or set up, except with the previous
special knowledge and consent of the director and council
unanimously granted and expressed.

2.

Taverns, ale-houses and tippling places already established
may continue for at least four years more, but in the meantime
they remain bound and obliged to provide themselves like other
honest trades in this place with proper and respectable burgher
dwelling houses for the embellishment and improvement of this
city of New Amsterdam, each according to his station, quality
and circumstances, pursuant to the ordinance and regulation for
buildings made by the director and council, with the knowledge
and advice of the city surveyors.

3.

Tavernkeepers and tapsters who for certain reasons are
allowed to continue this business for at least four years more
may change their trade, but may not transfer to others their
business of tapping or selling liquor, [371] nor hire or sell
their houses and dwellings to any one else for that purpose,
unless with the previous knowledge and full consent and permission of the director and council.

4.

Item. Tavernkeepers and tapsters henceforward shall not
sell, barter or tap to the Indians or natives any beer, wine,
brandy or spirituous liquors, nor provide the natives therewith
in the first, second or third hand, on pain of forfeiting their
business and of arbitrary correction at the discretion of the
judge.

5.

Item. To prevent all fighting and mischief they shall be obliged to notify the officer immediately in case any one be wounded or hurt at their house, on pain of forfeiting their business and one pound Flemish for every hour that the matter is concealed by the tapster or tavernkeeper after the wound or hurt has been inflicted.

6.

The ordinances heretofore published against night reveling at unseasonable hours and drinking to excess on the Sabbath shall be observed with more strict attention and care by the tavern-keepers and tapsters, to wit: they shall not admit or entertain any company in the evening after the ringing of the curfew-bell, nor sell or tap beer or liquor to any one, travelers or boarders alone excepted, on Sunday before three o'clock in the afternoon, when divine service is finished, under the penalty thereto provided by law.

7.

Item. They shall be bound not to receive, directly or indirectly, into their houses or cellars any wines, beer or strong liquors before these are entered at the office of the receiver and a permit therefor has been received, under forfeit of their business and such beer or liquors and, in addition, a heavy fine at the discretion of the court.

8.

Finally, all tavernkeepers and tapsters who are inclined to continue their business shall within the space of eight days after the publication and posting hereof send in and make known

their names and addresses to the director and council and also
solemnly promise before them punctually to observe in all its
parts what is enacted, or may hereafter be enacted, on the
subject of tapsters and tavernkeepers, and to conduct themselves
decently in their business as good and faithful subjects, etc.
Thus done in council, in Fort Amsterdam in New Netherland, the
10th of March A°. 1648.

[372] In council appeared Adriaen Dircksen, tavern keeper,
Martin Cregier, Jan Jansz Schepmoes, Jan Snediger, Philip
Geraerdsz, Seargeant Daniel Litsco, Gerrit Douman, Hendrick
Smith, Cornelis Volckersz, Abraham Pietersz, G[e]orge Rapalje
and Pieter Andriesen, all tavern keepers and inhabitants of
this city of New Amsterdam, who register their names and make
themselves known to the honorable general and council, in accordance with the ordinance issued on the 10th of March on the
subject of tavern keepers, promising on their manly troth to
observe said ordinance in all its parts as far as it lies in
their power. This 16th day of March anno 1648, in New Amsterdam in New Netherland.

[373] The honorable director general and council of New
Netherland having seen the reasonable petition of the curators
appointed over the estate of Seger Tonisen, deceased, for power
to collect all debts due to, and pay all demands against said
estate here in this country, said director general and council
have, therefore, considered it highly necessary for the benefit
of the creditors and co-administrators of said estate, that as

enough time has now elapsed, those who are indebted to said
estate shall pay up within six months in order that this being
done the curators may also satisfy and pay the creditors, on
pain, if they fail to do so, that the curators shall have power
to levy execution against them without being obliged to enter
any further proceedings on that account. Furthermore, if any
one in this country is indebted to said estate, or has any claim
against it, he must advise the curators thereof within the time
aforesaid in order to prove his claim before the commissaries;
in default whereof, those who appear afterward to present any
claim shall be barred from their right and action. This 30th
of March anno 1648.

Whereas the honorable director general is informed that one
Josep Brusto, merchant, residing at New Haven, within the limits
of New Netherland, has arrived here this day with his bark from
Virginia and that he has certain letters and goods in his vessel,
which goods are said to be consigned to Willem Westerhuysen, now
residing at New Haven aforesaid, on which goods apparently no
duty has been paid, and whereas said Westerhuysen heretofore
attempted to defraud the honorable Company of their duty with
his ship Beninjo; therefore, it is unanimously resolved and concluded in council that the fiscal shall demand of Brusto the
letters belonging to Westerhuysen; that the same shall be opened
and read by the secretary in the secretary's office, and that he
shall reseal them with wax without a signet as they were received
and hand them again to Brusto if they contain nothing prejudicial
or dis-advantageous to the honorable Company. This 30th of
March anno 1648, in New Amsterdam.

The honorable director general and council of New Netherland have ratified and approved what has been ordered and done by the appointed commissaries by order and command of the honorable general and council in laying out and surveying the lands and boundary line between Mr. van Twiller, Mr. [Dincklage ?], Cosyn Gerritsz and the path to the shore, so that everyone shall hereafter have to be satisfied and keep the peace. This 30th of March anno 1648, in New Amsterdam.

[374] Whereas Willem Harck, born in old England, at present a vassal and inhabitant of New Netherland, and provisionally schout and officer of New Flushing, being on Monday, the 30th of March, sent hither at the request of one Tomas Nuton, widower of Dorite Nuton, to Ritchert Smith and his wife, residing here in our city of New Amsterdam, to ask and demand of them as lawful father and mother the parents' will and consent to the marriage of said Tomas Nuton with their daughter Joon Smith, which being refused for reasons adduced by the girl's father, the aforesaid Willem Harck did, nevertheless, according to his own confession and sufficient testimony as provisional schout and officer of Flushing, not only presume to unite together on the following day said Tomas Nuton and Joon Smith, without the parents' knowledge or consent, by an unheard of and unwarranted sort of marriage in his own house, without any legal proclamation or marriage formalities, but also provided them instantaneously in his house with bed and room to consummate the marriage, without being authorized and empowered by any lawful superior to confirm any one in the marriage state, even though according to

Christian usage three proclamations and all marriage formalities
should have been previously observed, which as well as the
parents' will and consent were wanting in this indecent transaction, which was accomplished contrary to the express prohibition,
wherefore the aforesaid Ritchert Smith, as father, has made complaint to the honorable director general and requested legal
proceedings, not only on account of this indecent and unheard of
manner of marrying, but also for the sinister perversion of the
father's answer and intention, reporting on his return to his
daughter and Tomas Nuton that indeed the father would not consent
or allow their marriage, but nevertheless would bestow a word of
comfort (which the father denies) to wit: that he left it to the
girl's choice, as more fully appears by the examination and the
interrogatories taken in full council; all of which indecent
acts he, as provisional schout and deputed officer ought to
have prevented, hindered and opposed being performed by another,
yet being practiced and committed by himself they ought not and
cannot be suffered in any civilized city where law and justice
are administered. Therefore, we, the director general and
council, on the complaint and demand for justice by the offended
father, and especially for an example to others to prevent
further mischief by such improper modes of marriage, administering justice in the name of their High Mightinesses the Lords
States General, and his serene Highness, the Prince of Orange,
and the honorable directors, have condemned and sentenced, as
we do hereby condemn and sentence him, the aforesaid Willem
Harck, [375] to pay a fine of 600 Carolus guilders before he

shall be released from his arrest and confinement, further
dismissing him from his office and declaring the aforesaid
indecent marriage confirmation null and void. Done and
sentenced in full council, the 3d of April anno 1648, in New
Amsterdam in New Netherland.

Whereas Tomas Nuton, a resident of Flushing in New Netherland, contrary to all decency has presumed not only to marry
the daughter of Richert Smith without his knowledge or consent
and also without any proclamation or special consent of any
authorities, Joon Smith being a young girl and the marriage
being performed at Flushing by Schout Willem Harck secretly in
said schout's house, but also last Tuesday night to sleep with
said Joon Smith at the house of Willem Harck aforesaid, as
appears by the confessions of Tomas Nuton and Willem Harck, for
which reason said Ritchert Smith, being greatly aggrieved and
offended, has made complaint to the honorable director general
and requested proper remedy and justice, said matters have been
taken into further consideration by the honorable general and
council. Having considered everything that is to be considered
and done, they find the matter to be of serious consequence and
that, in case no timely provision be made herein, having the
children of decent people married by unlawful and unauthorized
persons against the will and consent of their parents may cause
great scandal and injury to an entire family. Therefore, the
honorable director general and council, administering justice,
as they do hereby, in the name of their High Mightinesses the

Lords States General, his Highness of Orange and the honorable
directors of the Chartered West India Company, condemn the said
Tomas Nuton and Joon Smith to pay a fine of 300 guilders, to be
applied according to the discretion of the honorable director
general and council, and to have their marriage after three consecutive proclamations approved by the honorable general and
council, as an example to others. Thus done in council, the
3d of April anno 1648, in Fort Amsterdam.

[376] In council Tomas Steyls, being heard on the complaint
made in writing by the honorable general, acknowledges that he
threw the sheriff [1] on the ground and did wrong and had never
before so acted, promising henceforth to behave as an honest
inhabitant should; praying, therefore, the honorable council to
be pleased to take the same into consideration.

The honorable council (without the honorable general),
having heard the confession and request of Tomas Steyls and his
promise of good behavior, have graciously pardoned the offense
committed by him, provided that the 50 guilders promised and
forfeited at Flushing be paid at the office of the Company, to
be applied at the discretion of the honorable director general
and council, and provided that he beg pardon of God, the council,
the honorable director and the sheriff of Flushing. Thus done,
the 8th of April anno 1648, in Fort Amsterdam, in New Netherland.

In council at Fort Amsterdam [appeared] Tomas Saal,
inhabitant at Flushing in New Netherland, being accused of
having prevented the schout at Flushing from performing his

---

[1] William Harck, sheriff of Flushing.

duty in arresting Tomas Steyls, which Tomas Saal acknowledges
that he kept the door shut so that no one could assist the
schout; prays mercy and promises never to do so again, being
very sorry for what he has done. The honorable director and
council, administering justice, have condemned the aforesaid
Tomas Saal to pay a fine of 25 guilders, to be applied at the
discretion of the council. Thus done the 8th of April anno 1648.

Tomas Nuton, widower of Dorite Nuton, deceased, residing
at Onckeway, being reconciled with Master Ritchert Smith, and
both parties being fully satisfied with regard to the marriage
of the latter's daughter Joons Smith, now the wife of said Tomas
Nuton, after the proper proclamations, without any objection
being made, Tomas Nuton and Joon Smith are confirmed in their
marriage state by the honorable director and council in the
presence of the above named Mr. Smith and Jan Dollingh. This
16th of April anno 1648, in Fort Amsterdam, in full council.

[377] Whereas from almost all countries, both in Europe
and these northern and southern parts of America, yes, even from
this province, and other places depending thereon, we hear and
receive nothing but sad and doleful tidings and rumors here of
severe inundations and floods, burning and pestilential fevers,
whereby thousands are swept away by a sudden death, so that
scarcely enough healthy persons remain alive to bury the dead;
elsewhere of hurricanes, storms and tempests and consequent
shipwrecks and destruction of both property and life, from which
no other conclusion can be drawn than that the Holy and Almighty
God of Israel, being justly provoked to anger and wrath on

account of our sins and those of other nations, threatens us
with a just retribution of the treasure of anger and just wrath,
caused by the spurning of the richness of His mercy, patience
and forbearance, abused by us so as to result in hardness of
heart instead of our reformation; which treasure of wrath and
just retribution, already raining from a sky laden with vengeance
on other places in this part of America, if it be not poured
down on us in a torrent, would at least drip on us and our
posterity, unless we turn to our God with the Ninevites in sack
cloth and ashes of unfeigned penitence, hating and abandoning
all wickedness, all false measures and evil practices, all
blasphemy and licentiousness in drunkenness, rioting, swearing,
lying, cheating and profanation of God's most holy name and the
sabbath, and many other abominations in vogue among us no less
than among other nations, wherefore, God's anger being justly
incited, He not only threatens and warns us with the exemplary
punishment meted out to others, but is visiting even ourselves
with loss of property and lives in consequence of severe storms
and shipwrecks and here in this province with inundations and
high water, commonly foreboding floods and being overrun by war,
pestilence and bad times, visiting with the first our sister
state of Brazil and with the second our allies and confederates
in the Caribbean Islands, yes, even our friends and vassals on
Curaçao and the islands thereabout, as a warning to us (praise
be the mercy of God) that we shall perish likewise unless we
repent, as we are no less sinners than they on whom we hear and
see fall, not the wrath of Siloah, but of Heaven, and unless we

heed this warning, not the elementary fire, but the pestilential
and feverish fire of the wrath of God will be hanging over our
heads. Therefore we, the director general and council, being
invited, inclined and obliged thereto according to the grace and
favor of God that is in us, pursuant to God's command, the example
of other laudable rulers, in order to conciliate ourselves and
our subjects with God by the means ordained by God himself and
to draw upon us and to continue to receive His gracious and
merciful favors instead of His just punishment [378], we have to
this end considered it highly necessary to proclaim and to order
a general day of fasting and prayer which shall be held in the
forenoon and afternoon of the first Wednesday in the month of
May, being the 6th of the aforesaid month, and thereafter a
monthly penitential sermon in the forenoon, to be held throughout
our province of New Netherland on every first Wednesday of each
month in succession. We therefore order and command all our
officers and commanders, as well as all vassals and subjects of
this province on the day and hour aforesaid to appear in the
church or where it is customary to hold divine service, in order,
after listening to and having been taught from God's holy word,
jointly and unanimously, with a humble and contrite heart to
invoke the name of the Lord and to pray and beseech Him that He
may be pleased to stop the torrents of His wrath poured out over
others and the clouds of His anger still pending over us and
change them into rivers and streams of grace and mercy, divert
from us and our allies, both at Curaçao and in the Caribbean
Islands, that all-devouring pestilence, those hot fevers, famines

and infertilities, and grant them and us health and fertile
seasons; that it may please Him to turn our sadness into joy
and to change the sad rumors reaching us from everywhere into
glad tidings and bless the fruits of the earth with early and
late rains, seasonable weather and luxuriant growth; that it may
please Him graciously to turn aside the storms and prevent the
shipwrecks and loss in life and property proceeding from them,
and henceforth to favor our navigation, industry and commerce,
both in and outside the country, with His safeguard and protection; that it may please Him to let wax and increase among us
the fear of His name and the knowledge and hatred of our own
sins, warding off from us all well merited punishments and
plagues which our sins crying unto heaven deserve; that it may
please Him, both here and in our dear fatherland, to keep the
light of the holy Gospel burning in the true and faithful
observance of His word and the holy sacraments and to grant a
fertile increase thereof, sending us pastors and ministers who
do not succumb, but who proclaim His glory and teach us our
duty; that it may please Him to take under His care and protection
the actual government, all high and low state officials, both
in our dear fatherland and here and elsewhere, and especially
the person of the honorable director general and the council
and officers of these and the Curaçao conquests, to attend them
with His wisdom and peaceful spirit in all their deliberations
and attacks, so as to plan and to decide nothing but what will
be serviceable to His glory, their salvation and the welfare of
the country. In order that the same may be the better practiced
and taken to heart, we prohibit and forbid on the aforesaid day

of fasting and prayer, during divine service, all exercise and practice of golf, tennis, hunting, fishing, sailing, plowing, sowing, mowing and many other unlawful games, such as throwing dice and drinking to excess, upon arbitrary correction and the penalty heretofore by law provided on the subject, and we further wish to admonish and pray all ministers of the holy gospel within our government to formulate their sermons and prayers to the aforesaid end. Thus done and decided in council, the 16th of April, in Fort Amsterdam in New Netherland.

[379] Whereas the ship Nieu Swol is at present again being made ready to be sent with provisions to Curaçao, for which much will be needed and whereas little money is available here to complete her outfit; therefore, it is unanimously resolved in council that a list of the debts which the honorable Company has outstanding here shall be handed to Mr. Dincklaghen and Mr. La Montagne and that they as commissaries shall be authorized to call upon and urge the debtors to make payment either in whole or in part, according to each person's circumstances. Thus done in Fort Amsterdam in New Netherland, the 17th of April anno 1648.

Whereas Jems Hallet, at present a prisoner, has heretofore made bold to run away from the Company's service without leave or permission and at Greenwich, within the jurisdiction of New Netherland, to steal divers goods; and furthermore has stolen a canoe from the Indians hereabout and therein, on St. Nicholas Eve, carried off a servant girl from her master's house, for which misdeed and offense he, Jems Hallet, on the third of last March, was condemned by the honorable general and council to be brought to the place where justice is usually executed, there to witness the punishment which was then and there inflicted and, in order to make satisfaction for the stolen goods, etc., to saw during an entire year, on condition that he should receive reasonable wages for said labor if he conducted himself well. And whereas, notwithstanding the mild sentence, the said Jems Hallet has now recently assisted one Hans Rootrock, who was confined for theft, to escape at night from jail, furnishing a rope with which the prisoner let himself down and thus escaped, for which reason we have been unable to administer proper justice to him; and whereas Jems Hallet attempted also to carry off Hans Rootrock's wife and run away with her; all of which acts are of evil consequence and may not and ought not to be tolerated in a land where it is customary to maintain justice;

Therefore, the honorable director general and council, administering justice in the name of their High Mightinesses, the Lords States General, his Serene Highness of Orange and the honorable directors of the West India Company, on the request of the fiscal, condemn said Jems Hallet to be brought to the place where justice is usually executed and there to be severely whipped with rods, and there to be severely whipped with rods, and in addition to be locked to a chain to saw or labor for the honorable Company in satisfaction as aforesaid, so long as the honorable director general and council shall think proper, as an example to others. Thus done and sentenced and put into execution, the 18th of April anno 1648, in New Amsterdam in New Netherland.

[380] Hendrick van Dyck, fiscal of New Netherland, ex officio plaintiff against Mr. Joseph Brusto, defendant. Plaintiff demands that defendant pay a fine of fl. 50, as he anchored with his sloop beyond the sign post and directly contrary to the ordinance published the 4th of June 1647. The defense of the defendant being heard, who could not produce any sufficient reasons why he had anchored beyond the sign post, as it was calm weather and he was going with the tide as he anchored near Mr. Allerton's house, said Mr. Brusto is therefore condemned to pay the fine of fl. 50 provided therefor by the ordinance, with the costs of the trial. Thus done in court at Fort Amsterdam in New Netherland, this 20th of April anno 1648.

The fiscal, plaintiff, against Davidt Provoost and Pieter Jacobsz, defendants. The fiscal, instituting his action in writing, concludes: Whereas Provoost arrived here from the north, heaved his anchor and drew near the shore and did not enter any goods within 48 hours after his arrival, notwithstanding he was notified so to do by the fiscal in person; therefore, demands the confiscation of his, the defendants', sloop and lading.

The defendants appearing in court acknowledge that they have done wrong and plead ignorance of the ordinance, and therefore pray light sentence.

Pursuant to the ordinance the honorable director general and council declare the sloop to be liable to confiscation, but inasmuch as the defendants plead ignorance and said ordinance was published in their absence, the case was therefore referred to Mr. Dincklagen and Paulus Leendersz, naval store keeper, to

settle and decide the difference between the defendants and the
fiscal, bearing in mind the poor, the church and the fiscal.

Whereas Antony Jansen van Zalee, residing on Long Island,
near the Narrows, on the North River, cultivates his land there
without properly fencing in the same or not fencing it at all,
wherefore the cattle belonging to the inhabitants of Gravesend
and that vicinity frequently damage the crops on the unfenced
land, which the owners cannot prevent as the cattle seek food
where they find a place open; and whereas said Antony finding
some cattle on his land ill-treats them both by beating and
setting on dogs to bite them, whereby great damage has already
been suffered, causing those of Gravesend to complain and demand
that Antony enclose his land; therefore, the honorable director
general and council having taken the same into consideration,
the said Antony Jansen is ordered to enclose his land and to
make the fence tight, on pain of forfeiting his right to the
ground should he not obey this order within one month from date.
This 20th of April 1648, at New Amsterdam.

[381] Whereas Cornelis Jacobsz Stille, Gerrit Jansen van
Oldenborch, Cornelis Claesen Swits and Leendert Aerden received
from the honorable Director Willem Kieft patents for the farms
situated beyond the Fresh Water, on condition that they annually
pay to the honorable Company the tithes on the date of the patent,
and whereas they have thus far paid nothing and made no preparation worth mentioning to improve the land and cultivate it with
zeal and industry for their own and the Company's profit, therefore, the honorable director general and council have thought it

highly necessary to warn said farmers to fence their lands and
to till them with all diligence in order that the Company may
receive their due, on pain, if they continue negligent, of being
deprived of the lands which will be given to others who regularly
pay the quitrent annually. Said farmers are informed of this by
the honorable director and council in court, the 20th of April
anno 1648, in Fort Amsterdam in New Netherland.

Whereas a letter from Vice Director Luycas Roodenborch of
Curaçao, dated the 19th of February, has been received here by
the honorable director and council by way of New England on the
14th of April, advising them that the ship <u>Groote Gerritt</u> arrived
at Curaçao completely disabled and damaged by a very severe storm
or hurricane, having been obliged to throw overboard the most
part of the cargo of provisions taken on board at Boston for
Curaçao, which was damaged by leakage and the great quantity of
water that was in the hold; also, that in consequence of great
sickness and mortality the ships <u>Cath</u> and <u>Liefde</u> must remain at
Curaçao and that there was scarcely a healthy person aboard said
ships; furthermore, that they were in want of everything at
Curaçao, especially of provisions, men and materials to repair
the ships and refit them for sea, without which they must remain
there idle and further deteriorate; therefore, the honorable
director general and council have unanimously resolved and concluded, for the best interest and advantage of the chartered
West India Company, to send thither with all possible despatch
the yacht <u>Swol</u>, formerly called <u>Beninjo</u>, under command of Paulus
Leendersz, at present naval store keeper, as captain, in which

yacht shall be shipped as many provisions and necessary materials
as can be collected at the present time. And whereas we have
here no permanent crew or sailors on the yacht in the service of
the Company to navigate said vessel, it is also decided to engage
by the public beat of the drum as many seamen as can be obtained
to man the yacht Swol and the other ships, and that on as good
terms as circumstances permit and only for this voyage. Thus
done in full council in Fort Amsterdam in New Netherland, the
20th of April anno 1648.

[Appointment of schout and schepens for the town of Flushing] [1]

[382] Whereas divers misunderstandings have heretofore arisen
among the inhabitants of New Flushing in New Netherland, the
said inhabitants have, therefore, referred the question to the
director general and council, to whose decision they have voluntarily submitted themselves; in like manner they have in
writing referred the election of schout and schepens there to
the said general and council, having only provisionally named
and proposed to the honorable director and council Jan Onderhil
as schout; Jan Tonsen, Jan Hicx, Willem Toorn, for schepens and
selectmen, and Jan Laurens, for clerk, before whom all civil
suits under 50 guilders shall be brought, and that pursuant to
the written order to that end granted to the inhabitants of
Flushing.

Therefore, after consideration of the matters herein to be
deliberated, for the greater tranquility of the province, and
the assured peace and unity of said village of Flushing is

---

1 Revised from Laws and Ordinances of New Netherland, p. 97.

Jan Onderhil by us chosen and appointed schout, and the said
persons schepens and clerk, provided that the schout and schepens
shall take the oath of allegiance and uprightness punctually to
follow in all civil cases the written rule and articles already
issued and enacted for them. Which being done, we charge and
command the inhabitants of our town of New Flushing to respect
said persons each in his quality, and to lend them a helping
hand in the execution of their office.

Thus done the 27th of April anno 1648, in Fort Amsterdam
in New Netherland.

[Ordinance for the better observance of the Sabbath] [1]
Petrus Stuyvesant, on the behalf of the High and Mighty
Lords the States General of the United Netherlands, his Highness
the Prince of Orange, and the honorable directors of the General
Chartered West India Company, director general of New Netherland,
Curaçao and the islands thereof, together with the honorable
council.

Whereas we see and find that, notwithstanding our well meant
laws and ordinances, heretofore promulgated for the observance
and sanctification of the Holy Sabbath in conformity to God's
holy command, they are not complied with and obeyed according to
our good intent and meaning, but that it is still profaned and
desecrated in divers ways, to the great scandal, offense and
reproach of the commonalty and foreign neighbors who frequent
this place, the contempt and disregard of God's Holy Word and of
our ordinances deduced therefrom; therefore, we, the director

---

[1] Revised from Laws and Ordinances of New Netherland,
pp. 98-99.

general and council aforesaid, in order to avert, as much as in us lies, from us and our subjects the wrath and chastisement of God to be apprehended from these and other transgressions, do hereby renew and amplify our previous edicts and ordinances, having, for the stricter observance thereof, with the pre-advice of the minister of the Gospel, deemed it expedient that a sermon shall be preached from the Sacred Scriptures and the usual prayers and thanksgiving offered from this time forward in the afternoon as well as in the forenoon; wherefore we request and command all our officers, subjects and vassals to frequent and attend the same; meanwhile, in conformity with our aforesaid ordinances, we forbid during divine service, all tapping, fishing, hunting, and other customary avocations, trading and business, either in houses, cellars, shops, ships, yachts, or in the streets and markets, under the penalty of forfeiting such wares, merchandizes and goods, or their redemption with the sum of 25 florins, until further order to be applied to the poor and the Church, and in addition thereto one pound Flemish to be forfeited as well by the buyers as the sellers, by the lessees and by the lessors, to be distributed, one-half to the officer, one-half at the discretion of the court. In like manner, also, we do hereby interdict and forbid all persons on the aforesaid day to spend their time to the shame and scandal of others in gross drunkenness and excess, on pain, if so found, of being arrested by our fiscal or any superior or inferior officer, and arbitrarily punished by the court.

Thus done and, after reconsideration, enacted and published the 29th April anno 1648, in New Amsterdam in New Netherland.

On the 3d of May 1648

The honorable director general protests in council against
Mr. Lubbert van Dincklagen, because he refuses to testify to the
truth of what occurred in council on the 2d of May between the
fiscal, Commissary Keyser and Pauwelis Leendersz, naval store
keeper.

[384] On the 11th of May 1648

Whereas Adriaen de Keyser, commissary, has hitherto
neglected to bring in the account which he ought to have had
ready last New Year, he is ordered and commanded in council to
make up and deliver his account as speedily as possible to the
honorable director.

[Ordinance further prohibiting the sale of intoxicating liquors
     to the Indians] [1]

Whereas, notwithstanding it has been repeatedly forbidden
by previous edicts to tap, give, barter or sell by the third or
fourth hand, directly or indirectly, any strong drink to the
Indians or natives of these parts, it is seen and observed by
daily experience that Indians are running drunk along the [streets
of the] Manhatans and that the people who reside at a distance
suffer serious annoyance from drunken Indians, whence new troubles
and wars, as heretofore, are to be apprehended; therefore, the
honorable director general and council have thought it necessary
to renew once more the previous ordinance and hereby most strictly
to forbid, as we hereby do, the giving, bartering or selling of
any strong liquors, by what name soever they may be called; and

---

[1] Revised from Laws and Ordinances of New Netherland, p. 100.

in case anyone after the date hereof be found [so offending],
were it even that the information be received from the Indians
(to whom for weighty reasons credit shall be given in such case)
he shall, in addition to the fine prescribed in the previous
ordinance, receive without any dissimulation an arbitrary corporal
punishment; for it is better that such evil disposed persons be
punished than that a whole country and people should suffer in
consequence of their acts.

Thus done the 13th May anno 1648, in council, in Fort
Amsterdam in New Netherland.

[385] In council the honorable general stated that Fiscal
van Dyck had given a promise of good and better behavior, which
the honorable council jointly hope will come to pass. Thereupon
it was unanimously resolved to allow the fiscal to continue for
the present in his office on condition that he will in the future
conduct himself as a good, faithful and vigilant fiscal should
and ought to do, in default whereof, if he act contrary hereto,
he shall be dismissed from his office. This 18th of May in
council. Present: the honorable director general, L: van Dincklagen,
second, La Montagne, Briant Nuton, etc.

Govert Aertsen appeared in council and requested a certificate
of the honorable director general and council, to be shown to
the magistrates in New England, that his name is Govert Aertsz
and not Govert Loockmans, the more so as he went some time ago
to Rhode Island with his sloop, where he was threatened to be
put into prison, it being said that he was Loockemans, and

Captain Clercq had told him, Govert Aertsen, that Lookmans had sold powder and lead there to the Indians and that they would have confiscated his sloop for that reason had he been Lookmans. Resolved in council to grant Govert Aertsz a certificate of identity, according to the aforesaid petition, this 25th of May anno 1648, in New Amsterdam in New Netherland.

Having seen the petition of the officers of the Burgher guard in regard to the issuing of a regulation about the musketry, whereby they remonstrate that there is a lack of guns among the citizens; therefore, the burghers must provide themselves with fire arms, for which purpose two or three months time is allowed them. Meanwhile the burghers who have no guns shall be provided out of the Company's magazine on condition that they shall keep the same clean and neat and return them in good condition when they are called in. Furthermore, a suitable guard house for the summer shall be provisionally built for them. This 23d of May anno 1648.

[386] Hendrick van Dyck, fiscal, ex officio, plaintiff, vs. Hans Hansen, defendant, on account of two metal gun chambers which the defendant assisted one Hans Bastiaen, a sailmaker, to remove, etc.

The Plaintiff, presenting his complaint in writing, demands execution. The defendant acknowledges that he assisted in carrying the chambers, but did not know where, or how, the sailmaker procured them, and proves by witnesses that the sailmaker had long ago offered the same for sale.

The honorable director general and council having seen the written complaint of the fiscal against Hans Hansen, an inhabitant here, and the case being considered, it is found to be of serious consequence, but inasmuch as said Hans Hansz has maintained a good name and reputation during his 14 years' residence in New Netherland, the aforesaid offense as well as his opposition to the honorable director are forgiven him, on condition that said Hans Hansz beg pardon in court of God and the magistrates, which Hans Hansen has done. Wherefore the offenses above mentioned are forgiven him and the fiscal's further demand is denied. This 26th of May anno 1648.

Barent Ennesen van Noorden, Company smith and corporal, at present a prisoner, being heard and examined in court regarding some gun barrels and gun locks which were sold by him to some persons, said prisoner confesses, without torture, that he sold some locks, barrels and guns belonging to the Company to Jacob Reynsen and Joost de Backer, [1] who had asked him to do so, as may be seen and is stated more at length in his deposition. Whereupon it was resolved to hear Jacob Reynsen and Joost de Backer, who, appearing in court, denied and contradicted everything. It was therefore decided to imprison said Jacob Reynsen and Joost de Becker and to search their houses, which was done forthwith, an inventory being taken at the house of Jacob Reynsz of his goods and peltries, which were immediately removed to the Company's warehouse. This 28th of May anno 1648, in New Amsterdam.

---

[1] Joost Teunissen, the baker.

[387] Joost Teunisz, baker, declares in court that he received one gun from the Company's corporal, on which he paid fl. 25; also purchased and received one lock from the corporal and, as the spring was broken, brought it to be repaired, but never got the lock back, Govert Loockemans having bought and received said lock from Barent. The second lock he purchased from Abraham Rycken, which lock he also took to Barent to be repaired, but never received or got it back, and that Lambert Clomp told him, the deponent, that he could not give the locks to any person but Loockemans, which said Loockemans had forbidden him. He declares further that he, the deponent, had never bought any locks, barrels, or guns from Corporal Barent except one lock, but finally acknowledges that Huybert Rogierse brought a barrel to his house, for which he paid Huybert fl. 12. This 28th of May anno 1648, in New Netherland.

Jacob Reynsen deposes in court that he never bought any gun barrels from the Company's corporal, but once purchased two gun barrels from one Claes Cramer in the month of July anno 1647, which he carried to the corporal, and that it took him three months before he could get them back from the corporal. Finally having received them, one of the barrels burst in his partner's hands up at Fort Orange while firing, when Carel van Bruggen came there. The stock belonging to said barrel Lambert Clomp made; the locks, being snaphances, were made by Abraham Rycken. [He] also [declares] that there are still two of the snaphances which they brought from Holland in the possession of his partmer, up above. Jacob Reynsz declares further that neither he nor his mate ever bought any gun barrels or locks from the corporal. Thus done in council, the 28th of May 1648, in New Amsterdam.

Jacob Reynsen being examined in court confesses that he bought five or six gun barrels from the Company's smith, but that he did not know that they were the Company's property as Barent, the smith, said that he looked up and bought here and there old barrels, which being repaired he sold to him, Jacob Reyntjes.

Jacob Reynsen also says and acknowledges that he brought six locks with him from Holland and that he did not buy more than two locks from Barent for fl. 16, which he paid him. Jacob Reynsen also acknowledges that he purchased and received three gun barrels from Cooltjes, [388] and that he brought with him in the ship De Princes about 70 lbs. of gun powder, which was stowed in prune barrels. Jacob Reynsen declares that he bought from Egbert van Borsum about 75 lbs. which is all the powder which he purchased here. The payment therefore he made to Abraham, the carpenter. This 29th of May 1648, in New Netherland.

In court was heard and examined Joost Teunisz, baker, at present a prisoner, who confesses voluntarily, without torture, that he brought 12 lbs. of powder from Holland and that he paid the smith fl. 25 on the gun; also that he would not meddle with powder and lead as his wife frequently spoke to him, the prisoner, against that trade. Joost is also asked in court where the gun is which he brought from Holland, and answers that it burst and the pieces, as he says, are lost. This 29th of May 1648, in New Amsterdam.

Having heard in court the confession of Jacob Reyntjes and the original letters which his partner wrote to him about the contraband trade in guns, powder and lead, from which truth and

clearness of the case are sufficiently manifest, the director
general and council have considered it necessary to send up a
boat, immediately and secretly, to have Jacob Jansz Schermerhoorn,
partner of Jacob Reynsen, arrested, as well as his brother, and
to take good care that his books and papers be secured. All the
merchandise, goods, papers and books of Schermerhoorn and his
brother, shall be taken under inventory in the presence of two
of the court of Rensselaerswyck and delivered to Commissary van
Bruggen, which being done, the prisoners shall immediately be
brought down in order to immediately proceed further against
them as the case may require. This 29th of May anno 1648, in
New Amsterdam.

[389] Whereas the honorable director general and the
honorable council have by experience seen and remarked that
contraband goods are very secretly imported here in New Netherland, which we according to honor and oath endeavor as much as
possible to prevent and to have the contraveners punished; and
whereas we daily expect a ship, or ships, from the fatherland,
we have resolved for the best interest and advantage of the
Company and the public good to station the ship De Liefde in
the bay behind the Sant Point [1] to watch for the ships, on which
ship the naval store keeper is appointed captain to execute
everything according to his orders and not to suffer any boats
or craft to board or leave said vessels and to convoy them to
their anchorage before Fort Amsterdam. This 19th of June
anno 1648, in New Netherland.

---

[1] Sandy Hook.

Written Proposition submitted to the
Officers of the council by the Honorable
Director General Stuyvesant.

It is known to me and to all your honors that since our
arrival here frequent complaints have been received from our
neighbors, the English and Swedes, as well as from our own subjects,
about the altogether too dangerous and prohibited trade in powder,
guns and lead carried on with the natives, whereby our persons,
although we protest our innocence before God, are accused and
suspected of conniving at this trade, not only by our neighbors,
the English and Swedes, but also by some of our vassals, and
that not without some semblance of justification and reason,
because the trade is carried on so generally, in regard to which
the fiscal, who by virtue of his office is most concerned therein,
has become either too lax or blind.

I have myself submitted to the council and the nine selectmen divers protests on the subject and requested their aid and
remedy to prevent such dangerous trade, wondering how and by
what means such large quantities of guns, powder and lead were
imported into the country, as by my own experience I observed
were now and then traded to the Indians here or sent elsewhere
to be sold to the Indians. Whereupon some plausible explanations
have been offered to me, to wit, that such merchandises were
discharged from the ships between this fort and the Sant Point
before the ships came to anchor in front of the Manhatans, either
by having such contraband goods, in watertight casks and boxes
purposely prepared thereto in the fatherland, thrown overboard
under the nose of a careless watchman and afterwards fished up

again as occasion offered, or else by having them concealed some-
where else in the country, which is large and extensive, in a
secret place, until a convenient time and opportunity.

There being no other remedy for this than to watch the ships
arriving from the fatherland as they come in, either in or outside the harbor, we have made use of the means at our command
[390] and sent thither the yacht De Liefde, under the command
of our naval store keeper, but without written resolution
adopted by all the members of the council, in order that it might
proceed more secretly, having reached our intention and decision
in this matter in connection with the ship directed to Govert
Loockermans and his partners, said person being, as the council
knows, according to reports more suspected than any one else.
Wherefore we have also put on board his arrived ship De Valckenier,
besides the fiscal, to whom the making of the discovery can not
well be entrusted, six soldiers and two of our prominent officers,
to wit, Secretary van Tienhoven and Ensign Bacxter, who with the
fiscal will for the first night keep good watch and guard. This,
now, serves to request advice as to what ought to be done next
in this case for our vindication, for the better knowledge of
what there is to the suspected case and for the promotion of the
public service. The 23d of June anno 1648.

Upon the proposition of the honorable general, pursuant to
the orders and instructions of the honorable directors, it is
resolved in council to have the ship De Valckenier unloaded down
to the keel as soon as possible and to have a watch kept by day
and night by some of the Company's officers and the fiscal in
order that no contraband or smuggled goods be brought on land

by day or night; also, that all goods shall be brought into the
Company's storehouse and there inspected and that every evening
during the unloading the hatches shall be sealed with the Company's
seal and the keys lodged in the council chamber. Thus done in
council the 23d of June. Present: the honorable general, Briant
Nuton, Paulus Leendersz and Adriaen d'Keyser.

Whereas it has come to our knowledge that some willful
persons not only deliberately and without apparent reason absent
themselves from the burgher guard, but also act sullenly and
disrespectfully toward their officers and refuse to pay the fixed
fine for neglect of duty; therefore, in order to prevent all
disorders and inconvenience, the honorable director and council
do hereby command every burgher duly to attend the burgher watch,
and if after the publication hereof any person deliberately and
intentionally neglects his watch without sufficient cause, the
officer of the watch is hereby authorized forthwith to levy
execution against him who neglects his guard duty, should he
refuse to pay voluntarily; and if execution be levied, the fine
shall be doubled, and if any one resist his officer he shall be
punished according to the merits of the case. Thus done and
published in Fort Amsterdam, the 23d of June, 1648, in New
Amsterdam.

[391] The 29th of June anno 1648

The crew of the <u>Valckenier</u> present a petition to the council
and request permission to sell, without hindrance, their entered
personal freight; [1] therefore, the honorable director general

---

[1] <u>Voering</u>; literally, lining.

and council, having seen the reasonableness of the request and
also that the freight amounts to little, have allowed the sailors
to sell their entered freight here, except the guns, which the
honorable Company shall appropriate and pay for at the discretion
of the council. Thus done and enacted in council, the 29th of
June anno 1648, in New Amsterdam.

Whereas a Spanish bark called Nostra Singnora Rosario,
laden with hides, captured in the Caribbean Islands by Hans
Wyer, the honorable Company's captain on the yacht De Cath, has
been brought up in front of this city of New Amsterdam, public
notice is hereby given by the ringing of the bell to every one,
of what state, rank or condition he may be, that if he has any
objection to make why said bark should not be declared a good
prize he must produce his reasons within one month after the
publication hereof, on pain in case of non-appearance within
said time of being debarred from his action. Thus done in
council, published and affixed in Fort Amsterdam, the 2d of July
anno 1648.

The 2d of July 1648

Hendrick van Dyck, fiscal, ex officio plaintiff against the
crew of the yacht De Cat, for the recovery of some pieces of
eight and a few pearls which they secured in capturing the bark
Nostra Senora Rosario and divided among themselves. The fiscal,
instituting his action in writing, demands restitution of the
aforesaid pieces of eight and pearls, maintaining that they
are not plunder.

Having seen the demand of the fiscal against the crew of the Kat, who captured the prize below Margarita and brought it up before the Manhatans, [setting forth that] said crew, contrary to the Company's Articles, found in said prize some pieces of eight and a few pearls which they divided among themselves and furthermore brought in no prisoners, as ordered by the Company, it appears that this would deserve a civil court punishment, but observing that we have very few men and that it is necessary to fit the vessel out again for the West Indies to procure salt and that consequently we should not be able to procure any men here, and this crew's term has long since expired, we have for the best interest and advantage of the Company considered it advisable to pardon them for this offense, on condition that their claim to the prize money from the captured bark be confiscated for the benefit of the Company. Therefore, the fiscal's further demand is dismissed. This 2d of July anno 1648, in New Amsterdam.

[392] Whereas this entire country (not only we but also our neighbors) is in great need of salt and there is not in our stores above ten schepels of salt, caused by the fact that the ships at Curaçao are all out of repair and in need of everything; therefore, it is considered highly necessary, both for the preservation of the ships at Curaçao and on account of the need of salt here, to fit out and despatch the captured prize to Curaçao to fetch salt and St. Martha's wood, so as to enable us before the coming winter to salt provisions both for this country and Curaçao, and to bring us as much St. Martha's wood as possible. Thus done and resolved, the 20th of July anno 1648, in New Netherland.

The 6th of July 1648

The fiscal, ex officio plaintiff against Jacob Reynsen, who escaped from prison, having been arrested for trade in contraband goods which he sold to the Indians and for buying guns, barrels and locks from the Company's smith, being Company's arms.

Said Jacob Reynsen, after being summoned, appeared in court and requested a copy of the fiscal's complaint and his other documents, in order to make answer thereto within three days.

The request of Jacob Reynsen is granted, but meanwhile he shall go to prison, whence he escaped.

The 8th of July 1648

Jacob Reynsen, at present a prisoner, being again heard in court, declares that in the year 1647 he stowed away in the water cask of Jan Heyn's bark ten staves of lead, without Jan Heyn's knowledge. He further confesses as regards the contraband trade that he did very wrong; therefore, prays the director general for a merciful and gracious sentence.

Whereas the excise on beer and wine is not promptly paid to the Company's office according to the rule and custom of the fatherland, the receiver is ordered to grant no permits to any one before and until he has been paid. We have, therefore, caused this to be published, so that every one shall govern himself accordingly. This 8th of July anno 1648, in Fort Amsterdam, in New Netherland.

[393] Jan Heyn presents a petition to the council, wherein he requests that his brother, Laurens Heyn, be allowed to come here with his merchandise from Virginia on condition that he pay the usual customs, on which petition it is ordered that the petitioner's brother shall be allowed to come hither with his goods on payment of the customary duty on the imported and exported goods. This 8th of July anno 1648, in Fort Amsterdam, in New Netherland.

Whereas it is rumored that Claes Bordingh, in October 1647, conveyed a quantity of guns up to Fort Orange, he is asked in council how many guns he took thither and from whom he had received them? To which Claes Bordingh answers that he has no recollection thereof, but as he refuses to confirm his assertion by an oath, notwithstanding that the director and council promise that if he declare the truth his name shall be withheld and that no harm shall come to him on that account, he is committed to prison and allowed time to bethink himself.

The 8th of July 1648

Abraham Willemsz, carpenter, appeared in court and declared on his manly troth, with offer of an oath, that he bought from Cornelis and Claes Jansz, sailors of the ship St. Beninjo, at New Haven toward the north, two kegs of powder, weighing about 70 lbs., for himself and Egbert van Borsum, jointly, which powder was resold here at the Manhatans to Jacob Reynsen. He declares further that he bought no guns or lead. This 8th of July 1648, in New Amsterdam.

The farmers residing on the island of Manhatans have jointly presented a petition to the honorable director general and council, wherein they set forth the unfavorable crop of this year, as well as many other reasons which make it impossible for them to pay the honorable Company this year the tenth of the crop. All of which being considered by the honorable director and council, they find said representation to be true; considering further that the tenth would for this year amount to very little and would hardly be worth the labor, they have remitted them the tithes of this year, 1648, on condition that if God should bless the tillage they will pay the tithes next year. Thus done and resolved in full council. Present: the honorable general, Mr. Dincklaghen, Mr. La Montagne, Briant Nuton, Paulus Leendersz, naval store keeper, and Adriaen Keyser, commissary. The 8th of July, in New Amsterdam in New Netherland.

[394] Petrus Stuyvesant, director general of New Netherland, Curaçao, Bonaire, Aruba and the dependencies thereof, and the honorable council, residing in New Netherland, having seen the letters of Jacob Reynsen and Jacob Jansz Schermerhoorn, written and signed with their own hands, as also their confessions made in council on the 8th of July, without torture, whereby it clearly appears that during their sojourn here in New Netherland, since March 1647, they have ventured to trade and traffic in guns, powder and lead and have sold the same in quantities to the Indians, to wit: Jacob Reynsen, residing here at the Manhatans, has continually bought up said contraband merchandise wherever he could get it and then sent it by vessels to his associate and partner, Jacob Schermerhoorn, at Fort Orange, where Schermerhoorn

lived and by whom, Schermerhoorn, the contraband goods were sold
to the Indians, all of which more clearly appears by the letters,
both of Jacob Reynsen and Schermerhoorn; which trade in powder,
lead and guns with the Indians was forbidden by the late Director
Willem Kieft and the council by ordinance of the 23d of February,
1645, on pain of punishment by death and forfeiture of all his
goods, if any one were found to have carried on that trade with
the Indians. Furthermore, the said Jacob Reynsen has dared to
solicit by trade with Barent Ennesz van Noorden, the Company's
smith, guns, locks and barrels, belonging to the honorable Company,
and thus, carrying off the honorable Company's arms, has sent
them to Fort Orange to his said partner, who sold them to the
Indians, as more fully appears in the letter written by Jacob
Reynsen and found in his house, wherein he says: "Partner, the
Company's smith has informed against me. Hide the guns, or otherwise there might be trouble." For this offense Jacob Reynsz was
imprisoned, which imprisonment he violated by breaking jail and
making his escape. Therefore, according to said ordinance, both
offenders would deserve to be put to death. However, considering
the petition and recommendation of several honest persons and
inhabitants of this place and the former good behavior of the
offenders, it is out of special favor and mercy resolved and concluded to moderate the sentence as much as it is possible and
justifiable, but yet to punish them as an example to others.
Therefore, the aforesaid director general and council, administering justice in the name of their High Mightinesses, the Lords
States General of the United Netherlands, his Highness of Orange

and the honorable directors of the Chartered West India Company, do condemn, as they hereby condemn, the above named Jacob Reynsen and Jacob Schermerhoorn to depart from here by the first ship and, furthermore, to remain banished from this province for five consecutive years. The director and council likewise declare all their goods, both peltries and others, here in New Netherland liable to confiscation, as they do hereby confiscate the same for the benefit of the honorable Company and those whom it concerns, and furthermore, they are to pay the costs of the suit [395] as an example to other violators of the public ordinances. However, it is to be noted that this course shall not be followed or held as a precedent in case any others, after publication hereof, shall be found to have transgressed the said ordinance, but these violators shall be punished without any regard or respect of persons, according to the tenor of said ordinance. Thus done in court in Fort Amsterdam, in New Netherland, the 9th of July 1648.

The honorable director general and council of New Netherland having seen the voluntary confession made and acknowledged without torture on the 28th and 29th of May and on the 8th of July by Barent Enessen van Noorden, smith and corporal of the Company, at present a prisoner, by which it appears that he, the prisoner, forgetting his honor and oath, has allowed himself to sell the honorable Company's guns, locks and barrels, handed and entrusted to him to be cleaned and repaired, to one Jacob Reyntjes and Joost Teunisz Backer, by which means the honorable Company's arms are alienated and rendered useless to them, which not only tends to the great damage and injury of the honorable Company, but also apparently to the final selling to the Indians of said arms, which have been thus sold and alienated, whence it follows that the Christians are weakened and the barbarians strengthened in arms, which is a matter of every great consequence and importance, that ought not to be tolerated or suffered in a country where it is customary to maintain justice. Therefore, we, Petrus Stuyvesant, director general of New Netherland, Curaçao, etc., and the council, wishing to administer justice, as we hereby do, in the name of their High Mightinesses, the Lords States General of the United Netherlands, his Highness of Orange, and the honorable directors of the Chartered West India Company, although the offender richly deserves corporal punishment, yet, considering that this is his first offense and crime and that he was induced to commit said offense by said persons, have therefore, out of special mercy modified the punishment and have condemned, as we do hereby condemn, the offender to remain one whole year confined in the smith's shop of the honorable Company, there to work during the year in compensation and in indemnification for the Company's arms sold and alienated by him, as an example to others. Thus done and resolved in council and published the 9th of July 1648, in Fort Amsterdam, in New Netherland. Present: the honorable director general, L. van Dincklage, La Montagne, Briant Nuton, Poulus Leendersz and A: Keyser.

[396] Every inhabitant of New Netherland is hereby notified and warned not to present, sell or loan any wine, beer, or strong drink to Barent Ennesz, smith of the honorable Company, during

his confinement in the smith's shop, without express consent of
the honorable director general. Neither shall any one be permitted
to give credit to said Barent Ennesz, on pain of such creditor
not being paid; likewise, whoever shall, without permission, ask
said Barent Ennesz to make, sell, or repair any arms, shall be
punished according to the circumstances of the case. Let every
one take warning and guard himself against loss. Thus done and
decreed in council, in Fort Amsterdam, in New Netherland, the
9th of July anno 1648.

The 13th of July anno 1648

Pieter van[der] Linden and his wife appeared in council and
requested payment and satisfaction from Jan Bentijn of a bond
and for some other goods, which said Bentijn received before
his departure for Holland on the promise that he would bring
with him other goods in their place, the bond amounting to two
beavers, and the linen for three shirts amounting to fl. 8 each;
also fl. 4 for other linen, so that the whole sum amounts to
fl. 44.

The bond signed by Bentijn being shown and read in council,
it is considered advisable, if the appearers swear that the debt
is just, that in such case they shall be paid out of the means
which Jan Bentijn has still here.

The appearers having verified by oath their demand and the
bond, it is ordered that Pieter van[der] Linden shall be paid
without contradiction out of Bentijn's effects. This 13th of
July anno 1648, in New Netherland.

Whereas it is found by experience that free traders do not hesitate, nor feel ashamed, to defraud the honorable Company both as regards the price and measure of goods, as is evidenced in the purchase of some cloth on account of the Company, which by calculation as compared by the correct invoice is found to be 1/3 short in the measure; also, that Hardenb[erch] will not let the Company have the canvas which they greatly need for less than 30 stivers, which he entered in the fatherland at 5½ stivers. On account of these and similar faults, it is judged and deemed advisable in council [397] that some of the chief officers with the fiscal be ordered to open the cases belonging to Verbruggen standing in the public store, and carefully to measure what is therein contained; to do the same also at Hardenberch's house, to discover how they handled this matter and to see if everything agrees with the invoice, and in case any fraud be found, such goods shall be taken to the public store until further order. This 13th of July anno 1648, in New Amsterdam.

Claes Bordingh, being heard for the second time in council, declares that he has had some guns from Egbert van Borsum and that they came from the ship St. Beninjo, which guns he carried up the river last harvest. Said Claes Bordingh is promised that no harm or injury shall happen to him nor to Egbert van Borsum on this account. This 13th of July anno 1648, in New Amsterdam in New Netherland.

Whereas some powder has been found with an Indian of Pasquaeskeck, he is examined as to where he got it. Says he

bought the same from the Indians at Pavonia, and as no more
could be learned the honorable council, the honorable general
being absent, let the Indian go. This 14th of July anno 1648,
in New Amsterdam.

The honorable council, in the absence of the honorable
general, have considered it necessary, pursuant to the director
general's order, to despatch the ship De Liefde for salt, which
is required here, and as provisions are wanted it is decided to
send the commissary to Stamford to buy provisions, for which
beavers shall be given him. This 15th of July 1648.

Pursuant to order, the honorable council, the general being
absent, opened in the public store all the cases shipped by
Gillis Verbruggen in the ship De Valckenier, and measured the
pieces of duffel and found the measure to be generally less than
is marked on the tags; nothing was found in the cases but what
is stated in the invoices; wherefore, we have permitted the
merchant to sell his goods without any hindrance. This 16th of
July anno 1648.

[398] On the 18th of July, at the request of the master of
the ship De Pynappel, the council, in the presence of the fiscal,
inspected the entire hold, room, cabin and other places and opened
provision casks, so that to the best of our knowledge not a
place in the ship escaped proper inspection. Nothing was found
that was not in the invoice, but everything agreed perfectly,
except 11 guns belonging to private persons, which were brought

ashore, so that the ship is declared free and the soldiers taken off her. Dated as above. Present: L. van Dincklaghen, La Montagne, Poulus Leendersz and the secretary.

On the 18th of July anno 1648

Whereas Mr. Isaack Allerton complains that the honorable Company will not readily be paid by Raef Ory for the freight of the yacht Groote Gerrit to Barbados, but that he as surety will apparently have to pay the freight, he, Allerton, therefore requests that he may be arrested here on his bond, on condition that he may depart on entering counter security. The honorable council, the general being absent, having seen Allerton's request, arrest said Allerton here, who offers as sureties Mr. Ritchert Smith and G[e]orge Bacxter, who promise to pay the honorable Company in case Raef Ory, or he, Allerton, do not pay.

In like manner the aforesaid Ritchert Smith and G[e]orge Bacxter offer themselves as sureties for Willem de Key for a sum of fl. 1200, which Raef Ory owes for freight on the ship De Bever, and in case said Ory or Mr. Allerton do not pay, Smith and Bacxter, promise to pay said sum.

In the margin was written: Present: Mr. Dincklaghen, Lieutenant Nuton, Poulus Leendersz and Adriaen d'Keyser.

Whereas on the night of the 21st, after the watch was posted, one Gerrit Jansen Slomp was stabbed to death at the house of Abraham Pietersz, tavern keeper on the island of Man-hatans, where he had been drinking, therefore, Abraham Pietersz is provisionally forbidden, pursuant to law, to tap or to entertain

company until further order. This 23d of July anno 1648, in
Fort Amsterdam in New Netherland. Present: Mr. Dincklagen,
La Montagne, Briant Newton, Paulus Leendersz and A: Keyser.
(The general being absent).

[399 Confession and declaration made in Council in the presence
of the Honorable Councilors, in the absence of the General,
of Johannes Roodenborch from Hamburg, at present arrested
for manslaughter committed on Gerritt Jansen Slomp after
the posting of the guard during the night between the
21st and 22d of July.

Johannes Roodenborch from Hamburg, aged 24 years, says:
Having the burgher watch last night, he went the rounds between
12 and 1 o'clock at night around Jan Damen's land and so came
past the house of Abraham Pietersz, tavern keeper, where he saw
light and heard singing, whereupon he, Roodenborch, in company
with Jan La Montagne, aged about 16 years, as roundsman, knocked
at Abraham Pietersen's house three several times in order to see
what people and noise were in the house so late. Thereupon
Abraham's wife got up in her shift and let him, Roodenborch, in,
who inquired what people she had in her house. Said woman
answered there were no people in her house; whereupon he went to
the back room to see who were there. The door being open, he
found that the light was out. He, Roodenborch, went into the
inside room, where Abraham Pietersz lay on his bed, undressed,
and took the lamp in order to see who were in the back room.
Abraham Pietersen's wife asked what he, Roodenborch, wanted in
the room and said that there was nobody there and closed the
door of the back room. He, Roodenborch, said to the woman that
he had to enter the room to see who were there, whereupon

Abraham got up from his bed and demanded who sent him, Roodenborch, there. He, Roodenborch, answered that he came there on his rounds to see what people and noise were there. Abraham replied, "The devil I care for you; let the fiscal come," and put out the lamp with his hand. He, Roodenborch, said, "I must see, nevertheless, who are there." Whereupon the said Roodenborch was thrown out of the house in the dark.

Johannes Roodenborch further deposes that when he was shoved out of the house, those inside tried to shut the door. He then pushed with his pike against the door so that it flew open again. Abraham Pietersz grasped the pike and wrested it from him, Roodenborch, whereupon he was obliged to take the gun of Jan La Montagne, whom he sent for the burgher guard while he himself remained before the door. While Jan La Montagne was going for the watch, one Gerritt Jansen Slomp suddenly ran from the door toward him, Roodenborch, cursing and swearing, and seized the gun Roodenborch had in his hand. He, Roodenborch, drew back and finally was obliged to give up the gun and defend his life. He could not reach the door or the gate of the clap-board fence, and in his flight he, Roodenborch, drew his sword and thrust it out behind him under his arm and touched Gerrit Slomp, who followed him, and who had taken or wrested away his gun. At that instant Gerrit Slomp threw down the gun. He, Roodenborch, took up the gun again and remained standing in front of the door. Finally he, Roodenborch, went himself to the guard house and got some burghers, to wit, Jacob Kip and others, who had left before him. Coming to the house of Abraham Pietersz, they found Jacob Leendersz and Paulus Heyman, who said

the man was dead, and went into the house of Abraham Pietersz
where the fiscal came, to whom he applied to be taken to the
appropriate place, but the fiscal refused and remained the rest
of the night drinking. There were present also in the room where
the dead man lay, Jacob L[eendersen] [400] and two soldiers, whom
the fiscal kept with him. In the morning [the aforesaid
Roodenborch] was put in prison in the fort. Thus done in council,
in [Fort] Amsterdam in New Netherland, the 22d of July anno 1648,
in New Amsterdam.

The original was signed by Johannes Roodenborch. Present:
Mr. Dinck[lage], La Montagne, B. Nuton, Paulus Leendersz and
A: Keyser.

Below was written: Attested by me, Cor: van Tienhoven,
Secretary.

Abraham Pietersen from Haerlem, tavern keeper, aged 47 years,
declares in council that Johannes Roodenborch knocked at his
door last night, to the best of his knowledge about 12 or one
o'clock, which said Roodenborch was let in by Abraham Pietersen's
wife and entered and went into the back room to see if there
were any people. Finally he, Roodenborch, returning where he,
the deponent, lay on his bed, took the lamp in order to return
to the back room. The deponent arose and pulled the door shut
and says that the lamp was blown out with his breath. The
deponent dragged him, Roodenborch, by force from the room and
said that he had no business there. Abraham Pietersz says that
he did not throw Roodenborch out of the door, but that they both
went to the door. Abraham Pietersz closed the lower door, at

which and over which door Roodenborch thrust with the pike, which pike he grasped and retained, and he, the deponent, then went in again. He declares that he does not know how Gerrit Slomp was killed; also, that he did not hear that Roodenborch and said Slomp had any words, but as far as he knew Gerrit Slomp lay and slept in the corridor. Three other persons lay and slept in his back room, namely, Baes Jeuryaen, the chief boatswain of the Pynappel, and the steward of the Liefde. A short while after he was in his room, he, the deponent, heard Roodenborch say, "He is wounded," and coming out he found Gerrit Jansen Slomp before the door, between the fence and his house, near the gate. All of which he offers to confirm on oath. This 22d of July anno 1648, in Fort Amsterdam, in New Netherland. Was signed by Abraham Pietersz in the presence of Mr. Dincklagen, La Montagne, Briant Nuton, Paulus Leendersz and Adriaen Keyser.

Below was written: Acknowledged before me, Cor: van Tienhoven, Secretary.

[401] Jan La Montangne, aged 16 years, being heard in council, declares that about one o'clock last night, Johannes Roodenborch going the founds in company with him, La Montagne, and coming near the house of Abraham Pietersen, tavern keeper, they saw light in two rooms and heard a noise as of drunken people, for which reason Johannes Roodenborch knocked at the door. Being admitted by the above named Abraham's wife, he, Roodenborch, inquired if there were any people there. To which the woman and her husband replied that there were no people in the house. He, Roodenborch, wishing to investigate, took the lamp, which

went out; the deponent does not know whether it was blown out or
not, as he was waiting at the front door. Abraham demanded by
whose order he came there. Roodenborch answered that he was
going the rounds. Abraham replied, "I have nothing to do with
the rounds, let the fiscal come and examine." Roodenborch,
standing near the front door, was thrown out of the door by
Abraham Pietersz. Whereupon Roodenborch called to him, the
deponent, to fire, taking his, the deponent's gun, and said,
"Run to the guard and bring some men from there," which he, the
deponent did. Returning with Jacob Leendersz and Poulus Heymans,
they found Gerrit Slomp stabbed to death. All of which he
declares to be true. Thus done in the presence of Mr. Dincklagen,
Mr. La Montagne and Paulus Leendersz, naval store keeper, in
Fort Amsterdam, in New Netherland, the 22d of July anno 1648.
The original was signed by Jan La Montangne. Underneath was
written, Which I attest, Cor: van Tienhoven, Secretary.

Meuwes Jansen from Amsterdam, aged about 40 years, appeared
before the council and acknowledged and declared that last night,
not knowing how late it was, he was lying on the bed at the house
of Abraham Pietersz, tavern keeper, when the rounds came knocking,
the lamp or candle being burning in the back room and one or the
company still up, who hadn't yet finished drinking his beer.
This person blew out the candle when he heard the knocking. The
deponent says that he does not know for certain whether it was
Baes Jeuryaen or the chief boatswain of the Pynappel. The
deponent declares that he knows nothing more of the matter, nor
what trouble there was in the forepart of the house between

Johannes Roodenborch, the tavern keeper, and Gerrit Slomp. Thus
done in council. Present: Mr. Dincklagen, La Montagne, Briant
Nuton, Paulus Leendertsz and Adriaen Keyser, the 22d of July
anno 1648, in New Amsterdam in New Netherland.

The original was signed by Meus Jansen with his mark. Underneath was written: Which I witness, Cor: van Tienhoven, Secretary.

[402] Pieter Pietersz Costelyck, chief boatswain of the
ship Pynappel, being heard in council, declares as follows:

First, that he heard the knocking of the rounds at Abraham
Pietersen's door, and that he was then lying on the bed in the
back room with Meus Jansen; on hearing the knocking he blew out
the lamp in the back room. The deponent declares further that
he went to bed about an hour before the rounds knocked.

Said Pieter Pietersz Costelyck declares further that he
and others sat drinking at the house of Abraham Pietersz, tavern
keeper, on the 21st of July last, and that one Gerrit Jansen
Slomp also was drinking in the afternoon, who, being drunk,
annoyed and tried to pick a quarrel with him, the deponent, and
Baes Juryaen. Neither he nor Baes Juryaen being so disposed,
however, they turned him away with kind words. Finally, the
above named Gerrit Jansz became dead drunk and went to sleep
before the door. Toward evening they brought Gerrit Slomp
again into the house and laid him down in the hall, where he
remained sleeping until about the time the rounds came knocking
in the night, when the said Slomp made great noise and racket
in the hall aforesaid, so that it seemed as though a great many
people were in the house. All of which the deponent declares
to be true, offering to confirm this declaration on oath, this
23d of July 1648. The original was signed by Pieter Pietersz

Costelyck in the presence of Mr. Dincklagen, La Montagne, Briant
Nuton, Poulus Leendersz and A: Keyser, in Fort Amsterdam.
Below was written: Acknowledged before me Cor: van Tienhoven,
Secretary.

Jeuryaen Hendricksen from Osenbrugge, [1] house carpenter,
aged 36 years, declares in the presence of Mr. Dincklaghen and
Paulus Leendersz, at the request of the fiscal, that during the
night between the 21st and 22d of July he slept in the house of
Abraham Pietersz, where the deponent had sat drinking in company
with others and Gerrit Slomp, who, being drunk, joined them in
the afternoon. Declares that he knows nothing in the world of
any dispute, as he was highly intoxicated and does not even know
how much he spent. Thus done the 24th of July anno 1648, in New
Amsterdam. The original was signed with Juryaen Hendricksen's
mark, made by himself in the presence of the above named councilors.
Underneath was written: Acknowledged before me, Cor: van
Tienhoven, Secretary.

[433] Proposition submitted by the honorable Director
General to the Council

Whereas it is seen by
experience that nothing is
done by the fiscal to ob-
tain a decision as to what
is to be done with the
guns, about [   ] in number,
obtained from both of the

Resolved in council to pay
for the guns belonging to the
sailors what they cost in
Holland, and to restore their
guns to those domiciliated
here as settled burghers, on
condition that whenever a

---

[1] Osnabrück, Hanover.

ships and still remaining in the council chamber: in case no further claim is brought against these ships on that account we are of opinion that the guns at least are liable to confiscation.

2. Regarding the 13 guns and 13 bullet molds, and some other articles marked A C, which were seized without appearing on the invoice of the lading.

3. The purchased cloth which still lies in the council chamber and is found to be longer than indicated on the invoice.

4. In regard to the homicide while I was at Fort Orange, and the wounding of the gunner by Simon Courtbrant, a soldier, who ran away before my departure and since skulks at

burgher intends to depart he must produce his gun before the council.

Resolved, according to agreement, to pay 100 per cent as per the Company's invoice.

Resolved that the fugitives shall be summoned by beat of the drum.

Mespachtes, without any
inquiry being made of any
action started by the
fiscal, to the injury and
disrepute of justice.

5. The petition of
the free traders in favor
of the convicted Jacob Reynsen
and Schermerhoorn, that their
sentence of banishment may be
remitted.

Finally, the case of
Egbert van Borsum, who, being
still the Company's sworn servant
and master of the yacht _Prins_
Willem, in violation of his
honor and trust has purchased
guns and powder from the
smugglers at New Haven, and
has carried them, or caused
them to be conveyed, past
this place to Fort Orange.

On these five foregoing
propositions, especially, a
final conclusion is necessary.
Was signed: P. Stuyvesant, the
first of August anno 1648.

In council, being seen the petition of respectable burghers
residing in this city of New Amsterdam; also the petition and
conduct of Jacob Reynsen and Jacob Jansen Schermerhoorn, in
regard to certain [sentence of] banishment recently imposed upon
them for trading in contraband wares, the honorable director
general and council of New Netherland have, therefore, graciously
remitted said banishment to said Jacob Reynsen and Schermerhoorn
and declare them henceforth capable of going, coming and returning here as other respectable persons are permitted to do.
Thus done in Fort Amsterdam, the first of August anno 1648.
Present: the honorable general, Mr. Dincklage, La Montangne,
B. Nuton, P: Leendersz and Adriaen Keyser.

[404] Egbert van Borsum, being heard in council, declares
and acknowledges that in the year 1647, at New Haven, to the
north, he bought and received from the chief boatswain of the
Klinckert [1] and the cook of the ship Beninjo 50 guns at fl. 26
each, and that at the time there were still nine cases with guns
in the hold of the said Beninjo; also, that no one in the world
was associated with him, except Abraham Willemsz, at that time
a sailor. He also says that he bought from the same four kegs
of powder at one guilders, and three kegs of shot of 50 lb.
each at 12 stivers a pound. Thus done in the presence of the
honorable general, Mr. Dincklagen, Mr. La Montagne, Briant Nuton,
Paulus Leendersz and Adriaen d'Keyser, the 1st of August anno 1648.

---

[1] The name of a small vessel.

2 Whereas Fort Orange, situated on the North river of New
Netherland, near the colony of Renselaerswyck, last winter was
almost entirely washed away by the high water and is highly in
need of being repaired for the maintenance of the honorable
Company's limits and jurisdiction; and whereas the present condition both of the honorable Company and ourselves here does
not permit us to make the required repairs, much less to complete
them, Therefore the honorable director general and council for
reasons and considerations aforesaid, have resolved and concluded,
that it would be most advantageous and least expensive for the
said Company to permit some respectable inhabitants of New Netherland to build at their own expense houses in said Fort, against
the wall, run up with stone 12 feet high, especially as the
Hon. Mr. Kieft, the late director, and the council had long ago
permitted some to do the same thing. It is also resolved that
the ground shall at all times remain the property of the Company,
and that those who will build in the fort, shall not own more
than the buildings, or be able to sell more than the same,
whereunto the Company shall enjoy the preemption right.

Thus done and resolved in Council in Fort Amsterdam in New
Netherland, the 11th of August A⁰. 1648. Present: The Hon.
Director General, Mr. Dincklage, La Montagne, Brian Nuton,
Paulus Leendersen and Adriaen Keyser.

Fiscal van Dyck is ordered to place in confinement the
persons of Hendrick the tailor and Albert the carpenter and in
the meantime to inform himself more fully regarding the complaint

2 Revised from Doc. Rel. Col. Hist. N. Y., 14:92-93.

made by the officer of the burgher guard and then to institute his action against them in proper form. The 10th of August anno 1648.

The papers and information against Johannes Roodenborch being read and examined and the council having heard all the persons who persist in their first testimony, the fiscal is ordered to institute his suit against Johannes Roodenborch, who has again appeared without being summoned, and furthermore to inform himself of all particulars, to which end he will be assisted by Lieutenant Brian Nuton and Marten Cregier, lieutenant of the burgher company. This 10th of August anno 1648.

Having seen the written complaint of the fiscal against Egbert van Borsum and Abraham Willemsz on account of the purchase of contraband goods effected at New Haven on board the ship St. Beninjo, of which Cornelis Clasen Snoy was master, and whereas thus far it does not appear to us that the guns were sold by them to the Indians or savages, the fiscal is authorized to inquire further what has become of the guns and to whom they were sold and who were their confederates, especially as some officers of the Company are said to be involved. Therefore, the first purchasers of the said contraband goods are commanded to make at the request of the fiscal a full and true declaration to whom they sold the said contraband goods; and in case they refuse, then the promised impunity which the director and council gave in order to obtain further information and intelligence shall be null and void and they shall be considered as having sold them to the Indians, etc. Thus done in council. Present: the honorable general, Mr. Dincklaghen, Mr. La Montagne, Brian Nuton, Paulus Leendersz and Adriaen Keyser, the 15th of August anno 1648, in Fort Amsterdam in New Netherland.

[409] The 15th of August anno 1648

Fiscal van Dyck, plaintiff, against Hendryck the tailor,
and Albert the carpenter, for having molested the rounds on the
street and made use of abusive language at night, after the
guard had been posted.

The director and council having seen the fiscal's complaint
and the proofs thereof, as well as the declaration and report
of the burgher officers, the defendants are condemned to pay a
fine of fl. 50 to be applied 1/3 for the church, 1/3 for the
fiscal, and 1/3 for the watch, as an example to others, and in
case they be found hereafter repeating such offenses and mis-
demeanors they shall be punished corporally.

Whereas the grist mill has hitherto been nothing but a
burden to the honorable Company in consequence of the great and
necessary repairs which are constantly required, and the rent
derived from it is not sufficient to meet the expense, it is for
the best interest and profit of the honorable Company considered
necessary by the council that the honorable Company do not lease
the mill, but appoint a miller to have charge of it and give
him decent wages, say fl. 40 a month, on condition that the toll
shall be paid to the receiver, from which money the mill shall
be kept in repair and the miller paid. Thus done the 15th of
August anno 1648, in New Amsterdam in New Netherland.

The director general and council having seen with regret
the unseaworthiness of the yacht De Liefde and that she is bare
of all necessary equipment, which is not on hand nor to be had
here; also, that we have here neither materials nor carpenters

to repair, furnish and fit out for sea the said ship again and moreover provisions and men are lacking, the vessel being very leaky and absolutely requires to be sheathed, which for reasons above set forth cannot be done here; therefore, it is unanimously resolved in council to be most profitable and advantageous to the honorable Company to sell before winter the said ship at the first opportunity. If no purchasers be found, it is resolved to haul the little vessel on shore next winter and there to take down the running and standing rigging, therewith to fit out next spring the ships that may come out of the sea, as to all appearances these will also be destitute of everything. This 15th of August anno 1648, in Fort Amsterdam.

[410] [1] The honorable director general having exhibited in council the account of Andries Hudden, commissary at Fort Nassau, which is found to be obscure and not made out as clearly as it ought to be; therefore, it is resolved to order said commissary to come hither overland and personally to explain his account before the director and council. This 15th of August anno 1648.

Johannes Roodenborch from Hamburg, at present a prisoner, is examined and asked by the honorable courtmartial in what manner the manslaughter was committed by him on the person of Gerrit Jansen from Amsterdam. Johannes Roodenborch, being heard for the second time, persists in his confession and declaration made on the 22d of July last.

---

[1] Revised from <u>Doc</u>. <u>Rel</u>. <u>Col</u>. <u>Hist</u>. <u>N</u>. <u>Y</u>., 12:42.

Interrogatories on which said Roodenborch is further examined
  in court

1. Did Gerrit Jansen Slomp
come swearing toward him out
of the house of Abraham
Pietersz, tavern keeper, and
take his gun by force, and
did he call out to said Gerrit Jansen to keep away
from him?

Johannes Roodenborch from
Hamburg answers to the first:
Yes.

2. When he had lost the gun,
did Gerrit Jansen follow him
with it, and when he was running away could he not escape
through the door or gate of
the clapboards?

To the second he answers:
Yes.

3. Did he while retreating
draw his sword and stab back-
wards under his arm?

To the third he answers:
Yes, and that he drew his
sword because he thought that
Gerrit Jansz would take fright
and abandon the pursuit.

4. Had he any intention
at all to wound or kill
Gerrit Jansen?

To the fourth he answers that
he had not the least thought of
wounding or killing him.

5. Did he ever in his live   To the fifth he answers:
have any difficulty or quar-   No.
rel with the man whom he
killed?

6. Did he not hate   To the sixth he answers:
Gerrit Jansen?   No.

Which answers Johannes Roodenborch has given in the presence of
the court-martial, the same being confirmed by him on oath, so
truly help him God Almighty. Present: the honorable general,
Mr. Dincklagen, Mr. La Montagne, Briant Nuton, Lieutenant Paulus
Leendersz, naval store keeper, G[e]orge Bacxter, ensign, and
Sergeant Daniel Litschoe. Done in Fort Amsterdam in New Netherland, the 19th of August anno 1648.

[411] Hendrick van Dyck, fiscal, complains against Jan from
Leyden, freeman, defendant, for drawing a knife and resisting an
officer of the law. The fiscal's complaint and the evidence in
support thereof being heard in court, said Jan from Leyden is condemned to pay a fine of fl. 100 before his release from confinement,
as an example to other turbulent persons. Present: the honorable
general, Mr. Dincklagen, Mr. La Montagne, Briant Nuton and
Paulus Leendersz.

The honorable court-martial having seen and read all the
information taken by the fiscal against Johannes Roodenborch
from Hamburg, at present under arrest, and having duly considered
everything that is to be noted and observed, they find that it

does not appear from said information that the said prisoner
deserves any punishment for the homicide of Gerrit Jansen from
Amsterdam, committed on the night of the 21st of July; wherefore,
said Roodenborch is provisionally released on bail and allowed
to go about on the island of Manhatans. And in order that no
one may plead ignorance, every inhabitant of New Netherland is
hereby notified by the ringing of the bell, that if any person
know anything incriminating said Roodenborch, or tending to
exculpate the slain person he shall communicate the same to the
proper authorities within three consecutive court days, when
the honorable court-martial will proceed to the final disposition
of the case. Thus done and published in Fort Amsterdam, the 19th
of August anno 1648, in New Netherland.

Augustyn Heermans, free merchant on the island of Manhatans,
becomes bail for Johannes Roodenborch that he shall appear in
court when required on account of the manslaughter of Gerrit
Jansen from Amsterdam. This 19th of August anno 1648.

Resolved to renew until further order the Ordinance published the [23d of February] anno 1645 by the late director and
council, relative to the trade in powder and lead. This 19th
of August 1648.

[412] Whereas the Scotch merchants who came over in the
year 1648 in the ships _Pynappel_ and _Valckenier_ request permission
to return to the fatherland, the honorable director general and
council have granted their request and resolved and concluded
that the Scotch merchants who hereafter come over shall remain
during the term of three consecutive years in New Netherland.

This shall be published in due season and at a most convenient
opportunity. Thus done in council. Present: the honorable
director general, Mr. Dincklagen, Mr. La Montagne, Captain Nuton,
and Poulus Leendersz, the 19th of August anno 1648, in New Amsterdam in New Netherland.

Jan Jansz Damen appeared in council and produced two protested bills of exchange allowed to go to protest by the
honorable directors; one of fl. 1,000, the other fl. 350. He
demands payment and reimbursement for exchange and reexchange,
with loss and damage thereof. The honorable director general
and council, seeing the equity of the demand, promise to pay
promptly in the spring, to wit: fl. 350 in beavers and the
fl. 1,000 in other good currency, and in addition by way of
interest eight per cent of the amount, commencing from the date
of the bills of exchange. This 19th of August anno 1648, at New
Amsterdam. Present: the honorable director general, Mr. Dincklagen,
Mr. La Montagne, Briant Nuton and Poulus Leendersz.

[1] The honorable director general lays before the council a
message from Commissary van Brugge, who reports that Commander
Slechtenhorst, contrary to the notice served on him, proceeds
with the building under the walls of the Company's Fort Orange.
[Resolved,] that he pull down the same, and in case Slechtenhorst
offers opposition thereto, he[, van Brugge,] is to advise us
thereof, when more men will be sent from here for his assistance.

---

[1] Revised from Doc. Rel. Col. Hist. N. Y., 14:93.

This day, the 23d of August anno 1648, in New Amsterdam. Present, the honorable director, Mr. Dincklagen, La Montagne, Briant Nuton and Paulus Leendersz.

[413] Whereas the grist mill must be maintained at the Company's expense and yields little profit, it is, for the best advantage and benefit of the Company resolved to engage a miller at wages to be paid by the Company, provided that the toll for grinding shall be paid to the receiver of the Company's revenue; and whereas at present no better person than Abraham Pietersz from Haerlem is available, we have engaged him at fl. 40 per month, commencing on the date hereof. This 23d of August anno 1648, at New Amsterdam.

The honorable director general requests in writing a decision in the case of Symon Courtbrandt.

The honorable courtmartial having seen the writing and request of the honorable director general, Symon Courtbrandt is examined and confesses that he wounded the gunner and ran away on that account. However, having appeared again on his own account and submitted himself to the merciful sentence of the honorable courtmartial, and satisfaction being made to the gunner, the aforesaid Symon Courtbrandt is condemned to ride the wooden horse for two hours a day for three consecutive days, and in case he again commit any offense he shall be punished according to martial law. This 4th of September 1648. The director absent. Present: L. van Dinckla[gen], La Montagne, Brian Nuton, lieutenant, G[e]orge Bacxter, ensign, and D: Litschoe, sergeant.

The honorable director general and council order that the
goods belonging to the estates of Jan from Rotterdam and Pieter
Colet be sold to the highest bidder by Jan Damen and Olof Stevensz,
administrators, in the presence of Mr. Dincklagen and Mr. La
Montagne. The 10th of September 1648. Present: P. Stuyvesant,
L; van Dincklaghe, La Montagne, Paulus Leendersz.

[1] The honorable director general lays before the council a
despatch dated the 4th of September, sent by Commissary van
Brugge, regarding Commander Slechtenhorst in the colony of
Rensselaerswyck, who contrary to our order and command proceeds
with the building of the house near and under the walls of Fort
Orange and within a pistol shot thereof. Resolved, therefore,
that four to six soldiers be sent to the commissary for his
assistance and better execution of his orders to demolish the
house with the [414] smallest loss to the owners, and in case
Commander Slechtenhorst offer opposition Carel van Brugge shall
arrest him in the most civil manner and detain him so long in
confinement until he deliver to the commissary copies of his
commission and instructions, with the declaration that he, the
commander, has no other commission and instructions than those
he shall then have exhibited. Thus done the 10th of September
1648. Present: the honorable director, L: van Dincklagen,
La Montagne, Briant Nuton and Poulus Leendersz.

---

[1] Revised from Doc. Rel. Col. Hist. N. Y., 14:93.

Matys Capita is engaged by the honorable director general
and council as assistant commissary in the store in place of
Pieter Antony, at fl. 18 a month and fl. 100 a year board money.
This 10th of September 1648. Present: The honorable director,
L: Dincklagen, La Montagne, Brian Nuton and Poulus Leendersz.

Proposition submitted by the honorable director general to
the council on the 9th of September 1648 [1]

1. To read to the council
the letter received from
Swedish governor, and then
to hear the report of
Andries Hudden.

2. To decide thereupon
what advice we had best give
to the honorable directors for
the promotion of the public
interest and the prevention
of further encroachment and
usurpation, to which end
our last drafted dispatch
to the honorable directors,
shall be read by the
secretary.

---

[1] Revised from <u>Doc</u>. <u>Rel</u>. <u>Col</u>. <u>Hist</u>. <u>N</u>. <u>Y</u>., 12:42.

3. To abstract the account of Commissary Hudden.

Commissary Adriaen Keyser and Cornelis van Tienhoven, secretary, are authorized to abstract summarize the account of Hudden, and to make a report thereof to the honorable director and council.

4. Regarding the previously published ordinance to mark the beavers, copy whereof has also gone to the fatherland and which according to the previous resolution is to go into effect immediately after the departure of the Pynappel.

Resolved in council that the ordinance shall take effect and be put in force immediately after the sailing of the Pynappel.

5. How shall the goods purchased of Olof Stevensz be employed to the best advantage of the Company.

Resolved to barter a considerable quantity of duffels for good seawan, and seawan for beavers, and to entrust the remainder to a good and reliable friend, to dispose thereof for the benefit of the Company, and to pay him a decent remuneration.

7. In regard to the last petition of Martie Tymens

for the appointment of
guardians over her
minor child.

8. The regulation of loose   [415] Resolved to wait yet a
seawan.   while and to consult the honorable
                                   directors once more on the subject.

9. Whether it is advisable   On this point a notice shall
to publish an ordinance   be posted that all persons, with-
obliging all Scots or   out any exception, who in the
merchants who come to   future shall come hither, shall
trade to remain in the   be warned that they must continue
country three consecutive   to reside three years in this
years?   country.

10. To publish an ordin-   Resolved to publish an ordinance that no one shall   ance to this effect.
bring any guns into the
country, except with per-
mission of the honorable
directors, and then neither
to give nor to sell them to
any person except to the
Company at two beavers a
piece.

11. Whereas with God's   Resolved to leave the fort
help we still hope to start   in its old form with four
doing some work on the   bastions, and to repair it.

fort, how the council think
it ought to be rebuilt, as
it has been with four
bastions, or enlarged to
five?

12. By what means are the   Resolved to communicate this
inhabitants to be induced to matter to the Nine Men and to
lend a helping hand to that   order them to take up among
work, agreeable to the   them a collection of about
orders of the Board of   5,000 or 6,000 guilders.
XIX?

Thus done and resolved in council, in Fort Amsterdam, in
New Netherland, the 9th of September anno 1648. Was signed:
P. Stuyvesant, L: van Dincklaghe, La Montagne, and Brian Newton.

Marretie Jans, widow of Dirck Cornelisz from Wensveen,
appeared before the council and requested that the honorable
director general and council legally appoint and commission
two respectable men to be tutors and guardians of her minor son,
named Cornelis Dircksz; not only to look after his person and
education, but to take good care especially of the property and
effects coming to her above named son by inheritance from his
aforesaid father, deceased; to administer the same to the best
advantage and profit of the aforesaid Cornelis Dircksz, and to
keep and render thereof a correct account.

The honorable director general and council having seen and
heard the reasonable request of Marretie Jans, widow of the said
Dirck Cornelisz, the said director general and council have
appointed and commissioned, as they do hereby appoint and commission, Michiel Jansz and Olof Stevensz, burghers and inhabitants
of this city of New Amsterdam, to be guardians and tutors of the
above named Cornelis Dircksz and all his property and effects,
both here in New Netherland and elsewhere, who, having received
the same under benefit of inventory, shall have legal administration of said property during the minority of Cornelis Dircksen,
aforesaid, collect and pay all debts due to or by the estate,
and perform all that upright and faithful guardians and administrators are allowed and bound to do; which they have sworn to
do before the honorable director general and council. Thus done
on the 14th of September anno 1648, in New Amsterdam, in New
Netherland. Present: The honorable general, L: Dincklagen,
La Montagne, B. Nuton and Poulus Leendersz.

[Ordinance obliging Scotch merchants and petty
traders to reside three years in New Netherland] 1

[416] Whereas the honorable director general and council
have seen and by experience observed that several of the Scotch
merchants and petty traders who from time to time come over in
the ships from the fatherland do and aim at nothing else than
solely to spoil trade and business by their underselling, dispose
of their goods with the utmost speed, give 11 or **12 guilders** in
loose seawan for one beaver and, when sold out, go back again

---

1 Revised from Laws and Ordinances of New Netherland,
pp. 101-2.

in the ships the same year in which they came, without bestowing or conferring any benefit on the country, all the burdens whereof, on the contrary, the inhabitants who own property must bear;

Therefore, to prevent such destroyers of trade, it is judged proper and profitable for New Netherland and the inhabitants thereof and it is hereby ordained that henceforth those merchants, scots and petty traders who come over in any ships from Patria with the intention to trade here either with Christians or heathens by the large or small measure, ell or weight, shall not be permitted to carry on any business in the least on shore here unless they take up their abode here in New Netherland for three consecutive years and, in addition, build in this city of New Amsterdam a decent burgher dwelling, each according to his circumstances and means. All merchants and others who bind themselves to transact business in a burgher house and to remain three years in the country shall be admitted, but no one else, the skipper or merchant of his own or his master's ship alone excepted, but these shall not be at liberty to keep any shop on shore. Thus done in the presence of the honorable director general, Mr. Dincklagen, Mr. La Montagne, Briant Nuton and Paulus Leendertsen, this 18th of September A⁰. 1648, in New Amsterdam.

Ordinance for the better enforcement of the ordinance against fires [1]

The honorable director general and council of New Nether land, for the purpose of preventing all calamities from fire, order and command the firewardens to visit every house in this

---

[1] Revised from Laws and Ordinances of New Netherland, p. 102.

city of New Amsterdam and to see to it that every one is keeping
his chimney properly clean by sweeping, and to oblige those who
are in default immediately to pay the fine of three guilders,
to be applied according to the ordinance to this effect published
on the 21st of January 1648. Thus done and ordained in council
in Fort Amsterdam in New Netherland, the 28th of September 1648.
Present: the honorable director general, L. Dincklage, La
Montagne, Briant Nuton, Paulus Leendertsen.

[Ordinance for the recovery of wages due to Indians] [1]
[417] 28 September anno 1648

Whereas great complaints are daily made by Indians and natives
to the honorable director general and council that some inhabitants of New Netherland put the natives to work and employ them
in their service and frequently dismiss them without pay after
the work is performed and persist, against all public law, in
refusing to pay the Indians for their labor, which Indians
threaten, if they are not remunerated and paid, to pay themselves,
or to revenge themselves by other improper means; Therefore,
the honorable director general and council, in order to put a
stop to this and to prevent as much as possible, in good time,
all mischief, warn all inhabitants who are indebted to the
Indians for wages or otherwise to pay them without contradiction,
and if in future they employ them they shall be bound to pay
them on the representation and complaint of the Indians, who for
good reasons shall in that case be competent witnesses; on pain
of paying such fine as in the circumstances of the case shall
be found proper.

---

[1] Revised from *Laws and Ordinances of New Netherland*, p. 103.

Thus done in council and published the 28th September 1648, in New Amsterdam. Present: the honorable director general, L. van Dincklagen, La Montagne, B. Nuton and Paulus Leendertsen.

Whereas Hans Loodwyck and Jacob Hendricksz from Benschop have contrary to the order and custom of New Netherland, without the knowledge of the honorable director general and council, secretly run away, they are by the ringing of the bell summoned to defend themselves on account of their desertion. This 28th of September 1648.

The 5th of October 1648

Antony Crol is by the honorable director general and council appointed master of the yacht De Liefde at fl. 50 per month, commencing on the date hereof.

The deacons presenting a petition to the council request thereby that the honorable director general and council be pleased to favor the deaconry with a donation, as God has granted their honors a valuable prize and the confiscation of Jacob Reynsen's peltries. Therefore, the honorable director general and council have unanimously resolved that fl. 500 be allowed and paid to the deacons when the account is made up and the books are closed. This day, the 5th of October anno 1648, in New Amsterdam.

[418] Whereas Jan Tonisz, at present a prisoner, has confessed without torture that, notwithstanding the former light sentence passed on him on the 12th of March last for drawing a knife and assaulting Cornelis Dircksen Hoochlandt, he has since dared to accuse Herry Breser, an Englishman, of theft, for which,

not being able to prove the same properly, he was condemned by
the director and council to make reparation to the person whom
he had unjustly accused; and whereas he, the prisoner, scorning
both sentences and orders of the director and council, has
moreover deserted his service and duties and run away, taking
with him the Company's scow or ferry boat; all of which acts,
tending to disobedience and contempt of justice, can not and
ought not to be tolerated in a well regulated state and government where laws and justice prevail, but ought to be rigorously
punished as an example to others; Therefore, the director and
council, administering justice in the name and on behalf of the
High and Mighty lords the States General, his Serene Highness
the Prince of Orange, and the honorable directors of the
Chartered West India Company, have, notwithstanding he richly
deserves corporal punishment, as a special favor, in view of
his office and because, according to his declaration, he never
withdrew from this jurisdiction, condemned and sentenced as they
do hereby condemn and sentence, the aforesaid Jan Tonisen, at
present a prisoner, to the penalty of doing 150 days' work at
his usual trade, to wit: 100 days for the honorable Company and
50 days for the church wardens, at such labor as the honorable
director and council or the church wardens shall order him to do.
And in order hereafter to prevent his desertion and to put this
sentence into effect the prisoner is ordered to furnish sufficient security for his service, obedience and labor, and in
default thereof to be kept securely in confinement on bread and
water. The further demand of the fiscal is denied. Thus done

on the 12th of October anno 1648, in New Amsterdam. Present:
the honorable director general, Mr. Dincklagen, La Montagne,
B. Nuton and the naval store keeper.

[Ordinance against fugitives from service] [1]

Whereas the honorable director general and council daily
see and observe that some of the inhabitants of New Netherland
harbor in their houses and dwellings the Company's servants and
other their domestics when they run away from their lords and
masters, also those who come hither from our neighbors across
the borders, whereby many servants, when they are dissatisfied
with their employment, are afforded a means and opportunity to
run away, which is of daily occurence; therefore, in order that
the honorable director general and council may prevent and
hinder such practices as much as is possible and practicable,
the honorable director general and council hereby notify and
warn all persons against harboring or entertaining any persons
in the service either of the Company or of other private
individuals residing here or elsewhere, and against lodging them
at most longer than 24 hours; and if any one shall be found to
have acted contrary hereto, he shall by way of fine forfeit
fl. 150, to be paid to whomsoever will make the complaint or be
entitled thereto. Thus done in council, the 6th of October 1648.
Present: the honorable director general, L. Dincklagen, La Montagne,
B. Nuton and P. Leendersz.

---

[1] Revised from Laws and Ordinances of New Netherland,
p. 104.

[419] Hendrick van Dyck, <u>ex officio</u>, plaintiff, against
Johannes Roodenborch, for manslaughter committed on the person
of Gerrit Slomp, during the night of the 21st of July.

The honorable director general and the court martial, having seen the demand of the fiscal and the informations taken on
the 22d of July respecting the aforesaid accident and having considered the evidence and the fiscal's complaint and all that is
to be done and observed in this case, find that the homicide was
accidentally committed by said Roodenborch in going the rounds,
he, coming past Abraham Pietersen's tavern at night after the
posting of the watch and the ordinary ringing of the bell, having
knocked, as he was bound to do on hearing a noise, and thus, as
more fully appears by the informations, the mishap unexpectedly
occurred. And whereas on the 19th of August last for every one's
satisfaction a notice was published that if any one knew anything to the inculpation of Roodenborch and in defense of the
slain man he was to present it within the next three court days,
which have now long since passed, and whereas nothing has been
produced by the fiscal or any one else against said Roodenborch;
therefore, the fiscal's demand is completely granted and the
above named Roodenborch acquitted of the manslaughter, as we
have taken into consideration the fact that the same was committed in the performance of his duty and while going the rounds.
Thus done and acquitted the 6th of October anno 1648, in Fort
Amsterdam in New Netherland, by the honorable director general
and the court martial, at which were present: the Honorable
Director Petrus Stuyvesant, Mr. van Dincklagen, second in
authority, La Montagne, Briant Nuton, captain lieutenant; George
Bacxter, ensign; and Daniel Litschoe, sergeant.

Whereas the honorable Company's expenses are daily increasing and their officers and councilors are daily dunned and applied to for payment of what the honorable Company owes to others, which is hardly possible unless the Company be first satisfied and paid their old and outstanding debts; therefore, the director general and council authorize and order Fiscal van Dyck and the receiver, Roelof Jansz de Haes, to demand from Commissary Keyser an abstract of the accounts of the debtors from the Book of the Colonists and to present this to all debtors and demand payment; or, in default thereof, in the name of the Company and their representatives here to notify and serve notice on those who for the present are unable to pay the whole, to pay so much as any one in his present state and condition may be able to pay, and for the balance to charge a reasonable yearly interest at 8 per cent per annum, to be paid each half year, the first interest to be due on the first of May next, and thereafter every six months four guilders per hundred. Thus done and resolved in council in Fort Amsterdam, the 15th of October anno 1648, in New Netherland. Present: P. Stuyvesandt, L. van Dincklagen and Paulus Leendersz.

[420] The 19th of October anno 1648

The guardians of the surviving orphan children of Claes Ja[nsen from Emden], baker, are authorized and ordered by the honorable director general to sell to the highest bidder for the best advantage and profit of the minor children the goods left by their aforesaid father, deceased.

The 26th of October anno 1648

Whereas it is considered highly necessary by the council
to appoint another qualified person in the place of Jan Stevensz,
precentor, and for the present we have not been able to find on
the island of Manhatans a more suitable person than Piter vander
Linden for the said office of [precentor or] reader, we have
therefore engaged said Pieter vander Linden as reader and have
allowed him therefor fl. 150 annually, and that until another
competent person be sent from Holland.

[Order to Commissary van Brugge to proceed with the repairs of
    Fort Orange and to demolish all buildings within cannon
    shot of the fort] [1]

Whereas by divers letters from our Commissary van Bruggen,
the testimony of others and personal reports of the inhabitants
of the colony we are informed of the usurpation of power and
improper procedure which Commander van Slechtenhorst practices,
not only with reference to his own inhabitants, as, contrary to
legal practice and the granted Exemptions, he forbids them on
the heaviest fine to appeal from his court, but also against the
servants and vassals of the Company itself, to the disparagement
of the charter granted by their High Mightinesses and infraction
and nullification of the Freedoms granted to the patroons, in
obscuring and hemming in the Company's fort by various structures,
in plowing up the old gardens and fields situated near the dry
moat of the fort and heretofore always used by the commissaries,
and especially in trying to prevent, as far as lies in his power,
the necessary repairs of the fortress, as he himself sneeringly

---

[1] Revised from Doc. Rel. Col. Hist. N. Y., 14:101-2.

styles it, because it can be entered by night as well as by day, being severely damaged in the latter part of last winter by the extraordinary high water and floods. As for that reason neces- sary repairs were required, we ordered and commanded our com- missary there, not only to repair it, but to put it in a proper state of defense, to wit, to surround it with a wall of stone, instead of timber, so as to avoid the annual expense and repairs. This being already begun, Commander Slechtenhorst, contrary to a former but never enforced privilege, prohibited the quarrying of stone and the cutting of timber within the limits of the colony and forbade the farmers and inhabitants to cart the same, all according to the tenor of his ordinance, without the knowledge or consent of us and the council of New Netherland; without designating, however, how far the limits of the colony extend, or pointing out where the Company may cut its wood or fetch the stone. This was never before done by any chief officer of the colony, or tolerated by any director and council, our predecessors, as it tends not only to the palpable belittling of their authority and general commission, but especially to the violation, infraction and nullification of the Chartered West India Company's supreme jurisdiction, which extends as well over the colony of Renselaerswyck as over others. If this be tolerated, other colonies, such as Heemstede, Flushing, Gravesend and others, would be expecting still more. Proceeding on that basis, the honorable Company would finally be deprived of firewood and timber necessary for ships, churches, forts and other buildings, or become obliged to beg these from their vassals and subjects and, what is worse and more to be apprehended, have to purchase

th n at the highest price and consequently, through our lack of
vigilance cause their supreme jurisdiction to be degraded and
changed to subordinate jurisdiction, contrary to the charter
from their High Mightinesses and to the infringement of the
Company's prerogatives. Being bound by commission and oath to
maintain both we, therefore, do hereby authorize and earnestly
command our commissary to proceed with the repairs of the fortress
and to that intent and **purpose** to cause timber to be cut, stone
to be quarried in and hauled from the mountains, cliffs and
plains in any part of New Netherland where it may be most convenient
for him or the Company, except only the bouweries and plantations
which are already fenced and cultivated, or may be hereafter
fenced or cultivated, within which he or any of the Company's
vassals shall not be at liberty to cut timber or quarry stone,
unless with previous knowledge of the proprietor or occupant.
And in case the jealousy of the commander may constrain the
inhabitants of the colony and hinder them from lending a helping
hand to the work with their horses and wagons, we order our
commissary to have a wagon made for himself and to use therefor
the horses of Mr. Jonas Bronck, now on the bouwery of Corler,
against whom the Company has a just claim in consequence of an
honest debt; this, however, is to be with the previous knowledge
of the Reverend Domine Megapolensis, his agent and attorney,
and an account is to be kept of what they cart and earn each day
in the Company's service. And we also, in like manner, authorize
and charge the commissary especially to maintain the Company's
high jurisdiction, ancient and previous use of the gardens and
lands situated under the fort, and not to cede the smallest iota

thereof, unless the commander exhibit to him, according to our
previous demand, later or other order and commission from their
aforesaid High Mightinesses, our Sovereigns, the lords directors,
our superiors and patroons, an authentic copy whereof he shall
transmit to us, so that we may then otherwise order. Finally,
in order to maintain the jurisdiction of the fort, the resolution
we last sent for the removal of the houses built within musket
or small cannon shot shall be peremptorily executed, if not
already obeyed. Thus done in Council in Fort Amsterdam in New
Netherland, the 2d of November anno 1648.

[422]   The 9th of November anno 1648

Whereas the yacht De Cath, of which Jeuryaen Andries[sen]
was master, arrived here from Curaçao with a cargo inside Sandy
Hook, otherwise called Godyns Point, in a [safe] port and, the
wind being contrary, tried to tack to before Fort Amsterdam,
said yacht, in tacking, stranded on a sand bank with such force
that notwithstanding all effort it could not be brought off,
except the effects which were in and on her, inclusive of the
masts; only, by the splitting of the ship, a quantity of salt
was dissolved. The effects and merchandise being calculated
against the monthly wages earned by the crew of the said ship,
the proceeds according to the inventory were found to amount
to more than the accrued wages; and whereas the ship's crew
appearing in a body before the council request a final settlement
according to maritime law, it is therefore resolved and concluded
in council to furnish a proper account to all the members of the
crew of the yacht De Cath, who shall be paid and satisfied by

the honorable director at Amsterdam, on condition that they shall
continue in the Company's service until their bounden time shall
have expired. This day, the 9th of November 1648. Present: The
honorable general, Mr. Dincklagen, Briant Nuton and Paulus
Leendersz.

The 23d of November anno 1648

Jeuryaen Andriesz, late master of the yacht De Cath,
presents to the council a petition requesting a settlement of
his account and his discharge, or other employment, whereupon
the following apostil is entered on the petition: The petitioner
shall be granted a final account and whereas there is no
employment for him here at present he is discharged, but
attention will be paid to his future employment, for which his
person remains recommended. The apostil is granted in the presence
of the honorable director general, the honorable deputy and
Brian Nuton.

The honorable director general and council having seen the
complaint of Pieter Wolphersz, guardian of the children of Claes
Jansz, baker, that Geertie Nannincx, widow of the said Claes
Jansz, collects the outstanding debts and alienates and sells
the property; therefore, for the reasons aforesaid, the court
messenger is ordered to notify Geertie Nannincx that henceforth,
without the knowledge of Pieter Wolphersz, she must not undertake to collect any debts or to alienate any property, on pain
of other measures being taken in the matter. Present: the
honorable general, Mr. Dincklagen, La Montagne, Brian Nuton
and Paulus Leendersz.

[423] On the 15th of December anno 1648

The honorable director general and council observing that
Skipper Antony Crol, heretofore put on the ship *De Liefde*, does
not conduct himself as he ought in his service and office, inasmuch as he scarcely once looks after said ship, whereby the
Company's affairs and service are greatly neglected; it is therefore unanimously resolved to dismiss said Antony Crol from his
office and to revoke the commission and instructions already
granted to him and to pay him one month's wages for the trouble
he has taken, going back and forth, and loss of time. And whereas
it is necessary to put a competent person on said ship, we, the
undersigned, have appointed Jeuryaen Andriesz to be skipper and
master and have allowed him fl. 50 per month, commencing on this
date and ending when he shall again arrive here, discharge all
his cargo and render an account of his receipts. Present: the
honorable general, L. van Dincklagen, La Montagne, Briant Nuton
and Paulus Leendersz.

1 Whereas the honorable director general and council of New
Netherland have long before this warned the commonalty by an
ordinance that their lots on the island of Manhatans were laid
out too large and bigger than they can be built on by some
inhabitants; and whereas some persons desire to build and scarcely
a spot is to be found hereabouts on which a house can be conveniently erected; therefore, the director general and council
aforesaid think it advisable to notify all persons once more
and for the last time to erect proper buildings on their lots,

---

1 Revised from *Laws and Ordinances of New Netherland*, p. 105.

or, in default thereof, the director general and council shall
assign suitable places to those who are inclined to build houses
in this city of New Amsterdam, and allow the present proprietors
a reasonable indemnity for them at the discretion of the surveyors.
Let every one be warned hereby and those who intend to build will
please give their names to the secretary, which being done,
proper measure will be taken. Thus done in council and published
and posted the 15th of December anno 1648, in New Amsterdam, in
New Netherland. Present: the honorable general, Mr. Dincklagen,
La Montangne, Brian Nuton and Paulus Leendersz.

[424] The last of December

The petition and documents presented to the council by the
crew of the Jonge Prins van Deenemarcken being seen, the director
and council decide that the sailors are in a manner free of the
ship De Jonge Prins van Deenemarcken in her present condition
and, when she is so repaired as to be considered fit to carry
merchandise, they are bound to assist with God's help to bring
her to the place whence they first sailed and where they were
engaged, that is, to Amsterdam in the Netherlands. Meanwhile,
being apprehensive for the ship and goods in consequence of the
threats of the supercargo and his lack of care for the same,
they are allowed to have an inventory taken thereof and to
attach the same, in order to be paid therefrom at a more convenient time. Thus done, the last of December anno 1648.
Present: the honorable general, the deputy, van Dinckl gen,
L. Montagne, Briant Nuton and Poulus Leendersz.

[425] Anno 1649

The 2d of January

Cornelis Melyn presented to the council a letter from their
High and Mighty Lords the States General of the United Provinces
of the Netherlands and one from his Highness the Prince of Orange
to the honorable director general. Having seen and read therein
the commands of the aforesaid High and Mighty Lords and his
princely Highness of Orange, we humbly acknowledge that we are
ready to execute and obey their honors' orders and commands in
every respect. We have therefore provisionally granted permission
to Cornelis Melyn to support himself in New Netherland like other
inhabitants, whereupon he has taken the proper oath of fidelity
before the council. Present: the honorable director general,
van Dincklagen, second in authority, La Montagne and Fiscal van
Dyck. Below was written: To my knowledge, and signed, Cor:
van Tienhoven, secretary.

The 16th of January

Resolved and concluded in council to send out notice to
hold a general day of fasting and prayer on February first next
ensuing to thank and praise God for the peace concluded and
secured between the King of Spain and our dear fatherland; also
to pray God Almighty that the same may redound to the glory of
God, the welfare of the fatherland and the prosperity of its
inhabitants. Present: the honorable general, L. Dincklagen,
La Montagne, Briant Nuton, Poulus Leendertsz. To my knowledge:
Cor: van Tienhoven, secretary.

1 Whereas the select man have at divers times requested by
petition to have a delegation sent to the fatherland to address
our superiors on some weighty matters, and whereas the English
villages on Long Island which are under the jurisdiction of
their High Mightinesses ought also according to our best judgment
to be consulted about this important matter, in order that hereafter they may not plead ignorance thereof, it is resolved in
council to summon them by letter to appear on the appointed day.
Thus done and approved. Present: the honorable general, the
honorable deputy, La Montagne, Briant Nuton, Poulus Leendersz.
This day, the 21st of February.

2 [426] On the 4th of March anno 1649 met and appeared at
the request of the honorable director general in the hall of
Fort Amsterdam the honorable general, L. Dincklagen, Fiscal van
Dyck, La Montagne, Briant Nuton, Ensign Bacxter, Paulus Leendersz,
Commissary Keyser, Sergeant Litschoe.

Next, the burgher officers: Jacob Couwenhoven, Captain;
Martin Crigier, Lieutenant; Philip Geraerdy, Pieter Cock,
sergeants; Borger Jorisen, Augustyn Heerman, ensigns; by whom
in a joint meeting and session the following was resolved and
did occur.

Mr. Lubbert van Dincklagen protests in council against the
honorable director because he has heretofore done and still does
many things without his previous knowledge; also, because he has
caused Adriaen vander Donck to be placed under arrest without

---

1 Revised from <u>Doc</u>. <u>Rel</u>. <u>Col</u>. <u>Hist</u>. <u>N</u>. <u>Y</u>., 14:109.
2 Revised from <u>Doc</u>. <u>Rel</u>. <u>Col</u>. <u>Hist</u>. <u>N</u>. <u>Y</u>., 14:110-11.

consulting him. Thus protested. Present: all the aforesaid
officers and burghers.

At the aforesaid meeting was read the part of Adriaen vander Donck's Journal in which vander Donck writes that at the
house of Melyn he heard Mr. Dincklagen say that he had violated
his oath in the case and that things did not go so straight in
Holland and that among the States there were also some who are
perjurers.

Mr. Dincklagen denies having ever said what vander Donck
has stated in his Journal to the detriment of their High
Mightinesses and demands proof thereof.

Mr. Dincklagen requests a copy of the Journal written by
Verdonck and taken out of the house of Michiel Jansen by the
director without his, Dincklagen's, knowledge; against which
he protests also.

The director gives for answer that it will be furnished to
him, Dincklagen, at the proper time when the ships shall sail
for Holland and that because he can not have a copy now, as it
contains things which must first be proved.

The 4th of March. Present: the above mentioned councilors
and burghers.

The farmers on the island of Manhatans request by petition
a free pasture on the island of Manhatans between Schepmoes'
plantation and the fence of the large Bouwery No. 1.

The request is provisionally granted to the petitioners,
with the promise that no new plantations will be made or granted
between the said fences.

The 4th of March anno 1649

1 Follow the opinions of the honorable councilors and
burghers respecting the Journal written by Adriaen vander Donck.

Mr. Dincklaghen is of opinion that Adriaen vander Donck
shall be heard respecting the writing and provisionally be
released on bail.

La Montagne advises that Verdonck be heard according to
law.

Briant Nuton is of opinion that Verdonck shall be heard
in his place of confinement.

[427] Paulus Leendertsz is of opinion that Adriaen vander
Donck shall be examined by commissaries in his place of
confinement.

Commissary Keyser is of opinion that vander Donck ought to
be brought here and then examined.

Burghers

Jacob Wolpertsen says this matter does not concern him and
therefore he ought to be excused from voting.

Marten Cregier says that vander Donck ought to be heard
in confinement.

Gorge Bacxter, ensign, as above.

Augustyn Heerman says, as vander Donck is a co-member of
the board of Nine Men, he can not advise in the matter.

Sergeant Litscho thinks that it is best that Verdonck
remain in confinement until he be examined.

Jan Evertsen Bout says inasmuch as vander Donck is a
burgher, he ought to be treated as a burgher.

---

1 Revised from <u>Doc</u>. <u>Rel</u>. <u>Col</u>. <u>Hist</u>. <u>N</u>. <u>Y</u>., 14:111-12.

Philip Geraerdy says that vander Donck must receive what he has paid.

Pieter Cock says that vander Donck must remain in confinement until he has been examined.

Borger Jorisz _ut_ _supra_, the same as Pieter Cock.

The honorable director general is of opinion that for the removal of all differences and disputes it would be necessary to summon two deputies from each colony and village in New Netherland to hold a _land_ _dach_ to deliberate on the highly necessary delegation for the best interest of the country in general.

Mr. Dincklaghen says that he will not meddle with the matter and is of opinion that one ought to wait until the lords States shall have taken measures.

Fiscal van Dyck thinks it advisable to summon two or three persons from the surrounding English and other villages to assist with those of the Manhatans in deciding what is best for the public in regard to the delegation to the fatherland.

La Montagne, _ut_ _supra_

Briant Nuton, _ut_ _supra_

Gorge Bacxter, _ut_ _supra_

Adriaen Keyser, _ut_ _supra_

Poulus Leendersz, _ut_ _supra_

Daniel Litschoe, _ut_ _supra_

Martin Crigier, _ut_ _supra_

Augustyn Heerman refers it to the board of Nine Men

Borger Jorisen, Philip Geraerdy and Pieter Cock agree in opinion with the fiscal, as above.

Poulus Leendertsz and Adriaen d'Keyser are ordered and appointed a committee to investigate the case of Adriaen vander Donck in the presence of the honorable fiscal, the 5th of March anno 1649, in New Amsterdam, New Netherland.

[428] The 6th of March anno 1649

In council is presented a certain petition of Adriaen vander Donck, on which the director and council have caused the following apostil to be made:

The petitioner is ordered by plurality of votes to remain in confinement until he be examined and shall have answered the interrogatories, pursuant to the resolution of March 4, anno 1649, in New Amsterdam, New Netherland.

[1] The 8th of March

The honorable director general produces in council and exhibits to the members a writing and after reading it to them asks their opinion whether said writing should not be read to the entire commonalty when met.

Mr. Dincklagen refuses to express his opinion thereon.

Fiscal van Dyck states that he considers it well and advisable that it be read to the commonalty.

La Montagne, *ut supra*

Briant Nuton, *ut supra*

Adriaen Keyser, commissary, *ut supra*

Paulus Leendertsz, *ut supra*

---

[1] Revised from *Doc*. *Rel*. *Col*. *Hist*. *N*. *Y*., 14:113.

The 11th of March

Whereas on the 9th of March last one Symon Walingen vant
Bilt was found dead at Pavonia near Paulus Hoeck, having been
killed, as it appears from the arrows and the wound in his head,
by the Indians, without our knowing, however, of which nation,
the opinion thus far being that they must have been outsiders,
either Raretangs, or Indians from the south, who committed this
crime from motives of avarice, since they took from the house
in which the slain man lived 300 gl. in strung seawan, 4 beavers
and 5 otters, together with a small quantity of trading cloth
or duffel, which theft no doubt was the cause of the slaying of
the man, who was found dead outdoors, about a pistol shot from
the door or path with a small ladder [1] in his hand. And whereas
the slain man, without the knowledge of the court and contrary
to the general ordinance, was removed by private individuals from
the place where he was found dead and brought from the other
side to the Manhatans before this city, no small commotion was
thereupon caused among the inhabitants as well as among the
Indians, the more so as some of our nation began to take hold
of them and others to scold them, so that a general flight of
the Indians from the Manhatans followed and this rumor spread
everywhere. Therefore, before it flares up further, it is by
us, the director and council, judged advisable in the best
interest of the country at first not to make any commotion
about this murder, but to make every effort and use all diligence
to set at rest the natives and the inhabitants, to cause the

---

[1] leertie (piece of leather?) [Penciled note of
A. J. F. VanLaer].

body to be buried in the most civil manner possible and to
notify the Christians not to show any signs of vengeance. Thus
done and resolved in council the 11th of March. Present: the
honorable director and all the members of the council.

[429] [1] Proposition submitted in writing by the honorable
director to the ordinary councilors and other officers, the
15th of March anno 1649.

The ordinary councilors and other superior and inferior
officers are aware that we, by virtue of our office and commission,
have quite recently caused one Adriaen van der Donck to be
guarded in his usual residence or confinement, [2] on account of
a slanderous writing drawn up in the form of a Journal, and found
at the house of Michael Jansen, wherein he has grossly slandered
not only some superior and inferior officers, but also their
High Mightinesses themselves, or at least many among the Lords
States are suspected and accused of perjury; as appears by the
original thereof.

Authentic extracts of which having been read by the Commissioners to the aforesaid Van der Donck and a categorical
answer demanded, the said Van der Donck responded in contempt
of the court, in a dubious, or at least in an immaterial manner,
nevertheless affirming in plain and distinct words the injurious
and defamatory accusation partly expressed by him in writing to
me, and partly read to others out of the Journal, tending to the
special defamation both of our Sovereigns and the Councillors

---

1 Revised from Doc. Rel. Col. Hist. N. Y., 14:113-14.
2 Gijselinge - Debtor's Prison. This note, and the translation from here to the end of this document is by B. Fernow.

sent hither, to the maintenance of whose most illustrious renown
we are pledged by our commission and the Laws of Netherland and
by honor, oath and conscience

Therefore my opinion in regard to the equivocal deposition
that has been taken is, that **the deponent** be ordered and constrained
to prove and establish or to revoke what he has injuriously
written or spoken against the Honble Lords States and officers
here; and in the meanwhile, until further information, that he
absent himself from our Council and the Assembly of the elected
Select Men (_gemeents mannen_). On which points, besides this, we
also request the written opinions of the other Councillors and
officers, hereby excusing and holding myself guiltless of the
charge which may be brought against me, either here or hereafter,
that I knew of the defamation and injury of my Sovereigns, and
did not punish or notice them. Done Manhatans. (Signed)

P. STUYVESANT.

Votes on the proposition of the Honble Director given by
the Honble Councillors, dated 15th of March A^o. 1649.

Lubbert **van Dincklage**, the Vice Director, says he will
not have any thing to do with the Director's proposition,
refuses to sign.

Hendrick van Dyck, fiscal, is of opinion, that Van der Donck
shall not appear at the board of the Director and Council, or
at the Assembly of the Nine men until he shall have proved the
writing drawn up in the form of a Journal. (Signed)

H. VAN DYCK, fiscal.

La Montagne is of opinion that Verdonck shall not appear in the session of the Council until the decision of the suit. (Signed) LA MONTAGNE. Brian Nuton votes like La Montagne. (Signed) BRIAN NEWTON. Adriaen Keyser, Commissary, votes as the Fiscal has done. (Signed) A. KEYSER. Paulus Leendersen, naval storekeeper, votes and in the case of Verdonck is of the same opinion as the Fiscal. (Signed) PAULUS LEENDERTSEN VAN DE GRIFT.

Director and Council have by plurality of votes decided that Adriaen van der Donck shall not attend the session of the Council or the Assembly of the Select Men when they meet, until he shall have duly verified what he has written in defamation of the Honble States and of the officers and Councillors here. This 15th of March A°. 1649. New Amsterdam.

[1] 23 March

Thus the process of the fiscal, plaintiff, and Tielman Willekens, merchant of the suspected Prince of Denmark, has been pending before us for a long time and is now fully documented. Thus Tielman Wilkens appeared personally in the assembly and was asked by the gentlemen director if he had anything more to submit in the defense of his ship and goods; Also if he had received copies of both commissions, one in Latin and the other in German, from his lawyer.

Tielman answered that he had nothing further to submit at this time and that the Commissions were handed to him by his lawyer.

---

[1] Translation by Robert Van Niel.

The fiscal, plaintiff, vs. Tielman Willekens as merchant
from the ship The Young Prince of Denmark suspected of sneaky
smuggling.

The plaintiff answered all questions and all pieces were
seen by both parties. The plaintiff, under benefit of perfect
inventory, was allowed to appoint two out of the Council, such
as Mr. Dincklaghen and Commissioner Keyser, who with two whom
the merchant Willekens would wish to commission thereto to take
possession of the ship, and at the proper time to give a receipt
of the receivership. In case Tielman Willekens refuses, the
fiscal will be permitted to select two impartial citizens who
will be paid out of the goods. Done 23 March in council; present
were the honorable General, L. van Dincklagen, La Montangne,
Paulus Leendertsz van die grift, and Briant Nuton.

[431] Thus the ship De Liefde lays helpless and urgently
needs to be sent to the West Indies for salt which is urgently
needed here; and that several ships' carpenters such as Lambert
Moll, Jan Claesz van Bellecum, and Harck Syboltsz will not work
on said ship belonging to the gentlemen directors of the United
West India Company, for less than four guilders per day above
the cost of materials, which is an unheard of wage. Thus the
gentlemen directors and the council have resolved and decided
to command the aforementioned ships' carpenters, with the first
as their spokesman, to take themselves to the ship in order that
they there as carpenters may suitably fix the ship, and in
accordance with the work done they will be paid for their labor
as two honest and impartial persons shall find suitable. Done

this 23 March 1649, New Amsterdam, New Netherlands. Was signed:
P. Stuyvesandt, L. van Dincklagen, Hendrick van Dyck, fiscal,
La Montagne, Briant Nuton, Paulus Leendersz van die Grift, and
A. Keyser.

The fiscal, Hendrick van Dyck, plaintiff, vs. Tielman
Willekens, defendant. The defendant is questioned in full assembly
in which two Select Men were present, namely Olof Stevensz and
Michiel Jansz, if he had anything further to present in defense
of his ship and goods. To this was answered, no, nothing other
than what he had previously submitted in writing. All of which
in addition to the judgment of the defendants own confession,
and all assembled documents, also including the original commissions and everything that might serve as material evidence, and
being carefully weighed on various judgment days, so it is that
the gentlemen director and councillors of New Netherland can
derive no other decision out of the confession of the defendant
Willekens and other witnesses, than that the ship, first named
The Gray Stallion, destined for Guinea was equipped and outfitted
at Amsterdam by one Hectoor Pietersz and Gerrit Ferraers, the
officers and sailors needed on this ship were acquired under the
announcements and charter of their High Mightinesses in Amsterdam.
According to their declaration in the amount of 30 to 36 heads,
all inhabitants and subjects of the United Netherlands Provinces.
Except for the assistant merchant, the barber, and at the most
three or four others, they received their money in hand, also
six hundred bars of iron in the galliot and a wharf lighter full
of bars was also loaded into the ship The Gray Stallion. In

addition there were other Guinea goods, also the ship's provisions,
beans and irons for the negroes, everything in sufficient quantity
to judge by the declarations of the sailors. All this is not
denied nor evidence to the contrary presented by the defendant
Willekens, but only that the remaining Guinea goods were bought
by him, the defendant, and Gerrit Feraers in Amsterdam. From
there with three small yachts he was sent to Glückstadt on the
Elbe from that [432] port to Kiel with one Evers van Kil in the
aforementioned ship The Gray Stallion, then renamed The Young
Prince of Denmark, is transferred without the defendent Willekens
declaring, much less proving, that the aforementioned Guinea
cargoes or the iron bars, the provisions, and the other mercantile
goods were loaded in Amsterdam, or any recognition being paid to
the Honorable Company or the duties were paid to the country.
With which ship and galliot the majority of the officers and
sailors disguised and greased black, took to sail on 4 July 1646
and ran out of the Zuider Zee to the Elbe, and from there proceeded under two Danish Commissions both of one date, one in
German and the other in Latin. The German indicating that the
honorable persons also creditors of Glückstadt, namely captain
and skipper Tielman Willekens and Arent Gerritsz, and sealed with
the royal arms but not signed and therefore false. The Latin
commission in its own words, sub ductu navarcha seu Capitanej,
itidem subiditj et civis Nostrj Arnoldj Gerseny, sealed with the
same royal arms and signed Christianus in a broken Roman script,
without any other subscription or post script in ordination of
the high named royal majesty as is the princely style and is
usual on their commissions. This by no means slight suspicion

of wrong doing, or at least that they were not obtained in good
faith, is more clearly indicated in the commissions themselves,
compared with the testimonial letter of Tielman Willekens and the
declaration of the people, both commissions indicating with clear
and direct words that they were given and executed on the honorable
inhabitants and sureties of Glückstadt signed on 16 June 1646
which, according to the testimonial letters and declarations of
the sailors, is false. Both the captain and the skipper of the
aforementioned ship The Prince of Denmark, namely Tielman
Wilkens and Arendt Gerritsz with their families first left
Netherlands the next 4th of July for Glückstadt. And the aforementioned Willekens first was accepted as a creditor of Glückstadt
on the 15th of July according to his own testimonial letter signed
by the Count and Governor Pents. From this the plaintiff concludes that the commercial swindle and the misleading of his
royal majesty are clear enough, even though both commissions
were good and obtained in good trust though this is not proved,
no foreigner may equip ships and assemble people without the
foreknowledge of the High or subordinate governments. When in
this matter the Nomine offitie seeks from the defendant clear
and sufficient evidence both about the equipping of the ship and
the galliots, and the recruitment of the people, to indicate
that such occurred with prior knowledge and consent of the High
Sovereign of the United Netherlands or subordinate magistrates
of A'dam., as well as that the goods and mercantile products
were reported and paid proper duties and fees, the defendant
does not answer these matters, even refusing to verify this

with his oath. Thus we the Director and Councillors mentioned
before, having listened to the justice of the claim, in part
with the self confession of the accused and the testimony of
sailors (433), In part out of the commissions and the matter
itself after calling God's holy name, could find no other than
that the ship and goods as a notorious smuggler are confiscable
and forfeit as a consequence of their High Mightinesses' announcements and charter of the West India Company decreeing that none
of the natives or inhabitants of the United Netherlands or those
from outside these lands shall be permitted to sail or negotiate
on the coasts and lands of Africa from the Tropic of Cancer to
the Cape of Good Hope, America, etc., and so whoever shall undertake to sail or negotiate in any places within the forementioned
limits without consent of the Company will suffer loss of ship
and goods, Article 45 of the ordinances of their High Mightinesses:
that the above and all other rights will be maintained and
enforced by all agencies, officers, and subjects of the United
Netherlands without direct or indirect hindrance both in and out
of the United Netherlands on pain of being punished as hinderers
of the general welfare and transgressors against her ordinances
and being punished in body and goods. With the power of the
highly considered High Mightinesses' announcements and given
charter considered, that by these and similar indirections,
dodges, frauds, and smugglings their High Mightinesse's, our
sovereign, announcements are being violated, the Netherlands'
commerce, the soul of our fatherland, is diverted by its own
subjects, the noble Company suffers in its charter, its

recognition and the land's duties are shorted, we declare the
above named ship and goods, under benefit of inventory, forfeited
and **confiscable,** just as we confiscate it with this announcement
for the profit of the noble company and all that belongs to it,
with this reservation: that the indicated true debts on behalf
of the ship or made in other ways will be paid under suitable
receipt, the defendant will be given a suitable inventory and
scrip certificates and an authentic copy of this sentence and
the documents of the Proceedings. Done on the 23d, resumed on
24 March 1649 in Fort Amsterdam in New Netherland. Present were
the honorable Director General, L. van Dincklagen, La Montagne,
Paulus Leendertsz, Briant Nuton, A. Keyser who have all signed
the draft in my presence. Signed Cor. van Tienhoven, Secretary.

31 March

In assemblage after deep deliberation it was unanimously
and collegially resolved that the sailors of the confiscated
ship The Young Prince of Denmark should be paid here the total
monthly wages which they have earned, after the ship's debts
have first been paid. Present were the honorable Director
General and all the Councillors.

[434] The fiscal asks for the second time that Tielman
Willekens, merchant, of the ship The Prince of Denmark, shall
provide a list of debts and credits made on behalf of the ship.

Willekens answers that as soon as he has received the papers
of the court proceedings he will submit these others.

Since the honorable director general and the Councillors of
New Netherland have noted that Tielman Willekens, up to now,
remains in failure and has remained unwilling to surrender his

account in order to show his known debts, thus all creditors are hereby warned that these will not be paid out of the confiscated goods unless they can produce a verification signed by Tielman's own hand to establish the authenticity of the debt; meanwhile Tielman Willekens remains under arrest and will not be allowed to depart for 24 hours. Done this 12 April 1649, New Amsterdam, New Netherland.

Anthony Crol, skipper of the ship The Prince of Denmark, appeared before the gathering and sought for himself and the remaining ship's personnel that their account might be given to Tielman Willekens so that they might obtain their earnings. Tielman Willekens answers that when he has received the papers of the court proceedings, he will then settle with the sailors, especially since they are finished. The Director and Council order that Tielman Willekens shall give the skipper and all other sailors shall provide individual extracts of the account, showing the debts and credits and properly signed by him. Failing to do this, Tielman Willekens will remain in arrest until he has provided each of the ship's personnel with a private accounting. 12 April 1649, New Amsterdam.

April 21

The fiscal Van Dyck, Nomine Offitie, presents action against the ship and goods of Gerrit Vastrick because of a case of firelocks. So it is that I, the undersigned, as Director and primary judge of the country, affix and make known under oath and assisted by the testimony of unimpeachable witnesses: first that I have been ordered by two letters from the noble gentlemen directors to try to obtain at moderate prices powder, lead, and firelocks from sources outside the noble Company, until it will be in a better position to supply these and to meet the eventuality of a new war, and not to dispose of any unless there is a request from the colony of Renselaersyck which has been advised that such must be highly urgent, but that beyond this there will have to remain a shortage for the time being. To this end it was that Mr. Gerrit Vastrick was asked by me here on 2 and 3 August 1648 if he, upon his return, would bring 20 to 30 firelocks for the account of the Company and he was promised for his risk, advance of money, and freight, a premium of fifty percent or two beavers to be paid here. This agreement was closed in public in my garden in the presence of the Secretary Tienhoven and others.

[435] Second, that many times both in and out of the council I have said to councillors as well as freemen that I had asked Vastrick to do this so that the freemen who are often seeking guns, would also be able to obtain them for a reasonable price. So that by these I declare that whatever is commissioned and is wrongly done in this matter has been done by our purposeful request.

Third, I declare that Vastrick had just arrived here when he informed me that he had brought along 30 firelocks at my request, and asked where I wished these brought. I asked that these would be delivered to the Commissioner, and so that the fiscal would be informed of the quantity of the same, he and other councillors, including even the alternate (deputy)

Dincklagen, [were present] last Monday morning before the first
goods were unloaded from the ship. Thus we declare that something both wrong and suspect has occurred with the forementioned
30 firelocks, on my commission for which all impartial men and
judges hope to answer. The fiscal in accordance with his office
made the result into the proper charge with a plurality of
voices, I myself not voting, etc. This 21 April 1649, New
Amsterdam, in assembly declared by the honorable Director General
and was signed P. Stuyvesant.

The fiscal submitted his charge in writing in last instance
against the skipper of the little ship Prince William.

The skipper appeared and said that in the ship a case of
firelocks was transported by the merchant Vastrick, and that it
is his duty to take over whatever is transported by his merchant
who had also told him that he had commands and orders of the
gentlemen directors for this.

Gerrit Vastrick being heard in assembly answered that on
the request and order of the gentlemen directors he had brought
the case with firelocks in which were 30 pieces to New
Netherland.

The honorable Director General and Councillors have seen
the written charge drawn up against Cornelis Coenraetsz van
Campen, skipper on the ship Prince William, concerning a certain
case of firearms of 30 pieces brought here by this same ship,
and delivered into the warehouse of the Company. And it is
understood by the Director General and the council in full
assembly that the affair concerning these will remain in suspension until further orders from the gentlemen directors, with

the understanding that the forementioned skipper **in view of**
the fiscal's charge and action will post substantial bail, for
which Mr. Peter Stuyvesant who is providing bail for him wants
him kept under close guard, the more so, declares the Director
General, since the aforementioned firelocks were brought along
on his order for the account of the Company. Thus was done on
21 April 1649 in New Netherland. Present were Mr. P. Stuyvesant,
La Montagne, and Briant Nuton.

[436] Thus on the 4th **of Kay the ship** The Young Prince
of Denmark by public auction to the highest bidder will be sold,
for the greatest necessity, decency and profit of the Company
and also to maintain the reputation of this country among its
neighbors. It is considered advisable by the Director General,
Mr. Dincklagen, and the fiscal Van Dyck, that if this ship is
sold in the neighborhood of five thousand guilders, not counting
a few hundred either way, to take half ownership in this ship
with someone else, and with this ship to seek our indebtedness
in freight or some other manner. This 3 May 1649 in New
Amsterdam.

In assembly it was unanimously agreed to sell to the highest
bidder the sugar of the ship The Prince of Denmark for loose
seawan and the elephant tusks for strung **seawan,** beavers, or money.
Also to sell the ship in true value such as beavers, strung
seawan, or silver money. This 3 May. Present were all the
Councillors.

The Distinguished Director General and Councillors of New
Netherland. All those who see, read, or hear this, Salute. Let

it be known how that the noble gentlemen directors of the
Chartered West India Company in order to benefit and favor their
conquest of New Netherland above all others, have, upon our
serious remonstrance concerning the heavy tobacco taxes, by
their latest letter dated 29 January, notified us and made known
that henceforth the tobacco cultivated and produced within
New Netherland will not pay heavier or more taxes within the
district under their jurisdiction, than the very worst tobacco
of the Caribbean Islands; namely, forty five stivers per 100.
Hereby the highly regarded directors our patrons not only signify
and show their favorable disposition toward this their conquest,
since this tobacco is so much worthier and expensive than others,
but also their good intention and hope that by these means
others will be attracted and the population, cultivation, and
growth will be stimulated, which we have thought essential to
show in good time and to make known. So that any already residing under our government, or who might yet wish to come in during
this favorable time, may have knowledge of this, we have decreed
that this adopted resolution of our patrons will be published
and displayed not only here on Manhattan, but also in all other
colonies and villages of this Jurisdiction so that everyone will
best know how to regulate his cultivation and agriculture.

This was done in our meeting this 21 April 1649, New
Amsterdam.

[437] [1] This day underwritten the honorable director general
went to the house of Domine Backerius and there, in his capacity
as director, told the minister not to read himself, or have read
by any of the church officers, from the pulpit in the church or
elsewhere, at the request of any of the inhabitants, any writing,
petition, or proposal regarding the public administration and
general government, whether in general or particular, before
and until such writings shall be signed either by the honorable
director himself, or by the secretary by order of the director
and council, without intending hereby **any ecclesia**stical affairs,
which are left to the full disposal of the aforesaid minister
and consistory and which he shall be free to regulate according
to church ordinances and the duty of a godly minister, wherein
said honorable director general offers him all aid and assistance
as far as they concern him as chief **magi**strate of the country.
Thus done in the presence of Councilor La Montagne and Secretary
Tienhoven, this 8th of May 1649.

[2] Whereas it is daily observed that, contrary to honesty,
the orders of the Lords States General and the ordinance caused
to be published by the late director general and council on the
12th of June anno 1646, great abuses are committed in the writing
and procuring of depositions by private persons who are neither
pledged thereto by oath nor qualified thereto by official authority,
whereby frequently many things are written to the advantage of
those who have the papers drawn up, interspersed with sinister,
obscure and dubious words, oftentimes contrary to the intention

---

1 Revised from <u>Doc</u>. <u>Rel</u>. <u>Col</u>. <u>Hist</u>. <u>N</u>. <u>Y</u>., 14:114.
2 Revised from <u>Laws</u> <u>and</u> <u>Ordinances</u> <u>of</u> <u>New</u> Netherland, p. 108.

of the witnesses, to the great prejudice and damage of the parties;
therefore, in order to prevent this result, dangerous in a
republic, and to promote the knowledge of the truth necessary in
all courts, we annul and declare invalid, as we do hereby annul
and declare invalid, all affidavits, interrogatories, or other
instruments serving as evidence, which are written by private
individuals and not confirmed by oath before the court here or
other magistrates, as we do also from now on annul all depositions
which are not written by the secretary or the person authorized
thereto, as well as contracts, wills, agreements and other important
documents, unless in case of need it should be impossible to call
on such person. Thus, this 8th of May 1649, it is resolved in
council to renew the ordinance published on June 12, 1646. The
original is signed by P. Stuyvesant, H. van Dyck, fiscal,
La Montagne, Briant Nuton, A. Keyser. Mr. Dincklagen refuses
to sign.

[438] The 14th of June 1649

Jacob Loper presents a petition dated the 14th of June,
requesting permission to go the South River of New Netherland
with the hired bark and the goods. And whereas the said Looper
married the daughter of Cornelis Melyn, in view of the letter
written by the honorable directors, dated the 27th of January
1649, the honorable director general is of opinion that the
request can not be granted, in view of the above mentioned
letter.

Mr. Dincklagen is of opinion that Loper may be granted his
request, provided he do nothing detrimental to the Company.

La Montagne, in view of the letter from the directors, has scruples about the matter.

Briant Nuton ditto.

Thus submitted at the meeting of the honorable director general and council inasmuch as Cornelis Melyn has caused the director and the members of the government to be summoned by mandamus to appear at 's-Graven Haage or to send a deputy on a suitable day to sustain and justify the sentence pronounced against Melyn.

The honorable director general and council having seen all the documents and papers produced by Arnoldus van Hardenbergh as plaintiff and Abraham Planck as defendant and having carefully considered and noted all the circumstances that are to be taken into consideration, they find that the goods consigned to Abraham Planck in the absence of Arnoldus van Hardenberch have been received by the said Planck, that he signed an obligation therefor, dated October 4, 1647, and made payment thereon, without having made any complaint to us about signing the said obligation and making payment thereon on account; also, that he acknowledges having signed the obligation with his own hand. Therefore, the honorable director general and the council condemn the said Abraham Planck, as they do hereby, to satisfy and pay the contents of the aforesaid obligation to Arnoldus van Hardenberch, providing that the amount paid thereon is to be deducted. Thus done in council, the 28th of June 1649, at New Amsterdam in New Netherland.

Govert Loockemans, plaintiff, against Aryana Cuvelje, defendant. The documents produced by the parties having been examined and everything having been carefully weighed and considered, the defendant is condemned to pay a fine of six hundred guilders, to be applied as is proper. This 28th of June 1649. [1]

[439] Johannes Backerius, minister in this city of New Amsterdam, appeared before the council and requested his discharge, in order that he may return to the fatherland. Therefore, the honorable director general and council having considered the urgent request, can not refuse said Backerius his dismissal. The said director general and council have accordingly granted him leave to depart for the fatherland. This 6th of July 1649. [2]

Whereas Willem Albertsen Blauvelt, captain of the frigate La Garce, sailed from New Netherland under commission of the honorable director, the said Blaeuvelt in the year 1648, before the 20th of December, captured a bark coming from Porto Bello, laden with some piece-goods, as appears from the invoice of the supercargo, and whereas the said goods or a part thereof have been sent up by Blaeuvelt, this is publicly read to every one, in order that if any one had any reason why the goods are not a good prize, he may make the same known. In default of appearance before the conclusion of the third publication the same shall be declared a good prize at the requisition of the fiscal. Published this 6th day of July.

Whereas Willem Blauvelt, deputy commissary of the late honorable Director Willem Kieft, captain of the frigate La Garce,

---

[1] The record has by mistake July 28, 1649.
[2] Revised from Doc. Rel. Col. Hist. N. Y., 14:115.

for private owners has sent up a small prize named <u>De Hoop van een Beter</u>, laden with 28 cases of indigo and a quantity of linen and hides, specified in detail in the invoice, which goods were captured in the Bay of Campeachy, according to the letter of the said captain and his supercargo, on the 30th of January 1648, about ten months before the commencement of the peace in the West Indies, we can therefore, at the request of the common owners and the complaint of the fiscal, not judge and conclude otherwise than that the same and the goods laden therein ought to be declared a good prize, as we hereby do declare the same to be a good prize, provided no contrary proof be produced by the defendant within the term of the last proclamation, which is extended for good reasons, exempting provisionally the few hides which were captured after or about the commencement of the peace in the West Indies and which until further proof will be stored in the Company's warehouse. As to the remaining goods, which are mostly wet and subject to decay and of which some, such as indigo and linen, have already been spoiled, the interested parties are under proper benefit of inventory allowed to accept the merchandise and, [440] the Company's duties being deducted, to receive the same pro rato, provided that each person give a proper bond and security for the restitution of the merchandise received or the true value thereof, in case this decision may either here or elsewhere be changed afterwards. Thus done in Fort Amsterdam in New Netherland, in full council, the 7th of July 1649.

Whereas yesterday, being the 6th of July of this current
year, there arrived here before New Amsterdam a Spanish bark
from the West Indies, sent up as a prize for the joint owners
by Captain Willem Blauvelt and whereas it appears from his
letters as well as the letters from the supercargo, Daniel Roggen,
that the aforesaid bark with its lading was captured in the river
of Tobasco in Campeachy Bay on the 22d of April 1649, being about
five months after the peace ought to have commenced in the West
Indies and consequently was taken in violation of the said
articles of peace and the placards to various effects of their
High Mightinesses our sovereigns, published, as we are informed
everywhere in the United Netherlands, providing that any damage
which by way of hostility should be done by either side within
the limits of the Chartered West India Company after the 19th of
November 1649, [1] would be repaired without delay, and whereas
it is our bounden duty to obey the said articles of peace and
the ordinances issued by their aforesaid High Mightinesses, our
sovereign lords, we cannot declare the aforesaid bark and lading
prizes since according to the articles of peace they must be
restored to the rightful owners. And whereas the owners are
unknown to us, we cannot restore the same to them and as the bark
is very leaky and unfit, so that it is to be feared that many
goods must be damaged, or may still be damaged or depreciated,
the director and council, in the best interest of the rightful
owners, have thought fit to have the same stored in the warehouse
and properly inventoried under the supervision of two members of
the council and two of the pretended owners, until further

---

[1] Apparently a mistake for November 19, 1648.

opportunity and better knowledge of the circumstances. Thus done, the 7th of July 1649, at New Amsterdam.

The 17th of July 1649

It is resolved in council to appraise the goods of the prize De Hoop belonging to the Company for so far as its share and right is concerned according to the price at which the owners have sold their goods, and after the goods have been appraised to deliver them to the servants (of the Company) upon credit. Date as above.

[441] Having heard in council Philip de Truy, court messenger, who reports that he handed to the Nine Men a copy of a petition dated the 21st of June and the apostil of the 5th of July, concerning the petition of Cornelis van Tienhoven, presented by them on the 14th of July last and by order of the director and council summoned the Nine Men for the second time to produce the aforesaid petition in council within twice twenty-four hours, which has not been done. This 17th day of July anno 1649, at New Amsterdam.

Declares that he served the aforesaid summons on the Nine Men for the third time. Date as above.

19 July

Philip de Treuy, court messenger, appearing in council, declares that under date of the fifth of July he received from the Nine Men a copy of a certain petition, dated the 21st of June, which petition (being an authentic copy), with the apostil thereon, he again delivered on the 12th of July to one of the Nine Men, to wit, Augustyn Hermans, standing in front of the

council chamber, or more specifically, the lodging of the honorable
director general. Having presented and delivered the same into
his hands, he received for answer from said Augustyn Heermans:
"Pray, keep the same for a while, until I ask you for it. I
must go to the wedding." Therefore, he kept the petition and
the apostil thereon for him.

He further declares that on the 15th of July last he _de
novo_ received orders from the director to serve the said notice,
which he did the same day on the aforesaid Augustyn Hermans,
Jacob Wolphertsz, Olof Stevensz and Arnoldus van Hardenberch.

On the 17th ditto he for the third time served the said
notice on the aforesaid four representatives of the commonalty,
upon which third notice Augustyn Heerman on the 19th of July
handed me a certain writing in the form of an answer, which I
have delivered to the honorable director. This day, the 19th
of July 1649, in Fort Amsterdam.

Propositions made by the chiefs of the savages dwelling
about the Manhatans, namely, Seysegeckkimus, Oratannin, Willem
of Tappen and Pennekes of Achter Col, on the last named date in
the council chamber in Fort Amsterdam, in the presence of Domine
Johannes Megapolensis, minister of Renselaerswyck, Arent van
Curler and Johannes van Twiller [1]

1. Pennekeck, chief of Achter Col, making a speech in the
Indian tongue (being translated), said that the Southern Minquas
had asked them to live in all friendship with the Dutch, which
they promised to do and to that end they had brought a present

---

[1] Revised from _Doc. Rel. Col. Hist. N. Y._, 13:25.

here to the honorable director general.

[422] 2. That an Indian of Mechgachkamic had lately involuntarily and unknowingly committed an offense at Paulus Hoeck. They requested therefore that we would excuse the same.

3. Pennekeck said the tribe called Raretanoos, formerly living at Wiqaeskeck, had no chief. They therefore spoke for them and they would, like them, be our friends and through him sent their greetings to the director, whereupon he threw down three beavers as a present.

4. That Meyterma, chief of Neyick, and his people were included in this agreement and like them would be and remain our friends, throwing down three beavers.

5. For those of Remahenonck as above, with a like present.

6. Pennekeck threw down two beavers and declared in the name of all that their heart was sincere and that they sought to live with us in friendship, forgetting on one side as well as the other what had passed.

7. Pennekeck said: "I wish you could see my heart, then you would be sure that the words I speak are sincere and true. He threw down two beavers, saying, "That is my confirmation."

8. The honorable director had in former times desired to speak with them; it was done now and they had shown their good intentions and were now awaiting what he would do, laying down upon this article two beavers.

9. Pennekeck said, although the honorable director general could not understand them, they did not doubt his good intentions.

10. In conclusion Pennekeck said: It is the wish of the Minquas that we and you should be and remain friends, for which we are ready.

The honorable director general first caused the chiefs to be thanked for having come to visit him with offers of neighborly friendship and told them that he was pleased to hear such a request. He promised them that nothing whatever would be wanting on our part and that he was willing to live with them in mutual friendship and neighborly intercourse. No cause for complaints would be given and if any one injured them they should report the same to the director, in order that they should receive justice according to the circumstances of the case. In token of his good will he accepted their presents on the aforesaid propositions with thanks and in due time he would return the compliment. A small present of about 20 guilders was then given to the common Indians and some tobacco and a gun to the chief Oratanin, and so the Indians departed, well pleased. This day, [blank].

[Ordinance to enforce the law respecting

weights and measures] [1]

[443] The honorable director general and council of New Netherland daily observing that their ordinance heretofore made and enacted respecting weights and measures [2] is not duly complied with by some, whereby the good inhabitants may be greatly

---

[1] Revised from Laws and Ordinances of New Netherland, pp. 109-10.
[2] See Ordinance of April 11, 1641.

defrauded; Therefore, the honorable director general and council
notify all wholesale and retail traders, as well as bakers and
all others who sell anything by the yard, measure or weight, to
use no other yard, measure or weight in delivering or receiving
than the legal Amsterdam ell, weight and measure. And in order
that everything may proceed in orderly fashion, the honorable
director and council have thought fit hereby to give notice to
all inhabitants and traders to procure and to provide themselves
between this date and the first of August next with the legal
Amsterdam ell, weight and measure. Meanwhile, those who at the
present time have any weights shall bring them into the Company's
warehouse in the fort, to be there weighed and measured, so that
in the future no subject may suffer any loss thereby. And in
order that everything may be attended to and followed with
greater zeal by all and every one, the fiscal, Hendrick van Dyck,
is hereby commanded and authorized after the expiration of the
first of August next to inspect all ells, weights and measures
as often as he shall think proper, and whoever shall then be
found not to use the legal ell, weight or measure shall pay such
fine as is thereto provided by law in our fatherland. Let every
one be warned hereby and guard himself against loss. Thus done
in council the 17th of July; resumed and posted the 19th of
July 1649, at New Amsterdam in New Netherland.

On the 23d of July Cornelis van Tienhoven presented in
council a certain remonstrance and petition, put in writing on
the 23d of July, upon which it is resolved by the honorable

director general and council that the petitioner's request is
reasonable and fair. Consequently, the accusers, whoever they
may be, are expressly ordered and commanded within the space of
eight days to prove their accusations by sufficient and irreproachable testimony before commissaries appointed thereto, or
in default thereof to be held and declared such as the court
according to law shall find proper. Thus done in council in
Fort Amsterdam, New Netherland, the 23d of July 1649. Present:
the honorable director general, L. van Dincklagen, who refused
to sign; H. van Dyck, La Montagne, Briant Nuton.

[Resolution to retain and engage the Rev. Johannes Megapolensis
    as minister of the church at New Amsterdam] [1]

[444] Whereas Domine Johannes Backerius at his urgent
request and, as he declares, with the consent of the Classis,
wherein the despatches of the honorable directors concur, has
received from us license and dismissal to depart with the first
ships for the fatherland and whereas in the meantime this congregation would remain destitute of spiritual nourishment,
namely, the preaching of the Holy Gospel and the lawful par-
ticipation of the blessed sacraments; Therefore, we, the director
and council, wishing to promote according to our ability the
honor of God and the welfare and salvation of men, can not consent that this congregation shall or is to remain bereft of a
pastor.

---

[1] Revised from Doc. Rel. Col. Hist. N. Y., 14:116.

Therefore, on the instructions from the honorable directors, we have resolved, as we do hereby resolve, earnestly and urgently to solicit and entreat the Reverend Domine Johannes Megapolensis, late minister in Renselaerswyck, who, having obtained his dismission there, is now here and prepared to depart with the first ships for the fatherland, and seriously and urgently to inquire if he could not be induced and persuaded, for the glory of God, the upbuilding of His church and the salvation of men, to supply here the preaching of the Divine Word and the administration of the holy sacraments, to which, as we are already informed, his reverence offers no small reasons for refusal. Meanwhile, the extreme need of the churches imperatively demands that at least one clergyman remain in this province among the Dutch nation, both for this capital and Renselaer's colony, were it only for administering baptism to the children who are commonly presented here every Sunday at the Manhatans alone for baptism, sometimes one, sometimes two, yes, even three or four together. Therefore, we can at this time not accept his excuses, but hereby resolve, if possible, to endeavor to retain him blanda vi et quasi nolens volens, and we shall try to justify him to the best of our ability both to the reverend Classis and the honorable patroon, from whom he has already received his dismissal and settlement of accounts. We consider this to be most necessary for the glory of God, the service of His church and the salvation of men. Thus done in our council, this 2d day of August. Present: the Honorable Director General Petrus Stuyvesant, L. van Dincklaghe, H. van Dyck, La Montagne and Briant Nuton.

These are the resolutions which were passed during my directorate in New Netherland since the 27th of May 1647 until the 2d of August 1649.

[Signed]   P. Stuyvesant   <u>vidit</u>

INDEXES

Compiled by Kenneth Scott, Ph.D., F.A.S.G.

The following have been omitted because they appear so frequently: New Amsterdam, Fort Amsterdam, New York, New Netherland, Manhattan, and O'Callaghan.

Numbers refer to documents, and not to pages. Some numbers have been omitted in the typescript.

Since -sen, -ssen, and -sz are interchangeable male patronymic endings, the -ssen and -sz endings are omitted as variants.

INDEX OF PERSONS

INDEX OF PLACES

640

INDEX OF SHIPS